Long Island's

Prominent South Shore Families:

Their Estates and Their Country Homes

in the Towns of Babylon and Islip

Raymond E. and Judith A. Spinzia

VirtualBookworm

College Station, Texas

2007

"Long Island's Prominent South Shore Families: Their Estates and Their Country Homes in the Towns of Babylon and Islip" by Raymond E. and Judith A. Spinzia ISBN 978-1-58939-964-8.

Library of Congress Control Number: 2007920290.

Published 2007 by Virtualbookworm.com Publishing Inc., P.O. Box 9949, College Station, TX 77842, US.

Manufactured in the United States of America.

Also by Raymond E. and Judith A. Spinzia

Long Island: A Guide to New York's Suffolk and Nassau Counties
(*with* Kathryn E. Spinzia)

Long Island's Prominent North Shore Families:
Their Estates and Their Country Homes, Volumes I and II

offered as tribute to our Island
which grows and is nurtured by its people

Table of Contents

Acknowledgments . . . . *vi*

Factors Applicable to Usage . . . . *viii*

Introduction . . . . *ix*

Maps of Long Island Estate Areas . . . . *xi*

Surname Entries A – Z 1

Appendices:

    Architects 305

    Civic Activists 311

    Estate Names 314

    Golf Courses on Former South Shore Estates 320

    Landscape Architects 321

    Maiden Names 323

    Occupations 337

    Rehabilitative Secondary Uses of Surviving Estate Houses . . . 348

    Statesmen and Diplomats Who Resided on Long Island's South Shore . . 350

    Village Locations of Estates 352

    America's First Age of Fortune: A Selected Bibliography . . . 359

    Selected Bibliographic References to Individual
    South Shore Estate Owners 366

Biographical Sources Consulted 387

Maps Consulted for Estate Locations 388

Illustration Credits 389

The authors are sincerely indebted to the following for their assistance:

Ruth Albin, Curator, Babylon Village Museum, Village of Babylon Historical and Preservation Society, Babylon, NY

Victoria Aspinwall, Long Island Studies Institute, Hofstra University, Hempstead, NY

Cathy Ball, Librarian, Long Island Room, Smithtown Library, Smithtown, NY

Wallace W. Broege, Director, Suffolk County Historical Society Museum, Riverhead, NY

James Connell, President, Bayport Heritage Association, Bayport, NY

Constance Gibson Currie, former President, Sayville Historical Society, Sayville, NY

Carey Davis, Babylon Village Museum, Village of Babylon Historical and Preservation Society, Babylon, NY

Louise Dougher, former Director, Greenlawn–Centerport Historical Association, Greenlawn, NY

Carl Ilardi, Historian/Archivist, The Admiralty, West Bay Shore, NY

David Kerkhof, Reference Librarian, Suffolk County Historical Society, Riverhead, NY

Thomas A. Kuehhas, Director, Oyster Bay Historical Society, Oyster Bay, NY

Gary Lawrance, AIA, Architect

Raymond Lembo, Archivist, East Islip Historical Society, East Islip, NY

Richard Martin, Suffolk County Historian, Great River, NY

Rodney G. Marve, Assistant Director, Bay Shore–Brightwaters Public Library, Brightwaters, NY

Gasper Merced, Sayville, NY

Dr. Natalie A. Naylor, Director Emerita, Long Island Studies Institute, Hofstra University, Hempstead, NY

E. Lee North, Historian, Village of Brightwaters, Brightwaters, NY

Florence Olsson, Director, Bayport Heritage Association, Bayport, NY

Eric Gordon Ramsay III, President, Eric Gordon. Ramsay, Jr. Associates, LLC, Bay Shore, NY

John S. Rienzo, Jr., Librarian/Archivist, Dowling College, Oakdale, NY

Mark H. Rothenberg, Senior Reference Specialist and Historian, Suffolk Cooperative Library System and Patchogue – Medford Library, Patchogue, NY

Coleen A. Smisek, Head Librarian, Adult Reference Services, Bay Shore – Brightwaters Public Library, Brightwaters, NY

Thomas B. Smith, Historian, Town of Babylon, North Babylon, NY

Debra Willett, Associate Director, Long Island Studies Institute, Hofstra University, Hempstead, NY

Alice Zaruka, former President, Babylon Village Museum, Village of Babylon Historical and Preservation Society; current Historian, Village of Babylon, Babylon, NY

We would especially like to thank:

Frederic Lawrence Atwood, Barbara Gulden Black, Marjorie Wilson Candiano, John Vanderveer Gibson, Frank Gulden III, Harry W. Havemeyer, Louise Gulden Henriksen, William R. Hulse, Peter G. Johnston, Jr., Matthew Morgan, Helena Parsons Hallock Pless, Eric Gordon Ramsay III, Raymond Joseph Terry, Peter Titus, and Douglas Thomas Yates, Sr. for reviewing entries pertaining to their families and for providing invaluable genealogical information.

Raymond E. and Judith A. Spinzia

Even though an individual may not have used Sr., Jr., I, II, etc., they have been added to the surnames in an attempt to designate relationships and alleviate confusion. In some instances, birth dates have been calculated using the age at the time of death as given in *The New York Times* obituary.

Current street and village designations are given with the exception of Montauk Highway (Route 27A), which changes names several times from West Main Street, Main Street, East Main Street, and South Country Road as it passes through the various villages. To alleviate confusion we have chosen to use South Country Road, its original name, as the sole designation for the street.

The exact street address of some houses could not be determined due to the diminution of the estates by subdivision. In these cases, the road on which a major portion of the estate bordered has been recorded as the address. It should also be noted that some of the subsequent owners may not have lived in the estate's main house but rather in a service building that had been converted into a residence. To aid in tracing the estate properties, these owners have been included in the hope that this will prove useful to future researchers.

The Spinzias

Introduction

Previously studded with estates and grand hotels, the quiet, year-round villages in the Towns of Babylon and Islip today suggest little of the past and the seasonal frenzy of social activity that was the "Hidden Gold Coast" on the South Shore of Long Island. To many who pick up this volume, the concept of an estate area, a "Gold Coast," in this section of the South Shore of Long Island will be a new concept. In truth it is an old reality; preceding the development of Long Island's North Shore Gold Coast by some forty years. Spending the Spring and Autumn months in this area of western Suffolk County on the land that slopes down to the Great South Bay with the Atlantic Ocean visible on the horizon beyond Fire Island was such a social phenomenon that the *Brooklyn Daily Eagle* and local newspapers announced the rental intentions and seasonal arrivals of families. When houses were sold; when houses were renovated; when new houses were built, that was news.

The South Shore estate owners built their homes, generally more modest than those that would be built in the estate area of the North Shore, conveniently close to the main roads and actually financed railroad spurs to serve the South Shore communities where their homes were located. The plank roads gave way to gravel roads which eventually gave way to paved roads. Families who had moved their households in wagons and carriages and boats soon had automobiles. The arrival of fleets of moving vans heralded the summer season. The seasonal visitors enjoyed the congenial socialization of the seaside environment so much that families who rented soon became families that owned homes to which they escaped from the very different world of the city. Coming out to the Island primarily from Brooklyn and Manhattan, they tended to build near their friends thus establishing streets of country homes that could almost be labeled as "Manhattan streets" and "Brooklyn streets."

The North Shore Gold Coast extended eastward along the Island's North Shore from the Queens / Nassau boundary for approximately twenty five miles to the Village of Centerport in Suffolk County and some fifteen miles southward from the shoreline of the Long Island Sound, an area of approximately three hundred and seventy-five square miles. The South Shore Gold Coast began at the Nassau / Suffolk border and extended eastward about sixteen miles to the Bayport / Blue Point village boundary and about one mile southward from South Country Road to the shore of the Great South Bay, an area of approximately sixteen square miles. The expanse of the North Shore area and the relative exclusivity of its residents created a significantly different social structure from that of the South Shore.

A closely knit, but ethnically and religiously diverse and tolerant, social and business community evolved on the South Shore as families settled in for the season. They were predominately sugar plantation owners and sugar refiners, merchants, shipping magnets, attorneys, capitalists, and investment bankers. Curtiss–Wright aeroplanes, the New York Central Railroad, Gulden mustard, Domino sugar, Entenmann bakery, Moran tugboats, Adams and Chicle chewing gum, Doxsee clams, Lorillard and American Tobacco, deMurias and Bachia cigars, Abraham and Straus, Arnold and Constable, Singer sewing machines, Bon Ami cleanser, Republic Pictures, and Pinkerton National Detective Agency are names still recognizable today; they were the businesses of South Shore families.

With the notable exceptions of William Collins Whitney, Benjamin Sumner Welles III, August Belmont, Perry Belmont, George Scott Graham, Meyer Robert Guggenheim, Sr., Walter Hines Page, Sr., Regis Henri Post, Sr., Robert Barnwell Roosevelt, Sr., George Campbell Taylor, and Landon Ketchum Thorne, Jr., few South Shore Gold Coast residents served in national politics. Unlike their counterparts who lived in the North Shore's Gold Coast area, those living on the South Shore were more likely to serve at the local level.

Their sons and daughters grew up along the shore, socialized, and married. They, in turn, brought their families to the South Shore. Today, many of their descendents still live on the South Shore, having chosen to live on Long Island year-round; the island so aptly described in Hal B. Fullerton's promotional campaign for the Long Island Rail Road as the "Blessed Isle."[1]

Raymond E. and Judith A. Spinzia

Endnotes

1. For additional information on the prominent families of Long Island's South Shores and the social history of Long Island's South Shore see Harry W. Havemeyer, *Along the Great South Bay from Oakdale to Babylon: The Story of a Summer Spa 1840-1940* (Mattituck, NY: Amereon House, 1996); Harry W. Havemeyer, *East on the Great South Bay: Sayville and Bellport 1860-1960* (Mattituck, NY: Amereon House, 2001); Harry W. Havemeyer, *Fire Island's Surf Hotel and Other Hostelries on Fire Island Beaches in the Nineteenth Century* (Mattituck, NY: Amereon House, 2006); and Harry W. Havemeyer, "The Story of Saxton Avenue," *Long Island Forum* (Winter, February 1, 1990 and Spring, May 1, 1990). For information on Long Island's North Shore estates see Edward A. T. Carr, Michael W. Carr, and Kari-Ann R. Carr, *Faded Laurels: The History of Eaton's Neck and Asharoken* (Interlaken, NY: Heart of the Lakes Publishing, 1994); Robert B. Mackay, Anthony K. Baker, and Carol A. Traynor, eds., *Long Island Country Houses and Their Architects, 1860-1940* (New York: W. W. Norton & Co., 1997); Liisa and Donald Sclare, *Beaux-Arts Estates: A Guide to the Architecture of Long Island* (New York: The Viking Press, 1980); and Raymond E. and Judith A. Spinzia, *Long Island's Prominent North Shore Families: Their Estates and Their Country Homes.* vols. I, II (College Station, TX: VirtualBookworm, 2006).

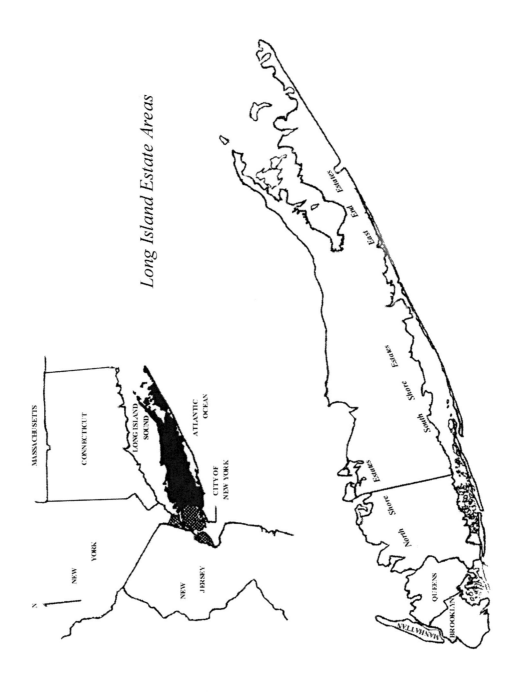

Long Island Estate Areas

South Shore Estate Area

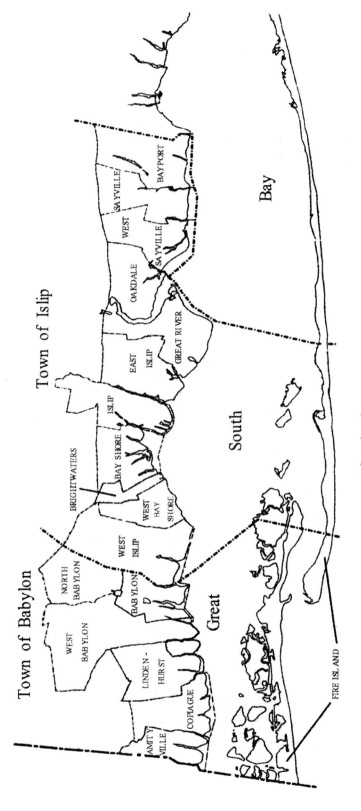

Adams, John Dunbar (1849-1934)

Occupation(s):   industrialist -   president and chairman of board, American Chicle Co.
                                                        (chewing gum manufacturer) (which merged with
                                                        Beeman Chemical Co.; W. J. White & Sons of
                                                        Cleveland, OH; S. T. Britten of Toronto, Canada;
                                                        Kisme Gum Co. of Louisville, KY; and J. P. Primley
                                                        of Chicago, IL, to form American Chicle Co.)

Marriage(s):   Susan Burchell

Address: South Country Road, Bay Shore
Name of estate: *Woodlea*
Year of construction: c. 1902
Style of architecture: Modified Neo-Tudor
Architect(s):
Landscape architect(s):
House extant: no; destroyed by fire, c. 1955*
Historical notes:

The house was built by Dr. Alfred Ludlow Carroll.

It was purchased from Mrs. Carroll by Adams, who called it *Woodlea*.

The *Brooklyn Blue Book and Long Island Society Register, 1918* lists Mr. and Mrs. John Dunbar Adams as residing at *Woodlea* in Bay Shore.

He was the son of Thomas and Martha Dunbar Adams, Sr. His brother Thomas Adams, Jr., who married Emma Mills and, subsequently, Elizabeth Flood, resided at *Ardmore* in West Bay Shore. His brother Horatio married Mary Hartwell Carter and resided at *Appledale* in Glen Cove.

In 1917, John Dunbar and Susan Burchell Adams' son Dunbar married Edith Temple Gracie, the daughter of Archibald and Constance Elise Schack Gracie of Manhattan. Archibald, who was the last man rescued when the *Titanic* sunk, died several months later due to the effects of exposure caused by the accident. Archibald's will stipulated that his estate was to be divided equally between his daughter Edith and his wife. Edith died during World War I while Dunbar was serving in the army. Mrs. Gracie accused Mr. and Mrs. John Dunbar Adams of entering her daughter's house and stealing Edith's will which left Edith's estate entirely to her mother. After a lengthy court trial, which finally ended in 1922, the Adamses were exonerated but agreed to pay Mrs. Gracie $75 per week as her share of the estate. In 1925 Mrs. Gracie married Count Humbert Aguirre de Urbino who, it turned out, was not a count but instead a dishwasher who absconded with Mrs. Gracie's jewelry which was valued at $5,000. [*The New York Times* January 7, 1929, p. 26.]

[See following entry for additional family information.]

In 1929 Mr. and Mrs. John Dunbar Adams donated their son Dunbar's 1912 Simplex racing car to the Smithsonian Institution.

*In the 1950s, the house became Mimi's Awixa Pond Restaurant.

rear facade

Adams, Thomas, Jr. (1846-1926)

Occupation(s): industrialist - president, Adams & Sons (chewing gum manufacturer) (which merged with Beeman Chemical Co.; W. J. White & Sons of Cleveland, OH; S. T. Britten of Toronto, Canada; Kisme Gum Co. of Louisville, KY; and J. P. Primley of Chicago, IL, to form American Chicle Co.)
president, American Chicle Co.

Marriage(s): M/1 – 1871-1925 – Emma Mills (d. 1925)
M/2 – 1926-1926 – Elizabeth Flood (b. 1884)

Address: South Country Road, West Bay Shore
Name of estate: *Ardmore*
Year of construction: c. 1905
Style of architecture: Mediterranean Villa
Architect(s):
Landscape architect(s):
House extant: yes
Historical notes:

The house, originally named *Ardmore*, was built by Thomas Adams, Jr.

The *Brooklyn Blue Book and Long Island Society Register, 1918* lists Mr. and Mrs. Thomas Adams [Jr.] as residing in Bay Shore [West Bay Shore].

He was known locally as "Tutti Frutti Adams." [Harry W. Havemeyer, *Along the Great South Bay From Oakdale to Babylon: The Story of a Summer Spa 1840 to 1940* (Mattituck, NY: Amereon House, 1996), p. 291.]

In 1896, an actress by the name of Myrtle Thurlow sued Adams for breach-of-promise. She claimed to have over one hundred letters in her possession that Adams had written to her in which he referred to her as "Dear Little Chick," "Darling Little Rosebud," and "My Dear Little Bluebird." [*The New York Times* August 18, 1896, p. 2.]

Elizabeth Flood Adams was the daughter of Thomas Flood of Manhattan.

[See previous entry of additional family information.]

Thomas and Emma Mills Adams, Jr.'s son George J. Adams, Sr. resided in Hempstead. Their daughter Florence, who married George Augustus Ellis, Jr., subsequently owned *Ardmore*.

The house is currently part of Southward Ho Country Club.

front facade, 2005

2

Aldrich, Spencer, Sr. (1854-1936)

Occupation(s):   attorney -   member. Blatchford, Steward, Griswold, and DaCosta;
                                       member, DeWitt, Lockman, and DeWitt
                        capitalist*
Civic Activism: trustee, St. Luke's Home for Aged Women, NYC

Marriage(s):   1876 – Hariette Holley Dall

Address: Bay Shore Avenue, Bay Shore
Name of estate: *Windermere*
Year of construction:
Style of architecture:
Architect(s):
Landscape architect(s):
House extant: unconfirmed
Historical notes:

   The *Long Island Society Register, 1929* lists Spencer and Hariette Holly Dall Aldrich [Sr.] as residing at *Windermere* on Bay Shore Avenue in Bay Shore.
   He was the son of Herman Daggett and Elizabeth Wyman Aldrich.
   Hariette Holley Dall Aldrich was the daughter of Austin Dall of Baltimore, MD.
   Spencer and Hariette Holley Dall Aldrich, Sr.'s daughter Louise married William Christen Meissner. Their daughter Mary married Charles Malcolm Fraser. Their daughter Helen married Talcott Hunt Clark. Their daughter Maude married Stanley Matthews. Their son Spencer remained a bachelor.
   *Upon the death of his father Spencer Aldrich, Sr. retired from the practice of law to administer his father's extensive real estate holdings, which included twenty-eight different trusts and legacies of Manhattan property.

Allen, Theodore (1838-1908)

Occupation(s):   politician -   Republican Ward Boss, Eighth Ward, Manhattan
                        gambler*

Marriage(s):   _____ Smith (d. 1903)

Address: Fairview Avenue, Bayport
Name of estate:
Year of construction:
Style of architecture: Victorian
Architect(s):   Isaac Henry Green II designed
                           alterations (for Allen)
Landscape architect(s):
House extant: no; destroyed by fire, 1911
Historical notes:

front facade

   In 1883, Allen purchased the Daniel Coger house.
   *The son of an Episcopalian clergyman, Allen's unsavory lifestyle was accented by his ownership of several illegal gambling establishments, a thriving bookie operation, and taverns that were patronized by criminals and prostitutes. In 1871, he was critically injured and permanently disfigured when a disgruntled gambler stabbed him several times in an ice pick and bit off a portion of his nose. [Harry W. Havemeyer, *East on the Great South Bay: Sayville and Bayport 1860-1960* (Mattituck, NY: Amereon House, 2001), pp. 71-73.]
   The house was subsequently owned by Allen's granddaughter Mrs. Clarence Owens.

3

Allgood, Andrew Perry de Forest (1885-1956)

Occupation(s):   engineer -   Lockwood and Green Engineers, Inc., NYC

Marriage(s):   M/1 – Laurie Smith
                                 M/2 – Dorothy _____

Address: *[unable to determine street address]*, Sayville
Name of estate:
Year of construction:
Style of architecture:
Architect(s):
Landscape architect(s):
House extant: unconfirmed
Historical notes:

In 1925, Allgood inherited $100,000 from a prominent Syracuse, NY, woman, who jumped or fell from the window of her Manhattan hotel room after having dinner with Allgood. Her will was contested by her two nieces, whose bequest amounted to only $100 each. Allgood agreed to a settlement of $10,000 to cover his legal fees. The nieces divided $25,000 between them and the balance of $65,000 went to a Syracuse hospital.

Allgood was killed when he was struck by a Manhattan bus as he was crossing Third Avenue at Thirty-second Street. [*The New York Times* January 25, 1956, p. 16.]

Laurie Smith Allgood was the daughter of Elward and Frances Cairns Smith, Sr., who resided in Sayville. Her sister Frances married Admiral Harry Alexander Baldridge, Sr. and also resided in Sayville, as did their brother Jewett, who married Virginia Woodhull Otto, and their brother Elward Smith, Jr., who married Ella Bailey. Their brother Irving was killed in World War I.

Allison, William Manwaring, Sr. (1869-1946)

Occupation(s):   capitalist -   president, William M. Allison & Co. (wholesale
                                              importer and exporter of drugs and spices)

Marriage(s):   Alice Crosby (d. 1952)

Address: 29 South Clinton Avenue, Bay Shore
Name of estate:
Year of construction:
Style of architecture: Victorian
Architect(s):
Landscape architect(s):
House extant: yes
Historical notes:

The *Long Island Society Register, 1929* lists Mr. and Mrs. William Manwaring Allison [Sr.] as residing at 29 South Clinton Avenue in Bay Shore.

In 1926 their son William Manwaring Allison, Jr. died at the age of twenty-one.

Their daughter Frances married Wilbur Kyle McAneny, the son of Samuel Wright McAneny of Fanwood, NJ.

front facade, 2005

Andrews, William Loring (1837-1920)

Occupation(s):   financier -   trustee, Bank for Savings, NYC;
                                                  director, Continental Insurance Co.
           writer -   *New Amsterdam, New Orange, New York*, 1898;
                                                  Fragments of American History, 1898;
                                                    Old Book Sellers of New York; A Trio of French Engravers, 1899;
Portraiture of American Revolutionary War; James Lyne's Survey, 1900;
Gossip About Book Collecting, 1900;
Paul Revere and His Engravings;
Iconography of Battery and Castle;
Treatyse of Fysshynge Wyth An Angle, 1903;
New York as Washington Knew It After the Revolution, 1906;
Sportsmen and Binder of Angling Books, 1907;
The Heavenly Jerusalem;
Catalogue of Early Printed Books Given to Yale University, 1912

Civic Activism: manager, House of Refuge, Randall's Island;
trustee, School District #1, Town of Islip;
member, executive board, Metropolitan Museum of Art, NYC;
a founder, Grolier Club, NYC;
a founder and president, Society of Iconophiles of New York

Marriage(s):   1860 – Jane Elizabeth Crane

Address: Oak Neck Lane, West Islip
Name of estate: *Pepperidges*
Year of construction:
Style of architecture: Colonial Revival
Architect(s):
Landscape architect(s):
House extant: yes
Historical notes:

William Loring Andrews was the son of Loring and Caroline C. Delamater Andrews.
Jane Elizabeth Crane Andrews was the daughter of Theodore Crane of New York.

front facade, 1903

Arnold, Alexander Duncan Cameron (b. 1891)

Occupation(s):

Marriage(s):   M/1 – 1911-div. 1919* – Evelyn Hollins Nicholas (b. 1895)
                        M/2 – 1918 – Katharine Weeks

Address: South Country Road, West Islip
Name of estate:
Year of construction:
Style of architecture:
Architect(s):
Landscape architect(s):
House extant: unconfirmed
Historical notes:

    Alexander Duncan Cameron Arnold was the son of Edward Miller Cameron of West Islip. After the death of their parents, Alexander and his brother Edward William Cameron were adopted by their aunt Annie Cameron Arnold and assumed the Arnold surname. Edward married Edith Isabelle Trenchard and resided at *Oknoke* in West Islip. [Harry W. Havemeyer, *Along the Great South Bay From Oakdale to Babylon: The Story of a Summer Spa 1840 to 1940* (Mattituck, NY: Amereon House, 1996), pp. 253-54.]

    Evelyn Hollins Nicholas Arnold was the daughter of Harry Ingersoll and Alice M. Hollins Nicholas, Sr. of *Virginia Farm* in North Babylon. Evelyn subsequently married Joseph H. Stevenson of Hewlett. Her brother Harry Ingersoll Nicholas II married Dorothy Snow and resided at *Rolling Hill Farm* in Muttontown. Her sister Beatrice married Edward Nicholl Townsend, Jr. of Manhattan. Her sister Reta married Uriel Atwood Murdock II and resided in Babylon. Her sister Daisy married Grosvenor Nicholas and resided in Old Westbury. Her sister Elsie married Alonzo Potter and resided at *Harbor House* in St. James.

    *In 1919, Evelyn filed for divorce. The court ruled that the 1918 Nevada divorce, secretly obtained by Alexander, was invalid and gave Evelyn custody of their two children. [*The New York Times* October 7, 1919, p. 19.] Presumably, Alexander had legal problems with his 1918 marriage to Katharine Weeks.

    [See other Arnold entries for additional family information.]

Annie Stuart Cameron Arnold estate, Clovelly,
rear facade, 2006

Arnold, Annie Stuart Cameron (d. 1945)

Civic Activism: bequeathed $50,000 and one-quarter of her estate residuary
                                          and a contingent interest in the remainder to St. Rose's
                                          Settlement of the Catholic Social Union, NYC;
                   bequeathed *Clovelly* to the Dominican Fathers of the Provence
                                         of St. Joseph*

Marriage(s):   William Arnold (1863-1891)
                               - merchant -   partner, Arnold, Constable & Co.
                                             (department store chain)

Address: South Country Road, West Islip
Name of estate: *Clovelly*
Year of construction: 1906
Style of architecture: Georgian Revival
Architect(s):
Landscape architect(s):
House extant: yes**
Historical notes:

    Annie Stuart Cameron Arnold demolished her father-in-law's house and built a new house, which she called *Clovelly*.

    She was the daughter of A. M. Cameron of Manhattan. Her brother Edward married Annie Caroll and resided in West Islip.

    William Arnold was the son of Richard and Pauline Bicar Arnold.

    [See other Arnold entries for additional family information.]

    *In 1948, the religious order sold *Clovelly* to Cadman H. Frederick, who subdivided its property for a housing development. [*The New York Times* September 18, 1948, p. 25.]

    **The house and the estate's greenhouse survive. The house is currently the Arnold Manor condominium. The greenhouse in now located on the SUNY Farmingdale campus.

front facade, nd

front facade, 2005

Arnold, Edward William Cameron (1887-1954)

Occupation(s):
Civic Activism: donated twenty-one ship models, dating from 1776-1875,
                         to the Museum of the City of New York

Marriage(s):   M/1 – Edith Isabelle Trenchard
                M/2 – Mary Knight

Address: South Country Road, West Islip
Name of estate: *Oknoke*
Year of construction:
Style of architecture:
Architect(s):
Landscape architect(s):
House extant: unconfirmed
Historical notes:

    The *Long Island Society Register, 1929* lists Edward William Cameron and E. Isabelle Trenchard Arnold as residing at *Oknoke* on South Country Road in West Islip.
    He was the son of Edward Miller Cameron of West Islip.
    Edith Isabelle Trenchard Arnold was the daughter of Edward and Mary Stafford Trenchard of Manhattan. Edith had previously been married to John Anthony Power, with whom she resided in Manhattan. John Anthony and Edith Isabelle Trenchard Power's daughter Mary married Samuel Walter Gregg, Jr. of Bradford, PA. Their daughter Patricia married M. Marshall Marston of Washington, DC.
    Edward William Cameron and Edith Isabelle Trenchard Arnold's thirty-three-year-old son Richard died in a fire while asleep in his three-room tenement apartment at 826 Ninth Avenue, Manhattan. [*The New York Times* April 23, 1945, p. 18.] Their son Frederick married Katherine L. Carney and resided in Babylon.
    [See other Arnold entries for additional family information.]

Arnold, Richard (1825-1886)

Occupation(s):   merchant -   partner, Arnold, Constable & Co. (department store chain)

Marriage(s):   M/1 – Pauline Bicar (d. 1875)
                M/2 – 1882-1886 – Georgina E. Bolmer

Address: South Country Road, West Islip
Name of estate: *The Crescent*
Year of construction: 1873
Style of architecture:
Architect(s):
Landscape architect(s):
House extant: no
Historical notes:

    The house, originally named *The Crescent*, was built by Richard Arnold.
    His father Aaron was a found of Arnold, Constable & Co.
    Pauline Bicar Arnold was the daughter of Noel J. Bicar of Manhattan.
    Richard and Pauline Bicar Arnold's son William inherited the house. Upon William's death, it was inherited by his wife Annie Stuart Cameron Arnold, who demolished the house and built a new house, which she called *Clovelly*.
    Georgina E. Bolmer Arnold was the daughter of M. T. Bolmer of Manhattan. Her sister Louise married Frederick A. Constable and resided in Manhattan.
    [See other Arnold entries for additional family information.]

Ash, Dr. Charles F. (1848-1937)

Occupation(s):	physician - dentist
Civic Activism:	president, First Dental Society of New York State;
	president, Second Dental Society of New York State;
	member, fund raising committee, Beekman Street Hospital,
	NYC (which became Beekman–Downtown Hospital
	after its merger with Downtown Hospital)
Marriage(s):	Lucretia Durfey
Address:	Penataquit Avenue, Bay Shore
Name of estate:	
Year of construction:	c. 1912
Style of architecture:	
Architect(s):	
Landscape architect(s):	
House extant: unconfirmed	
Historical notes:	

The house was built by Dr. Charles F. Ash on property he purchased from John Adolph Mollenhauer. [Harry W. Havemeyer, *Along the Great South Bay From Oakdale to Babylon: The Story of a Summer Spa 1840 to 1940* (Mattituck, NY: Amereon House, 1996), p. 371.]

Dr. Charles F. and Mrs. Lucretia Durfey Ash's son Prentice married Olive Louise Snow, the daughter of Elmer J. Snow, and resided in Mahwah, NJ. Their daughter Kathryn married Harry Carlson of Woodstock, IL, and resided in Englewood, NJ.

Asten, Thomas B. (1825-1895)

Occupation(s):	politician - president, NYC Board of Taxes and Assessments;
	*
Marriage(s):	
Address:	Saxon Avenue, Bay Shore
Name of estate:	
Year of construction:	
Style of architecture:	
Architect(s):	
Landscape architect(s):	
House extant: unconfirmed	
Historical notes:	

The house was built by Thomas B. Asten.
*He was a delegate to the 1864 Republican National Convention that nominated Abraham Lincoln.
Asten's daughter Louise married Frank Curtis.

Aston, W. K. (d. 1919)

Occupation(s):   capitalist -   extensive holdings in NYC and on Long Island

Marriage(s):

Address: south of Montauk Highway, Oakdale
Name of estate: *Peperidge Hall*
Year of construction: c. 1880
Style of architecture: French Chateau
Architect(s):   H. Edward Ficken designed
                            and reassembled the house
                            (for C. R. Robert, Jr.)*
Landscape architect(s):
House extant: no; demolished in 1940
Historical notes:

Peperidge Hall

The house, originally named *Peperidge Hall*, was built by Christopher Rhinelander Robert, Jr.

*Its interior had been removed from a chateau in Normandy, France. Robert brought the crated interior to Long Island and had it reassembled in his country house.

In 1896, Robert sold the estate to Aston, who unsuccessfully attempted to subdivide its property for a housing development in 1907.

Atwood, Frederic Lawrence (b. 1930)

Occupation(s):   attorney -   partner, Pelletreau and Pelletreau;
                                   partner, Fisher, Egan, and Golden, LLP, Patchogue
                               judge -   U. S. Magistrate, Federal Court, Nassau and Suffolk
                                       Counties
Civic Activism: trustee, Long Island Maritime Museum, West Sayville;
                      member, advisory committee, Long Island Community Foundation;
                      president, Seatuck Environmental Association, Islip;
                      trustee, Bayard Cutting Arboretum, Great River;
                      member of board, Southside Hospital, Bay Shore

Marriage(s):   1955 – Elizabeth Morse

Address: 272 Ocean Avenue, Islip
Name of estate:
Year of construction: 1961
Style of architecture: Ranch
Architect(s):
Landscape architect(s):
House extant: yes
Historical notes:

The house was built by Frederic Lawrence Atwood on a portion of his parents' estate.
Elizabeth Morse Atwood was the daughter of George Perley Morse of Brookhaven.
[See following entry for family information.]

Atwood, Kimball Chase, Jr.

Occupation(s):   financier -   secretary, president, and chairman of board, Preferred
                                               Accident Insurance Co.
Civic Activism: director, New York State Chamber of Commerce

Marriage(s):   1925 – Adela Overton Girdner (d. 1976)

Address: Ocean Avenue, Islip
Name of estate: *Mapleton*
Year of construction: c. 1890
Style of architecture: Shingle
Architect(s):   Isaac Henry Green II designed
                             the house (for Schieren)
Landscape architect(s): Olmsted
House extant: no; demolished in 1979*
Historical notes:

   The house, originally named *Mapleton*, was built by Charles Adolph Schieren, Sr.
   In 1926, it was purchased by Atwood, who continued to call it *Mapleton*.
   Kimball Chase Atwood, Jr. was the son of Kimball Chase and Caroline B. Hutchins Atwood, Sr.
   Adela Overton Girdner Atwood was the daughter of Dr. John
Harvey and Mrs. Adela Overton Pratt Girdner. Dr. Girdner was
one of the attending physicians at President Garfield's deathbed.
   Kimball Chase and Adela Overton Girdner Atwood, Jr.'s son
John married Judith Avery King of Portland, ME. Their son
Frederic married Elizabeth Morse, the daughter of George
Perley Morse of Brookhaven.
   *The garage, stable, and caretaker's apartment are extant and
are currently private residences. The estate's carriage house is
also extant. It was moved to Frederic Lawrence Atwood's
property.

west facade, c. 1908

Bachia, Richard Augustus, Jr. (1857-1930)

Occupation(s):   industrialist -   R. A. Bachia & Co., Long Island City (manufacturer
                                               of "fine" Havana cigars)

Marriage(s):   M/1 – Mary Teresa Rieliey (1860-1885)
                         M/2 – 1890 – Emily P. _____ (d. 1945)

Address: Montgomery Avenue, Bay Shore
Name of estate:
Year of construction:
Style of architecture: Mediterranean Villa
Architect(s):
Landscape architect(s):
House extant: no
Historical notes:

   The Long Island Society Register, 1929 lists Mr. and Mrs.
Richard A. Bachia [Jr.] as residing on South Country Road
in Bay Shore.
   Mary Teresa Rieliey Bachia was the daughter of James
and Teresa Rieliey.

side facade

Baker, William Dunham

Occupation(s):

Marriage(s):   Louise Thompson (d. 1966)

Address: 146 East Bayberry Road, Islip
Name of estate:
Year of construction: 1899-1900
Style of architecture: Moorish
Architect(s):   Grosvenor Atterbury designed the house
                           (for H. O. Havemeyer)*
Landscape architect(s): Nathan F. Barrett
                           (for H. O. Havemeyer)**

House extant: yes
Historical notes:

    The house was built by Henry Osborne Havemeyer as part of his "Modern Venice" development.
It was subsequently purchased by Baker.
    William Dunham and Louise Thompson Baker's daughter Elizabeth married Temple Eppes Dalrymple, the
son of Matthew Dalrymple of Carthage, NC. Their son William Thompson Baker, Sr. married Elizabeth
Baird, the daughter of William Parfitt Baird of Bay Shore.
    The house was later owned by Joseph Francis Dempsey, Jr.
    *The sales brochure for "Modern Venice" states that the Moorish-style architecture was suggested by
Louis Comfort Tiffany.
    **The sales brochure also states that "Modern Venice" would be devoid of trees and vegetation and that
Nathan F. Barrett was the landscape architect.

front facade, 2006

Baldridge, Harry Alexander, Sr. (1880-1952)

Occupation(s):   military -   admiral, United States Navy;
                                                      fleet ordinance officer, Pacific Fleet, 1913;
                                                        commander, Destroyer Division 20, World War I;
    instructor, Naval War College, Newport, RI, 1921-1923;
    director, Department of Seamanship and Flight Tactics, 1924 - 1928;
    director, aviation, United States Naval Academy, 1937-1952;
    director, Military Museum, United States Naval Academy, 1937-1952

                          intelligence agent -   director, Naval Intelligence Department, 1930-1932

Marriage(s):   M/1 – 1910-1911 – Rosalie McDermot (d. 1911)
                                   M/2 – 1914 – Frances Elward Smith

Address: Handsome Avenue, Sayville
Name of estate:
Year of construction:
Style of architecture:
Architect(s):
Landscape architect(s):
House extant: unconfirmed
Historical notes:

    Harry Alexander Baldridge, Sr. was the son of William and Anna Reynolds Baldridge of Albany, NY.
    Frances Elward Smith Baldridge was the daughter of Elward and Frances Cairns Smith, Sr., who resided in Bayport. Her sister Laurie married Andrew Perry de Forest Allgood and resided in Sayville. Her brother Jewett married Virginia Woodhull Otto of Patchogue. Her brother Elward Smith, Jr. married Ella Bailey and resided in Sayville. Her brother Irving was killed in World War I.

Ballard, Frederick E., Sr. (1854-1915)

Occupation(s):   financier -   member, Cyril de Cordova (stock brokerage firm)

Marriage(s):   Elizabeth B. Keeler

Address: Awixa Avenue, Bay Shore
Name of estate:
Year of construction:
Style of architecture:
Architect(s):
Landscape architect(s):
House extant: unconfirmed
Historical notes:

    Elizabeth B. Keeler Ballard's sister Emma married Frederick Gilbert Bourne and resided at *Indian Neck Hall* in Oakdale.
    Frederick E. and Elizabeth B. Keeler Ballard, Sr.'s daughter Helen married Walter Hayward Powers, Jr. Their daughter Grace married Philip Barnard Philipp.

Baruch, Bernard Mannes, Sr. (1870-1965)

Occupation(s):	financier - member, A. A. Housman and Co. (stock brokerage firm)
Civic Activism:	member, Council of National Defense, Wilson administration; commissioner, raw materials, minerals, and metals, 1916; chairman, Allied Purchasing Commission (later, War Industries Board) during World War I; member, U. S. delegation to Peace Conference, 1919; trustee and major benefactor, College of the City of New York; a founder, Camden Hospital, Camden, SC
Marriage(s):	1897 – Annie Griffen
Address:	Ocean Avenue, Bayport
Name of estate:	*Strandhome*
Year of construction:	1890
Style of architecture:	Shingle
Architect(s):	Isaac Henry Green II designed the house (for W. R. Foster, Jr.) George Browne Post designed the alterations (for Charles Alfred Post)

Landscape architect(s):
House extant: no; demolished in the 1950s
Historical notes:

The house, originally named *Strandhome*, was built by William R. Foster, Jr.

In 1888, it was purchased at public auction by the Produce Exchange Gratuity Fund. In 1890, the Fund sold the house to Charles Alfred Post, who also called in *Strandhome*. It was subsequently owned by his son Waldron Kintzing Post, who continued to call it *Strandhome*.

Baruch rented the house during the summers of 1915 and 1916.

He was the son of Simon and Belle Wolfe Baruch of Camden, SC. His brother Dr. Herman Benjamin Baruch, who resided in Dix Hills, married Rosemary Emetaz and, subsequently, Baroness Anna Marie Mackay of The Hague.

Annie Griffen Baruch was the daughter of Benjamin Griffen of New York.

Bernard Mannes and Annie Griffen Baruch, Sr. had three children, Belle, Renee, and Bernard Mannes Baruch, Jr.

Strandhome

Bates, William Graves (1860-1944)

Occupation(s):   military - general, United States Army
                                 attorney
Civic Activism: trustee, Grant Monument Association;
                                 treasurer, New York State Society of Colonial Wars;
                                 member, Citizen's Visiting Committee, Bay Shore High School

Marriage(s):   1899-1944 – Amy Rowan Scott (1865-1953)

Address: South Country Road, Bay Shore
Name of estate: *Evergreens*
Year of construction:
Style of architecture: Shingle
Architect(s):
Landscape architect(s):
House extant: unconfirmed
Historical notes:

front facade, c. 1903

    William Graves Bates was the son of Levi Miles and Martha Arnold Tucker Bates.
    Amy Rowan Scott Bates was the daughter of James Rowan Scott. She had previously been married to Effingham Lawrence Johnson, with whom she resided in Bay Shore.
    Effingham Lawrence and Amy Rowan Scott Johnson's daughter Amy married Herbert Groesbeck and resided in Manhattan.

Baxter, John Edward (1878-1958)

Occupation(s):   industrialist - president, Baxter, Kelly, & Faust, Inc. (textile manufacturers)
                                 financer - trustee, Dime Savings Bank of Brooklyn
Civic Activism -   director, Brooklyn Society for Prevention of Cruelty to Children;
                                 *

Marriage(s):   1902-1953 – Katherine Byrne (1879-1953)
                  - Civic Activism: regent, Brooklyn Circle of International Federation
                                        of Catholic Alumnae;
                                   a founder, Catholic Thrift Shop of Brooklyn;
                                   a founder, Villa de Sales Convalescent Home;
                                   director, Dr. White Memorial Catholic Settlement;
                                   chairman, Brooklyn Red Cross, home nursing chapter,
                                        during World War II;
                                   trustee, Brooklyn Girl Scout Council

Address: Clinton Avenue, Bay Shore
Name of estate:
Year of construction:
Style of architecture:
Architect(s):
Landscape architect(s):
House extant: unconfirmed
Historical notes:

    The *Long Island Society Register, 1929* lists the Baxters' residence as Clinton Avenue in Bay Shore.
    Their daughter Claire married Norman C. Hilborn, the son of Hedley H. Hilborn of Brooklyn and Belle Terre. Their daughter Ann married John de Lacey Regan, the son of John F. Regan of Brooklyn.
    *Because of his extensive civic activities, Baxter was made a Knight of St. Gregory in 1919 by Pope Pius X and a Knight of Malta in 1945 by Pope Pius XII.

Beard, Anson Mc Cook, Jr. (1909-1997)

Occupation(s):   financier -   investment banker

Marriage(s):   1934 – Roseanne Hoar

Address: 126 East Bayberry Road, Islip
Name of estate:
Year of construction: 1899-1900
Style of architecture: Moorish*
Architect(s):   Grosvenor Atterbury designed the house
                              (for H. O. Havemeyer)*
Landscape architect(s):   Nathan F. Barrett
                              (for H. O. Havemeyer)**

House extant: yes
Historical notes:

The house was built by Henry Osborne Havemeyer as part of his "Modern Venice" development.
It was owned by Richard Sturgis Perkins, Sr. and, subsequently, by Beard.

The *Social Register, 1945* lists Captain Anson Mc Cook and Mrs. Roseanne Hoar Beard [Jr.] as residing at 152 South Main Street, Southampton. The *Social Register, 1946* lists the Beards as residing in Islip. They later relocated to the West Hills section of Huntington and, subsequently, to 111 High Farms Road, Glen Head.

He was the son of Anson Mc Cook and Ruth Hill Beard, Sr., who resided on Gin Lane in Southampton. Ruth Hill Beard was the daughter of James Jerome Hill, a founder of the Great Northern Railroad. After her husband's death she married Pierre Lorillard and resided in Tuxedo Park, NY. Ruth's brother James Norman Hill married Marguerite Sawyer and resided at *Big Tree Farm* in Brookville. Her daughter Mary married Frederick C. Havemeyer II and resided in Tuxedo Park, NY.

Roseanne Hoar Beard was the daughter of Friend and Virginia Goffe Hoar, who resided at *Little Orchard* in Southampton.

Anson Mc Cook and Roseanne Hoar Beard, Jr.'s son Samuel married Patricia Dranow, the daughter of Harry Dranow of Manhattan and resided in Manhattan and Delaware and Clinton Corners, NY. Their son Peter married Mary Olivia Cochran Cushing, the daughter of Howard Gardiner Cushing, Sr. of Newport, RI. Their son Anson Mc Cook Beard, Jr. [III] married Jean Jones, the daughter of Gilbert E. Jones of Greenwich, CT, and resided in Greenwich, CT.

*The sales brochure for "Modern Venice" states that the Moorish–style architecture was suggested by Louis Comfort Tiffany.

**The sale brochure also states that "Modern Venice" would be devoid of trees and vegetation and that Nathan F. Barrett was the landscape architect.

front facade, c. 2006

Bedell, Walter Ellwood

Occupation(s):   financier -   partner, Woodworth, Lounsbery and Co. (stock
brokerage firm);
partner, Morris and Smith (stock brokerage firm)

Marriage(s):

Address: Saxon Avenue, Bay Shore
Name of estate:
Year of construction:
Style of architecture: Shingle
Architect(s):
Landscape architect(s):
House extant: unconfirmed
Historical notes:

front facade

   The *Long Island Society Register, 1928* lists
Mr. and Mrs. Walter Ellwood Bedell as residing
on Saxon Avenue in Bay Shore.

Behman, Louis C., Sr. (1855-1902)

Occupation(s):   capitalist -   partner, with Richard Hyde, Hyde and Behman
Amusement Co., which owned and operated
Volks Garden, Brooklyn; Park Bijou, Brooklyn;
Amphion Theatre, Brooklyn; Folly Theatre,
Brooklyn; Grand Opera House, Brooklyn; Gaiety
Theatre, Brooklyn; and Newark Theatre, Newark, NJ

Marriage(s):   M/1 – Margaret Scott (b. 1845)
                        - entertainers and associated professions -   stage singer
              M/2 – 1900-1902 – Evelyn P. Scott (1871-1942)

Address: 80 Seaman's Avenue, Bayport
Name of estate: *Lindenwalt*
Year of construction: 1900
Style of architecture: Shingle
Architect(s):   Clarence K. Birdsall designed
                      the house (for Behman)
Landscape architect(s):
House extant: yes
Historical notes:

Lindenwalt

   The house, originally named *Lindenwalt*, was built by Louis C. Behman, Sr.
   Louis C. and Margaret Scott Behman, Sr.'s daughter Marguerite, who remained unmarried, resided in
Bayport. She was the author of a children's book entitled *Lindenwood Tales*. Their son August married
Marjorie Downey and resided in *Lindenwalt*'s gatehouse. Their daughter Consuelo married Dr. Henry T.
Hagstrom of Brooklyn.
   Louis subsequently married his sister-in-law Evelyn P. Scott. Louis C. and Evelyn P. Scott Behman, Sr.'s
son Louis C. Behman, Jr. did not attain adulthood.

Belmont, August, Sr. (1816-1890)

Occupation(s):   financier -   president, August Belmont and Co. (investment
                                                         banking firm);
                                    agent for Rothschild banking interest in United States
                diplomat -   United States *Charge d' affaires* and, later, Minister
                                        to The Netherlands;
                                    Austrian Council General to the United States
                politician -   delegate, Democratic Convention, 1860*;
                                    chairman, National Democratic Committee,
                                    1864-1868

Civic Activism: helped raise and equip the first German regiment for the Union
                             during the Civil War

Marriage(s):   1849-1890 – Caroline Slidell Perry (1829-1892)

Address: Southern State Parkway, North Babylon
Name of estate: *Nursery Stud Farm*
Year of construction: c. 1868
Style of architecture: Modified Second Empire
                                with Colonial Revival elements
Architect(s):
Landscape architect(s):
House extant: no; demolished in 1935**
Historical notes:

    The twenty-four-room house, originally names *Nursery Stud Farm*, was built by August Belmont, Sr.
He was the son of Simon and Frederika Elsaas Belmont of Alzei, Rhenish Palatinate, Prussia.
    An avid breeder of thoroughbred horses, Belmont purchased 1,100 acres in North Babylon in 1864 to be used as a stud farm. Eventually there were thirty outbuildings, a one-mile racetrack with a grandstand, and five hundred acres of the farm property under cultivation.
    Caroline Slidell Perry Belmont was the daughter of Commodore Matthew Calbraith and Mrs. Jane Slidell Perry and a niece of Commodore Oliver Hazard Perry.
    The Belmonts' son Perry, who married Jessie Robbins, inherited *Nursery Stud Farm*. Their son Oliver Hazard Perry Belmont, who resided at *Belcourt* in Newport, RI, and at *Brookholt* in East Meadow, married Sallie Whiting and, subsequently, Alva Erskine Smith Vanderbilt, the wife of his close friend William Kissam Vanderbilt, Sr., who resided at *Idlehour* in Oakdale. Their son August Belmont, Jr. [II] married Elizabeth Hamilton Morgan, the daughter of Edward Morgan and, subsequently, Eleanor Robson, who, after August's death, resided in Syosset. Their son Raymond Rogers Belmont I, who was a bachelor, committed suicide in 1887 at the age of twenty-four. Their daughter Jane died at the age of twenty-one.
    [See other Belmont entries for additional family information.]
    *During the 1860 Democratic Convention, Belmont supported Stephen A. Douglas as a compromise candidate.

    During World War I a portion of the estate became the United States Army Air Corps' Camp Dam.
    **In 1935, the house was demolished by the Long Island State Park Commission. Part of the estate's property is now Belmont Lake State Park. The two cannons in front of the commission's headquarters in the park are from a British ship sunk at the Battle of Lake Erie by Commodore Oliver Hazard Perry during the War of 1812. They were recovered by Belmont from a Pittsburgh junkyard.

Nursery Stud Farm racetrack, c. 1930

18

Belmont, August, III (1882-1919)

Occupation(s):	financier -	partner, August Belmont and Co. (investment banking firm);
		director, Windsor Trust Co.;
		director, First National Bank of Hempstead
	capitalist -	treasurer, August Belmont Hotel Co.;
		director, Interborough–Metropolitan Co.;
		director, Cape Cod Construction Co.;
		treasurer, Park Row Reality Co.;
		director, Degon Reality & Terminal Improvement Co.;
		director, Degon Terminal Railroad Corp.

Marriage(s): 1906-1919 – Alice Wall deGoicouria (1885-1926)

Address: Saxon Avenue, Bay Shore
Name of estate:
Year of construction: 1880
Style of architecture: Colonial Revival
Architect(s): Isaac Henry Green II designed the
 1889 southwestern wing addition
 of a living room and four bedrooms
 (for E. S. Knapp, Sr.)
Landscape architect(s):
House extant: no
Historical notes:

The house, originally named *Awixa Lawn*, was built by Edward Spring Knapp, Sr.
In 1915, it was purchased by Belmont.
The *Brooklyn Blue Book and Long Island Society Register, 1921* incorrectly lists August and Alice W. deGoicouria Belmont, Jr. (III), as residing on Saxon Avenue in Bay Shore.
He was the son of August and Elizabeth Hamilton Morgan Belmont II. His brother Raymond Rogers Belmont II married Ethel Helen Linda, whose stage name was Ethel Loraine, Caroline Hubbard of Virginia, and, subsequently, Marie Muurling, the daughter of I. J. R. Muurling of Virginia. Raymond and Marie resided at *Belray Farms* in Middleburg, VA. His brother Morgan married Margaret F. Andrews.
Alice Wall deGoicouria Belmont was the daughter of Cuban-born Albert V. and Mary C. Wall deGoicouria of Islip. She subsequently married John D. Wing. Alice's sister Rosalie married W. Scott Cameron, with whom she resided at *Wee Home* on Gin Lane in Southampton, and, subsequently, Benjamin Curtis Allen of Philadelphia, PA.
August and Alice Wall deGoicouria Belmont III's daughter Bessie married Louis Felix Timmerman, Jr. and resided in Manhattan and on Shelter Island. Their daughter Cecelia married Gardiner Lothrop Lewis of Swampscott, MA. Their daughter Barbara married Robert Livermore, Jr. In 1955 the Belmont's forty-five-year-old daughter Alice, who had remained unmarried, committed suicide in her apartment on 113th Street in Manhattan. Their son August Belmont IV married Elizabeth Lee Saltonstall, the daughter of John L. Saltonstall of Topsfield, MA, and, subsequently, Louise Vietor, the daughter of George F. Vietor of Manhattan. Louise had previously been married to Francis L. Winston. August and Louise Belmont IV resided on Burtis Lane in Syosset.
[See other Belmont entries for additional family information.]
In 1923, Mrs. Belmont sold the estate, which consisted of a twenty-five-room main residence on nine acres with six hundred feet of shoreline on Awixa Creek, stables, and a five-car garage to John Allen Dillon, Sr.

Belmont, Perry (1851-1947)

Occupation(s):	attorney
	politician - member, 47th through 50th Congresses, 1881-1887
	diplomat - United States Minister to Spain, 1887-1888
	writer - *National Isolation: An Illusion*, 1924;
	Survival of Democratic Principle, 1926;
	Return to the Secret Party Funds, 1927;
	Political Equality, Religious Toleration, 1928;
	An American Democrat, 1940;
Civic Activism:	member, advisory board, American Defense Society
Marriage(s):	1899-1935 – Jessie A. Robbins (d. 1935)
Address:	Southern State Parkway, North Babylon
Name of estate:	*Nursery Stud Farm*
Year of construction:	c. 1868
Style of architecture:	Modified Second Empire
	with Colonial Revival elements
Architect(s):	
Landscape architect(s):	
House extant: no; demolished in 1935*	
Historical notes:	

Perry Belmont was the eldest son of August and Caroline Slidell Perry Belmont, Sr., from whom he inherited *Nursery Stud Farm*.

Jessie A. Robbins Belmont was the daughter of Daniel C. and Matilda L. Robbins of Brooklyn. She had previously been married to Henry T. Sloane. Henry T. and Jessie Robbins Sloane's daughter Jessie married William Earle Dodge of Manhattan and, subsequently, George Dustin Widner, Jr., with whom she resided in Old Westbury. The Sloanes' daughter Emily married Baron Amaury de la Grange and resided in Paris, France.

[See previous Belmont entries for additional family information.]

During World War I a portion of the estate became the United States Air Corps' Camp Dam.

*In 1935, the house was demolished by the Long Island State Park Commission. Part of the estate's property is now Belmont Lake State Park. The two cannons in front of the commission's headquarters in the park are from a British ship sunk at the Battle of Lake Erie by Commodore Oliver Hazard Perry during the War of 1812. They were recovered by August Belmont, Sr. from a Pittsburgh junk yard.

Nursery Stud Farm

August Belmont, Sr.'s estate, Nursery Stud Farm,
rear facade, 1935, during demolition;
servants' quarters on left

Betts, Roland Whitney (1877-1954)

Occupation(s):	financier - partner, Betts, Power, and King (produce exchange brokerage firm)

Marriage(s):   M/1 – 1905-1929 – Mabel Granbery (d. 1958)
  - Civic Activism: major, Motor Ambulance Corp of New York during World War I;
      president, auxiliary, Southside Hospital, Bay Shore
    M/2 – Olga ____

Address: Handsome Avenue, Sayville
Name of estate: *Sunneholm*
Year of construction:
Style of architecture:
Architect(s):
Landscape architect(s):
House extant: unconfirmed
Historical notes:

   The *Brooklyn Blue Book and Long Island Society Register, 1918* and *1921* lists Roland Whitney and Mabel Granbery Betts as residing at *Sunneholm* in Sayville.
   The *Long Island Society Register, 1929* lists Mabel Granbery Betts as residing on Handsome Avenue in Bayport [Sayville] and Roland as residing in Manhattan.
   He was the son of Edward and Emma Whitney Betts of Brooklyn. His brother Herbert married Jessica Watkins, the daughter of Albert Watkins. His sister Mrs. Paul Strayer resided in Rochester, NY.
   Mabel Granbery Betts was the daughter of Henry A. T. and Prudence Nimmo Betts of Norfolk, VA. In 1929, Mabel married Charles Edward Spratt. Her sister Mary married Frank Smith Jones and resided at *Beechwold* in Sayville.
   Roland Whitney and Mabel Granbery Betts' son Allan married Evelyn Ohman and reside in Laurel Hollow. Their daughter Louise married Frederick David Anderson, the son of Frederick and Florence Sweetland Anderson of Ottawa, Canada.

Bigelow, Edwin Hick (1886-1970)

Occupation(s):   financier -   partner, Dillon, Read, and Co. (investment banking firm)

Civic Activism: president, East Side Draft Board, NYC, during World War I;
                   member, building fund committee, Beekman–Downtown Hospital, NYC

Marriage(s):   Alice I. Blum (d. 1988)

Address: *[unable to determine street address]*, East Islip
Name of estate:
Year of construction:
Style of architecture:
Architect(s):
Landscape architect(s):
House extant: unconfirmed
Historical notes:

The *Long Island Society Register, 1929* lists the Bigelows as residing in East Islip.

He was the son of Elliot and Edwina Richards Bigelow.

Alice I. Blum Bigelow was the daughter of Edward Charles and Florence May Abraham Blum, who resided at *Shore Acres* in Bay Shore. After her divorce from Bigelow, Alice married Eugene Sinclair Taliaferro and resided at *The Wilderness* in Cove Neck. She subsequently married Ethelbert Warfield, with whom she resided in Oyster Bay. Her brother Robert married Ethel Halsey and resided in Bay Shore.

Edwin Hicks and Alice I. Blum Bigelow's son Edwin Richards Bigelow married Melissa Weston, the daughter of Herbert Weston of Southampton, and, subsequently, Joan Evelyn Turnburke, the daughter of Harry Milton Turnburke of Clearwater, FL, and resided in Denver, CO. Their daughter Florence married Norman Schaff, Jr. and resided in Westport, CT.

Blagden, Crawford, Sr. (1882-1937)

Occupation(s):   financier -   member, Clark, Dodge, and Co. (private investment firm);
                   member, Walker and Sons (stock brokerage firm)

Civic Activism: *

Marriage(s):   M/1 – 1911-1912 – Mary Hopkins (d. 1912)
                 M/2 – 1918-1937 – Mina E. MacLeond

Address: 109 Fire Island Avenue, Babylon
Name of estate:
Year of construction:
Style of architecture: Second Empire
Architect(s):
Landscape architect(s):
House extant: yes
Historical notes:

front / side facade, 2005

The *Long Island Society Register, 1929* lists Crawford and Mina E. MacLeond Blagden, [Sr.] as residing at 109 Fire Island Avenue, Babylon.

He was the son of Samuel P. and Julia G. Blagden of Manhattan.

Mary Hopkins Blagden was the daughter of Archibald and Charlotte Everett Hopkins.

Blagden's son Crawford Blagden, Jr. married Mary Kernochan, the daughter of Justice Frederic Kernochan of Tuxedo Park, NY.

*Crawford Blagden, Sr. and Grenville Clark, Sr. of Albertson are credited with being major supporters for the establishment of the Plattsburg, NY, training camps, which, during World War I, trained over 16,000 men to become army officers. [*The New York Times* January 13, 1937, p. 23.]

Blum, Edward Charles (1863-1946)

Occupation(s):	merchant -	chairman of board, Abraham & Straus (department store chain) (which merged into Federated Department Store Inc.)
	financer -	trustee, Dime Savings Bank of Brooklyn; trustee, Kings County Trust Co.; trustee, Security Safe Deposit Co.
	capitalist -	vice-president, Abrast Realty Co.; treasurer, Flatbush Avenue Realty Co.

Civic Activism: chairman of board, Brooklyn Institute of Arts and Sciences;
board member, French Hospital;
board member, Brooklyn Chamber of Commerce;
board member, National Council Economic League;
member, Red Cross Auxiliary during World War I;
president, Jewish Hospital of Brooklyn;
director, Brooklyn Federation of Jewish Charities;
director, Brooklyn League;
director, Juvenile Probation Association

Marriage(s): 1894-1946 – Florence May Abraham (1872-1959)
 - Civic Activism: member of board, American Women's Voluntary Services during World War I;
member, advisory committee, New York's World Fair, 1939;
president, Hebrew Educational Society Auxiliary;
vice-chairman, women's committee, Boston Symphony concerts in Brooklyn

Address: Penataquit Avenue, Bay Shore
Name of estate: *Shore Acres*
Year of construction: c. 1902
Style of architecture: Queen Anne
Architect(s):
Landscape architect(s):
House extant: no
Historical notes:

    The *Long Island Society Register, 1929* lists Edward Charles and Florence May Abraham Blum as residing at *Shore Acres* in Bay Shore.
    He was the son of Adolph and Ida Deutsch Blum of Manhattan.
    Florence May Abraham Blum was the daughter of the co-founder of Abraham and Straus Department Store, Abraham Abraham. Her sister Lillian married Simon Frank Rothschild and resided in Bay Shore. Her sister Edith married Percy S. Straus and resided in Manhattan and Red Bank, NJ.
    Edward Charles and Florence May Abraham Blum's daughter Alice married Edwin Hicks Bigelow and resided in East Islip. She later married Eugene Sinclair Taliaferro and resided at *The Wilderness* in Cove Neck. Alice subsequently married Ethelbert Warfield and resided in Oyster Bay. The Blums' son Robert married Ethel Mildred Halsey and resided in Bay Shore.
    [See following entry for additional family information.]

Blum, Robert Edward (1900-1999)

Occupation(s):	merchant -	vice president and secretary, Abraham & Straus (department store chain) (which merged with F. R. Lazarus, Shillito's, and Filene's of Boston in 1929 to form the holding company Federated Department Stores Inc.*)
		director, Federated Department Stores Inc.
	financer -	director, Equitable Life Assurance Society of the United States;
		trustee, Dime Savings Bank of Brooklyn;
		trustee, Kings County Trust Co.

Civic Activism: president of board, Brooklyn Institute of Arts and Sciences;
member, New York State Board of Social Welfare (Dewey administration);
treasurer, Lincoln Center for the Performing Arts, NYC;
trustee, The Wildlife Conservation;
member, New York City Municipal Art Commission (Lindsay administration)

Marriage(s): 1928-1991 – Ethel Mildred Halsey (1901-1991)
- journalist
artist - watercolorist
Civic Activism: a founder, Brooklyn Committee for Planned Parenthood;
president, Brooklyn Juvenile Guidance Center;
trustee, Mount Desert Hospital, Bal Harbor, ME;
a founder and president, Mount Desert Island Highway Safety Council, Bal Harbor, ME;
trustee, Mount Desert Biological Laboratory, Bal Harbor, ME

Address: Penataquit Avenue, Bay Shore
Name of estate:
Year of construction:
Style of architecture:
Architect(s):
Landscape architect(s):
House extant: unconfirmed
Historical notes:

The *Long Island Society Register, 1929* lists Robert Edward and Ethel Mildred Halsey Blum as residing in Bay Shore. They subsequently resided at *Slope Oaks* in the Roslyn area of Long Island's North Shore.
He was the son of Edward Charles and Florence May Abraham Blum of *Shore Acres* in Bay Shore.
Ethel Mildred Halsey Blum was the daughter of Dr. and Mrs. John T. Halsey.
Robert Edward and Ethel Mildred Halsey Blum's son John married Susanne Holcomb Jousseam Delatour, the daughter of Dr. Beeckman J. Delatour of South Worcester, NY. Their daughter Alice married Robert H. Yoakum and resided in Lakefield, CT.
[See previous entry for additional family information.]
*Federated Department Stores, Inc. currently owns and operates 992 stores in forty-five states, the District of Columbia, Guam, and Puerto Rico under the names Bloomingdale's, Famous – Barr, Filene's, Foley's, Hecht's, Kaufmann's, Lord & Taylor, L. S. Ayres, Macy's, Marshall Field's, Meier & Frank, Robinsons – May, Strawbridge's, and The Jones Store. It also owns and operates 721 bridal and formalwear stores in forty-seven states and Puerto Rico under the names of David's Bridal, After Hours Formalwear, and Priscilla of Boston.

Bohack, Henry C. (1865-1931)

Occupation(s):   merchant -   president, H. C. Bohack & Co. (grocery store chain
                                           of 740 stores)
                            capitalist -   president, Bohack Realty Corp.
                            financier -   director, People's National Bank of Brooklyn;
                                           director, Guarantee Title and Mortgage Co.;
                                         director, East New York Securities Co.;
                                         trustee, Hamburg Savings Bank of Brooklyn

Civic Activism: trustee, Wartburg Orphan Training School, Mount Vernon, NY;
                         director, Queensborough Chamber of Commerce

Marriage(s):   1885-1931 – Emma A. Steffens

Address: South Country Road and Greeley Avenue, Sayville
Name of estate:
Year of construction:
Style of architecture:
Architect(s):
Landscape architect(s):
House extant: yes
Historical notes:

   The Bohacks spent one summer in Sayville.

Bossert, Charles Volunteer (1888-1953)

Occupation(s):   industrialist -   partner, with his half brother John, Bossert Lumber
                                               Co., Brooklyn*
                            capitalist -   partner, with his mother Philippine and half brother
                                             John, Hotel Bossert, Brooklyn Heights
                                         president, Bossert Building Corp., Trenton, NJ

Marriage(s):   Natalie Taylor (d. 1977)

Address: *[unable to determine street address]*, Sayville
Name of estate:
Year of construction:
Style of architecture:
Architect(s):
Landscape architect(s):
House extant: unconfirmed
Historical notes:

   Charles Volunteer Bossert was named after the America Cup winner *Volunteer.*
   He was the son of Louis and Philippine Krippendorf Bossert, who resided at *The Oaks* in West Islip.
   Natalie Taylor Bossert was the daughter of Irving G. and Florence Rockford Taylor of Brooklyn.
   Charles Volunteer and Natalie Taylor Bossert's daughter Isabelle married Edward Peter Ruddy of Forest Hills, Queens. Their daughter Natalie married John Gildersleeve Heemans, Jr. of Brooklyn.
   [See following entry for additional family information.]
   *The Bossert Lumber Company, which was one of the largest lumber companies in the country, filed for bankruptcy during the Depression. [Liz Howell, *Continuity: Biography 1819-1934* (Sister Bay, WI: The Dragonsbreath Press, 1993), pp. 364-65.]

Bossert, Louis (1843-1913)

Occupation(s):   capitalist -   builder and owner, Hotel Bossert, Brooklyn Heights;
                                                    director, Estates of Long Island (real estate developer)
                        industrialist -   president, Bossert Lumber Co., Brooklyn;
                                                    president, Louis Bossert & Sons, Brooklyn (sash
                                                            manufacturer)
                        financier -   president, Broadway Bank of Brooklyn;
                                                    trustee, Germania Savings Bank

Civic Activism: trustee, Brooklyn Academy of Music

Marriage(s):   M/1 – 1869-1884 – Elizabeth Neger (d. 1884)
                                M/2 – 1885-1913 – Philippine Krippendorf (1859-1945)

Address: South Country Road, West Bay Shore
Name of estate: *The Oaks*
Year of construction: c. 1874-1876
Style of architecture: Stick Style
Architect(s):   Calvert Vaux designed the house
                                (for H. B. Hyde, Sr.)
Landscape architect(s):   Olmsted, with Jacob Weidenman
                                (for H. B. Hyde, Sr.)*

House extant: yes**
Historical notes:

    The forty-room house, situated on 365 acres, was originally named *Masquetux* before being renamed *The Oaks*. It was built by Henry Baldwin Hyde, Sr.

    The estate was inherited by his son James, who continued to call it *The Oaks*.

    In 1901, the estate and most of James Hazen Hyde's furniture were purchased by Bossert. [Liz Howell, *Continuity: Biography 1819-1934* (Sister Bay, WI: The Dragonsbreath Press, 1993), p. 221.]

    Louis Bossert was the son of Alois and Mary Bossert of Brooklyn.

    Elizabeth Neger Bossert was the daughter of Mathias Neger, a successful Brooklyn wine merchant.

    Louis and Elizabeth Neger Bossert's son John married Mary A. James and resided in Garden City and, later, in Jamaica, Queens. Their daughter Harriet married Frederick Max Huber, Sr. and resided in Bay Shore. Their daughter Josephine married Dr. Henry Moser of Brooklyn.

    Philippine Krippendorf was originally the Bossert children's piano teacher.

    Louis and Philippine's son Charles married Natalie Taylor and resided in Sayville. Their daughter Bienie married Carroll Trowbridge Cooney, the son of John J. Cooney of Brooklyn, and resided in Plandome.

    Louis Bossert died of a ruptured appendix half way between Honolulu and San Francisco, while returning from a round-the-world tour.

    [See previous entry for additional family information.]

    *Weidenman's landscape plans were awarded special honor at the 1876 Centennial Exhibition in Philadelphia, PA.

    **The house, which has been extensively modified over the years, is currently the clubhouse of the Southward Ho Country Club.

The Oaks

Louis Bossert estate, The Oaks
service building, front facade, 2005

Bourne, Alfred Severin, Sr. (1878-1956)

Occupation(s):
Civic Activism: donated Barnes Memorial Field, in memory of his wife, to Gunnery
         School, Washington, CT*;
         donated Bourne Field to Berkshire School, Sheffield, MA

Marriage(s):   1905-1955 – Hattie Louise Barnes (d. 1955)
         - Civic Activism: president, Garden Club, Washington, CT;
                          president, Sands Hill Garden Club,
                          Augusta, GA

Address: South Country Road, Oakdale
Name of estate:
Year of construction:
Style of architecture:
Architect(s):
Landscape architect(s):
House extant: unconfirmed
Historical notes:

     The *Brooklyn Blue Book and Long Island Society Register, 1918* lists Alfred S. and Hattie Louise Barnes Bourne [Sr.] as residing in Oakdale. The *Brooklyn Blue Book and Long Island Society Register 1921* lists their address as South Country Road, Oakdale.

     He was the son of Frederick Gilbert and Emma Sparks Keeler Bourne, who resided at *Indian Neck Hall* in Oakdale.

     Alfred Severin and Hattie Louise Barnes Bourne, Sr.'s son Alfred Severin Bourne, Jr. married Nancy H. Work and resided at *The Woodlands* on Oakwood Lane in Greenwich, CT. Their son Kenneth married Ann E. Clark, the daughter of Raymond P. Clark of Rochester, NY, and resided in Rochester. Their daughter Barbara married John B. Von Schiegell and resided in Pinehurst, NC. Their son Frederick Gilbert Bourne II died in infancy.

     [See other Bourne entries for additional family information.]

     *In 1958 the Gunnery School purchased Bourne's 140-acre Washington, CT, estate.

Bourne, Arthur Keeler, Sr. (1877-1967)

Occupation(s):	industrialist - director, Singer Sewing Machine Co.
	capitalist - president, Round Hill Resort, Lake Tahoe, CA
Civic Activism:	established Claire Louise Progressive Elementary School,
	San Gabriel, CA (now, Clairbourn School)
Marriage(s):	M/1 – 1903 – Ethel L. Hollins (d. 1970)
	M/2 – Emily Boxley Miller
	M/3 – Jean _____
Address:	South Country Road, Oakdale
Name of estate:	*Lake House*
Year of construction:	c. 1904
Style of architecture:	Colonial Revival
Architect(s):	Isaac Henry Green II designed
	the house (for A. K. Bourne, Sr.)
Landscape architect(s):	
House extant: yes	
Historical notes:	

The house, originally named *Lake House*, was built by Arthur Keeler Bourne, Sr.

He was the son of Frederick Gilbert and Emma Sparks Keeler Bourne of *Indian Neck Hall* in Oakdale.

Ethel L. Hollins Bourne was the daughter of Frank C. Hollins, a stockbroker who committed suicide in 1909. [*The New York Times* April 10, 1909, p. 9.] Her sister Daisy married Willard F. Smith and resided at *Ledgeland* in Lee, MA.

In 1922, at the age of eighteen, Arthur Keeler and Ethel L. Hollins Bourne, Sr.'s son Arthur Keeler Bourne, Jr. eloped with Beatrice Clancy, the daughter of John F. Clancy, an Astoria, Queens, general building contractor. Their marriage was shaky almost from the start. In 1924, Beatrice sued Arthur for separation on the charge of desertion and sued her mother-in-law for alienation of affections. In 1925, Beatrice had Arthur arrested and jailed for disorderly conduct, claiming that he had struck her. The arresting officer had to pursue Bourne for three city blocks before apprehending him. In spite of his having jumped bail on the desertion charge, Arthur's bail for the disorderly conduct charge was set at only $1,000. In 1926, after two years of legal battles, Arthur and Beatrice were reunited, but the reunion didn't end Arthur's legal problems. In 1927, he was involved in a fatal head-on automobile accident on Motor Parkway in the Village of Lake Success in which Frank A. Cotton of Indianapolis was killed. Bourne and the other driver Frank G. Brown, a cotton broker, accused each other of being drunk. [*The New York Times* June 25, 1925, p. 3; August 19, 1927, p. 19; August 20, 1927, p. 3; August 21, 1927, p. 27; and August 30, 1927, p. 10.]

In the midst of his son's problems, Arthur Keeler Bourne, Sr. had his own legal battles which involved suits and counter-suits with his brothers and sisters over the distribution of their father's inheritance.

[See other Bourne entries for additional family information.]

The house was purchased by LaSalle Military Academy. It is currently owned by the Joint Industry Board of the Electrical Industry.

front facade, 2005

Bourne, Frederick Gilbert (1851-1919)

Occupation(s):	industrialist -	president, Singer Sewing Machine Co;
		director, Diehl manufacturing Co.;
		director, Babcock & Wilcock Co.;
		director, Atlas Portland Cement Co.;
		director, Aeolian Piano & Pianola Co.;
		trustee, New York Phonograph Co.
	financier -	director, Knickerbocker Safe Deposit Co.;
		director, Bank of Manhattan Co.; Liberty National
		Bank; Knickerbocker Trust Co.; Albany Trust
		Co.; and Commercial Trust Co. of New Jersey
	capitalist -	director, Long Island Rail Road;
		director, Bourne & Co., Ltd. of New Jersey;
		director, Long Island Motor Parkway;
		director, Long Branch Rail Road Co.

Marriage(s): 1875-1916 – Emma Sparks Keeler (d. 1916)

Address: South Country Road, Oakdale
Name of estate: *Indian Neck Hall*
Year of construction: 1897-1900
Style of architecture: Modified Neo-Federal
Architect(s): Ernest Flagg designed the house, 1907 and 1908 alterations, and c. 1909
garage (for F. G. Bourne)
Alfred Hopkins designed the c. 1910 farm complex (for F. G. Bourne)
Isaac Henry Green II designed the c. 1904 gatehouse, c. 1905 boathouse,
and c. 1913 pump house (for F. G. Bourne)
Landscape architect(s): Olmsted (for F. G. Bourne)*
House extant: yes
Historical notes:

The house, originally named *Indian Neck Hall*, was built by Frederick Gilbert Bourne.
He was the son of The Reverend George Washington and Mrs. Harriet Gilbert Bourne of Boston, MA.
Emma Sparks Keeler Bourne's sister Elizabeth married Frederick E. Ballard, Sr. and resided in Bay Shore.
Frederick Gilbert and Emma Sparks Keeler Bourne's son Arthur Keeler Bourne, Sr., who resided at *Lake House* in Oakdale, married Ethel L. Hollins, Emily Boxley Miller, and, subsequently, Jean ____. Their son Alfred Severin Bourne, Sr. married Hattie Louise Barnes and resided in Oakdale. Their son George Galt Bourne, who resided in Lattingtown, married Helen Cole Whitney and, subsequently, Nancy Atterbury Potter, the daughter of Eliphalet N. Potter. Their daughter Florence married Anson Wales Hard, Jr., with whom she resided at *Meadowedge* in West Sayville, Robert Barr Deans, Sr., with whom she resided at *Yeadon* on Centre Island, and, subsequently, Alexander Dallas Thayer of Philadelphia, PA. The Bournes' daughter Marjorie also was married to Alexander Dallas Thayer. Their daughter Marion married Robert George Elbert, the son of George Cleveland and Emma Breuer Elbert of Frederick, MD, and resided at *Elbourne* in North Hills. Their daughter May married Ralph Beaver Strassburger and resided at *Normandy Farm* in Gwynedd Valley, PA. Their son Howard died at age twenty-five. He was a bachelor. Their son Kenneth did not attain adulthood.
[See other Bourne entries for additional family information.]
*The landscaping on the approximately two-thousand-acre estate consisted of the planting of 10,000 trees and shrubs, the creation of two artificial fresh water lakes, and the dredging of a three-mile canal system.
In 1925, the Bourne family sold the estate to a land development syndicate headed by Joseph P. Day.
In 1926, Clason Point Military Academy of The Bronx purchased the main house, the boathouse, the garage complex, the gatehouse, and the surrounding 154 acres and renamed the academy LaSalle Military Academy. [James Fordyce, "Frederick Bourne and Indian Neck Hall" *Long Island Forum* April 1987, p. 88.]
In 2001, the academy, then named LaSalle Center, sold it to St. John's University.
In 2006, the estate was purchased by the Joint Industry Board of the Electrical Industry.

Frederick Gilbert Bourne Estate, *Indian Neck Hall*

south facade, c. 1905

north facade, c. 1905

south facade, 1955

gatehouse, 1991

boathouse, 1991

30

Breese, William Laurence (1852-1888)

Occupation(s):   financier -   partner, Smith and Breese (stock brokerage firm)

Marriage(s):   1880 – Mary Parsons

Address: Great River Road, Great River
Name of estate: *Timber Point*
Year of construction: 1882
Style of architecture: Shingle
Architect(s):   Hart and Shape designed the
                                alterations, converting the
                                house to Colonial Revival
                                (for Timber Point Club)
Landscape architect(s): Martha Brooks Brown Hutcheson
                                (for Breese)

House extant: yes
Historical notes:

Timber Point, c. 1900

The house, originally named *Timber Point*, was built by William Laurence Breese.

He was the son of J. Salisbury and Augusta Eloise Lawrence Breese of Manhattan.

Mary Parsons Breese was the daughter of George M. Parsons of Columbia, OH. She subsequently moved to Great Britain and married Henry Vincent Higgins.

William Laurence and Mary Parsons Breese's daughter Eloise married Gilbert Heathcote Drummond Willoghby, the Earl of Ancaster. Their daughter Anna married Lord Alastair Robert Innes–Kerr. Both daughters resided in Great Britain. [Harry W. Havemeyer, *Along the Great South Bay From Oakdale to Babylon: The Story of a Summer Spa 1840 to 1940* (Mattituck, NY: Amereon House, 1996), pp. 130, 355, and 418.]

In 1905, the estate was purchased by Julian Tappan Davies, who continued to call it *Timber Point*. In 1923, his heirs sold the estate to the Great River Club, which changed its name to the Timber Point Club in 1925.

It was owned for a period of time by the Republican Party of Suffolk County before being purchased by Suffolk County. The house is currently the clubhouse of the county's Timber Point Country Club.

Bromell, Alfred Henry (d. 1925)

Occupation(s):

Marriage(s):   Estelle Knowles

Address: Little East Neck Road, Babylon
Name of estate:
Year of construction: 1902
Style of architecture: Mediterranean Villa
Architect(s):
Landscape architect(s):
House extant: no*
Historical notes:

The house was built by Jay Stanley Foster II.

It was subsequently owned by Bromell.

Estelle Knowles Bromell had previously been married to Jay Stanley Foster II.

At the time of his death the Bromells were residing on Centre Island.

*Only the carriage house is extant.

Brownlie, George

Occupation(s):   capitalist -   Manhattan real estate
                        politician -   mayor, Dearing Harbor, Shelter Island

Marriage(s):

Address: Little East Neck Road, Babylon
Name of estate: *Willow Close*
Year of construction: c. 1913
Style of architecture: Neo-Georgian
Architect(s):
Landscape architect(s):
House extant: yes
Historical notes:

   The house is currently the clubhouse of the Long
Island Yacht Club.

rear facade, 2005

Bruce–Brown, Ruth A. Loney (d. 1927)

Civic Activism: bequeathed $1,537,654 each to the New York Post Graduate Medical
                        School and Hospital and to the Home for Incurables*

Marriage(s):   George Bruce–Brown (1844-1892)

Address: Main Street and Route 111, Islip
Name of estate: *Bronhurst*
Year of construction: c. 1915
Style of architecture: Modified Neo-Federal
Architect(s):
Landscape architect(s):
House extant: yes
Historical notes:

   The house, originally named *Bronhurst*, was built by
Ruth A. Loney Bruce–Brown.
   Her sister Mary married Frederick Roosevelt and
resided in Manhattan. Her sister Alice married Harry S.
Abbot and resided in Pelham Manor, NY. Her brother
Henry resided in Mountain Lake, NJ.
   *Known as the Bruce–Brown Memorial Fund it was
established in memory of her husband George and her
sons William and David. An amateur automobile racer,
David was killed in 1912 in an auto accident in
Milwaukee, WI. [*The New York Times* November 21, 1928, p. 2.]

front facade

Bull, Henry Worthington (1874-1958)

Occupation(s):   financier -   partner, Edward Sweet and Co. (investment banking firm);
                                       partner, Bull Holden and Co. (stock brokerage firm);
                                       director, Fulton Trust Co., NYC

Civic Activism: president, National Steeplechase and Hunt Association

Marriage(s):   1904-1958 – Maria Maude Livingston

Address: St. Mark's Lane, Islip
Name of estate:
Year of construction:
Style of architecture:
Architect(s):
Landscape architect(s):
House extant: unconfirmed
Historical notes:

    The house was built by Parmenus Johnson.
    In 1880, it was purchased by E. B. Spaulding, who enlarged and modernized the house.
    In 1886, it was purchased by Robert Cambridge Livingston III.
    It was subsequently owned by Livingston's daughter Maria, who married Henry Worthington Bull.
    He was the son of William Lanman and Sara Newton Worthington Bull. As a sergeant in the Rough Riders, Bull participated in the engagements at Las Guasimas, San Juan Hill, and the siege of Santiago.
    Maria Maude Livingston Bull was the daughter of Robert Cambridge and Maria Whitney Livingston III. Her brother John married Clara M. Dudley and resided in Lawrence. Her brother Johnston married Natalie Havemeyer. Her brother Louis married Catherine Murphy and resided in Manhattan. Her brother Henry remained a bachelor. Her sister Caroline married Maxwell Stevenson, the son of A. L. Stevenson.

Burchell, George W. (1850-1926)

Occupation(s):   financier -   vice president, Queens Insurance Co. of America
Civic Activism: president, National Board of Fire Underwriters of New York;
                                       vice-president, New York Board of Fire Underwriters

Marriage(s):   Ellen Rushton Haviland (d. 1924)

Address: 46 Penataquit Avenue, Bay Shore
Name of estate:
Year of construction: 1897
Style of architecture: Shingle
Architect(s):
Landscape architect(s):
House extant: yes
Historical notes:

    George W. and Ellen Rushton Haviland Burchell's daughter Sarah married Harry Townsend Rounds. Their daughter Florence married Irving G. Day of Newark, NJ.

front facade, 2006

Burke, Charles Felix (1881-1937)

Occupation(s):	capitalist - advertising manager, William E. Harmon & Co. (Cincinnati, Detroit, and New York real estate developer);
	vice-president, Edmund G. and Charles F. Burke, Inc. (New York and Pittsburgh, PA, real estate development company)*
Civic Activism:	trustee, Denison University, Granville, OH;
	chairman, Gifts and Bequests Committee, Denison University;
	trustee, First Baptist Church of Pittsburgh;
	deacon, Riverside Church, NYC;
	director, Brooklyn Real Estate Board
Marriage(s):	Lorena M. Woodrow
Address:	island in Connetquot River, Oakdale

Name of estate:
Year of construction:
Style of architecture:
Architect(s):
Landscape architect(s):
House extant: unconfirmed
Historical notes:

Born in Bethel, OH, Charles Felix Burke was the son of Orville and Jennie Glenn Burke. His father Orville was associated with President Ulysses S. Grant in the tannery and leather firm of Grant–Burke–Medary. [*The New York Times* January 23, 1937, p. 17.]

Lorena M. Woodrow Burke had previously resided in Emporia, Kansas.

*Edmund G. and Charles F. Burke, Inc. were developers of major subdivisions in Manhattan, Howard Beach, Queens, Bergen Beach, Brooklyn, and on the site of Camp Upton in Yaphank. The Burkes purchased the William Kissam Vanderbilt, Sr. estate *Idlehour* and subdivided its property for a residential development. The furnishings from the main residence were sold by the firm through the American Art Galleries in New York City. In 1943, Charles' brother Edmund acquired *Beacon Towers*, the Sands Point estate of Vanderbilt's first wife Alva, demolished it, and created a housing subdivision on the estate's property. [*The New York Times* May 10, 1966, p. 45.]

Burke residence

Cameron, Edward Miller (d. 1895)

Occupation(s):   industrialist - president, Hygeia Distilled Water Co.
                                   financier -   member, Kerr and Co. (stock brokerage firm)

Marriage(s):   M/1 – _____ Arnold
                                   M/2 – 1891 – Annie Carll

Address: South Country Road, West Islip
Name of estate:
Year of construction:
Style of architecture:
Architect(s):
Landscape architect(s):
House extant: unconfirmed
Historical notes:

    Edward Miller Cameron died of a self-inflicted pistol wound to the heart. He was the son of A. M. Cameron of Manhattan. His sister Annie, who resided at *Clovelly* in West Islip, married William Arnold.
    Annie Carll Arnold was the daughter of Harvey Carll, who resided at *The Red Cottage* in West Islip.
    Edward and Annie Carll Cameron's sons Alexander Duncan Cameron and Edward William Cameron were adopted by their aunt Annie Arnold and assumed the surname of Arnold.

Carlisle, Jay Freeborn, Sr. (1868-1937)

Occupation(s):   financier -   partner, Mellick and Co. (stock brokerage firm);
                                        member, board of governors, New York Stock
                                              Exchange
Civic Activism: trustee, Southside Hospital, Bay Shore

Marriage(s):   1906-1937 – Mary Pinkerton (1886-1937)
                       - Civic Activism: member, fund raising committee,
                                          Southside Hospital, Bay Shore

Address: Suffolk Lane, East Islip
Name of estate: *Rosemary*
Year of construction: 1917
Style of architecture: Mediterranean Villa
Architect(s):   Trowbridge and Ackerman designed
                         the house (for Carlisle)
Landscape architect(s): Vitale, Brinkerhoff, and Geiffert
                         (for Carlisle)
House extant: no; demolished c. 1940
Historical notes:

    The house, originally named *Rosemary*, was built by Jay Freeborn Carlisle, Sr.
    Mary Pinkerton Carlisle was the daughter of Robert Allan and Anna E. Hughes Pinkerton, who resided at *Dearwood* in Bay Shore. Her sister Anna married Lewis Mills Gibb, Sr. and resided at *Cedarholme* in Bay Shore. Her brother Allan Pinkerton II married Franc Woolworth and resided in Bay Shore.
    Jay Freeborn and Mary Pinkerton Carlisle, Sr.'s son Jay Freeborn Carlisle, Jr. married Margaret Moffett, the daughter of Standard Oil president James A. Moffett, and resided in Brookville.
    In 1932, prior to the younger Carlisle's marriage to Margaret, his father foiled a plot to kidnap the young couple and hold them for $30,000 ransom. [*The New York Times* November 13, 1937, p. 5.]

Jay Freeborn Carlisle, Sr. Estate, *Rosemary*

courtyard

front facade

garden stairs

rear facade

Carroll, Dr. Alfred Ludlow (b. 1833)

Occupation(s):	physician
	writer - articles in numerous medical journals
Civic Activism:	a founder, New York State Medical Association;
	a founder, New York State Board of Health, 1872;
	secretary and president, New York State Board of Health
Marriage(s):	1862 – Lucy Johnson (d. 1909)
Address:	South Country Road, Bay Shore
Name of estate:	
Year of construction:	c. 1902
Style of architecture:	Modified Neo-Tudor
Architect(s):	
Landscape architect(s):	
House extant:	no; destroyed by fire, c. 1955*
Historical notes:	

The house was built by Dr. Alfred Ludlow Carroll.

Lucy Johnson Carroll was the daughter of Bradish and Louisa Anna Lawrence Johnson, Sr., who resided at *Sans Souci* in Bay Shore. Her brother Bradish Johnson Jr. married Amiee E. J. Gillard and resided at *Woodland* in East Islip. Her brother Effingham married Amy Scott and resided in Bay Shore. Her sister Helena married Schuyler Livingston Parsons, Sr. and resided at *Whileaway* in Islip.

Dr. Alfred Ludlow and Mrs. Lucy Johnson Carroll's son Bradish married Marian Bowers, the daughter of Henry Bowers of Manhattan.

The house was purchased from Lucy Johnson Carroll by John Dunbar Adams.

*In the 1950s, the house became Mimi's Awixa Pond Restaurant.

rear facade

Catlin, Dr. Daniel, Sr. (1908-2001)

Occupation(s):   physician -   surgeon

Marriage(s):   1937-1975 – Doris Havemeyer (1912-1975)

Address: Saxon Avenue, Bay Shore
Name of estate:
Year of construction: 1949
Style of architecture: Contemporary Ranch
Architect(s):
Landscape architect(s):
House extant: no; demolished in 2004
Historical notes:

    Dr. Daniel Catlin, Sr. was the son of Daniel K. Catlin of Dublin, NH.
    Doris Havemeyer Catlin was the daughter of Horace and Doris Anna Dick Havemeyer of *Olympic Point* in Bay Shore. Her sister Adaline married Richard Sturgis Perkins, Sr. and, subsequently, Laurance B. Rand of Southport, CT. Her brother Horace Havemeyer, Jr. married Rosalind Everdell and resided in Islip and, later, Dix Hills. Her brother Harry married Eugenie Aiguier and resides on the *Olympic Point* property in Bay Shore.
    Dr. Daniel and Mrs. Doris Havemeyer Catlin, Sr.'s son Daniel Catlin, Jr. married Dundeen Bostwick, the daughter of Dunbar Wright Bostwick of Shelburne, VT. Their son Loring married Susan Carol Johnson, the daughter of Charles Raymond Johnson of Litchfield, CT. Their daughter Doris, who married Douglas Thomas Yates, Jr., the son of Douglas Thomas and Margaret Louise Titus Yates, Sr. of Islip, resides in Vermont. Their daughter Leigh married Wayne Grant Quasha, the son of William H. Quasha of Glen Cove. Leigh subsequently married John R. French and resides in Greenwich, CT, and at *Windswept* in Bridgehampton. The Catlins' son Brian married Rosalie Hornblower, the daughter of Ralph Hornblower, Jr. Rosalie subsequently married Willits H. Sawyer III and resides in Cambridge, MA.

Catlin, John Bernsee, Sr. (1889-1952)

Occupation(s):   financier -   oil industry analyst, Guaranty Trust Co.

Marriage(s):   Helen Robb

Address: 127 Gillette Avenue, Sayville
Name of estate:
Year of construction:
Style of architecture:
Architect(s):
Landscape architect(s):
House extant: unconfirmed
Historical notes:

    The *Long Island Society Register, 1929* lists John Bernsee and Helen Robb Catlin as residing at 127 Gillette Avenue in Sayville.
    Their daughter Betty married John B. Whitehouse.

Ceballos, Juan Manuel, Sr. (1859-1913)

Occupation(s):   financier -   partner, Czarikow–Rionda (sugar brokerage firm);
                                                  president, J. M. Ceballos and Co. (investment
                                                      banking firm)
                         capitalist -   president, Brighton Pier and Navigation Co.;
                                                    vice-president, Development Company of Cuba;
                                                    vice-president, Edgewater Basin Co.
                         shipping -   vice president, Iron Steamboat Co.;
                                                    director, New York & Porto [Puerto] Rico
                                                   Steamship Co.

Civic Activism: director, International Banking Association

Marriage(s):   1886-1913 – Lulu Washington (d. 1934)

Address: South Country Road, Bay Shore
Name of estate: *Brookhurst Farm*
Year of construction:
Style of architecture: Modified Colonial Revival
Architect(s):
Landscape architect(s):
House extant: unconfirmed
Historical notes:

In about 1894, Ceballos purchased the ancestral home of John Mowbray.

The *Brooklyn Blue Book and Long Island Society Register, 1921* lists Mr. and Mrs. Juan M. Ceballos as residing on Main Road [South Country Road] in Bay Shore.

One month after the sinking of the battleship *USS Maine*, Ceballos was appointed by the Spanish government to a commission that was seeking a *rapprochement* between the governments of the United States and Spain. War broke out between the two nations when the commission's recommendations were rejected by both the Cuban dissidents and President McKinley. [Harry W. Havemeyer, *Along the Great South Bay From Oakdale to Babylon: The Story of a Summer Spa 1840 to 1940* (Mattituck, NY: Amereon House, 1996), pp. 261-62.]

Lulu Washington Ceballos was the daughter of Allan C. Washington.

Juan Manuel and Lulu Washington Ceballos, Sr.'s son Juan Manuel Ceballos, Jr., who resided at *Three Winds* in Old Westbury, married Maude Elizabeth Hammill and, subsequently, Evelyn Dunn. Their daughter Louisa married the Austro-Hungarian Council General to Canada, Dr. Charles Winter.

front facade, c. 1903

Childs, Eversley, Sr. (1867-1953)

Occupation(s): capitalist - director, Technicolor Motion Picture Corp.;
director, Technicolor, Inc.;
director, Long Island Lighting Co.;
director, Queens County Gas and Electric;
director, Kings County Gas Co.;

industrialist - president, Mica Roofing Co. (which merged with
Barrett Manufacturing Co.; later, with United
Coke and Gas Co.; and, subsequently, with
American Coal, becoming Barrett Co.);
vice president, Barrett Manufacturing Co.;
president and chairman of board, Bon Ami Co., Inc.;
chairman of board, Barrett Co.;
director, Boorum and Pease Co.;
director, Congoleum Nairn Inc.

Civic Activism: a founder, with General Leonard Wood, Childs Leprosarium in
Cebu, The Philippines, 1930;
donated, with his son Eversley Childs, Jr., thirty-four acres and
buildings in Setauket to the Salvation Army to establish a
children's home, 1942;
chairman of board, Leonard Wood Memorial

Marriage(s): M/1 – 1889 – Mary Shubrick Lockwood
M/2 – 1947-1953 – Alice Barnard

Address: Edwards Avenue, Sayville
Name of estate:
Year of construction: c. 1894
Style of architecture: Colonial Revival
Architect(s): Isaac Henry Green II designed
the house (for Childs)

Landscape architect(s):
House extant: yes
Historical notes:

The house was built by Eversley Childs, Sr.
In 1902, Childs moved to Long Island's North Shore.
The *Brooklyn Blue Book and Long Island Society Register, 1918* lists Eversley and Mary Shubrick
Lockwood Childs [Sr.] as residing at *Crane Neck Farm* in Setauket.
He was the son of William Harrison and Maria Eversley Childs, Sr. of Brooklyn.
Mary Shubrick Lockwood Childs was the daughter of Dr. Charles Edward Lockwood of Manhattan.
Eversley and Mary Shubrick Lockwood Childs, Sr.'s daughter Dorothy married Archibald McLaren. Their
son William Henry Harrison Childs II married Catharine Stuart Orland and resided in Kensington in the
Great Neck area of Long Island. Their son Eversley Childs, Jr. married Margherita Abbey and resided in
Garden City, and, subsequently, Georgiana A. Van Epps, with whom he resided at *Crane Neck Farm* in
Setauket.

Childs, William Hamlin (1857-1928)

Occupation(s):	industrialist - chairman of board, Bon Ami Co., Inc.;
	director, Congoleum Co.;
	director, Crucible Steel Co., of America
	capitalist - director, Loew's Inc. (motional picture studio and theaters);
	director, Technicolor Motion Picture Corp.
Civic Activism:	donated $250,000 for the improvement of the Downtown Community House, NYC;
	chairman, Brooklyn Bureau of Charities;
	president, Battery Park Association;
	vice-president, Park Association of NYC;
	chairman, subcommittee on Coal Tar Products and Raw Materials, Council of National Defense, during World War I
Marriage(s):	1881-1928 – Nellie White Spencer
Address:	Edwards Avenue, Sayville
Name of estate:	
Year of construction:	c. 1894
Style of architecture:	Colonial Revival
Architect(s):	Isaac Henry Green II designed house (for W. H. Childs)
Landscape architect(s):	
House extant: no; destroyed by fire, c. 1995	
Historical notes:	

The *Brooklyn Blue Book and Long Island Society Register, 1918* lists William Hamlin and Nellie Spencer Childs as residing at *Belle Haven* in Greenwich, CT.

He was the son of Gordon H. and Julia Richards Childs of Hartford, CT.

William Hamlin and Nellie White Spencer Childs' daughter Mary married Ernest G. Draper and resided in Greenwich, CT.

Clarkson, William Kemble (1849-1933)

Occupation(s):	capitalist - treasurer, Kemble Reality, Co.;
	industrialist - executive, Nassau Brewing Co.
Marriage(s):	Mary Augusta Brown (d. 1923)
Address:	32 Awixa Avenue, Bay Shore
Name of estate:	
Year of construction:	c. 1890
Style of architecture:	Shingle
Architect(s):	William H. Wray designed his own house
Landscape architect(s):	
House extant: yes	
Historical notes:	

side / front facade, 2005

The house, originally named *Whileaway*, was built by William H. Wray.

It was later owned by Fred C. Lemmerman and, subsequently, by Clarkson.

The *Brooklyn Blue Book and Long Island Society Register, 1921* lists William Kemble and Mary Augusta Brown Clarkson as residing in Bay Shore.

Their son Jesse Dunsmore Clarkson, who was a professor of history at Brooklyn College, married Mary R. Griffits and resided in Bay Shore.

In 2003, the house was purchased by Dr. Mark Foehr.

Clyde, William Pancoast, Sr. (1839-1923)

Occupation(s):   shipping -   a founder and president, Clyde Steamboat Co.,
                                                   Wilmington, DE (Atlantic coast shipbuilding
                                                   and shipping firm);
                                              president, Pacific Mail Steamship Co. (Pacific coast
                                                   shipbuilding and shipping firm)
                             capitalist -   president, Richmond & Danville Railroad;
                                              president, Richmond & West Point Terminal &
                                                   Warehouse Co.*

Marriage(s):   1865 – Emeline Field Hill

Address: South Country Road, West Islip
Name of estate:
Year of construction:
Style of architecture:
Architect(s):
Landscape architect(s):
House extant: unconfirmed
Historical notes:

    In the 1880s, Clyde purchased the Minor C. Keith house. [Harry W. Havemeyer, *Along the Great South Bay From Oakdale to Babylon: The Story of a Summer Spa 1840 to 1940* (Mattituck, NY: Amereon House, 1996), p. 179.]
    The *Brooklyn Blue Book and Long Island Society Register, 1918* lists William P. and Emeline F. Hill Clyde [Sr.] as residing at *Uplands* in New Hamburg, NY.
    He was the son of Thomas and Rebecca Pancoast Clyde of Delaware.
    Emeline Field Hill Clyde was the daughter of Marshall Hill of Philadelphia, PA.
    William Pancoast and Emeline Field Hill Clyde, Sr.'s son William Pancoast Clyde, Jr. married Dora Jesslyn Taylor, the daughter of Joshua Taylor of England. Their daughter Mabel married Metropolitan Opera singer William Wade Henshaw. Their son Marshall married Margery L. Buckin.
    *As a result of the Panic of 1893, Clyde sold his interest in the Richmond & West Point Terminal and Warehouse Co. to J. P. Morgan. [Jean Strouse, *Morgan: American Financier* (New York: Random House, 1999), p. 321.]

Colt, Robert Oliver (1812-1885)

Occupation(s):   capitalist -   a founder and president, South Side Railroad Co.,
                                                   Long Island (which merged with other small
                                                   lines to form the Long Island Rail Road)

Marriage(s):   Adelaide ____ (1835-1865)

Address: South Country Road, West Bay Shore
Name of estate:
Year of construction:
Style of architecture:
Architect(s):
Landscape architect(s):
House extant: unconfirmed
Historical notes:

    The Colts' daughter Amy married Cornelius DuBois Wagstaff and resided in West Islip.

Conover, Augustus Whitlock, Sr. (1847-1901)

Occupation(s):   merchant -   partner, with H. Schaus, William Schaus (art dealers)

Marriage(s):   Ettie _____ (1848-1911)

Address: Saxon Avenue, Bay Shore
Name of estate:
Year of construction: c. 1880
Style of architecture: Victorian
Architect(s):
Landscape architect(s):
House extant: no; demolished in 1932
Historical notes:

    The house was built by Daniel Conover.
    It was inherited by his son Augustus Whitlock Conover, Sr.
    Augustus Whitlock and Ettie Conover, Sr.'s son Augustus Whitlock Conover, Jr. died before attaining adulthood. Their daughter Lillian married William Phelps Jones.
    [See following entry for additional family information.]
    The house was purchased in 1912 by Franklyn Hutton, who later sold it to his brother Edward Francis Hutton.
    In 1921, it was purchased from E. F. Hutton by Philip Balch Weld.
    In 1930, the house was purchased from Weld by H. Cecil Sharp, who demolished it and built a new house on the site.

Conover, Daniel D. (1822-1896)

Occupation(s):   capitalist -   president, Forty-Second Street Railroad, NYC;
                               vice-president, Metropolitan Surface Railroad Co.,
                                  NYC;
                               land developer and builder, Town of Islip
          politician -   New York City Street Commissioner, 1857

Marriage(s):   1846-1896 – Catherine E. Whitlock (1822-1900)

Address: Saxon Avenue, Bay Shore
Name of estate:
Year of construction: c. 1880
Style of architecture: Victorian
Architect(s):
Landscape architect(s):
House extant: no; demolished in 1932
Historical notes:

    The house was built by Daniel D. Conover.
    Catherine E. Whitlock was the daughter of Samuel M. and Phebe T. Whitlock.
    Daniel D. and Catherine E. Whitlock Conover's daughter Catherine married Morris B. Place and resided in Manhattan. Their son Augustus inherited the house.
    [See previous entry for additional family information and history of estate.]

front facade, c. 1903

43

Corbin, Austin (1827-1896)

Occupation(s):   attorney

financier - a founder, Maklot and Corbin (banking firm);
              a founder, First National Bank of Davenport

capitalist - president, Long Island Rail Road;
              president, Philadelphia & Reading Rail Road;
              president, Chicago Railroad;
              president, Bay Ridge & Coney Island Rail Road;
              director, Lehigh Railroad;
              president, Manhattan Beach Hotel, Coney Island;
              president, Long Island Improvement Co.;
              president, Argyle Hotel, Babylon;
              president, Oriental Hotel;
              director, Western Union Telegraph Co.;
              director, Marine Railway Co.;
              director, Long Island Elevated Railroad

industrialist - director, Reading Coal & Iron Co.

Marriage(s):   1853 – Hannah Wheeler

Address: off Deer Park Avenue, North Babylon
Name of estate: *Deer Park Farm*
Year of construction: c. 1875
Style of architecture: Modified Tudor
Architect(s):
Landscape architect(s):
House extant: no
Historical notes:

Deer Park Farm, c. 1893

    The house, originally named *Deer Park Farm*, was built by Austin Corbin on his 1,000-acre estate.
He maintained a private zoo on the estate grounds.
    Corbin and his coachman died of injuries sustained in a coach accident in the driveway of his Newport, RI, estate.

Corse, Israel S. (1819-1885)

Occupation(s):   merchant - partner, Jonathan Thorn & Co. (leather merchants);
                          a founder and partner, Corse & Thompson (leather
                              merchants);
                          partner, Corse & Pratt (leather merchants)

Marriage(s):

Address: South Country Road, Sayville
Name of estate: *The Swamp*
Year of construction:
Style of architecture:
Architect(s):
Landscape architect(s):
House extant: no
Historical notes:

    Israel S. Corse was the son of Israel Corse.
    His daughter Katherine married Charles Lyman, the son of G. T. Lyman of Bellport.

Covell, Charles Heber, Sr. (1833-1915)

Occupation(s):   merchant -   specialty foods store

Marriage(s):

Address: Clinton Avenue, Bay Shore
Name of estate: *Villa Avalon*
Year of construction: c. 1902
Style of architecture: Neo-Tudor
Architect(s):
Landscape architect(s):
House extant: yes
Historical notes:

front / side facade, c. 1903

   The house, originally named *Villa Avalon*,
was built by Charles Heber Covell, Sr.
   His son Charles Heber Covell, Jr. married
Florence Allison.

Cox, George, Jr. (1857-1933)

Occupation(s):   financier -   partner, with Thomas Calender, Cox and Calender
                                       (foreign exchange stock brokerage firm);
                                       vice-president, Dime Savings Bank of Brooklyn
                                       (later, Dime Savings Bank of New York; now,
                                       The Dime)

Marriage(s):   Eona Johnson

Address: Argyle Avenue, Babylon
Name of estate:
Year of construction:
Style of architecture:
Architect(s):
Landscape architect(s):
House extant: unconfirmed
Historical notes:

   The *Long Island Society Register, 1929* lists Mr. and Mrs. Cox [Jr.] as residing in Babylon.
   He was the son of George and Eliza Van Sant Cox, Sr. His brother Thomas resided in Center Moriches.
   George and Eona Johnson Cox, Jr.'s daughter married Lawrence Marcellus Bainbridge and resided in
Montclair, NJ, and Nassau Point, NY.

Cox, Stephen Perry

Occupation(s):

Marriage(s):   E. Jane Stoppani

Address: Fairview Avenue, Bayport
Name of estate: *Arcadia*
Year of construction: 1888
Style of architecture:
Architect(s):   Isaac Henry Green II designed
                              the house (for C. F. Stoppani, Sr.)
Landscape architect(s):
House extant: no
Historical notes:

The house, originally named *Arcadia*, was built by Charles F. Stoppani, Sr.

It was inherited by his daughter Jane, who married Stephen Perry Cox. The Coxes continued to call it *Arcadia*.

The *Brooklyn Blue Book and Long Island Society Register, 1918* lists Stephen Perry and E. Jennie [Jane] Stoppani Cox as residing at *Arcadia* in Bayport.

She had previously been married to ____ Harris. The Harries' daughter May married Louis H. Hamersly Jr., who was the brother-in-law of John Ellis Roosevelt and Robert Barnwell Roosevelt, Jr. *[See Roosevelt entries for additional Hamersly family information.]* Mrs. Cox' brother Charles F. Stoppani, Jr. married Evelyn Henry and resided in Bayport. Her brother Joseph married Ida Maloney and resided at *Liberty Hall* in Bayport.

In 1919, Cox sold the house to John J. O'Connor, who defaulted on its property taxes.

The house was purchased by Martin Thomas Manton. In 1939, Manton lost the house for failure to pay its property taxes.

Creamer, Frank D., Sr. (d. 1913)

Occupation(s):   politician - sheriff, Kings County, NY, 1898
                            capitalist - treasurer, Borough Construction Co.;
                                          treasurer, Sanitary Co. of Boston
                            merchant -   president Frank D. Creamer & Co. (brick and
                                          building supplies)

Marriage(s):   Lulu Murray (d. 1912)

Address: 712 South Country Road, Islip
Name of estate:
Year of construction:
Style of architecture: Queen Anne
Architect(s):
Landscape architect(s):
House extant: yes
Historical notes:

front facade, c. 1900

In 1921, the Creamers' son Frank D. Creamer, Jr., who married Laura Calderwood, was indicted for allegedly restraining trade by exchanging bids and prices with other building material suppliers, thereby creating a fixed price for building supplies within the industry. [*The New York Times* February 1, 1921, p. 27.] Their son Joseph Byron Creamer, Sr. married Ellen Juliette Moffit and resided in Islip.

[See following entry for additional family information.]

The house currently houses The Gatsby Restaurant.

Frank D. Creamer, Sr.'s house, 2006

Creamer, Joseph Byron, Sr. (1885-1930)

Occupation(s):	merchant -	director, Frank D. Creamer & Co. (brick and building supplies); president, Frank Byron Co.
	capitalist -	director Phoenix Reclamation Co.; director, Brooklyn Ash Removal Co.

Marriage(s):   1913-1930 – Ellen Juliette Moffit (d. 1941)

Address: South Country Road, Islip
Name of estate:
Year of construction:
Style of architecture:
Architect(s):
Landscape architect(s):
House extant: unconfirmed
Historical notes:

   The *Long Island Society Register, 1929* lists J. Byron and Ellen Juliette Moffit Creamer [Sr.] as residing on Main Street [South Country Road], Islip.
   He was the son of Frank D. and Lulu Murray Creamer, Sr. of Islip.
   Ellen Juliette Moffit Creamer was the daughter of William Henry Moffitt, who also resided in Islip.
   Joseph Byron and Ellen Juliette Moffit Creamer, Sr.'s daughter Lou Ellen married Conway Cohalan, the son of New York State Supreme Court Justice Denis O'Leary Cohalan, Sr.
   [See previous entry for additional family information.]
   In 1924, Mrs. Creamer sold the house and twelve acres to Andrew Lazare of Woodmere. [*The New York Times* October 3, 1924, p. 36.]

Crothers, Gordon

Occupation(s):   industrialist - member, Dennison Manufacturing Co.,
                                          Framingham, MA (now, a subsidiary
                                          of Avery–Dennison paper products
                                          manufacturer)

Marriage(s):   Marie G. Johnson (1896-1977)

Address: Ocean Avenue, Islip
Name of estate: *La Casetta*
Year of construction:
Style of architecture:
Architect(s):
Landscape architect(s):
House extant: unconfirmed
Historical notes:

   The *Social Register, Summer 1946* lists Gordon and Marie G. Johnson Crothers as residing at *La Casetta* in
Islip. The *Social Register, Summer 1950* lists their address as Ocean Avenue, Islip.
   Gordon Crothers was the son of The Reverend Dr. Samuel McChord and Mrs. Louise M. Bronson Crothers
of Cambridge, MA. His sister Helen remained unmarried.
   Marie G. Johnson Crothers was the daughter of Bradish and Aimiee E. J. Gaillard Johnson, Jr. of
Woodland in East Islip. Her brother Aymar, who inherited *Woodland*, married Marion K. Hoffman. Her
brother Bradish G. Johnson married Emma M. Grima and resided in Islip. Marie had previously been married
to William Hamilton Russell, Jr., with whom she resided in Islip. William Hamilton and Marie G. Johnson
Russell, Jr.'s daughter Amie married Don Cino Tomaso Corsini, the eldest son of Don Emmanuele and
Donna Maria Carolina Corsini of Florence, Italy. Their daughter Joan married Malcolm Scollay Low, the son
of Benjamin R. C. Low of Manhattan. Their son The Reverend William Hamilton Russell III married Joan
Schildhauer, the daughter of Clarence Henry Schildhauer of *White Oak* in Owings Mills, MD; Diane Sawyer
Fenton; and, subsequently, Elizabeth Buck Truslow, the daughter of Francis Adams and Elizabeth
Auchincloss Jennings Truslow of *The Point* in Laurel Hollow.

Robert Fulton Cutting's house, Westbrook Farm

48

Cutting, Robert Fulton (1852-1934)

Occupation(s):	capitalist -	director, St. Louis, Alton & Terre Haute Railroad;
		director, Cairo Short Line (which merged into Illinois Central Railroad;
		director, Florida Central & Peninsular Railroad (which merged into Seaboard Air Railway Co.);
		director, International Telephone & Telegraph;
		director, All America Cables, Inc.;
		director, Manhattan Storage & Warehouse Co.
	financier -	director, American Exchange Securities Co.;
		director, American Exchange National Bank;
		director, Manhattan Safe Deposit Co.;
		director, Church Properties Fire Insurance Corp.;
		director, Church Pension Corp.

Civic Activism: president, Metropolitan Opera & Real Estate Co;
president, board of trustees, Cooper Union, NYC;
president, Association for Improving the Condition of the Poor;
a founder and chairman of board, Suburban Homes (provided
 low income housing);
president, board of trustees, New York Trade School;
member, executive committee, Relief of Belgium, in NYC, during
 World War I;
a founder and president, Citizens Union (civic reform);
a founder and chairman, Bureau of Municipal Research

Marriage(s): M/1 – 1874-1875 – Natalie Schenck (d. 1875)
M/2 – 1883 – Helen Suydam

Address: South Country Road, Great River
Name of estate:
Year of construction: c. 1860s
Style of architecture: Neo-Tudor
Architect(s):
Landscape architect(s):
House extant: no; demolished in c. 1900*
Historical notes:

   The house, originally named *Westbrook Farms*, was built by Robert L. Maitland.
   In 1873, Mr. Maitland sold it to Dr. George L. Lorillard. It was later owned by Robert Fulton Cutting and, subsequently, by his brother William Bayard Cutting, Sr. They were the sons of Fulton and Elise Justine Bayard Cutting of Manhattan.
   Natalie Schenck Cutting was the daughter of Noah H. Schenck of Brooklyn.
   Helen Suydam Cutting was the daughter of Charles and Ann White Schermerhorn Suydam of Bayport. Her brother Walter married Jane Meiser Suydam and resided at *Manowtasquott Lodge* in Blue Point.
   Robert Fulton and Helen Suydam Cutting's daughter Helen married Lucius Wilmerding and resided in Far Hills, NJ. Their daughter Elizabeth married Stafford McLean. Their daughter Ruth married Reginald L. G. Auchincloss, the son of Edgar Sloan Auchincloss of Manhattan. Their son Fulton married Mary J. Amory, the daughter of Francis Inman and Grace Minot Amory of Boston, MA, and resided in North Hills and, later, in Brookville. Their son Charles married Helen McMahon, the daughter of John T. McMahon of Flushing.
   *After the Spanish American War, the house was used by the federal government as a convalescent home for returning servicemen and, then, demolished. [Harry W. Havemeyer, *Along the Great South Bay From Oakdale to Babylon: The Story of a Summer Spa 1840 to 1940* (Mattituck, NY: Amereon House, 1996), p. 148.]

Cutting, William Bayard, Sr. (1850-1912)

Occupation(s):	attorney	
	capitalist -	president, St. Louis, Alton & Terre Haute Railroad;
		director, Illinois Central Railroad;
		director, Southern Pacific Railroad Co.;
		director, Norfolk & Southern Railway Co.;
		director, Oxnard Sugar Co. (later, American Beet Co.)
	financier -	trustee, United States Trust Co.;
		director, American Exchange National Bank;
		director, Commercial Union Assurance Co.;
		director, Commercial Union Fire Insurance Co.

Civic Activism: president, Improved Dwellings Association (provided low income housing);
president, New York Chamber of Commerce;
director, Suburban Homes Co. (provided low income housing);
director, Metropolitan Opera, NYC;
director, American Museum of Natural History, NYC;
director, Metropolitan Museum of Art, NYC;
trustee, Columbia University, NYC;
trustee, General Theological Seminary, NYC;
trustee, Episcopal Church Board of Domestic and Foreign Missions

Marriage(s): 1877-1912 – Olivia Peyton Murray (1855-1949)
- Civic Activism: established traveling fellowships, Columbia Univ., NYC;
established memorial scholarship in her son Bronson's
name, Harvard Univ., Cambridge, MA;
trustee, East Islip Public School District;
a founder, woman's auxiliary, Episcopal Diocese of
New York's Board of Missions

Address: South Country Road, Great River
Name of estate: *Westbrook Farm*
Year of construction: 1886
Style of architecture: Modified Neo-Tudor
Architect(s): Charles Coolidge Haight designed the
house and 1884 east gatehouse
(for W. B. Cutting, Sr.)
Isaac Henry Green II designed the barns
[unconfirmed] and gatehouse [confirmed]
(for W. B. Cutting, Sr.)
Landscape architect(s): Olmsted, 1887-1894 (for W. B. Cutting, Sr.)
Beatrice Jones Farrand designed the animal
cemetery (for W. B. Cutting, Sr.)
House extant: yes
Historical notes:

rear facade, 2005

William Bayard Cutting, Sr., purchased the Robert L. Maitland / George L. Lorillard estate. After residing in the former Lorillard house for approximately a year, Cutting built a new house on the property, which he called *Westbrook Farm.*

He was the son of Fulton and Elise Justine Bayard Cutting of Manhattan.

Olivia Peyton Murray Cutting was the daughter of Bronson and Ann Eliza Peyton Murray of Manhattan.

William Bayard and Olivia Peyton Murray Cutting, Sr.'s son William Bayard Cutting, Jr. married Lady Sybil Cuffe. Their daughter Justine married George Cabot Ward. Their daughter Olivia married Henry James, who resided at *Greenleaves* in Cold Spring Harbor. Their son Bronson, a bachelor, was killed in an airplane crash. He was a United States Senator from New Mexico.

The estate is now the Bayard Cutting Arboretum. The house is open to the public

Dahl, George W.

Occupation(s):

Marriage(s):   Amabel Bancker Cox

Address: 22 South Ocean Avenue, Bayport
Name of estate:
Year of construction: 1881
Style of architecture: Neo-Italianate
Architect(s):
Landscape architect(s):
House extant: yes
Historical notes:

    The house was built by Joseph W. Meeks, Jr. In 1916, Mrs. Meeks sold it to Dahl.
    The *Long Island Society Register, 1929* lists George W. and Amabel Bancker Cox Dahl as residing on Ocean Avenue in Bayport.
    Amabel Bancker Cox Dahl's brother Harold Newton Cox of Southold invented the Cox method of taking colored motion pictures. [*The New York Times* March 16, 1936, p. 17.]

Dana, Richard Turner (1876-1928)

Occupation(s):   civil engineer -   assistant engineer, Erie Railroad;
                                             chief engineer, Construction Service Co.

Marriage(s):   1902-1928 – Mary R. Meredith (d. 1943)

Address: Suffolk Lane and South Country Road, East Islip
Name of estate:
Year of construction:
Style of architecture: Colonial Revival
Architect(s):
Landscape architect(s):
House extant: yes
Historical notes:

    The *Long Island Society Register, 1929* lists Richard T. and Mary R. Meredith Dana as residing in East Islip.
    He was the son of Richard Starr and Florence Turner Dana.
    Mary R. Meredith Dana was the daughter of William Tuckey and Mary R. Watson Meredith. Her sister Gertrude married J. Osgood Nichols.
    Richard Turner and Mary R. Meredith Dana's daughter Mary married William C. Kopper, the son of Philip W. Kopper of Manhattan.

front facade

Davies, Julien Tappan (1845-1920)

Occupation(s):   attorney - partner, Davies, Stone, and Auerbach;
                                              partner, Davies, Auerbach, Cornell, and Barry
                financier - vice-president, New York Title Guarantee & Trust Co.;
                                              trustee, Mutual Life Insurance Co. of New York;
                                              director, Bond and Mortgage Trust Co.

Civic Activism: vice-president, Bar Association of the City of New York;
                                  president, Saint David's Society, 1900-1903;
                                  a founder, Young Men's Municipal Association, 1871;
                                  member, board of managers, Foreign and Domestic Mission Society,
                                        Protestant Episcopal Church in the United Sates of America;
                                  trustee, St. George's School, Newport, RI

Marriage(s):   1869 – Alice Martin

Address: Great River Road, Great River
Name of estate: *Timber Point*
Year of construction: 1882
Style of architecture: Shingle
Architect(s):   Hart and Shape designed the alterations, converting the
                                  house to Colonial Revival (for Timber Point Club)
Landscape architect(s):   Martha Brooks Brown Hutcheson (for Breese)
House extant: yes
Historical notes:

    The house, originally named *Timber Point*, was built by William Laurence Breese.
    In 1905, the estate was purchased by Davies, who continued to call it *Timber Point*.
    He was the son of Judge Henry E. and Mrs. Rebecca Waldo Tappan Davies of New York.
    Alice Martin Davies was the daughter of Henry H. Martin of Albany, NY. Her brother Henry married Justine de Peyster, the daughter of Johnston de Peyster. Her brother Frederick Townsend Martin was a bachelor. Her brother Bradley Martin, Sr. married Cornelia Sherman. Her sister Anna married General William B. Rochester.
    Julien Tappan and Alice Martin Davies' daughter Ethel married Archibald d'Gourlay Thatcher and resided at *Pondcroft* in Old Westbury. Their son Julien Townsend Davies, Sr. married Marie Rose de Garmendia and resided at *Casa Rosa* in West Islip.
    [See following entry for additional family information.]
    In 1923, the Davieses' heirs sold the estate to the Great River Club, which in 1925 changed its name to the Timber Point Club. It was owned for a period of time by the Republican Party of Suffolk County. The house is currently the clubhouse of the county's Timber Point Country Club.

Timber Point, c. 1900

Timber Point, c. 1925

Davies, Julien Townsend, Sr. (1870-1917)

Occupation(s):	attorney - partner, Davies, Auerbach and Cornell
	capitalist - president and director, Bancroft Reality Co.;
	director, Maplewood Hotel Co.
Civic Activism:	vice-president of board, Southside Hospital, Bay Shore;
	member, executive committee, Suffolk County Taxpayers' Good
	Roads Association

Marriage(s):	1891-1917 – Marie Rose de Garmendia

Address:	South Country Road, West Islip
Name of estate:	*Casa Rosa*
Year of construction:	
Style of architecture:	
Architect(s):	
Landscape architect(s):	
House extant:	unconfirmed
Historical notes:	

In 1901, Julien Townsend Davies, Sr. purchased the Francis Peabody Magoun house and called it *Casa Rosa*.

He was the son of Julien Tappan and Alice Martin Davies of *Timber Point* in Great River.

Julien Townsend and Marie Rose de Garmendia Davies, Sr.'s daughter Alice married Henry Sellers McKee II, the son of Wood McKee of Woodmere, and resided in Babylon. Their daughter Phebe married Walter J. Sutherland, Jr. Their son Julien Townsend Davies, Jr., who resided in Flower Hill, married Faith de Moss Robinson, Marie O'Connor Quinn, and, subsequently, Ida Pasquali.

[See previous entry for additional family information.]

deCoppet, Andre H. (1891-1953)

Occupation(s):   financier -   president, deCoppet and Doremus (stock
                                                brokerage firm)
                               industrialist -   president, Haitian–American Development Co.*
                               capitalist -   owner, Dauphin, a sugar plantation in Haiti

Marriage(s):   M/1 – 1920 – Clara W. Barclay
                              M/2 – 1931 – Muriel Johnson
                              M/3 – 1943-1953 – Eileen Johnston (d. circa 1995)

Address: South Country Road, Islip
Name of estate: *The Willows*
Year of construction: c. 1925
Style of architecture:
Architect(s):
Landscape architect(s):
House extant: no
Historical notes:

    The house was built by William H. Moffitt.
    In 1925, it was purchased by deCoppet, who called it *The Willows*.
    The *Long Island Society Register, 1929* lists Andre H. and Clara W. Barclay deCoppet as residing at *The Willows* on South Country Road, Islip.
    He was the son of Edward T. deCoppet of New York.
    Clara W. Barclay deCoppet was the daughter of Henry Anthony Barclay. She had previously been married to Jose Victor Onativia, Jr. and, subsequently, John Lord Boatwright of Richmond, VA. Jose and Clara Onativia, Jr.'s daughter Clara married Francis Bacon Gilbert, the son of Clinton Gilbert of Manhattan. Their daughter Jacqueline married Philippe Joseph Berthet of Paris, France. Jose Victor Onativia, Jr. subsequently married Clarisse Coudert Nast, the former wife of Conde Nast, who resided at *Sandy Cay* in Sands Point.
    Muriel Johnson was the daughter of Goodwin Johnson of San Francisco, CA. She had previously been married to Raymond Belasco. She subsequently married George Hopper Fitch of Manhattan.
    Andre H. and Muriel Johnson deCoppet's daughter Diane married George Simpson, the son of William Simpson of London, England, and resided in London. She subsequently married Richard Russell and resides in Manhattan and South Carolina. Their daughter Laura remained unmarried.
    Eileen Johnston deCoppet was the daughter of George Johnston of Islip. She subsequently married Prince Wilhelm Zu Wied of Albania.
    *During World War II, the Haitian–American Development Co. played a major role in developing substitute fibers to be used in the manufacture of rope to eliminate the dependence on hemp.

de Forest, James G. (d. 1903)

Occupation(s):   financier -   trustee, Atlantic Mutual Insurance

Marriage(s):   Julia T. _____ (d. 1875)

Address: South Country Road and de Forest Avenue, West Islip
Name of estate:
Year of construction:
Style of architecture:
Architect(s):
Landscape architect(s):
House extant: unconfirmed
Historical notes:

    In 1885, James G. and Julia T. de Forest's infant daughter died. In 1905, their son Frederick died.

deGoicouria, Albert V. (1849-1930)

Occupation(s):	financier - stockbroker; trustee, New York Stock Exchange
Civic Activism:	president, New York Athletic Club, NYC
Marriage(s):	Mary Cecelia Wall (d. 1904)
Address:	South Country Road, Islip
Name of estate:	
Year of construction:	
Style of architecture:	
Architect(s):	
Landscape architect(s):	
House extant: unconfirmed	
Historical notes:	

Albert V. and Mary Cecelia Wall deGoicouria's daughter Rosalie married W. Scott Cameron, the son of A. Scott Cameron, and, subsequently, Benjamin Curtis Allen of Philadelphia, PA. Their daughter Alice married August Belmont III, with whom she resided in Bay Shore. Alice subsequently married John D. Wing.

Delaney, John Hanlon (1871-1952)

Occupation(s):	publisher - owner, weekly printing trade journal; manager, *The Morning Telegraph*, NYC*
	industrialist owner, commercial printing plant; treasurer, bottle manufacturer
	politician - commissioner, Department of Plant and Structure, NYC, 1918-1919; commissioner, Rapid Transit, NYC, 1919-1921; commissioner, New York City Docks, 1921-1924; commissioner, Board of Transportation, NYC, 1924-1941**
Civic Activism:	trustee, St. John's University, Brooklyn
Marriage(s):	1903-1944 – Eleanor Gertrude Leary (d. 1944) - Civic Activism: president, St. Mary's Hospital Aid Association, Brooklyn
Address:	Fairview Avenue, Bayport
Name of estate:	
Year of construction:	c. 1912
Style of architecture:	
Architect(s):	
Landscape architect(s):	
House extant: unconfirmed	
Historical notes:	

The house was built by John Hanlon Delaney.

He was the son of John and Mary Curran Delaney of Manchester, VT.

*According to Harry Popik, a 2005 candidate for Manhattan Borough President, the use of the name "Big Apple" for New York City first appeared in *The Morning Telegraph* in which an apple graphic was featured in the column head for "Around the Big Apple" with John J. Fitz Gerald. Fitz Gerald refers to the city as "the apple" in his column of February 18, 1924. [electronic source, November 8, 2005.]

**As commissioner of the Board of Transportation Delaney was the chief architect of New York City's unified transit system, earning him the nickname "Mr. Transit."

Dempsey, Joseph Francis, Jr.

Occupation(s):   attorney - member, Shearman, Sterling and Wright, NYC

Marriage(s):   1941 – Phebe Thorne (d. 1981)*

Address: 146 East Bayberry Road, Islip
Name of estate:
Year of construction: 1899-1900
Style of architecture: Moorish
Architect(s):   Grosvenor Atterbury designed the house
                                (for H. O. Havemeyer)**
Landscape architect(s):   Nathan F. Barrett
                                (for H. O. Havemeyer)***

House extant: yes
Historical notes:

The house was built by Henry Osborne Havemeyer as part of his "Modern Venice" development.
It was owned by William Dunham Baker and, subsequently, by Dempsey.
He was the son of Joseph Francis and May E. Dempsey, Sr. of Great River.
Phebe Thorne Dempsey was the daughter of Francis Burritt and Hildegarde Kobbe Thorne, Sr. of
Brookwood in East Islip. Phebe's sister Julia married Dennis McCarty. Her brother Oakleigh Thorne II, who
resided at *Valley Ranch* in Cody, WY, married Peggy N. Schroll and, subsequently, Lisa L. Bellows. Her
brother Francis Burritt Thorne, Jr. married Ann C. Cobb, the daughter of Boughton Cobb of Manhattan, and
resided in Bay Shore.
*Long Island's Phebe Dempsey Golf Tournament is held in Phebe's honor.
Joseph Francis and Phebe Thorne Dempsey, Jr.'s daughter Elizabeth married C. F. Linday Hewitt and
resides in Cold Spring Harbor.
After the Dempseys' separation, Joseph relocated to Great River and Phebe moved to Stony Brook.
[See following entry for additional family information.]
**The sales brochure for "Modern Venice" states that the Moorish-style architecture was suggested by
Louis Comfort Tiffany.
***The sales brochure also states that "Modern Venice" would be devoid of trees and vegetation and that
Nathan F. Barrett was the landscape architect.

front facade, 2006

Dempsey, Joseph Francis, Sr. (1886-1950)

Occupation(s):   attorney - partner, Cary and Caroll (which merged with Shearman, Sterling
                                        and Wright);
                                    partner, Shearman, Sterling and Wright, NYC
                        capitalist -   president, National Hotel Corporation of Cuba;
                                    president, Rye Ridge Realty Corp.;
                                    director, Fifth Avenue Building Co.;
                                    director, Holmens Newsprint Corporation;
                                    director, R. W. Goelet Estates, Inc.;
                                    director, Goelet Reality Co.;
                                    director, Rhode Island Corporation;
                                    director, Uddeholm Company of America;
                                    director, National City Realty Corp.;
                                    director, Classical Cinematograph Corp.;
                                    director, Telfair Stockton & Co., Inc.;
                                    director, Ritz–Carlton Hotel Corp.;
                                    director, Mark Cross Company;
                                    director, Mortbon Corporation of New York;
                                    director, Manchester Land Co.
                        industrialist -   director, Pacific Molasses Company, Ltd.;
                                    director, Commercial Molasses Corp.
                        financier -   director, Lawyers Mortgage Guarantee Corp.

Marriage(s):   May E____
                      - Civic Activism: director, Brooklyn Free Kindergarten Society, Inc.

Address: Great River Road, Great River
Name of estate:
Year of construction:
Style of architecture:
Architect(s):
Landscape architect(s):
House extant: unconfirmed
Historical notes:

   Joseph Francis and May E. Dempsey, Sr.'s daughter Susan married Anthony Hugh Barnes, the son of Sir
George and Lady Barnes of Prawls, Stone Tenterden, Kent, England. Their son John married Margaret
Leighton Moore, the daughter of Dr. David Dodge and Mrs. Margaret Leighton Hatch Moore of Islip. Their
son Joseph Francis Dempsey, Jr. married Phebe Thorne and resided in Islip.
   [See previous entry for additional family information.]

*Seaside Hospital for Sick Children
(later, Trinity Sea Side Home),
Great River Road, Great River
– built by Alva Smith Vanderbilt*

deMurias, Fernando Enrique (d. 1926)

Occupation(s):   industrialist -   manufacturer of Cuban cigars

Marriage(s):

Address: 44 Douglas Avenue, Babylon
Name of estate:
Year of construction:
Style of architecture: Modified Dutch Colonial Revival
Architect(s):
Landscape architect(s):
House extant: yes
Historical notes:

Fernando Enrique deMurias was the son of Ramon and Clara Gardin deMurias of Manhattan and Havana, Cuba. Fernando's sister Sylvia married Dr. Albert Vander Veer, Jr. and resided at *Alkmaar Cottage* in Point of Woods on Fire Island.

His son Ramon deMurias II married Polly Fenno Keppler, the daughter of Chester H. Keppler, and, subsequently, Ann Carlin Borden, the daughter of General William Ayres Borden, with whom he resided in Babylon.

The house was subsequently owned by Henry Chester Hepburn.

front facade, 2006

Dick, Adolph M. (1894-1956)

Occupation(s):   architect -   partner, Fuller and Dick*
Civic Activism   trustee, Southside Hospital, Bay Shore

Marriage(s):   bachelor

Address: Ocean Avenue, Islip
Name of estate:
Year of construction: 1931
Style of architecture: Neo-Georgian
Architect(s):   Adolph M. Dick designed his own house
Landscape architect(s):
House extant: no; demolished in 1960s
Historical notes:

The house was built by Adolph M. Dick.

The *Long Island Society Register, 1929* lists Adolph M. Dick as residing in Islip.

He was the son of John Henry and Julia Theodora Mollenhauer Dick, who resided at *Allen Winden Farm* in Islip.

[See other Dick family entries for additional family information.]

*Dick designed the original Islip Town Hall; the wings were added at a later date.

Dick, John Henry (1851-1925)

Occupation(s):   industrialist -   director, The National Sugar Refining Co.
                                 financier -   vice president, Manufacturers National Bank, Brooklyn

Marriage(s):   1886-1925 – Julia Theodora Mollenhauer (1863-1931)

Address: Ocean Avenue, Islip
Name of estate: *Allen Winden Farm**
Year of construction: c. 1880s
Style of architecture: Victorian
Architect(s):   Isaac Henry Green II designed the
                              c. 1889 alterations (for W. Dick)
                        Alfred Hopkins designed the garage
                              and stables (for John Henry Dick)
Landscape architect(s):
House extant: no; demolished in 1960s**
Historical notes:

   The house was built by Charles A. Tucker.

   It was later owned by William Dick, his son John Henry Dick, and, subsequently, by William Karl Dick, all of whom called in *Allen Winden Farm*.

   *Allen Winden is German for "all winds."

   The *Brooklyn Blue Book and Long Island Society Register, 1918* lists J. Henry and Julia T. Mollenhauer Dick as residing at *Allen Winden Farm* in Islip.

   He was the son of William and Anna Maria Vagts Dick. His sister Anna Margaretha married J. Adolph Mollenhauer and resided at *Homeport* in Bay Shore.

   Julia Theodora Mollenhauer Dick was the daughter of John and Doris Siems Mollenhauer of Bay Shore. Her brother J. Adolph married Anna Margaretha Dick and resided at *Homeport* in Bay Shore. Her brother Frederick married May Craig. Her brother Henry married Sarah W. Howe.

   John Henry and Julia Theodora Mollenhauer Dick's son William Karl Dick married Madeline Force and, subsequently, Virginia K. Conner. Their daughter Doris married Horace Havemeyer, Sr. and resided at *Olympic Point* in Bay Shore. Their daughter Julia married William Kingsland Macy, Sr. and resided in Islip. Their son Adolph remained a bachelor.

   [See other Dick family entries for additional family information.]

   **Garage and stables are extant.

rear facade

Dick, William (1823-1912)

Occupation(s):   financier -   president, Manufacturers National Bank, Brooklyn;
                                       vice president, Mechanics Bank of Williamsburg
                                            (which merged with Citizen Trust Co.; then
                                            became Manufacturers Trust Co; then, Hanover
                                            Bank; then, Manufacturers Hanover Bank);
                                        vice-president, Nassau Trust Co.;
                                        trustee, German Savings Institution
          industrialist -   partner, Dick & Meyer Corp. (Brooklyn sugar
                                        refiners);
                                        director, American Sugar Refining Co.

Marriage(s):   1848-1898 – Anna Maria Vagts (1819-1898)

Address: Ocean Avenue, Islip
Name of estate: *Allen Winden Farm**
Year of construction: c. 1880s
Style of architecture: Victorian
Architect(s):   Isaac Henry Green II designed the
                           c. 1889 alterations (for W. Dick)
                     Alfred Hopkins designed the garage
                           and stables (for John Henry Dick)
Landscape architect(s):
House extant: no; demolished in 1960s**
Historical notes:

   The house was built by Charles A. Tucker.
   It was later owned by William Dick, his son John Henry Dick, and, subsequently, by William Karl Dick,
all of whom called in *Allen Winden Farm.*
   *Allen Winden is German for "all winds."
   [See other Dick family entries for additional family information.]
   **Garage and stables are extant.

rear facade

Dick, William Karl (1888-1953)

Occupation(s):   industrialist -   director, Bates International Bag Co.;
                                        director, Bates Valve Bag Corp.;
                                        director, Hecker Products Corp.;
                                        director, The National Sugar Refining Co.;
                                      director, New Hampshire–Vermont Lumber Co.;
                                      director, St. Regis Paper Co.;
                                      director, Regis Kraft Co. of Canada;
                                      director, Shenandoah Rayon Corp.
                    capitalist -   director, Citizens Development Inc.;
                                        director, Citizens Water Supply, Newtown, NY;
                                        director, Cord Meyer Development Co.;
                                      director, Eastern State Corp.;
                                      director, St. Lawrence Railroad
                    financier -   director, Irving Trust Co.;
                                        director, Standard Capital Co.

Civic Activism: trustee, Boys' Club of New York;
                    director, American Red Cross Disaster Committee;
                    trustee, Southside Hospital, Bay Shore

Marriage(s):   M/1 – 1916 – Madeleine Force (1893-1940)
                    M/2 – 1941-1953 – Virginia Kenniston Conner (1910-1985)

Address: Ocean Avenue, Islip
Name of estate: *Allen Winden Farm**
Year of construction: c. 1880s
Style of architecture: Victorian
Architect(s):   Isaac Henry Green II designed
                        the c. 1889 alterations
                        (for W. Dick)
                    Alfred Hopkins designed the
                        garage and stables
                        (for John Henry Dick)
Landscape architect(s):
House extant: no; demolished in 1960s**
Historical notes:

Allen Winden Farm

The house was built by Charles A. Tucker.

It was later owned by William Dick, his son John Henry Dick, and, subsequently, by William Karl Dick, all of whom called in *Allen Winden Farm.*

*Allen Winden is German for "all winds."

The *Long Island Society Register, 1929* lists William Karl and Madeleine Force Dick as residing in Islip. He was the son of John Henry and Julia Theodora Mollenhauer Dick.

[See other Dick family entries for additional family information.]

Madeline Force Dick was the daughter of William H. Force of Brooklyn. She had previously been married to John Jacob Astor IV, who died aboard the *Titanic*. After her divorce from Dick, she married Enzo Fiermonte, a middle-weight prizefighter.

William Karl and Madeleine Force Dick's son William married Virginia Middleton French, the daughter of Francis O. French of Newport, RI. Their son John Henry Dick [II] remained a bachelor.

Virginia Kenniston Conner Dick was the daughter of Edwin Solon Connor of Akron, OH. She subsequently married Frederick S. Moseley, Jr.

William Karl and Virginia Kenniston Conner Dick's daughter Direxa married Christopher Farrell Dearie. Their son Will Kenniston Dick married Sandra Freeman Mueller.

**Garage and stables are extant.

Dillon, John Allen, Sr. (1885-1950)

Occupation(s):   industrialist - sales agent, American Car and Foundry Co.

Marriage(s):

Address: Saxon Avenue, Bay Shore
Name of estate:
Year of construction: 1880
Style of architecture: Colonial Revival
Architect(s):   Isaac Henry Green II designed the
         1889 southwestern wing addition
         of a living room and four bedrooms
         (for E. S. Knapp, Sr.)
Landscape architect(s):
House extant: no
Historical notes:

 The house, originally named *Awixa Lawn*, was built by Edward Spring Knapp, Sr.
 In 1915, Mrs. Knapp sold the estate to August Belmont II.
 In 1923, Mrs. Belmont sold the estate, which at that time consisted of a twenty-five-room main residence on nine acres, six hundred feet of shoreline on Awixa Creek, stables, and a five-car garage, to Dillon.
 John Allen Dillon, Sr. committed suicide in his Manhattan apartment located at 280 Park Avenue. [*The New York Times* April 12, 1950, p. 31.]
 His son John Allen Dillon, Jr. married Mary Stewart Cocken, the daughter of William York Cocken of Pittsburgh, PA.

Dodson, Robert Bowman (1849-1938)

Occupation(s):   financier - director, National City Bank;
             partner, Fahnestock and Co. (stock brokerage firm)
Civic Activism: established the Robert B. and Mary W. Dodson Fund (to improve
         the condition of the poor)

Marriage(s):   Mary Wells (d. 1942)

Address: Oak Neck Road and South Country Road, West Islip
Name of estate: *Kanonsioni**
Year of construction: c. 1903
Style of architecture: Queen Anne
Architect(s):   Kirby, Petit, & Green designed
         the house (for Dodson)
Landscape architect(s): Harold Truesdel Patterson (for Dodson)**
House extant: no; demolished in c. 1950
Historical notes:

 The house, originally named *Kanonsioni*, was built by Robert Bowman Dodson.
 He was the son of Christian B. and Harriet Warren Dodson of Geneva, IL.
 Mary Wells Dodson was the daughter of John Augustus and Elizabeth Tobias Wells.
 **Kanonsioni* is an Algonquian word for "longhouse."
 **Babylon Historical Society has Patterson's landscape plans.

Kanonsioni, c. 1906

Doxsee, James Harvey, Sr. (1825-1907)

Occupation(s):   industrialist -   a founder, James H. Doxsee and Sons (processors of
                                         canned clams, clam broth, and clam chowder)*

Marriage(s):   M/1 – ____ Whitman
                    M/2 – Almira S. Jennings (d. 1910)
                        - Civic Activism: treasurer, Woman's Christian Temperance
                                       Union, Islip

Address: Ocean Avenue, Islip
Name of estate:
Year of construction:
Style of architecture:
Architect(s):
Landscape architect(s):
House extant: unconfirmed
Historical notes:

    *Doxsee started the clam business in Islip in 1865, incorporating it into James H. Doxsee and Sons in 1897. Its directors, at the time of incorporation, were James Harvey Doxsee, Sr., John C. Doxsee, and Henry Smith Doxsee. [*The New York Times* January 10, 1897, p. 8.] In 1901, the Islip facility was closed and a new factory was established in Oracoke, NC, by Henry Smith Doxsee. In 1919, Robert Doxsee, Sr. opened a factory on Meadow Island near Point Lookout. In 1933, operations were moved to Point Lookout, where they remain today. Operating under the corporate name of Doxsee Sea Clam Company, Inc., the Point Lookout facility produces clam products for restaurants and retail stores under the brand name Offshore Seafood.
    The house was rented by Roland Redmond. [Harry W. Havemeyer, *Along the Great South Bay From Oakdale to Babylon: The Story of a Summer Spa 1840 to 1940* (Mattituck, NY: Amereon House, 1996), p. 173.]

Drummond, Howard (1882-1947)

Occupation(s):   financier -   partner, Carlisle, Mellick and Co. (stock brokerage firm)

Marriage(s):   M/1 – Elizabeth Newall (1880-1916)
                    M/2 – 1920-1947 – Lulu Hyde (d. 1958)

Address: South Country Road, Bay Shore
Name of estate: *Little House*
Year of construction:
Style of architecture:
Architect(s):
Landscape architect(s):
House extant: unconfirmed
Historical notes:

    Howard Drummond was the son of John L. and Jemima Drummond of Manhattan.
    Howard and Elizabeth Newall Drummond's daughters Elizabeth, age nineteen, and Dorothy, age sixteen, were killed when their automobile was struck by the Riverhead Express train of the Long Island Rail Road. The accident occurred at an unprotected crossing at Suffolk Avenue in Bay Shore. [*The New York Times* August 22, 1926, p. 1.]
    Lulu Hyde Drummond was the daughter of Richard Hyde, who resided in Bay Shore. She had previously been married to Vincent B. Hubbell, Sr. Her sister Lillian married Quentin Field Feitner, the son of Thomas L. and Mary C. Moore Feitner of Manhattan, and, subsequently, George B. Wagstaff, with whom she resided in Bay Shore. Their brother William married Grace M. Riopel and resided at *White Cottage* in Bay Shore. Their sister Mary married Sidney Dillon Ripley, Sr. and resided at *The Crossroads* in Uniondale.

Duval, Henry Rieman (1843-1924)

Occupation(s):   industrialist -   chairman of board, Ornard Sugar Co. (which merged
into American Beet Sugar Co.);
president, American Beet Sugar Co.;
director, American Car and Foundry Co.
capitalist -   president, Florida Central & Peninsular Railroad (which
merged into Seaboard Air Railway Co.);
director, Atcheson, Topeka & Sante Fe Railroad;
director, Sonora Rail Road Co.;
director, Kansas City Southern Railway Co.;
director, Sante Fe Pacific Railroad;
president, South Bound Railroad
financier -   trustee, Mutual Life Insurance Co.

Marriage(s):   1878 – Anne Gordon

front facade

Address: Suffolk Lane, East Islip
Name of estate: *Farmouth*
Year of construction:
Style of architecture: Shingle
Architect(s):
Landscape architect(s):
House extant: no; demolished in 1952*
Historical notes:

The house was built by Lee Johnson.
In 1885, it was purchased by Duval, who called it *Farmouth*.
He was the son of John Rawlings and Elizabeth Warfield Rieman Duval of Baltimore, MD.
Anne Gordon Duval was the daughter of John Hanson Thomas Gordon of Baltimore, MD.
Henry Rieman and Anne Gordon Duval's son Rieman married Elizabeth Williams, the daughter of Charles P. Williams of Stonington, CT, and resided in East Islip. Their daughter Nannie married John Haskins Wilcox and resided at *Mulberry Hill* in Easton, MD.
*The house was severely damaged by fire during World War II.

Eastwood, John H.

Occupation(s):   industrialist -   receiver, J. & R. Kingsland Paper Mills, Franklin, NJ

Marriage(s):   Margaret Spence (d. 1946)

Address: Montgomery Avenue, Bay Shore
Name of estate:
Year of construction: 1899
Style of architecture: Neo-Dutch Colonial
Architect(s):   Clarence K. Birdsall designed the house
(for Nathaniel Myers)
Landscape architect(s):
House extant: unconfirmed
Historical notes:

The house was built by Nathaniel Myers.
It was subsequently owned by Eastwood.
He was the adopted son of John Eastwood of Bellville, NJ, from whom he inherited $700,000 in 1911.
Margaret Spence Eastwood was the daughter of Oscar and Jane Ahearn Spence.

Eaton, James Waterbury, Sr.

Occupation(s):   publisher -   secretary and treasurer, Babylon Publishing Co.
                     industrialist -   director, Eaton–Hough Co., NY (manufacturers of
                                      computing and adding machines, comptometers,
                                      and typewriters);
                                      a founder, Kerosene Safety Engine Co., Jersey City, NJ;
                                      director, Greenmountain Product Co. of Babylon
                                      (manufacturer of carbonated waters and medicines)
                     financier -   director, Bank of Babylon
                     writer -   *Babylon Reminiscences*, 1911;
                                 *History of the First Presbyterian Church, Babylon, Long
                                 Island*, 1912

Marriage(s):   Elizabeth Bross (d. 1940)

Address: Eaton Lane, West Islip
Name of estate:
Year of construction:
Style of architecture:
Architect(s):
Landscape architect(s):
House extant: unconfirmed
Historical notes:

   James Waterbury and Elizabeth Bross Eaton, Sr.'s daughter Elizabeth married Meyer Robert Guggenheim, Sr. of *Firenze Farm* in North Babylon. Their son James Waterbury Eaton, Jr. married Matilda Brown and resided in Cold Spring Harbor.

Edwards, Edward (1831-1897)

Occupation(s):   capitalist -   Long Island real estate developer (built Edwardsville
                                     section of Patchogue)

Marriage(s):

Address: Fairview Avenue, Bayport
Name of estate: *White House*
Year of construction: 1881
Style of architecture: Modified Second Empire
Architect(s):
Landscape architect(s):
House extant: no; destroyed by fire in 1940s
Historical notes:

   The house, originally named *White House*, was built by Edward Edwards.
   In 1883, it was purchased by John R. Ely.
   Cyrus E. Staples purchased the house in 1890.
   In 1902, Staples sold it to William Kintzing Post and his brother Regis H. Post, Sr., who, in turn, sold it to James H. Snedecor in 1925.

front facade

Egly, Henry Harris (1893-1958)

Occupation(s):	financier - vice-president, Dillon Read and Co. (investment banking firm);
	trustee, Lincoln Savings Bank, Brooklyn
Civic Activism:	chairman, securities division, Securities and Exchange Commission, 1938-1939;
	trustee and chairman, underwriting committee, Beekman–Downtown Hospital, NYC (which was formed by the merger of Beekman Street Hospital and Downtown Hospital);
	trustee, Adelphi College (now, Adelphi University, Garden City);
	member, executive committee, New York Group of Investment Bankers Assoc.
Marriage(s):	1916 – Matilda Anna Pasfield
Address:	101 West Bayberry Road, Islip
Name of estate:	
Year of construction:	1899-1900
Style of architecture:	Moorish
Architect(s):	Grosvenor Atterbury designed the house (for H. O. Havemeyer)*
Landscape architect(s):	Nathan F. Barrett (for H. O. Havemeyer)**

House extant: yes
Historical notes:

   The house was built by Henry Osborne Havemeyer as part of his "Modern Venice" development. It was later owned by Egly.

   He was the son of Louis and Emma Bertha Maturnas Egly of Brooklyn.

   Henry Harris and Matilda Anna Pasfield Egly's daughter Jean married Harold Cole, the son of Charles Cole of Cold Spring Harbor. Their daughter Patricia remained unmarried.

   By 1939 the Eglys had relocated to Stewart Avenue in Garden City.

   *The sales brochure for "Modern Venice" states that the Moorish-style architecture was suggested by Louis Comfort Tiffany.

   **The sales brochure also states that "Modern Venice" would be devoid of trees and vegetation and that Nathan F. Barrett was the landscape architect.

front facade, 2006

Elder, George Waldron, Sr. (1860-1916)

Occupation(s): industrialist - manager, shipping department, Havemeyers
& Elder (sugar refinery, 1862-1891)*

Marriage(s): 1881-div. 1904 – Ellen Therese Cadwell (d. 1939)

Address: *[unable to determine street address]*, Bay Shore
Name of estate:
Year of construction:
Style of architecture:
Architect(s):
Landscape architect(s):
House extant: no
Historical notes:

   George Waldron Elder, Sr. was the son of George William and Mathilda Adelaide Waldron Elder. His sister Anne married Henry Norcross Munn. His sister Louisine married Henry Osborne Havemeyer and resided at *Bayberry Point* in Islip. His sister Adaline married Samuel Twyford Peters and resided at *Windholme* in Islip.
   Ellen Therese Cadwell Elder was the daughter of S. W. Cadwell.
   George Waldron and Ellen Therese Cadwell Elder, Sr.'s son George Waldron Elder, Jr. married Juanita Stewart and resided in Bellport.
   *In 1891 the sugar refining division of Havemeyers & Elder was merged into the American Sugar Refining Company. The remaining property, not used in the sugar refining business, was retained by Havemeyers & Elder as a Brooklyn real estate holding company until the 1950s.

Ellis, George Augustus, Jr. (1875-1942)

Occupation(s): financier - a founder and partner, E. F. Hutton (investment
banking firm)
Civic Activism: trustee, Southside Hospital, Bay Shore

Marriage(s): 1900-1942 – Florence Vance Adams (d. 1957)

Address: South Country Road, West Bay Shore
Name of estate: *Ardmore*
Year of construction: c. 1905
Style of architecture: Mediterranean Villa
Architect(s):
Landscape architect(s):
House extant: yes
Historical notes:

side / rear facade, c. 1909

   The house, originally named *Ardmore*, was built by Thomas Adams, Jr.
   It was subsequently owned by his daughter Florence and son-in-law George Augustus Ellis, Jr., who continued to call it *Ardmore*.
   The *Brooklyn Blue Book and Long Island Society Register, 1918* lists George Augustus and Florence V. Adams Ellis, Jr. as residing at *Admoor* [*Ardmore*] in Bay Shore [West Bay Shore].
   Florence Vance Adams Ellis' brother George J. Adams, Sr. resided in Hempstead.
   George Augustus and Florence Vance Adams Ellis, Jr.'s son George Adams Ellis married Georgia Williams, the daughter of Charles P. Williams of Stonington, CT, and subsequently, Margaret C. Richards. Their daughter Jean married M. F. Summers.
   The house is currently part of Southward Ho Country Club.

Ely, John R. (d. 1895)

Occupation(s):   industrialist -   partner, with his brother Henry, Ely Brothers
                                        Rectifiers and Distillers, Brooklyn

Marriage(s):

Address: Fairview Avenue, Bayport
Name of estate:
Year of construction: 1881
Style of architecture: Modified Second Empire
Architect(s):
Landscape architect(s):
House extant: no; destroyed by fire in 1940s
Historical notes:

The house, originally named *White House*, was built by
Edward Edwards.
   In 1883, it was purchased by John R. Ely.
   Ely's son George was declared insane and institutionalized
in an Amityville sanitarium. [*The New York Times* October 19, 1895,
p. 9.]
   In 1890, the house was purchased by Cyrus E. Staples.
   In 1902, Staples sold it to William Kintzing Post and his
brother Regis H. Post, Sr., who, in turn, sold it to James H.
Snedecor in 1925.

White House

Ennis, Thomas

Occupation(s):   financier -   partner, Ennis and Stoppani (odd-lot brokerage firm
                                          specializing in grain futures)

Marriage(s):

Address: *[unable to determine street address]*, Bayport
Name of estate:
Year of construction:
Style of architecture:
Architect(s):
Landscape architect(s):
House extant: unconfirmed
Historical notes:

   *Because of alleged irregularities in their 1903, 1909, and 1916 stock transactions, arrest warrants were
issued for both Ennis and his partner Charles F. Stoppani, Jr. As a result, the firm of Ennis and Stoppani
declared bankruptcy. [Harry W. Havemeyer, *East on the Great South Bay: Sayville and Bayport 1860-1960* (Mattituck, NY:
Amereon House, 2001), p. 82; *The New York Times* November 8, 1903, p. 20; April 14, 1909, p. 1; April 16, 1909, p. 5; April 22, 1909,
p. 5; April 28, 1909, p. 18; May 5, 1909, p. 7; and May 22, 1909, p. 1.]

Entenmann, Robert

Occupation(s):   industrialist -   chairman of board, Entenmann's Inc.*
                                     capitalist -   owner, Martha Clara Vineyards, Riverhead**
                                     financier -   director, First Long Island Investors, Inc.

Marriage(s):   Jacqueline _____

Address: Meadow Farm Road, East Islip
Name of estate:
Year of construction: 1927
Style of architecture: Colonial Revival
Architect(s):   Philip Cusack designed the
                              house (for R. W. Morgan, Sr.)

Landscape architect(s):
House extant: yes
Historical notes:

    The house was built by Robert Woodward Morgan, Sr.
    It was later owned by Robert Allan Pinkerton II and, subsequently, by Entenmann.
    He was the son of William and Martha Clara Schneider Entenmann, Jr.
    *Entenmann's bakery was purchased in 1978 by Warner–Lambert Company. In 1982, it was purchased by General Foods Corporation. In 1985, General Foods was acquired by Phillip Morris and Entenmann's became part of Kraft Foods. In 1995, Entenmann's was acquired by CPC International. [*The New York Times* September 30, 1996, sec. B, p. 8.] It is currently part of George Weston Bakeries.
    **Entenmann named the vineyard after his mother.

Evers, Cecil C. (d. 1936)

Occupation(s):   financier -   vice-president and secretary, Lawyers Mortgage Co.;
                                       director, The Mortgage–Bond Co. of New York

Marriage(s):

Address: 87 Argyle Avenue, Babylon
Name of estate:
Year of construction: c. 1907
Style of architecture:
Architect(s):
Landscape architect(s):
House extant: yes
Historical notes:

    Cecil C. Evers was residing in Elmsford, NY, at the time of his death. [*The New York Times* July 17, 1936, p. 17.]

front / side facade, 2006

Fairchild, Julian Douglas (1850-1926)

Occupation(s):	financier -	a founder and president, Kings County Trust Co.;
		president, Capital Surplus;
		vice-president, Mortgage Bond Co.;
		director, Metropolitan Casualty Co.;
		director, Pacific Fire Insurance Co.;
		director, Nassau Fire Insurance Co.;
		vice-president, Mortgage–Bond Co.;
		director, Lawyers Title Insurance & Trust Co.;
		director, National City Bank of Brooklyn;
		director, Metropolitan Plate Glass Insurance Co.;
		director, Bedford Bank;
		trustee, East River Savings Bank
	capitalist -	director, Eagle Warehouse & Storage Co.;
		president, Union Ferry Co.;
		director, Queens Electric Light & Power Co.
	industrialist -	secretary, Quinnipiac Fertilizer Co.
	politician -	treasurer, Democratic Campaign Committee, Kings County, 1923*

Civic Activism: regent, Long Island College Hospital, Brooklyn;
trustee, Brooklyn Institute of Arts and Sciences;
president, Brooklyn Central Dispensary

Marriage(s): 1879 – Florence Irene Bradley

Address: Awixa Avenue, Bay Shore
Name of estate:
Year of construction: 1894
Style of architecture: Queen Anne
Architect(s):
Landscape architect(s):
House extant: no
Historical notes:

The house was built by Emil H. Frank, Sr.
In 1904, it was purchased by Fairchild.
The *Brooklyn Blue Book and Long Island Society Register, 1918* lists Julian D. and Florence I. Bradley Fairchild as residing in Bay Shore.
He was the son of Douglas and Lydia Hawley Fairchild.
Florence Irene Bradley Fairchild was the daughter of Charles Leeman Bradley of New Haven, CT.
Julian Douglas and Florence Irene Bradley Fairchild's son Julian Percy Fairchild, Sr., who resided in Glen Cove, married Helen Louise Fitch, the daughter of Ezra C. Fitch of Boston, MA, and, subsequently, Ruth Callender.
*In 1894, Fairchild refused the Democratic nomination for mayor of Brooklyn and, in 1896, he also refused the party's nomination for comptroller of New York City.

front facade, c. 1894

Flint, Sherman

Occupation(s):	financier - stockbroker
Marriage(s):	1899 – Margaret Olivia Slocum (d. 1946)
Address:	St. Mark's Lane, Islip
Name of estate:	*Evershade*
Year of construction:	
Style of architecture:	
Architect(s):	
Landscape architect(s):	Beatrix Jones Ferrand, designed landscape plan, 1912 (for Flint) [landscape plan not executed]
House extant: unconfirmed	
Historical notes:	

Sherman Flint was the son of Dr. Austin and Mrs. Elizabeth McMaster Flint, Sr. of Manhattan. His brother Dr. Austin Flint, Jr. married Marion Wing and resided at *Box Hill Farm* in Muttontown. His sister Ann remained unmarried.

Margaret Olivia Slocum Flint was the daughter of Joseph Jermain Slocum, Sr., who was Russell Sage's partner and brother-in-law. Russell Sage was married to Margaret Olivia Slocum, known as Olivia, who, after Mr. Sage's death, embarked on a philanthropy that distributed an estimated $80 million.

Sherman and Margaret Olivia Slocum Flint's daughter Margaret married Thomas Emerson Proctor II, the son of James Howe Proctor of Boston, MA. The Flints' son Austin died in 1919 prior to attaining adulthood.

Ford, Malcolm W.

Occupation(s):	capitalist - Long Island real estate developer
	journalist - editor, several sporting publications
Marriage(s):	c. 1895-div. 1898 – Jeanette Graves
Address:	*[unable to determine street address]*, Babylon
Name of estate:	
Year of construction:	
Style of architecture:	
Architect(s):	
Landscape architect(s):	
House extant: unconfirmed	
Historical notes:	

Malcolm W. Ford was the son of Gordon Leicester and Emily Ellsworth Ford of Brooklyn. His obsession with sports led his father to disinherit him.

Jeanette Graves Ford was the daughter of Robert Graves of *Treborcliffe* in Lloyd Harbor, who made his fortune as a wallpaper manufacturer. Jeanette's sister Lorraine married David Donald Carroll of Bennettsville, SC, and, subsequently, Oliver Russell Grace, with whom she resided at *Yellowbanks* in Cove Neck.

Fortescue, Granville Roland (1875-1952)

Occupation(s): military - member, Rough Riders – wounded at San Juan Hill;
saw action in Philippines, 1898-1901;
served as President Theodore Roosevelt's military attaché
in Japan;
special agent, Cuban Rural Guard;
active duty in France, 314 Field Artillery, during World
War I

journalist - war correspondent, *London Standard*, during Riff War in
Spanish Morocco;
war correspondent, *London Daily Telegraph* during
World War I;
editor, *Liberty Magazine* (fiction)

writer - *At the Front with Three Allies: My Adventures in the Great War*,
1914; *Russia, the Balkans and the Dardanelles*, 1915; *What of the
Dardanelles? An Analysis*, 1915; *Forearmed: How to Build a
Citizen Army*, 1916; *France Bears the Burden*, 1917; *Delor*, 1915
(a play); *Love and Live*, 1921 (a play); *The Unbeliever*, 1925
(a play); *Frontline and Dead Line: The Experiences of a War
Correspondent*, 1937

Marriage(s): 1910-1952 – Grace Hubbard Bell (1883-1979)

Address: McConnell Avenue, Bayport
Name of estate: *Wildholme*
Year of construction: c. 1873
Style of architecture: Eclectic with Italianate elements
Architect(s):
Landscape architect(s):
House extant: no; destroyed by fire in 1958*
Historical notes:

In 1873, Robert Barnwell Roosevelt, Sr. purchased the two-hundred-acre farm of Daniel Lane and remodeled its farm house into his country residence *Lotos Lake*. It was subsequently owned by Granville Roland Fortescue, who called *Wildholme*.

Granville Roland Fortescue was the only Roosevelt to be buried in Arlington Cemetery. He was the illegitimate son of Robert Barnwell and Marion Theresa O'Shea Roosevelt, Sr., who resided at *Lotos Lake* in Bayport. His brother Kenyon, a bachelor, resided in Sayville. His sister Maude married Ernest W. S. Pickhardt and resided in London, England.

Grace Hubbard Bell was the daughter of Charles John and Roberta Wolcott Hubbard Bell of *Twin Oaks* in Washington, DC. Grace's sister Helen married Julian Ashton Ripley, Sr. and resided at *Three Corner Farm* in Muttontown.

Granville Roland and Grace Hubbard Bell Fortescue's daughter Marion married Daulton Gillespie Viskniskki, the son of journalist Guy Thomas and Virginia Gillespie Viskniskki of Montclair, NJ, and resided in Canterbury, OH. Their daughter Helen married Julian Louis Reynolds, heir to the Reynolds aluminum and tobacco fortune. In 1966, the Reynoldses' twenty-nine-year-old son Richard accidentally walked into the moving propeller of a plane that he was inspecting for possible purchase.

The Fortescue's sixteen-year-old daughter Grace (Thalia) married naval lieutenant Thomas Hedges Massie, the son of a Winchester, KY, shoe store proprietor, and, subsequently, Robert Uptigrove. [For a detailed account of the murder trial of Grace Fortescue and her son-in-law Thomas Hedges Massie see Harry W. Havemeyer, *East on the Great South Bay: Sayville and Bellport 1860-1960* (Mattituck, NY: Amereon House, 2001), pp. 37-46, 207-225; *The New York Times* April 30, 1932, pp. 1, 16.] [For a discussion of the Fortescue family see Raymond E. Spinzia, "Those Other Roosevelts: The Fortescues" *The Freeholder*, 11(Summer 2006), pp. 8-9, 16-22.]

*In 1953, the house and its furnishings were severely vandalized. In 1954, it was sold to real estate developer Maurice Babash. While he was demolishing it, the house was destroyed by fire.

Fortescue, Kenyon (1870-1939)

Occupation(s):   attorney -   partner, Roosevelt and Kobbe

Marriage(s):   bachelor

Address: *[unable to determine street address]*, Sayville
Name of estate:
Year of construction:
Style of architecture:
Architect(s):
Landscape architect(s):
House extant: unconfirmed
Historical notes:

    Kenyon Fortescue was the illegitimate son of Robert Barnwell and Marion Theresa O'Shea Roosevelt, Sr. *[See previous entry for additional family information.]*

Foster, Andrew D. (1826-1907)
(aka Forsslund)*

Occupation(s):   capitalist -   owner, Delavan Hotel, Foster Avenue, Sayville;
                                     owner, Foster House Hotel, South Main Street, Sayville

Marriage(s):   1853-1907 – Ann Eliza Brown (1834-1918)

Address: 302 Foster Avenue, Sayville
Name of estate: *Greycote*
Year of construction: c. 1883
Style of architecture: Colonial Revival
Architect(s):   Isaac Henry Green II designed the house
                     (for A. D. Foster)

Landscape architect(s):
House extant: yes
Historical notes:

    The house, originally named *Greycote*, was built by Andrew D. Foster.
    *He was the son of Peterson Forsslund of Sweden.
    Andrew D. and Ann Eliza Brown Foster's daughter Amelia married Dr. George A. Robinson and resided in Bayport. Their daughter Ann married Dr. ____ Haines. Their daughter Amy was a Broadway actress. Their daughter Louise, a writer whose books were set in Sayville, married Carey Waddell and resided in Sayville.

front facade, 2006

Foster, Jay Stanley, II (1877-1925)

Occupation(s):   attorney
                                   financier -   president, Bowery Bank
Civic Activism: *

Marriage(s):   M/1 – 1904-div. 1912 – Jennie Rice Morgan
                                   M/2 – Estelle Knowles

Address: Little East Neck Road and South Country Road, Babylon
Name of estate:
Year of construction: c. 1890
Style of architecture: Mediterranean Villa
Architect(s):
Landscape architect(s):
House extant: no**
Historical notes:

    The house was built by Jay Stanley Foster II.

    He was the son of John S. and Carrie O. Foster. His brother William resided at *Strandhome* in Bayport with his common-law-wife Lulu Benoit. His sister Karolyn married Eugene C. Savidge.

    *In 1921, Jay Stanley Foster II donated Argyle Park to the Village of Babylon. In 1927, his sister Karolyn donated the park's ornamental stone steps, gates, and waterfalls to the village.

    [See following entry for additional family information.]

    Estelle Knowles Foster subsequently married Alfred Henry Bromell, with whom she continued to reside at the Babylon estate.

    **Only the carriage house is extant.

Argyle Park, 2005

side / front facade, 1945

front facade, 1976

rear facade, 1976

south facade, 1976

front facade, c. 1894

Foster, William R., Jr.

Occupation(s):   attorney - partner, Foster and Wentworth;
                                         attorney for New York Produce Exchange

Marriage(s):   Lulu Benoit

Address: Ocean Avenue, Bayport
Name of estate: *Strandhome*
Year of construction: 1880
Style of architecture: Shingle
Architect(s):   Isaac Henry Green II designed
                                the house (for W. R. Foster, Jr.)
                             George Browne Post designed the
                                alterations (for C. A. Post)
Landscape architect(s):
House extant: no; demolished in 1950s
Historical notes:

   The house, originally named *Strandhome*, was built by William R. Foster, Jr.
   He was the son of John S. and Carrie O. Foster.
   [See previous entry for additional family information.]
   William R. Foster, Jr. allegedly swindled $68,000 from the Produce Exchange Gratuity Fund with
fraudulent mortgages and fled to France and Switzerland with his common-law-wife Lulu Benoit. In 1898, he
was arrested in France and extradited to the United States, at which time he finally married Lulu. The
majority of his debt was paid by his father, where upon William and Lulu returned to France and remained
there living off his inheritance.
   In 1888, *Strandhome* was purchased at public auction by the Produce Exchange Gratuity Fund which sold
it in 1890 to Charles Alfred Post. It was subsequently owned by Waldron Kintzing Post. Both Charles Post
and Waldron Post continued to call the estate *Strandhome*.
   Bernard Mannes Baruch, Sr. rented the house during the summers of 1915 and 1916.

Strandhome

Frank, Emil H., Sr. (1843-1919)

Occupation(s):   financier -   president, Frank and DuBois (marine insurance
                                                       firm

Marriage(s):   Paula Van Glahn (1864-1906)

Address: Awixa Avenue, Bay Shore
Name of estate:
Year of construction: 1894
Style of architecture: Queen Anne
Architect(s):
Landscape architect(s):
House extant: no
Historical notes:

The house was built by Emil H. Frank, Sr.
His brother was General Paul Frank.
Emil H. and Paula Van Glahn Frank, Sr.'s son
Emil H. Frank, Jr. remained a bachelor. Their
daughter Adele married Hobart Weekes, the son
of Bradford G. and Gladys Onderdonk Weekes,
Sr. of Oyster Bay. Their daughter Florence
remained unmarried. Their son Harold married
Alice Heath and resided in Chicago, IL. Their
daughter Grace married Paul Revere Smith and
resided in Staten Island. Their son George
married Louise Van Anden, the daughter of
William M. and Alice H. Frost Van Anden, Sr.
of Islip.
In 1904, the house was purchased by Julian
Douglas Fairchild.

front facade

Frothingham, John Sewell

Occupation(s):   capitalist -   director, Brooklyn Warehouse & Storage Co.
                        financier -   director, Home Life Insurance Co.
Civic Activism: member, board of regents, Long Island College Hospital, Brooklyn

Marriage(s):   Katharine Kent (d. 1930)

Address: Penataquit Avenue, Bay Shore
Name of estate:
Year of construction:
Style of architecture:
Architect(s):
Landscape architect(s):
House extant: unconfirmed
Historical notes:

The *Brooklyn Blue Book and Long Island Society Register, 1918* and *1921* list Katharine Kent
Frothingham as residing in Bay Shore.

Garben, Dr. Louis F., Sr. (d. 1964)

Occupation(s):	physician
Civic Activism:	chairman, mediation committee, Suffolk County Medical Society
Marriage(s):	Sarlta Moore
Address:	89 West Bayberry Road, Islip
Name of estate:	
Year of construction:	1899-1900
Style of architecture:	Moorish
Architect(s):	Grosvenor Atterbury designed the house (for H. O Havemeyer)*
Landscape architect(s):	Nathan F. Barrett (for H. O. Havemeyer)**

House extant: yes
Historical notes:

   The house was built by Henry Osborne Havemeyer as part of his "Modern Venice" development.
   It was later owned by Dr. Louis F. Garben, Sr.
   Dr. Louis F. and Mrs. Sarlta Moore Garben, Sr.'s son Robert resided in Dix Hills. Their son Dr. Allan C. Garben married Nancy Hendrickson, the daughter of Glenn Hendrickson of Brightwaters. Their son Bruce resided in Islip. Their son Dr. Louis F. Garben, Jr. resided in Glen Ridge, NJ.
   *The sale brochure for "Modern Venice" states that the Moorish-style architecture was suggested by Louis Comfort Tiffany.
   **The sales brochure also states that "Modern Venice" would be devoid of trees and vegetation and that Nathan F. Barrett was the landscape architect.

front / side facade, 2006

Gardiner, Robert David Lion (1911-2004)

Occupation(s):   financier -   member, Empire Trust Co.
                                        capitalist -   extensive commercial real estate holdings
                                        intelligence agent -   Naval intelligence officer during
                                                            World War II

Marriage(s):   1961-2004 – Eunice Bailey Oakes
                                     - British fashion model

Address: South Country Road, West Bay Shore
Name of estate: *Sagtikos Manor*
Year of construction: 1692
Style of architecture: Colonial
Architect(s):
Landscape architect(s):
House extant: yes
Historical notes:

    In 1692, Stephanus Van Cortlandt purchased 1,200 acres of land, extending from the Great South Bay northward to the middle of the Island, from the Secatogue Indians. He received a manorial grant for the land in 1697 and built his manor house the same year, naming it *Sagtikos*, an Algonquian word meaning "snake that hisses." In 1707, Van Cortlandt's heirs sold the manor along with its extensive lands to Timothy Carle [Carll], a wealthy Huntington farmer. In 1758, the manor was purchased for £1,200 by Jonathan Thompson of Setauket, a wealthy farmer and judge. In 1772, Thompson gave the manor house and 1,207 acres as a wedding gift to his son Isaac, who married Mary Gardiner of East Hampton. The last member of the Thompson/Gardiner family to own the house was Robert David Lion Gardiner, the Sixteenth Lord of the Manor.

    The house, which is on the National Register of Historic Places, was purchased by Suffolk County in 2002 and is open to the public.

front facade, 2006

rear / side facade, 2006

Garner, Thomas, Jr. (d. 1869)

Occupation(s):   industrialist -   partner, with his brother William, Garner
                                                    & Co. (cotton mills)

Marriage(s):   Harriet H. Amory (d. 1907)

Address: South Country Road, Bay Shore
Name of estate:
Year of construction:
Style of architecture:
Architect(s):
Landscape architect(s):
House extant: unconfirmed
Historical notes:

   He was the son of Thomas and Frances M. Thorn Garner, Sr.
   Harriet H. Amory Garner was the daughter of Jonathan Amory of Boston, MA.
   In 1878, Harriet filed suit against her brother-in-law William Thorn Garner for failure to disburse
$1 million she and her daughter Fanny inherited from her father-in-law. [*The New York Times* December 27, 1878,
p. 8.]
   [See following Garner entries for additional family information.]

Garner, Thomas, Sr. (d. 1867)

Occupation(s):   industrialist -   president and partner, with his brother William,
                                                    Garner & Co. (cotton mills)

Marriage(s):   Frances M. Thorn

Address: South Country Road, Bay Shore
Name of estate:
Year of construction:
Style of architecture:
Architect(s):
Landscape architect(s):
House extant: unconfirmed
Historical notes:

   Thomas and Frances M. Thorn Garner, Sr.'s son Thomas Garner, Jr. married Harriet H. Amory and also
resided in Bay Shore.
   Their son William Thorn Garner married Macellite Thorne of New Orleans, LA. Their daughter Frances
married Francis Cooper Lawrance, Sr. and resided at *Manatuck Farm* in Bay Shore. Their daughter Ann
remained unmarried.
   [See other Garner entries for additional family information.]

Garner, William Thorn (1842-1876)

Occupation(s):   industrialist -   partner, with his brother Thomas Garner & Co.
                                            (cotton mills);
                                              president, Harmony Mills (cotton mills);
                                              president, W. T. Garner & Co. (cotton mills)

Marriage(s):   Macellite Thorne (1846-1876)

Address: South Country Road, Bay Shore
Name of estate:
Year of construction:
Style of architecture:
Architect(s):
Landscape architect(s):
House extant: unconfirmed
Historical notes:

    William Thorn Garner was the son of Thomas and Frances M. Thorn Garner, Sr. After the death of their parents, William and his brother Thomas summered at their parents' estate in Bay Shore.
    William Thorn and Macellite Thorne Garner both perished in a yachting accident off Staten Island, NY, when their yacht the *Mohawk* was caught in a squall with all its sails set. In 1878, the yacht was purchased by the Coast and Geodetic Survey. Renamed the *Eagre*, it saw service in the Atlantic from 1878 to 1903.
    The Garners' daughter Macellite married Henri Charles Joseph le Tonnelie, the Marquis de Breteuil. Their daughter Edith married Count Leon von Molthe–Hvitfield and resided in Paris, France. Their daughter Florence married Sir William Gordon–Cumming, Baronet of Gordonstoun in Scotland. When accused of cheating at cards, William sued for slander. His position in British society was ruined when the jury found him guilty. [*The New York Times* May 21, 1930, p. 22; for further information on the trial and Florence's unhappy marriage to William, see Harry W. Havemeyer, *Along the Great South Bay From Oakdale to Babylon: The Story of a Summer Spa 1840 to 1940* (Mattituck, NY: Amereon House, 1996), pp. 209-10.]
    [See, also, preceding Garner entries for additional family information.]

Mohawk

Gibb, Howard, Sr. (1855-1905)

Occupation(s):   merchant -   president, Frederick Loeser & Co., Brooklyn
                                                              (formerly, H. Batterman Department Store)

Marriage(s):   M/1 – Mary Louise ____
                                      M/2 – Elizabeth Rossiter

Address: Ocean Avenue, Islip
Name of estate:
Year of construction: c. 1889
Style of architecture: Colonial Revival with Shingle elements
Architect(s):
Landscape architect(s):
House extant: no
Historical notes:

The house was built by Leander Waterbury.

It was subsequently owned by Howard Gibb, Sr.

He was the son of John and Harriet Balsdon Gibb, who resided at *Afterglow* in Islip.

Mary Louise Gibb subsequently married ____ Vernet and resided in France.

Howard and Mary Louise Gibb, Sr.'s daughter Minnie married Count Henri de Moy and resided in France.

The *Brooklyn Blue Book and Long Island Society Register, 1918* lists Elizabeth Rossiter Gibb as residing in Manhattan.

She was the daughter of Lucius Rossiter. Her brother E. V. W. Rossiter, who was vice-president of the New York Central & Hudson River Railroad, married Estelle Hewlett, the daughter of J. Lawrence Hewlett of Great Neck, and resided in Flushing, Queens.

[See following Gibb entries for additional family information.]

In 1898, the house was purchased by Henry Gerland Timmerman. It was later owned by Timmerman's daughter Grace, who married Orvill Hurd Tobey. Both the Timmermans and the Tobeys called the house *Breeze Lawn.*

front / side facade, c. 1903

Gibb, John (1829-1905)

Occupation(s):	capitalist -	partner, Mills & Gibb (importers of lace and linen)
	merchant -	president, Frederick Loeser & Co., Brooklyn (formerly, H. Batterman Department Store)
	financier -	trustee, Brooklyn Trust Co.
Civic Activism:		president, auxiliary, Adelphi College, Brooklyn (later, Adelphi University, Garden City);
		trustee, Adelphi Academy, Brooklyn

Marriage(s):   M/1 – 1852-1878 – Harriet Balsdon (d. 1878)
                           M/2 – 1882 – Sarah D. Mackay

Address: Ocean Avenue, Islip
Name of estate: *Afterglow*
Year of construction: c. 1890
Style of architecture: Shingle
Architect(s):
Landscape architect(s):
House extant: no; demolished in c. 1950
Historical note:

Afterglow, c. 1901

The house, originally named *Afterglow*, was built by John Gibb.

Born in Scotland, he was the son of James Gibb.

John and Harriet Balsdon Gibb's son Howard Gibb, Sr. married Elizabeth Rossiter and resided in Islip. Their son Lewis Mills Gibb, Sr. married Anna Pinkerton and resided at *Cedarholme* in Bay Shore. Their son Walter married Florence Althea Swan and resided at *Old Orchard* in Glen Cove. Their son Henry married Grace Dwight, the daughter of Frederick and Antoinette R. McMullen Dwight of *Tanglehedge* in Seabright, NJ, and resided in Morristown, NJ. Their son John Richmond Gibb, Sr. married Emily Mathews, who subsequently married John's brother Arthur, with whom she resided at *Gageboro* and at *Iron Action* in Glen Cove. Their daughter Ada married William Van Anden Hester, Sr. and resided at *Willada Point* in Glen Cove. Their daughter Florence married Herbert Lee Pratt, Sr. and resided at *The Braes* in Glen Cove.

Sarah Mackay Gibb's sister Annie married S. Perry Sturges and resided in Brooklyn.

[See other Gibb entries for additional family information.]

In 1909, the house was purchased by John Barry Stanchfield, Sr. It was inherited by Stanchfield's daughter Alice, who married Dr. Arthur Mullen Wright. Both the Stanchfields and the Wrights continued to call the house *Afterglow*.

living room, c. 1903

83

Gibb, Lewis Mills, Jr. (b. 1902)

Occupation(s):	merchant - president, Frederick Loeser & Co., Brooklyn (formerly, H. Batterman Department Store)
	capitalist - director, Pinkerton National Detective Agency

Marriage(s):   M/1 – 1927 – Patty Carroll Pease
                                  M/2 – 1943 – Jean Regan

Address: Dover Court, Bay Shore
Name of estate: *Cedarholme*
Year of construction: 1903
Style of architecture: Shingle
Architect(s):
Landscape architect(s):
House extant: yes
Historical notes:

The house, originally named *Cedarholme*, was built by Lewis Mills Gibb, Sr.

It was subsequently owned by his son Lewis Mills Gibb, Jr., who continued to call it *Cedarholme*.

The Long Island Society Register, 1929 lists Lewis Mills and Patty Carroll Pease Gibb [Jr.] as residing in Islip [Bay Shore].

She was the daughter of W. Albert and Martha C. Rodgers Pease, who resided in Hempstead.

Jean Regan Gibb was the daughter of Thomas J. and Aurora Sala Regan, who resided in Old Westbury. She had previously been married to Rigan McKinney of New York and Cleveland, OH.

Lewis Mills and Jean Regan Gibb, Jr.'s daughter Jean married Philip O'Donnell Lee, the son of Augustus Wilson Lee of Frederick, MD.

[See other Gibb entries for additional family information.]

The house was later owned by Charles H. Tenney.

front facade, 2005

Gibb, Lewis Mills, Sr. (1868-1912)

Occupation(s):   capitalist -   partner, Mills & Gibbs (importers of lace and linen);
                    merchant -   partner, Frederick Loeser & Co., Brooklyn (formerly,
                                        H. Batterman Department Store)

Marriage(s):   1900-1912 – Anna Pinkerton (d. 1942)
                        - Civic Activism: member, fund raising committee for construction
                                        of Southside Hospital, Bay Shore

Address: Dover Court, Bay Shore
Name of estate: *Cedarholme*
Year of construction: 1903
Style of architecture: Shingle
Architect(s):
Landscape architect(s):
House extant: yes
Historical notes:

The house, originally named *Cedarholme*, was built by Lewis Mills Gibb, Sr.

The *Brooklyn Blue Book and Long Island Society Register, 1918* lists Anna Pinkerton Gibb as residing at *Cedarholme* in Bay Shore.

She was the daughter of Robert Allan and Anna E. Hughes Pinkerton, who resided at *Dearwood* in Bay Shore. Her brother Allan Pinkerton II married Franc Woolworth and also resided in Bay Shore. Her sister Mary married Jay Freeborn Carlisle, Sr. and resided at *Rosemary* in East Islip.

[For additional family information see preceding Gibb entries.]

The house was later owned by Lewis Mills Gibb, Jr., who continued to call it *Cedarholme*, and subsequently, by Charles H. Tenney.

Gibson, Frederick E. (1908-1977)

Occupation(s):   capitalist -   president, F. E. Gibson Builders, Inc.;
                                        partner, Hempstead Park Acres (builders)
Civic Activism: president and chairman of board, Long Island Home Builders Association;
                    director, Suffolk County American Cancer Society;
                    member, Long Island Hospital Planning and Review Board;
                    member; advisory board, Southside Hospital, Bay Shore

Marriage(s):   Jean Giusti

Address: 87 Saxon Avenue, Bay Shore
Name of estate:
Year of construction:
Style of architecture:
Architect(s):
Landscape architect(s):
House extant: unconfirmed
Historical notes:

He was the son of William Robert Gibson, Sr., the founder and developer of the Gibson section of Valley Stream.

Frederick E. and Jean Giusti Gibson's son Gregory Martin Gibson married Carol Eugenia Epp and resided in Sayville and, later, in Brightwaters. Their son William Robert Gibson III married Lois Ann Bang, the daughter of Henry R. Bang.

Gibson, Gregory Martin

Occupation(s):   capitalist -   vice-president, F. E. Gibson Builders, Inc.*
                            politician -   mayor, Brightwaters, 1985

Marriage(s):   1959 – Carol Eugenia Epp (b. 1937)

Address: Concourse West, Brightwaters
Name of estate:
Year of construction:
Style of architecture:
Architect(s):
Landscape architect(s):
House extant: unconfirmed
Historical notes:

   Gregory Martin Gibson was the son of Frederick E. Gibson of Bay Shore.
   Carol Eugenia Epp Gibson was the daughter of Harold B. and Claira Moran Epp of Bay Shore.

Gibson, John James (1871-1936)

Occupation(s):   financier -   president, South Side Bank, Bay Shore (which merged into
                                           Franklin National Bank);
                                           director, First National Bank and Trust Co., Bay Shore
                            pharmacist
Civic Activism: president, Bay Shore Board of Education;
                            president, Bay Shore–Brightwaters Community Association

Marriage(s):   1904-1936 – Lavonne Jeanette Cushman (1868-1944)

Address: 45 Ocean Avenue, Bay Shore
Name of estate:
Year of construction:
Style of architecture: Neo-Colonial Revival
Architect(s):
Landscape architect(s):
House extant: yes
Historical notes:

   John James Gibson, Sr. was the son of Samuel Burr
and Rhoda Jane Reybert Gibson. His sister Aletta
married Raymond Hallock Terry and resided in Bay
Shore. His sister Mary married William Henry Brown
and resided in Bay Shore. His sister Anna married
Harry Mortimer Brewster and also resided in Bay
Shore. His brother Jesse married Addie May Hutton.
His brother Earle married Helen Smith, the daughter
of Allan and Anna Powell Petit Smith.
   John James and Lavonne Jeanette Cushman Gibson's
son John Joseph Gibson married Cornelia Lott
Vanderveer and resided in West Islip and Bay Shore.
   [See following entry for additional family information.]

front facade, 2006

Gibson, John Joseph (1910-1971)

Occupation(s):   attorney -   member, Green and Hurd, NYC;
                                    member, Hurd, Hamlin, and Hubbell, NYC;
                                    general counsel, Johnson & Johnson, New Brunswick, NJ
         industrialist -   vice-president, secretary, and treasurer, Johnson &
                                    Johnson, New Brunswick, NJ
         financier -   chairman of board, South Side Bank, Bay Shore (which merged
                                    into Franklin National Bank);
                                    director, Franklin National Bank, Franklin Square

Civic Activism: chairman of board, Islip Town Planning Board;
                       trustee, Southside Hospital, Bay Shore

Marriage(s):   1934-1971 – Cornelia Lott Vanderveer (1909-1988)

Address: 99 South Awixa Avenue, Bay Shore
Name of estate:
Year of construction: 1951-1953
Builder: Louis Bartos
Style of architecture: Colonial Revival elements
Architect(s):   Herbert W. Korber
Landscape architect(s):
House extant: yes
Historical notes:

     The house was built by John Joseph and Cornelia Lott Vanderveer Gibson.
     John Joseph Gibson was the son of John James and Lavonne Jeannette Cushman Gibson of Bay Shore.
     Cornelia Lott Vanderveer Gibson was the daughter of John and Gertrude Van Siclen Lott Vanderveer, who resided at *Sunnymead* in West Islip.
     [See previous entry for additional family information.]
     The John Joseph Gibson family resided in the gardener's cottage on the John Vanderveer estate *Sunnymead* in West Islip from 1935 to 1945. In 1945 they moved into the *Sunnymead's* main residence and resided there until 1953.
     The South Awixa Avenue house was subsequently owned by their son John Vanderveer Gibson.

Sunnymead, rear facade, 1930s

99 South Awixa Avenue, front facade, 2006

Goodrich, William W. (1833-1906)

Occupation(s):   attorney -   judge, New York State Supreme Court, 1896;
                                          chief justice, New York State Appellate Court
                              financier -   director, Kings County Bank
                              capitalist -   director, Port Jefferson Co. (real estate developer)
                              politician - member, New York State Assembly, 1865, 1870

Civic Activism: chairman, International Maritime Conference;
                              president of trustees, Brooklyn Homeopathic Hospital;
                              director, Philharmonic Society;
                              member, Brooklyn Board of Education, 1876

Marriage(s):   Frances Wickes (1836-1904)
                        - Civic Activism: a founder, New England Kitchen (raised money
                                              for Union hospitals during Civil War);
                                            manager, Long Island College Hospital, Brooklyn

Address: Saxon Avenue, Bay Shore
Name of estate:
Year of construction:
Style of architecture:
Architect(s):
Landscape architect(s):
House extant: unconfirmed
Historical notes:

    William W. Goodrich was the son of David and Mary Wenton Goodrich.
    Frances Wickes Goodrich was the daughter of Henry N. Wickes of Albany, NY.
    William W. and Frances Wickes Goodrich's daughter Jessie married Clinton Lawrence Rossiter and resided at *Old Field Acres* in Setauket. Their daughter Mabel married The Reverend Edward A. George, pastor of the First Congregational Church, Ithaca, NY. Their son Henry married Madeline C. Lloyd and resided at *Windygates* on Sakonnet Point in Rhode Island.

Gordon, Edward

Occupation(s):   financier -   president, Edward Gordon and Co.

Marriage(s):

Address: 80 Montgomery Avenue, Bay Shore
Name of estate:
Year of construction:
Style of architecture: Modified Shingle
Architect(s):
Landscape architect(s):
House extant: yes
Historical notes:

front facade, 2006

    The house was built by Charles Robinson Smith.
    It was subsequently owned by Gordon.
    The fifteen-room house, with nine bedrooms, six fireplaces, and five-and-a-half bathrooms, was for sale in 2006. The asking price was $1,490,000; the annual taxes were $18,055.

Graham, George Scott (1850-1931)

Occupation(s): attorney - partner, Graham and L'Amoreaux;
                            district attorney, Philadelphia, PA, 1880-1899
                capitalist - director, Electric Light Co., Philadelphia, PA;
                            director, Pennsylvania Heat, Light, & Power Co.
                industrialist - Smokeless Powder & Chemical Co.
                financier - director, Columbia Avenue Trust
                politician - member, United States Congress, 1913-1931

Marriage(s):   M/1 – 1870 – Emma M. Ellis
                M/2 – 1898-1931 – Pauline M. Clarke

Address: South Country Road, Islip
Name of estate: *Lohgrame*
Year of construction: 1910
Style of architecture: Modified Mediterranean
Architect(s):
Landscape architect(s):
House extant: no
Historical notes:

The house, originally named *Beautiful Shore*, was built by William Henry Moffit.
In 1915, it was purchased by Walter George Oakman, Sr.
In 1918, Mrs. Oakman sold the house to Graham, who called it *Lohgrame*.
He was the son of James Henry and Sarah Jane Scott Graham of Philadelphia, PA.
Emma M. Ellis Graham was the daughter of Charles Ellis. George Scott and Emma M. Ellis Graham's daughter Ethel married C. P. Wentz. Their daughter Blanche married Erskine Bains.
George Scott and Pauline M. Clarke Graham's daughter Marion married Graham Williams.

Green, Isaac Henry, II (1859-1937)

Occupation(s): architect - *[See Architects appendix for selected list of South Shore
                            commissions]*
                financier - president, Oysterman's National Bank, Sayville
Civic Activism: member, Board of Education, Sayville Public Schools, Sayville

Marriage(s):   1884-1937 – Emma Louise Hibbard (1865-1945)

Address: Brook Street, Sayville
Name of estate: *Brookside*
Year of construction: 1896-1897
Style of architecture: Tudor
Architect(s):   Isaac Henry Green II designed his own house
Landscape architect(s):
House extant: no; destroyed by fire in 1970
Historical notes:

The house, originally named *Brookside*, was built by Isaac Henry Green II.
He was the son of Samuel Willet and Henrietta Vail Green of Riverhead and Sayville.
Emma Louise Hibbard Green was the daughter of William and Emma Louise Hibbard of Bayport.
Isaac Henry and Emma Louise Hibbard Green II's daughter Henrietta married I. Howard Snedecor, the son of Isaac Scudder and Sarah Elizabeth Homan Snedecor, and resided in Bayport. Their daughter Beatrice married Edward H. Rogers and resided in Westhampton Beach.
A portion of the estate's property was purchased by Suffolk County and is now the county's "water park," Brookside County Park.

Gregory, William Hamilton, Jr. (1903-1962)

Occupation(s):	financier - partner, Gregory and Sons (investment banking firm)
	capitalist - chairman of board, Susquehanna & Western Railroad
	industrialist - director, Hycon–Caribbean Petroleum;
	director, Eastern Air Devices;
	director, Crescent Petroleum Corp.
Civic Activism:	trustee, Hewitt School for Girls, NYC (formerly, Miss Hewitt's Classes)
Marriage(s):	1929-1962 – Edith A. Crowley
Address:	Meadow Farm Road, East Islip
Name of estate:	*Creekside*
Year of construction:	1929
Style of architecture:	Neo-Federal
Architect(s):	William Hamilton Russell, Jr. designed
	the house (for J. K. Knapp II)
Landscape architect(s):	Charles Wellford Leavitt and Sons
	(for H. K. Knapp II)
House extant: yes	
Historical notes:	

The house, originally named *Creekside*, was built by Harry Kearsarge Knapp II.
In 1939, it was purchased by Gregory, who continued to call it *Creekside*.
He was the son of William Hamilton and Elizabeth Mitchell Gregory, Sr.
William Hamilton and Edith A. Crowley Gregory, Jr.'s son William Hamilton Gregory III married Elsie Bacon Lovering, the daughter of Joseph Sears Lovering, Sr. of Islip. Their daughter married Theodore C. Baer, Jr.

Guastavino, Rafael, Jr. (1872-1950)

Occupation(s):	capitalist - president, construction firm that specialized in
	ecclesiastical timbrel arch tile work
Marriage(s):	1909-div. c. 1941 – Elsie Seidel (1888-1982)
Address:	143 South Awixa Avenue, Bay Shore
Name of estate:	
Year of construction:	1912
Style of architecture:	Mediterranean Villa
Architect(s):	Rafael Guastavino, Jr.
Landscape architect(s):	
House extant: yes	
Historical notes:	

front / side facade, 2005

Rafael Guastavino, Jr. designed his own residence.
Elsie Seidel Guastavino subsequently married Randolph Mann and resided in Nyack, NY, and Fort Lauderdale, FL.
The house was subsequently owned by the Guastavinos' daughter Louise, who married Frank Gulden, Jr.
The sixteen-room house on 1.2 acres, with a 230-foot water frontage, was for sale in 2005. The asking price was $1.95 million.
A postcard mailed from Spain and dated April 12, 1912, indicated that the Guastavinos missed the fateful maiden voyage of the *Titanic*, due to travel scheduling, and planned to return to America on its second transatlantic voyage.

Guggenheim, Meyer Robert, Sr. (1885-1959)

Occupation(s):   industrialist -   member, executive committee, American Smelting
                                                     & Refining Co.;
                             secretary and vice president, U. S. Zinc Co.;
                             director, Guggenheim & Sons;
                             director, Guggenheim Exploration Co.
               diplomat -   United States Ambassador to Portugal, 1953-1954*
               financier -   director, American Smelting Securities Co.

Civic Activism: trustee, National Symphony Orchestra, Washington, DC;
                          trustee, Guggenheim Foundation

Marriage(s):   M/1 – 1905-div. 1915 – Grace L. Bernheimer
                         M/2 – 1915-1928 – Margaret Gibbs Miller Weyher (b. 1896)
                         M/3 – 1928- 1937 – Elizabeth Bross Eaton (b. 1903)
                         M/4 – 1938-1959 – Rebecca Pollard (1904-1994)

Address: Deer Park Avenue, North Babylon
Name of estate: *Firenze Farm***
Year of construction:
Style of architecture: Colonial Revival
Architect(s):
Landscape architect(s):
House extant: unconfirmed***
Historical notes: *front facade*

The *Long Island Society Register, 1929* lists Colonel and Mrs. M. Robert Guggenheim as residing on Deer Park Avenue in Babylon.

He was the son of Daniel and Florence Shloss Guggenheim, who resided at *Hempstead House* in Sands Point. His brother Harry, who resided at *Falaise* in Sands Point, married Helen Rosenberg, Caroline Morton, and, subsequently, Alicia Patterson. His sister Gladys married Roger W. Straus and resided in Manhattan.

*Guggenheim's diplomatic career was a disaster; his ambassadorship lasted barely a year. Known within State Department circles for "not having anything above his shoulders," he was also generally known for his indifferent work habits, gambling, habitual womanizing, and social *faux pas*. In his first ambassadorial speech he insulted his Portuguese guests by saying that his preference for an ambassadorial posting would have been for Great Britain but Portugal would do. A few months later, at a state banquet, he began flipping utensils at the dinner table. When a piece of silverware landed in the cleavage of an elderly guest, Guggenheim reached over and retrieved it from the between the dignitary's breasts. [Irwin and Debi Unger, *The Guggenheims* (New York: Harper Collins Publishers, 2005), pp. 186-89.]

Grace L. Bernheimer Guggenheim was the daughter of Jacob Bernheimer of Manhattan. She subsequently married Martin E. Snellenberg of Philadelphia, PA.

Meyer Robert and Grace L. Bernheimer Guggenheim, Sr.'s son Daniel Guggenheim II suffered from heart disease, as did most of the male line of the Guggenheim family, and died at the age of eighteen while a student at Phillips Exeter Academy. Their son Meyer Robert Guggenheim, Jr. married four times. His first wife Helen Claire Allyn was the daughter of Alfred Warren Allyn of Montreal, Canada. His second wife was his secretary and his fourth wife was Shirlee McMullen.

Guggenheim's conversion to Catholicism and his Roman Catholic ceremony marriage to Margaret Gibbs Miller Weyher, the daughter of Casper F. Weyher of Scranton, PA, stunned the Jewish community as did his subsequent marriage to Elizabeth Bross Eaton, the daughter of James Waterbury and Elizabeth Bross Eaton, Sr. of West Islip. Their Lutheran church wedding was devoid of guests. Elizabeth Guggenheim's brother James Waterbury Eaton, Jr. married Matilda Brown and resided in Cold Spring Harbor.

Rebecca Pollard Guggenheim was the daughter of Andrew W. Pollard. She had previously been married to William Van Lennep, Jr. After Guggenheim's death she married John A. Logan.

**Guggenheim's Babylon and Washington, DC, houses and his four yachts were all named after his mother, as was his parents' estate in New Jersey.

***In 1933, the house, which was located on 531 acres, was damaged by fire.

Gulden, Charles, II (1911-1994)

Occupation(s):   industrialist -   president, Charles Gulden, Inc. (manufacturer of mustard)

Marriage(s):   M/1 – 1933-1941 – Samantha Gaynor Isham (1915-1941)
                                         M/2 – 1942-1949 – Faith Hollins
                                         M/3 – 1957-1991 – Mary Faran Bulkley (d. 1991)

Address: 88 East Bayberry Road, Islip
Name of estate:
Year of construction: 1899-1900
Style of architecture: Moorish*
Architect(s):   Grosvenor Atterbury designed the house
                                (for H. O. Havemeyer)*
Landscape architect(s):   Nathan F. Barrett
                                  (for H. O. Havemeyer)**

House extant: yes
Historical notes:

    The house was built by Henry Osborne Havemeyer as part of his "Modern Venice" development.
It was later owned by Charles Gulden II.
    He was the son of Frank and Augusta Henes Gulden, Sr. of Islip.
    Samantha Gaynor Isham Gulden was the daughter of Ralph H. and Marion Gaynor Isham. Samantha's
grandfather New York City Mayor William J. Gaynor resided at *Deepwells* in St. James.
    Charles and Samantha Gaynor Isham Gulden II's son Charles Gulden III married Katherine A. Keogh, the
daughter of Thomas Keogh of Larchmont, NY. Their son Michael married Mary Jean Summers, the daughter
of Maurice Francis Summers, and resides in Mill Neck.
    Faith Hollins Gulden was the daughter of Gerald Vanderbilt and Virginia Kobbe Hollins, Sr. of *The Hawks*
in East Islip. She had previously been married to Arthur W. Little. Faith's sister Phylis married John
Grissom. Her brother John remained a bachelor. Her brother Gerald Vanderbilt Hollins, Jr. married Elizabeth
Armour, the daughter of Lester Armour of Chicago, IL.
    Mary Faran Bulkley Gulden was the daughter of David Tod and Mary F. Boyd Bulkley, who resided at *Rip
Wa Leta* in Ridgefield, CT.
    *The sales brochure for "Modern Venice" states that the Moorish–style architecture was suggested by
Louis Comfort Tiffany.
    **The sale brochure also states that "Modern Venice" would be devoid of trees and vegetation and that
Nathan F. Barrett was the landscape architect.
    The house was subsequently owned by Walter Livingston Titus, Jr.

front facade, 2006

Gulden, Charles, Sr. (d. 1916)

Occupation(s):   industrialist -   a founder, Charles Gulden, Inc. (manufacturer of mustard)
                                  financier -   director, Germania Bank of the City of New York;
                                                   trustee, Citizen Savings Bank

Marriage(s):   Mary C. Kellers (d. 1929)

Address: Clinton Avenue, Bay Shore
Name of estate: *Netherbay*
Year of construction: c. 1890s
Style of architecture: Queen Anne
Architect(s):
Landscape architect(s):
House extant: yes
Historical notes:

   Charles and Mary C. Kellers Gulden, Sr.'s son Frank Gulden, Sr. married Augusta Henes and resided in Bay Shore. Their daughter Margaret married Walter Livingston Titus, Sr. and resided in Babylon.
   [See other Gulden entries for additional family information.]
   The house is currently The Open Gate, a nursing facility.

front facade, 1997

Gulden, Frank, Jr. (1906-1989)

Occupation(s):   industrialist -   president and chairman of board, Charles Gulden, Inc.
                                            (manufacturer of mustard)

Marriage(s):   1932-1989 – Louise Guastavino (1914-2004)

Address: 143 South Awixa Avenue, Bay Shore
Name of estate:
Year of construction: 1912
Style of architecture: Mediterranean Villa
Architect(s):   Rafael Guastavino, Jr.
Landscape architect(s):
House extant: yes
Historical notes:

   The house was built by Rafael Guastavino, Jr.
   It was subsequently owned by his daughter Louise, who married Frank Gulden, Jr.
   He was the son of Frank and Augusta Henes Gulden, Sr. of Islip.
   Frank and Louise Guastavino Gulden, Jr.'s daughter Barbara married John Frederick Black, the son of Helen Baxter Black of Bay Shore, and resides in Easton, MD. Their daughter Louise married Rudolph Henriksen, the son of Christian and Jesse Stumme Henriksen of Islip, and resides in Islip. Their son Frank Gulden III married Jennie Giruc, the daughter of Stanley and Mary Korol Giruc of Bay Shore, and resides in Vero Beach, FL, and Point O' Woods, NY.
   [See other Gulden entries for additional family information.]
   The sixteen-room house on 1.2 acres, with a 230-foot water frontage, was for sale in 2005. The asking price was $1.95 million.

Gulden, Frank, Jr. (1906-1989)

Occupation(s):   industrialist -   president and chairman of board, Charles Gulden, Inc.
                                      (manufacturer of mustard)

Marriage(s):   1932-1989 – Louise Guastavino (1914-2004)

Address: 89 East Bayberry Road, Islip
Name of estate:
Year of construction: 1934-1935
Style of architecture: Mediterranean Villa
Architect(s):   Rafael Guastavino, Jr. designed the house
                          (for Gulden)

Landscape architect(s):
House extant: yes
Historical notes:

 The house was built by Frank Gulden, Jr.
 He was the son of Frank and Augusta Henes Gulden, Sr. of Islip.
 Louise Guastavino Gulden was the daughter of Rafael and Elsie Seidel Guastavino, Jr. of Bay Shore.
 [See Gulden and Guastavino entries for additional family information.]

front facade, 2006

Gulden, Frank, Sr. (1879-1961)

Occupation(s):	industrialist - chairman of board, Charles Gulden, Inc. (manufacturer of mustard)
Civic Activism:	president, board of trustees, Southside Hospital, Bay Shore; trustee, St. John's Hospital, Brooklyn; chairman, executive committee, Episcopal Church Charity Foundation; trustee, Berkeley Divinity School, New Haven, CT; vice-president, Boys Club of New York; trustee, Hofstra University, Hempstead; chairman, local chapter, New York State Temporary Emergency Relief Committee during the Depression; member, Emergency Committee of the Red Cross during World War II
Marriage(s):	1902-1961 – Augusta Henes (d. 1969)
Address:	137 West Bayberry Road, Islip
Name of estate:	
Year of construction:	1899-1900
Style of architecture:	Moorish*
Architect(s):	Grosvenor Atterbury designed the house (for H. O. Havemeyer)
Landscape architect(s):	Nathan F. Barrett (for H. O. Havemeyer)**

House extant: yes; but substantially altered
Historical notes:

The house, originally named *Bayberry Point*, was built by Henry Osborne Havemeyer as his own residence in his "Modern Venice" development.

It was owned by Gulden from the late 1920s to the late 1940s, at which time he relocated to 117 West Bayberry Road.

He was the son of Charles and Mary C. Kellers Gulden, Sr., who resided at *Netherbay* in Bay Shore.

Augusta Henes Gulden was the daughter of Julia Henes.

Frank and Augusta Henes Gulden, Sr.'s daughter Augusta married Carrick F. Cochran, the son of Dr. Robert W. Cochran of Sarasota, FL. Their son Frank Gulden, Jr. married Louise Guastavino and resided in Islip and Bay Shore. Their daughter Julia married Eric Gordon Ramsay, Sr. and resided in Brightwaters. Their son Charles Gulden II, who married Samantha Gaynor Isham, Faith Hollins, and, subsequently, Mary Faran Bulkley, resided in Islip and, later, in Cold Spring Harbor.

[See other Gulden entries for additional family information.]

*The sales brochure for "Modern Venice" states that the Moorish–style architecture was suggested by Louis Comfort Tiffany.

**The sale brochure also states that "Modern Venice" would be devoid of trees and vegetation and that Nathan F. Barrett was the landscape architect.

The house was subsequently owned by Dr. David Dodge Moore.

front facade, 2006

Gunther, William Henry, Jr. (1851-1901)

Occupation(s):   merchant -   partner, C. G. Gunther's Sons (fur dealer)*

Marriage(s):   1878-1901 – Mary R. Hatch

Address: Awixa Avenue, Bay Shore
Name of estate:
Year of construction: 1887
Style of architecture:
Architect(s):
Landscape architect(s):
House extant: unconfirmed
Historical notes:

    William Henry and Mary R. Hatch Gunther, Jr.'s son William Henry Gunther III was killed in Cuba during the Spanish American War.
    *C. G. Gunther's Sons, which was founded by William's grandfather Christian G. von Gunther, was one of the largest fur dealers in the country. [*The New York Times* February 16, 1901, p. 7.]

Haff, Albert D. (1870-1954)

Occupation(s):   financier -   chairman of board, Bank of Babylon
                       attorney -   partner, Haff and Farrington, Jamaica, NY

Marriage(s):   Josephine Farrington

Address: Cameron Avenue and Montrose Avenue, Babylon
Name of estate:
Year of construction:
Style of architecture:
Architect(s):
Landscape architect(s):
House extant: unconfirmed
Historical notes:

    Albert D. Haff was the son of John P. and Phoebe J. Pearsall Haff.
    Albert D. and Josephine Farrington Haff's daughter Madalene married _____ Van Nostrand and resided in West Islip.
    Albert was residing at 240 Secatogue Lane, West Islip, at the time of his death.

Haight, Gilbert Lawrence, Jr.

Occupation(s):

Marriage(s):

Address: 1646 Ocean Avenue, Amityville
Name of estate:
Year of construction:
Style of architecture: Colonial Revival
Architect(s):
Landscape architect(s):
House extant: unconfirmed
Historical notes:

Haight residence

    Gilbert Lawrence Haight, Jr. was the son of Gilbert Lawrence and Gladys Cook Haight, Sr.
    In 1954, Gilbert Lawrence Haight, Jr.'s three-year-old, adopted son Robert fell off the Haight's schooner into the Amityville River and drowned. [*The New York Times* June 5, 1954, p. 19.]

Hallock, Gerard, III (1905-1996)

Occupation(s):	financier - vice-president, Morgan Guaranty Trust Co.
Civic Activism:	trustee, Southside Hospital, Bay Shore;
	president, board of trustees, Hewlett School of East Islip;
	trustee, Boys' Club of New York City;
	trustee, Pinkerton Foundation (devoted to helping troubled children)

Marriage(s):   1937 – Marion Wharton (1908-1989)
                  - Civic Activism: member, auxiliary, Southside Hospital, Bay Shore;
                                 member, South Shore Garden Club

Address: St. Mark's Lane, Islip
Name of estate:
Year of construction: 1924
Style of architecture: Ranch
Architect(s):
Landscape architect(s):
House extant: no; demolished in 1980s
Historical notes:

Pleasure Island

    The house, originally named *Pleasure Island*, was built by Schuyler Livingston Parsons, Jr.
    It was then owned by his niece Marion and her husband Gerard Hallock III, who enlarged the house and moved it to the mainland in the 1970s. [Schuyler Livingston Parsons, Jr. *Untold Friendships* (Boston: Houghton Mifflin Co., 1955), p. 98.]
    Gerard Hallock III was the son of Gerard and Mary Adele Harlan Page Hallock, Jr. of Great Barrington, MA. His brother Harlan married Juliet Townshend, the daughter of Raynham and Juliet S. Adee Townshend of New Haven, CT. His brother Richards married Nancy Juelg and resided in Baltimore, MD.
    Marion Wharton Hallock was the daughter of Richard and Helena Johnson Parsons Wharton, who resided at *Whileaway* in Islip. Marion's brother Richard T. Wharton, Sr., who married Mara di Zoppola, the daughter of Count Andrea Alexsandro Mario and Countess Edith Mortimer di Zoppola of Mill Neck, inherited *Whileaway*.
    Gerard and Marion Wharton Hallock III's son Gerard Peter Hallock married Joanne Scheerer Babcock, the daughter of John Bodine Babcock, Sr. of Sharon, CT, and, subsequently, Judith Schneider. Their daughter Helena married John Anthony Pless, Jr., the son of John Anthony and Madelaine Sichel Pless, Sr. of Holland and France, and resided in Islip. Their daughter Lisa married Harry Kaye.

Harbeck, Charles T.

Occupation(s):   writer - *Bibliography of the History of the United States Navy*,
                                              c. 1908*

Marriage(s):   Sophia Child (d. 1918)

Address: Irish Lane, East Islip
Name of estate:
Year of construction:
Style of architecture:
Architect(s):
Landscape architect(s):
House extant: unconfirmed
Historical notes:

   Charles T. and Sophia Child Harbeck's son Dr. Charles J. Harbeck married Irene Brouwer, the daughter of
T. A. Brouwer of *Pinewold* in Westhampton. Their daughters Mildred and Helen remained unmarried and
resided together in a brownstone in Manhattan. In 1932, Mildred, age thirty-five, committed suicide in the
Manhattan residence.
   *Harbeck's naval history collection consisted of fifteen hundred books and ship logs, forty-six naval
medals, numerous historic prints, portraits of virtually all of the nation's prominent naval officers, documents
and letters, including one letter written by John Paul Jones. [*The New York Times* August 20, 1916, p. SM6.]

Harbeck, Charles T.

Occupation(s):   writer - *Bibliography of the History of the United States
                                              Navy*, c. 1908

Marriage(s):   Sophia Child (d. 1918)

Address: Suffolk Lane, East Islip
Name of estate:
Year of construction:
Style of architecture:
Architect(s):   Isaac Henry Green II designed
                                    the 1909 house
                                    (for Bradish Johnson, Jr.)
Landscape architect(s):   Olmsted, 1915
                                    (for Bradish Johnson Jr.)
House extant: first house on the site was destroyed by fire in 1905;
                        second (1909) house and gatehouse on the site are extant
Historical notes:

   The first house on the site was built by James Boorman Johnston.
   In 1880, it was purchased from Johnston by Harbeck.
   [See previous entry for Harbeck family information.]
   In 1882, Bradish Johnson, Jr. purchased the house from Harbeck and called it *Woodland*. After it was
destroyed by fire, Johnson built a second house on the site, which he also called *Woodland*.
   The estate was subsequently inherited by his son Aymar Johnson, who continued to call it *Woodland*.
   In 1946, Mrs. Aymar Johnson sold the estate to the Hewlett School of East Islip.
   In 2006, the school sold the estate to a developer. The main residence and gatehouse are extant as private
residences but the estate property was subdivided for a housing development.

Hard, Anson Wales, Jr. (1886-1935)

Occupation(s):	financier - stockbroker
Marriage(s):	M/1 – 1908-1932 – Florence Bourne (1886-1969)
	M/2 – 1933-1935 – Katherine Potter
Address:	South Country Road, West Sayville
Name of estate:	*Meadow Edge*
Year of construction:	c. 1908
Style of architecture:	Neo-Colonial Revival
Architect(s):	Isaac Henry Green II designed the house and carriage house (for Hard)
Landscape architect(s):	Charles Wellford Leavitt and Sons (for Hard)

House extant: yes
Historical notes:

The house, originally named *Meadow Edge*, was built by Anson Wales Hard, Jr.
He was the son of Anson Wales Hard, Sr. of Lawrence.
Florence Bourne Hard was the daughter of Frederick Gilbert and Emma Sparks Keeler Bourne, who resided at *Indian Neck Hall* in Oakdale. She later married Robert Barr Deans, Sr., with whom she resided at *Yeadon* on Centre Island, and, subsequently, Alexander Dallas Thayer of Philadelphia, PA.
[See Bourne entries for additional family information.]
Anson Wales and Florence Bourne Hard, Jr.'s son Frederick married Hildegarde Stevenson, the daughter of Joseph H. and Hildegarde Kobbe Stevenson. Their daughter Florence married William M. Walthers, Jr. Their son Anson Wales Hard III died before attaining adulthood.
Katherine Potter Hard had previously been married to Joseph W. Hemmersley Avery. After her divorce from Hard, she married Joseph W. Wear of Philadelphia, PA.
In 1966. the estate was sold to Suffolk County. The main residence and its surrounding grounds are the county's West Sayville Golf Course. The carriage house is the headquarters of the Long Island Maritime Museum.

front facade, 1992

rear facade, 1992

Havemeyer, Harry Waldron (b. 1929)

Occupation(s):	industrialist - executive vice-president, The National Sugar Refining Co.*
	writer - *Merchants of Williamsburgh*, 1989;
	       *Along the Great South Bay from Oakdale to Babylon, the Story of a
	           Summer Spa 1840 to 1940*, 1996;
	       East on the Great South Bay: Sayville and Bayport 1860-1960, 2001;
	       *Fire Island's Surf Hotel and Other Hostelries on Fire Island Beaches
	           in the Nineteenth Century*, 2006

Civic Activism:	trustee, Union Theological Seminary, NYC; member, executive council, Episcopal Church of the United States of America; treasurer, Episcopal Diocese of New York

Marriage(s):	1951 – Eugenie Aiguier
	  - Civic Activism: vice-chairman, board of trustees, Kirkland College**;
	                     trustee, Vassar College, Poughkeepsie, NY;
	                     trustee, Hamilton College, Clinton, NY

Address:	Saxon Avenue, Bay Shore
Name of estate:	
Year of construction:	1960
Style of architecture:	20th century Contemporary
Architect(s):	Francis Day Rogers of Rogers and Butler designed the house (for H. W. Havemeyer)
Landscape architect(s):	
House extant: yes	
Historical notes:	

    The house was built by Harry Waldron Havemeyer.
    He is the son of Horace and Doris Anna Dick Havemeyer, Sr., who resided at *Olympic Point* in Bay Shore.
    Eugenie Aiguier Havemeyer is the daughter of Dr. James Edward and Mrs. Virginia Light Aiguier of Bala–Cynwyd, PA.
    Harry Waldron and Eugenie Aiguier Havemeyer's daughter Ann married Tom Richard Strumolo, the son of Richard A. Strumolo of Middlebury, CT, and resides in Norfolk, CT. Their daughter Linden married David Scott Wise, the son of Harry H. Wise, Jr. of Hartsdale, NY, and resides in Manhattan. Their daughter Adaline married Stuart N. Siegel, the son of William Siegel of Mount Vernon, NY, and also resides in Manhattan. Their daughter Eugenie married Julian Pollak, the son of Dr. Victor Pollak, and resides in San Francisco, CA. Their daughter Catherine married Daniel Singer, the son of Jack Singer, and resides in Manhattan. Their daughter Tanya married Dr. Steven Sanford and resides in Greensboro, VT.
    [See following Havemeyer entries for additional family information.]
    *Claus Doscher, who lived in Sayville and was president of North Side Bank in Brooklyn, was a founder of New York Refining Company, which subsequently merged into The National Sugar Refining as did Mollenhauer Sugar Refining Company, founded by John Mollenhauer, who lived on Awixa Avenue in Bay Shore.
    **Kirkland College was a liberal arts college for women which coordinated with Hamilton College in Clinton, NY. It existed for ten years, from 1968 to 1978.

south facade, 2005

Havemeyer, Henry, Sr. (1838-1886)

Occupation(s):	industrialist - president, Havemeyer & Vegelius (tobacco); trustee, Havemeyer Brothers (later, Havemeyer Sugar Refining Co.)
	capitalist - president, Long Island Rail Road; constructed Rockaway Beach Iron Pier; established ferry from Jersey City, NJ, to Hunter's Point, Queens

Marriage(s):   Mary Jane Moller (d. 1889)

Address: South Country Road, West Islip
Name of estate: *Sequatogue Farm**
Year of construction:
Style of architecture: Shingle
Architect(s):
Landscape architect(s):
House extant: no
Historical notes:

The house was built by ____ Bergen.
In 1880, it was purchased by Havemeyer, who called it *Sequatogue Farm*.
He was the son of New York City Mayor William Frederick and Mrs. Sarah Agnes Craig Havemeyer, Sr.
Mary Jane Moller Havemeyer was the daughter of Brooklyn sugar refiner William Moller.
In 1884, Mary successfully sued Henry, claiming that he was a "habitual drunkard" and unfit to control his finances. [*The New York Times* June 7, 1884, p. 8 and June 3, 1886, p. 5.]
The house was subsequently owned by Charles Francis Hubbs, who continued to call it *Sequatogue Farm*.
*The estate was named for the *Sequatogue* [also, *Secatogue*] Indians, who lived in this area of Long Island.

Havemeyer, Henry, Sr. (1838-1886)

Occupation(s):   *[See previous entry.]*

Marriage(s):   Mary Jane Moller (d. 1889)

Address: Captree Island Boat Basin, West Islip
Name of estate: *Armory*
Year of construction: 1880
Style of architecture:
Architect(s):
Landscape architect(s):
House extant: no
Historical notes:

In 1879, Havemeyer purchased the Whig Inlet House, also known as Stone's Hotel, and converted it into his summer residence.
[See other Havemeyer entries for family information.]
In 1883, Havemeyer leased the house to the Argyle Hotel for use as an adjunct hotel. It was during the first summer as a hotel that President Chester A. Arthur and some of his cabinet member vacationed at the *Armory* for several days. [Harry W. Havemeyer, *Along the Great South Bay From Oakdale to Babylon: The Story of a Summer Spa 1840 to 1940* (Mattituck, NY: Amereon House, 1996), pp. 83-4.]

Havemeyer, Henry Osborne (1847-1907)

Occupation(s):   financier -   director, Williamsburgh Trust Co.
                                          industrialist -   managing partner, Havemeyers & Elder (sugar refinery 1862-91)*
                                                            founder and president, American Sugar Refining Co.**
                                          capitalist -   developer, "Modern Venice," Islip residential housing development

Civic Activism: donated 200 feet of shoreline to the Town of Islip for use as a public beach;
                                        donated works of art to the Metropolitan Museum of Art, NYC***

Marriage(s):   M/1 – 1870 – Mary Louise Elder (1847-1897)
                           M/2 – 1883-1907 – Louisine Waldron Elder (1855-1929)
                                   - writer -   "The Suffrage Torch, Memories of a Militant." *Scribner's Magazine*, 1922; "The Prison Special, Memories of a Militant." *Scribner's Maga*zine, 1922; "The Waking of Women." (typescript of speech), 1924-1925; *Sixteen to Sixty: Memoirs of a Collector*
                               Civic Activism: donated works of art to the Metropolitan Museum of Art, NYC***;
                                             active in Woman's Suffrage Movement

Address: 137 West Bayberry Road, Islip
Name of estate: *Bayberry Point*
Year of construction: 1899-1900
Style of architecture: Moorish
Architect(s):   Grosvenor Atterbury designed
                                the house (for H. O. H)****

Landscape architect(s): Nathan F. Barrett
                                (for H. O. H.)*****

House extant: yes, but substantially altered
Historical notes:

home of H. O. Havemeyer, left foreground; home of H. Havemeyer, Sr., right background

The house, originally named *Bayberry Point*, was built by Henry Osborne Havemeyer as his own residence in his "Modern Venice" development.

He was one of ten children of Frederick Christian and Sarah Louise Henderson Havemeyer.

Mary Louise Elder Havemeyer was the daughter of George and Hanna Riker Elder.

Louisine Waldron Elder Havemeyer was the daughter of George William and Mathilda Adelaide Elder. Her sister Anne married Henry Norcross Munn. Her brother George married Therese Cadwell and resided in Bay Shore. Her sister Adaline married Samuel Twyford Peters and resided at *Windholme* in Islip.

Henry Osborne and Louisine Waldron Elder Havemeyer's daughter Adaline married Peter Hood Ballantine Frelinghuysen. Their son Horace married Doris Anna Dick and resided at *Olympic Point* in Bay Shore. Their daughter Electra married James Watson Webb, Sr. and resided at *Woodbury House* in Syosset and in Old Westbury before relocating to Shelburne, VT.

[See other Havemeyer entries for additional family information.]

*In 1891 the sugar refining division of Havemeyers & Elder was merged into the American Sugar Refining Company. The remaining property, not used in the sugar refining business, was retained by Havemeyers & Elder as a Brooklyn real estate holding company until the 1950s.

**Havemeyer's Sugar Trust was second only to the Standard Oil Trust. The American Sugar Refining Co. controlled more than fifty-percent of the nation's sugar refining. [Frances Westzenhoffer, *The Havemeyers: Impressionism Comes to America* (New York: Harry N. Abrams, Inc. Publishers, 1986), p. 69.]

***The Havemeyers donated 1,912 paintings and art objects to the Metropolitan Museum of Art. [Westzenhoffer, p. 11]

****The sales brochure for "Modern Venice" states that the Moorish-style architecture was suggested by Louis Comfort Tiffany.

*****The sales brochure also states that "Modern Venice" would be devoid of trees and vegetation and that Nathan F. Barrett was the landscape architect.

The house was later owned by Frank Gulden, Sr. and, subsequently, by Dr. David Dodge Moore.

Havemeyer, Horace, Jr. (1914-1990)

Occupation(s):   industrialist -   president, The National Sugar Refining Co.;
                                      director, Amalgamated Sugar Co.
                            financier -   director, The New York Trust Co. (later,
                                        Chemical Bank, then, Chase Bank, and
                                      now, J. P. Morgan Chase)

Civic Activism: member of board, Huntington Hospital, Huntington;
                              member of board, Drew University, Madison, NJ;
                              trustee, East Woods School, Oyster Bay Cove;
                              a founder, Bayberry Yacht Club

Marriage(s):   1939-1990 - Rosalind Everdell (b. 1917)

Address: 68 East Bayberry Road, Islip
Name of estate:
Year of construction: 1899-1900
Style of architecture: Moorish
Architect(s):   Grosvenor Atterbury designed the house
                            (for H. O Havemeyer)*
Landscape architect(s): Nathan F. Barrett (for H. O. Havemeyer)**
House extant: yes; but altered
Historical notes:

   The house was built by Henry Osborne Havemeyer as part of his "Modern Venice" development.
   It was later owned by his grandson Horace Havemeyer, Jr.
   Rosalind Everdell Havemeyer was the daughter of William R. and Rosalind Romeyn Everdell, who resided in Manhasset.
   The Havemeyers' daughter Rosalind married Christopher du Pont Roosevelt, the son of Franklin Delano and Ethel du Pont Roosevelt, Jr. of Woodbury, and resides in Lyme, CT. Their son Horace Havemeyer III married Eugenie C. Cowan and resides in Manhattan. Their son William Everdell Havemeyer married Jane Litzenberg and also resides in Manhattan. Their son Christian Havemeyer, who resides at *The Reward* in Chestertown, MD, is a bachelor.
   [See other Havemeyer entries for additional family information.]
   *The sale brochure for "Modern Venice" states that the Moorish-style architecture was suggested by Louis Comfort Tiffany.
   **The sales brochure also states that "Modern Venice" would be devoid of trees and vegetation and that Nathan F. Barrett was the landscape architect.

front facade, 2006

Havemeyer, Horace, Sr. (1886-1956)

Occupation(s):   industrialist -   president, Havemeyers & Elder (sugar refinery 1862-1891)*;
                                               director, Remington Arms Co.;
                                               director, Cuban–American, Cape Cruz, Manati, Great
                                                         Western, Central Romana, San Domingo, Sante Fe,
                                                         Warren–Cuba Cane, W. J. McCahan, and South
                                                         Puerto Rico Sugar Company (sugar cane and sugar
                                                         beet companies);
                                               director, Savannah Sugar Refining Co.;
                                               president, Scranton & Lehigh Coal Co.
                        capitalist -   director, Lackawanna & Western Railroad;
                                               director, Brooklyn Eastern District Terminal
                        shipping -   director, American–Hawaiian Steamship Co.
                        financier -   director, Bankers Trust Co.;
                                               director, International Acceptance Bank, Inc;
                                               director, Lackawanna Securities Co.

Civic Activism: trustee, Metropolitan Museum of Art, NYC;
                        trustee, Frick Museum, NYC;
                        sugar and food consultant to federal government during World War I

Marriage(s):   1911-1956 – Doris Anna Dick (1890-1982)

Address: 117 West Bayberry Road, Islip
Name of estate:
Year of construction: 1899-1900
Style of architecture: Moorish
Architect(s):   Grosvenor Atterbury
                           designed the house
                           (for H. O. Havemeyer)**
Landscape architect(s):   Nathan F. Barrett
                           (for H. O. Havemeyer)***
House extant: yes, but substantially altered****
Historical notes:

     The house was built by Henry Osborne Havemeyer as part of his "Modern Venice" development.
     After his marriage, Horace Havemeyer, Sr., resided in the house next to his widowed mother. He continued to reside there until 1918, when he built *Olympic Point* in Bay Shore.
     [See following entry for family information.]
     *In 1891 the sugar refining division of Havemeyers & Elder was merged into the American Sugar Refining Company. The remaining property, not used in the sugar refining business, was retained by Havemeyers & Elder as a Brooklyn real estate holding company until the 1950s.

     In the late 1940s Frank Gulden, Sr. relocated to this house from 137 Bayberry Road.
     **The sales brochure for "Modern Venice" states that the Moorish-style architecture was suggested by Louis Comfort Tiffany.
     ***The sales brochure also states that "Modern Venice" would be devoid of trees and vegetation and that Nathan F. Barrett was the landscape architect.
     ****The flat roof style was eliminated by a subsequent owner.

front facade, 2006

Havemeyer, Horace, Sr. (1886-1956)

Occupation (s):	industrialist -	president, Havemeyers & Elder (sugar refinery 1862-1891)*;
		director, Remington Arms Co.;
		director, Cuban–American, Cape Cruz, Manati, Great Western, Central Romana, San Domingo, Santa Fe, Warren–Cuba Cane, W. J. McCahan, and South Puerto Rico Sugar Company (sugar cane and sugar beet companies);
		director, Savannah Sugar Refining Co.;
		president, Scranton & Lehigh Coal Co.
	capitalist -	director, Lackawanna & Western Railroad;
		director, Brooklyn Eastern District Terminal
	shipping -	director, American–Hawaiian Steamship Co.
	financier -	director, Bankers Trust Co.;
		director, International Acceptance Bank, Inc.;
		director, Lackawanna Securities Co.
Civic Activism:		trustee, Metropolitan Museum of Art, NYC;
		trustee, Frick Museum, NYC;
		sugar and food consultant to federal government during World War I

Marriage(s):　　　　　1911-1956 – Doris Anna Dick (1890-1982)

main staircase

Address:　　　　　　Saxon Avenue, Bay Shore
Name of estate:　　　*Olympic Point*
Year of construction:　1917-1919
Style of architecture:　Modified Cotswold
Architect(s):　　　　Harrie T. Lindeberg designed the house
　　　　　　　　　　(for Horace Havemeyer, Sr.)
　　　　　　　　　Alfred Hopkins designed the farm complex
　　　　　　　　　　(for Horace Havemeyer, Sr.)
Landscape architect(s):　Olmsted Brothers (for Horace Havemeyer, Sr.)
House extant:　no; demolished in 1948**
Historical notes:

　　The house, originally named *Olympic Point*, was built by Horace Havemeyer, Sr.

　　He was the son of Henry Osborne and Louisine Waldron Elder Havemeyer, who resided at *Bayberry Point* in Islip.

　　Doris Anna Dick Havemeyer was the daughter of John Henry and Julia Theodora Mollenhauer Dick, who resided at *Allen Winden Farm* in Islip. Her brother William Karl Dick, who married Madeline Force and, subsequently, Virginia K. Conner, also resided at *Allen Winden Farm* in Islip. Her sister Julia married William Kingsland Macy, Sr. and resided in Islip. Her brother Adolph, a bachelor, resided in Islip.

　　Horace and Doris Anna Dick Havemeyer, Sr.'s daughter Doris married Dr. Daniel Catlin, Sr. and resided in Bay Shore. Their daughter Adaline married Richard Sturgis Perkins, Sr. and, subsequently, Laurance B. Rand of Southport, CT. Their son Horace Havemeyer, Jr. married Rosalind Everdell and resided in Islip and, later, in Dix Hills. Their son Harry married Eugenie Aiguier and resides on the *Olympic Point* property in Bay Shore.

[See other Havemeyer entries for additional family information.]

　　*In 1891 the sugar refining division of Havemeyers & Elder was merged into the American Sugar Refining Company. The remaining property, not used in the sugar refining business, was retained by Havemeyers & Elder as a Brooklyn real estate holding company until the 1950s.

　　**Horace Havemeyer, Sr. engaged E. W. Howell & Co. to demolish the house in 1948 and build a smaller Colonial-style house on the property for his family.

Horace Havemeyer, Sr. Estate, *Olympic Point*

south facade

south and west facade

SOUTH

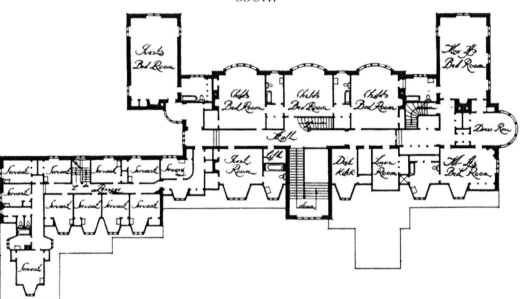

EAST   *second floor plan*   WEST

west facade

north facade

106

Hawley, Edwin (1850-1912)

Occupation(s):   capitalist* -   director, Southern Pacific Railroad;
                                          president, Minneapolis & St. Louis Railroad;
                                          director, Chesapeake & Ohio Railroad;
                                          director, Iowa Central Railroad;
                                          director, Missouri, Kansas & Texas Railroad;
                                          director, Toledo, St. Louis, & Western Railroad;
                                          director, Chicago & Alton Railroad
                        shipping -   director, Pacific Mail Steamship Co.

Marriage(s):   bachelor

Address: (Effingham Park section), Babylon
Name of estate:
Year of construction: c. 1900
Style of architecture: Colonial Revival
Architect(s):
Landscape architect(s):
House extant: no
Historical notes:

front facade

*Hawley was president or director of forty-one companies.

James Hazen Hyde's private railroad car "Bay Shore" was purchased by Hawley.

Hawley died intestate in 1912. Since there was no will, his $25 million estate was divided among his relatives.

Hayward, Frank Earle, Sr. (1867-1923)

Occupation(s):

Marriage(s):   1905-1923 – Kathleen Gilbert (d. 1960)

Address: Green Avenue, Sayville
Name of estate: *Joy Farm*
Year of construction: c. 1892
Style of architecture: Shingle
Architect(s):
Landscape architect(s):
House extant: unconfirmed
Historical notes:

rear facade

The house, originally named *Joy Farm*, was built by Frank Earle Hayward, Sr.

The *Brooklyn Blue Book and Long Island Society Register, 1918* lists Frank Earle and Kathleen Gilbert Hayward [Sr.] as residing at *Joy Farm* in Sayville.

He was the son of New York City Tax Commissioner John N. Hayward. His brother William Tyson Hayward, Sr. married Martha Eugenia Wemple. They resided at *The Anchorage*, also on Green Avenue in Sayville.

Kathleen Gilbert Hayward was the daughter of K. L. Gilbert of Patchogue. She subsequently married Admiral P. McCullough and resided in North Plainfield, NJ.

Frank Earle and Kathleen Gilbert, Sr.'s son Frank Earle Gilbert, Jr. moved to California.

[See other Hayward entries for additional family information.]

Hayward, William Tyson, Jr.

Occupation(s):   industrialist - oil

Marriage(s):   Jane Louise Bauman

Address: Cedar Lane, Babylon
Name of estate:
Year of construction:
Style of architecture:
Architect(s):
Landscape architect(s):
House extant: unconfirmed
Historical notes:

    The *Long Island Society Register, 1929* lists William Tyson and Jane Louise Bauman Hayward, Jr. as residing on Cedar Lane in Babylon.
    He was the son of William Tyson and Martha Eugenia Wemple Hayward, Sr., who resided at *The Anchorage* in Sayville.
    William Tyson and Jane Louise Bauman Hayward, Jr.'s son William Tyson Hayward III married Beverly Marion Frost, the daughter of John Patterson Frost of Winnipeg, Canada. Their daughter Janet married Eugene Kelly of Bermuda.
    [See other Hayward entries for additional family information.]

Hayward, William Tyson, Sr. (1857-1921)

Occupation(s):   industrialist -   president, Jay C. Wemple Co. (manufacturer of
                                        window shades)

Marriage(s):   Martha Eugenia Wemple (1861-1937)
                        - Civic Activism: chairman, American Red Cross, in Sayville,
                                      during World War I

Address: Green Avenue, Sayville
Name of estate: *The Anchorage*
Year of construction: 1892
Style of architecture: Shingle
Architect(s):   Isaac Henry Green II
                        designed the house
                        (for W. T. Hayward, Sr.)

Landscape architect(s):
House extant: no*
Historical notes:

front facade, c. 1892

    The house, originally named *The Anchorage*, was built by William Tyson Hayward, Sr.
    The *Brooklyn Blue Book and Long Island Society Register, 1918* lists William Tyson and Martha Eugenia Wemple Hayward [Sr.] as residing at *The Anchorage* in Sayville.
    He was the son of New York City Tax Commissioner John N. Hayward. His brother Frank Earle Hayward, Sr. married Kathleen Gilbert and resided at *Joy Farm*, also on Green Avenue.
    Martha Eugenia Wemple Hayward was the daughter of Jay C. Wemple of Brooklyn.
    William Tyson and Martha Eugenia Wemple Hayward, Sr.'s son William Tyson Hayward, Jr. married Jane Louise Baumann and resided in Babylon. Their son Dudley also resided in Babylon.
    [See other Hayward entries for additional family information.]
    In 1920, Hayward sold the house to developer Emil Kupler.
    *Kupler cut the house in half and sold it as separate residences. He also subdivided the property for a housing development.

Heckscher, Charles Augustus, Jr. (1850-1936)

Occupation(s):   capitalist -   Florida fruit grower

Marriage(s):   Emelia I. Thebaud

Address: *[unable to determine street address]*, Islip
Name of estate:
Year of construction:
Style of architecture:
Architect(s):
Landscape architect(s):
House extant: unconfirmed
Historical notes:

The Long Island Society Register, 1929 lists Charles A. and Emelia I. Thebaud Heckscher, Jr. as residing in Islip.

He was the son of Charles Augustus and Georgiana Coster Heckscher of Manhattan. His brother John married Mary Travers and, subsequently, Virginia Otis.

Charles Augustus and Emelia I. Thebaud Heckscher, Jr.'s. daughter Georgiana married John H. Tweed and resided in Manhattan.

Heins, John Lewis, Sr. (1844-1929)

Occupation(s):   capitalist -   president, Brooklyn City and Newtown Railroad Co.;
                                          president and chairman of board, Coney Island and
                                              Brooklyn Railroad Co. (which merged into
                                              Brooklyn Rapid Transit Co.);
                                          director, DeKalb Avenue and North Beach Railroad Co.
                      financier -   director, National City Bank of Brooklyn;
                                          director, Long Island Safe Deposit Co.

Marriage(s):   M/1 – 1871 – Eliza Anna Zundt
                           M/2 – 1907-1929 – Margaret Boscher (1875-1934)

Address: South Country Road, West Islip
Name of estate:
Year of construction:
Style of architecture:
Architect(s):
Landscape architect(s):
House extant: unconfirmed
Historical notes:

John Lewis Heins, Sr. was the son of Carsten and Anna Evers Heins.

His daughter Helen married George Walsh and, subsequently, John Conway of Salem, MA. His daughter Marguerite married R. M. Mansfield. His son John L. Heins, Jr. resided in Garden City.

Hepburn, Henry Charles, Jr. (1825-1912)

Occupation(s):   financier -   stockbroker
Civic Activism: election inspector, Town of Babylon;
                             trustee, Town of Islip Schools

Marriage(s):   Elizabeth Sarah Eytinge (1829-1915)

Address: South Country Road, Babylon
Name of estate: *The Firs*
Year of construction:
Style of architecture:
Architect(s):
Landscape architect(s):
House extant: unconfirmed
Historical notes:

    Henry Charles Hepburn, Jr. was the son of Henry Charles and Maria Chardavoyne Hepburn, Sr.
    An intimate friend of Daniel Webster and President Chester A. Arthur, Hepburn was, at the time of his death, reputed to be the oldest telegrapher in the world. [*The New York Times* June 16, 1915, p. 11.]
    Elizabeth Sarah Eytinge Hepburn was the daughter of Solomon and Mary Anne Miller Eytinge.
    Henry Charles and Elizabeth Sarah Eytinge Hepburn, Jr.'s son Henry Chester Hepburn married Silvie Livingston Strong and resided in Babylon.
    [See following entry for additional family information.]

Hepburn, Henry Chester

Occupation(s):   financier -   stockbroker

Marriage(s):   1911 – Silvie Livingston Strong (1873-1935)

Address: 44 Douglas Avenue, Babylon
Name of estate:
Year of construction:
Style of architecture: Modified Dutch Colonial Revival
Architect(s):
Landscape architect(s):
House extant: yes
Historical notes:

    Henry Chester Hepburn purchased the Fernando Enrique deMurias house.
    He was the son of Henry Charles and Elizabeth Sarah Eytinge Hepburn, Jr., who resided at *The Firs* in Babylon.
    Silvie Livingston Strong Hepburn was the daughter of James H. S. and Georgiana Louisa Berryman Strong of Babylon. She had previously been married to Richard Bailey Post. The Posts' daughter Aletla married John Timothy McMahon and resided in the Manhasset area of Long Island, as did her sister Elizabeth, who remained unmarried.
    The *Long Island Society Register, 1929* lists Silvie Strong Hepburn as residing at 44 Douglas Avenue, Babylon.
    [See previous entry for additional family information.]

front facade, 2006

Hobbs, Charles Buxton (1863-1944)

Occupation(s):   attorney -   partner, Gifford, Hobbs, and Beard

Marriage(s):   1894 – Mary E. Minor

Address: Great River Road, Great River
Name of estate: *River Croft*
Year of construction: c. 1902
Style of architecture: Shingle
Architect(s):
Landscape architect(s):
House extant: no; demolished in 1960
Historical notes:

River Croft

    The house, originally named *River Croft*, was built by Charles Buxton Hobbs.
    The *Brooklyn Blue Book and Long Island Society Register, 1918* lists Charles Buxton and Mary E. Minor Hobbs as residing at *River Croft* in Great River.
    He was the son of Edward and Ellen Buxton Hobbs.

Hodges, George W., Sr. (1869-1935)

Occupation(s):   financier -   partner, Remick, Hodges and Co. (investment
                                 banking firm)
Civic Activism: vice-president, Private Bankers Association;
                     president, Investment Bankers' Association;
                     director, New York State Bankers Association;
                     president, Better Business Bureau of New York City;
                     assistant director, Government Loan Organization during
                          World War I

Marriage(s):   1905 – Maita Angus Marvin
                     - Civic Activism: regent, New Jersey Daughters
                                     of the American Revolution

Address: 117 Awixa Avenue, Bay Shore
Name of estate:
Year of construction:
Style of architecture: Shingle
Architect(s):
Landscape architect(s):
House extant: unconfirmed
Historical notes:

    The house was built by Rudolph Oelsner, who by 1906 had relocated to Long Island's North Shore. It was later owned by Hodges.
    He was the son of Joseph Francis and Caroline Elizabeth Andrews Hodges.
    In 1923, Hodges sold the house to James P. Kelly, who called it *Awixaway*.

Hollins, Gerald Vanderbilt, Sr. (1886-1955)

Occupation(s):   financier -   Charles D. Halsey (investment banking firm)
Civic Activism: donated a portion of his estate to the Town of Islip for a
                                     nature preserve

Marriage(s):   1907-div. 1937 – Virginia Kobbe (1890-1948)

Address: Bay View Avenue, East Islip
Name of estate: *The Hawks*
Year of construction: c. 1912
Style of architecture: Modified-Shingle
Architect(s):   Isaac Henry Green II designed the
                                 house (for G. V. Hollins, Sr.)

Landscape architect(s):
House extant: yes
Historical notes:

    The house, originally named *The Hawks*, was built by Gerald Vanderbilt Hollins, Sr.
    The *Long Island Society Register, 1929* lists Gerald Vanderbilt and Virginia Kobbe Hollins [Sr.] as residing at *The Hawks* in East Islip.
    He was the son of Harry Bowly and Evelina Meserole Knapp Hollins, Sr., who resided at *Meadow Farm* in East Islip.
    Virginia Kobbe Hollins was the daughter of Gustav and Carolyn Wheeler Kobbe of Bay Shore. She subsequently married Henry Morgan, with whom she continued to reside in East Islip. Her sister Hildegarde married Joseph Stevenson and, subsequently, Francis Burritt Thorne, Sr., with whom she resided at *Brookwood* in East Islip. Her sister Carol married Robert Woodward Morgan, Sr. and also resided in East Islip. Carol subsequently married George Palen Snow of Syosset. Virginia's sister Beatrice married Raymond D. Little. Her brother George married Marjorie W. Goss.
    Gerald Vanderbilt and Virginia Kobbe Hollins, Sr.'s son Gerald Vanderbilt Hollins, Jr. married Elizabeth Armour, the daughter of Lester Armour of Chicago, IL. Their daughter Faith married Arthur W. Little and, subsequently, Charles Gulden II and resided in Islip. Their daughter Phyllis married John Grissom. Their son John remained a bachelor.
    [See other Hollins entries for additional family information.]

Harry Bowly Hollins, Jr. residence, Crickholly, c. 1912

Hollins, Harry Bowly, Jr. (1882-1956)

Occupation(s):	financier - partner, H. N. Whitney, Goadby and Co. (stock brokerage firm)
	industrialist - director, Perkin Elmer Corp. (optical instrument manufacturer);
	director, Marcaibo Oil Exploration Co.
Civic Activism:	member, Red Cross Auxiliary during World War I
Marriage(s):	1904-1956 – Lilias Livingston (1882-1976)
Address:	131 Bay View Avenue, East Islip
Name of estate:	*Crickholly*
Year of construction:	c. 1907
Style of architecture:	Neo-Georgian
Architect(s):	Cross & Cross designed the house (for H. B. Hollins, Jr.)

Landscape architect(s):
House extant: yes
Historical notes:

The house, originally named *Crickholly*, was built by Harry Bowly Hollins, Jr.

The *Long Island Society Register, 1929* lists Harry B. and Lilias Livingston Hollins, Jr. as residing at *Crickholly* in East Islip.

He was the son of Harry Bowly and Evelina Meserole Knapp Hollins, Sr., who resided at *Meadow Farm* in East Islip.

Lilias Livingston Hollins was the daughter of Henry Beekman and Frances Redmond Livingston, Jr. of Bay Shore.

Harry Bowly and Lilias Livingston Hollins, Jr.'s son Harry Bowly Hollins III married Elizabeth Wolcott Elkins, the daughter of William M. Elkins of Elkins Park, PA, and, subsequently, Elizabeth Jay of Sands Point. Their son Robert married Lorraine Young, the daughter of B. Loring Young of Weston, MA. Their daughter Evelina married Henry L. Hoguet and resided in Katonah, NY. Their daughter Hope remained unmarried.

[See other Hollins entries for additional family information.]

In 1999, the 6,500-square-foot, eighteen-room house on 4.1 acres was for sale. The asking price was $550,000; the annual taxes were $16,679.

front facade, 1999

113

Hollins, Harry Bowly, Sr. (1854-1939)

Occupation(s):	financier -	a founder, with H. Duncan Wood, H. B. Hollins and Co. (stock brokerage firm);
		a founder, Knickerbocker Trust Co.;
		president, Central Railroad & Banking Co. of Georgia;
		president, International Bank of Mexico;
		director, Corporation Trust Co. of America;
		director, North American Safe Deposit Co.
	capitalist -	director, Central Union Gas Corp.;
		director, Union Gas Co.;
		director, Long Island Motor Parkway, Inc.
	industrialist -	director, Havana Tobacco Co.

Marriage(s):   1877-1935 – Evelina Meserole Knapp (1853-1935)

Address: Hollins Lane, East Islip
Name of estate: *Meadow Farm*
Year of construction: c. 1880
Style of architecture: Shingle
Architect(s):
Landscape architect(s): Olmsted (for H. B. Hollins, Sr.)
House extant: no
Historical notes:

The house, originally named *Meadow Farm*, was built by Harry Bowly Hollins, Sr.

The *Long Island Society Register, 1929* lists Harry B. and Evelina Knapp Hollins [Sr.] as residing at *Meadow Farm* in East Islip.

He was the son of Frank and Elizabeth Coles Hollins. His sister Alice married Harry Ingersoll Nicholas, Sr. and resided in North Babylon.

Evelina Meserole Knapp Hollins was the daughter of William K. and Maria Meserole Knapp, who resided in Islip. Her sister Maria remained unmarried.

Harry Bowly and Evelina Meserole Knapp Hollins, Sr.'s son Harry Bowly Hollins, Jr. married Lilias Livingston and resided at *Crickholly* in East Islip. Their son Gerald married Virginia Kobbe and resided at *The Hawks* in East Islip.

Harry Bowly and Evelina Meserole Knapp Hollins, Sr.'s Manhattan residence is currently the Argentine Consulate.

[See other Hollins entries for additional family information.]

Meadow Farm

114

Hollister, Buell, Sr. (1883-1966)

Occupation(s):	financier -	partner, Hollister and Babcock (stock brokerage firm); partner, Pyne, Kendall and Hollister (stock brokerage firm)
	capitalist -	chairman of board, Cornell–Dublilier Electric Corp.; president, Cayuga & Susquehanna Railroad; director, Stentor Electric
	industrialist -	president, Inde Gold Mining Co.; chairman of board, Dubilier Condenser Corp.
Civic Activism:	trustee and treasurer, Southside Hospital, Bay Shore	

Marriage(s):   1912-1963 – Louise R. Knowlton (1886-1963)

Address: St. Mark's Lane, Islip
Name of estate:
Year of construction:
Style of architecture:
Architect(s):
Landscape architect(s):
House extant: unconfirmed
Historical notes:

The *Brooklyn Blue Book and Long Island Society Register, 1921* lists Mr. and Mrs. Buell Hollister [Sr.] as residing on St. Mark's Lane, Islip.

He was the son of Henry Hutchinson and Isabelle Howell Hollister, Sr. of Islip.

Louise R. Knowlton Hollister was the daughter of Danford and Minnie B. Jones Knowlton of Manhattan. Her sister Edith married Allan Appleton Robbins and resided at *Dolancothy Lodge* in Locust Valley. Her sister Natalie married J. Insely Blair and resided in Tuxedo, NY. Her sister Madeleine, who married John E. Cowdin, also resided in Tuxedo, NY.

Buell and Louise R. Knowlton Hollister, Sr.'s son Buell Hollister, Jr. married Eileen Bramwell, the daughter of Gerald A. Bramwell.

[See following entry for additional family information.]

Hollister, Henry Hutchinson, Sr. (1842-1909)

Occupation(s):	financier -	partner, Hollister and Babcock (stock brokerage firm)
Civic Activism:	secretary, Fraunces Tavern, NYC	

Marriage(s):   M/1 – Isabelle Howell
               M/2 – Anne Willard (d. 1918)

Address: St. Mark's Lane, Islip
Name of estate:
Year of construction:
Style of architecture:
Architect(s):
Landscape architect(s):
House extant: unconfirmed
Historical notes:

The house was built by John Dean Johnson.

In 1886, it was purchased by Hollister, who remodeled and expanded the house.

Hollister's son Henry Hutchinson Hollister, Jr. married Hope Shepley. His son Buell married Louise R. Knowlton and resided in Islip. His daughter Louise married Richard E. Forest of Philadelphia, PA, and, subsequently, Landon Barrett Valentine, with whom she resided in Islip.

[See previous entry for additional family information.]

Hoppin, Bayard Cushing (1884-1956)

Occupation(s):   financier -   a founder and partner, Abbott, Hoppin and Co. (stock
                                                     brokerage firm);
                                                     a founder and partner, Hoppin Brothers and Co. (stock
                                                   brokerage firm)
                             capitalist -   director, Beekman Estates (real estate development firm)

Civic Activism: chairman of board, Southside Hospital, Bay Shore;
                                        trustee, Seamen's Church Institute of New York

Marriage(s):   M/1 – 1910 – Helen Lispenard Alexandre
                              M/2 – Laurette Kennedy

Address: Suffolk Lane, East Islip
Name of estate:
Year of construction:
Style of architecture:
Architect(s):
Landscape architect(s):
House extant: unconfirmed
Historical notes:

The *Long Island Society Register, 1929* lists Bayard Cushing and Helen L. Alexandre Hoppin as residing on Pavilion Lane [Suffolk Lane] in Islip [East Islip].

He was the son of William Warner and Katharine Beekman Hoppin, Sr. of Manhattan. His brother William Warner Hoppin, Jr. married Mary Gallatin and resided at *Friendship Hill* in Old Brookville. His brother Gerard married Rosina Sherman Hoyt and resided at *Four Winds* in Oyster Bay Cove. His sister Katharine married A. Wright Post and resided at *White Lodge* in Bernardsville, NJ. His sister Esther married Dr. Eugene Hillhouse Pool and resided in Lattingtown.

Helen Lispenard Alexandre Hoppin was the daughter of John E. and Helen Lispenard Webb Alexandre of *Spring Lawn* in Lenox, MA. Her sister Civilise married Frederick Schenck, the son of J. Frederick Schenck of *Valleyhead* in Lenox, MA.

Howell, Carlton Bell (b. 1907)

Occupation(s):   capitalist -   owner, Horse Happy Farm, Schaefferstown, PA (riding academy)

Marriage(s):   1934-1977 – Elizabeth Huber

Address: 108 East Bayberry Road, Islip
Name of estate:
Year of construction: 1899-1900
Style of architecture: Moorish
Architect(s):   Grosvenor Atterbury designed the house
                              (for H. O Havemeyer)
Landscape architect(s):   Nathan F. Barrett (for H. O. Havemeyer)
House extant: yes
Historical notes:

The house was built by Henry Osborne Havemeyer as part of his "Modern Venice" development.
It was owned by Edwin Thorne III and, subsequently, by Howell.
He was the son of James Frederick and Adele Cornwell Widdifield Howell, Sr. of Brightwaters.
Elizabeth Huber Howell was the daughter of Frederick Max and Harriet Louise Bossert Huber, Sr. of Bay Shore. *[See Huber entry for additional family information.]*
Carlton Bell and Elizabeth Huber Howell's daughter Daphne married J. T. M. Born, the son of Theodore Born of Bay Shore.

Howell, Elmer Brown (1889-1954)

Occupation(s):	capitalist -	partner, E. W. Howell & Co. (construction firm)*
	financier -	vice-president, Suffolk County Federal Savings & Loan Assoc.;
		director, Babylon National Bank & Trust Co.
Civic Activism:		secretary, Town Economy League Economic Council;
		chairman, Board of Appeals;
		member, Babylon School Board

Marriage(s):   1912 – Frances Rogers

Address: Little East Neck Road, Babylon
Name of estate:
Year of construction:
Style of architecture:
Architect(s):
Landscape architect(s):
House extant: unconfirmed
Historical notes:

Elmer B. Howell was the son of Elmer W. and Kizze Brown Howell of Babylon.
*See following entry for a list of E. W. Howell & Co.'s South Shore commissions.

Howell, Elmer W. (1860-1954)

Occupation(s):	capitalist -	partner, E. W. Howell & Co. (construction firm)*

Marriage(s):   1887 – Kizze Brown

Address: Little East Neck Road, Babylon
Name of estate:
Year of construction:
Style of architecture:
Architect(s):
Landscape architect(s):
House extant: unconfirmed
Historical notes:

Kizze Brown was the daughter of George S. Brown.
*Among E. W. Howell & Co.'s South Shore commissions were: Jay Freeborn Carlisle, Sr.'s *Rosemary* in East Islip; George T. Turnbull's *The Pines* in West Islip; William Henry Moffitt's *Beautiful Shore* in Islip; Landon Ketchum Thorne, Sr.'s indoor pool at *Thorneham* in West Islip; as well as the house of Adolph Dick in Islip; a New England-style house on Horace Havemeyer, Sr.'s. *Olympic Point* estate in Bay Shore; and an addition to William Dick's *Allen Winden Farm* in Islip.

Howell, James Frederick, Sr. (b. 1860)

Occupation(s):   politician -   Brightwaters Village Clerk, 1924-1954

Marriage(s):   M/1 – 1889-div. 1899 – Greta Hughes
                                 M/2 – 1900-1951 – Adele Cornwell Widdifield

Address: *[unable to determine street address]*, Brightwaters
Name of estate:
Year of construction:
Style of architecture:
Architect(s):
Landscape architect(s):
House extant: unconfirmed
Historical notes:

   James Frederick Howell, Sr., the son of James Bruen and Mary Ann Bowen Howell, was a member of Theodore Roosevelt's Rough Riders.
   Greta Hughes Howell subsequently married Herbert Witherspoon, star basso of the Metropolitan Opera.
   Adele Cornwell Widdifield was the daughter of John and Mary Widdifield. Her sister Mary married Harry Packer Wilbur of Key West, FL.
   James Frederick and Adele Cornwell Widdifield Howell's son Carleton married Elizabeth Huber, the daughter of Frederick Max and Harriet Louise Bossert Huber, Sr. of Bay Shore.

Hubbard, Harmanus B.

Occupation(s):   attorney

Marriage(s):   1861-1915 – Margaret G. McKay (1842-1915)
                         - Civic Activism: manager, Home for Aged Men, Brooklyn

Address: Penataquit Avenue, Bay Shore
Name of estate: *Oakhurst*
Year of construction:
Style of architecture: Queen Anne
Architect(s):   Harry G. Hardenburg designed
                         the house (for Thurber)
Landscape architect(s):
House extant: no
Historical notes:

   The house was built by Fred C. Thurber.
   It was subsequently owned by Hubbard, who called it *Oakhurst*.
   The *Brooklyn Blue Book and Long Island Society Register, 1918* lists H. B. Hubbard as residing at *Oakhurst* in Bay Shore.
   Margaret G. McKay Hubbard was the daughter of Samuel McKay.
   Harmanus B. and Margaret G. McKay Hubbard's daughter married W. C. Cannon.

front facade, c. 1897

Hubbs, Charles Francis (1867-1935)

Occupation(s):	industrialist - president, treasurer and chairman of board, Charles F. Hubbs & Co. (paper manufacturer);
	president, Hubbs & Corning Co., Baltimore, MD (paper manufacturer);
	president, Hubbs & Hastings Paper Co., Rochester, NY (paper manufacturer);
	president, Hubbs & Howe Co., Cleveland, OH (paper manufacturer);
	president, Interstate Cordage & Paper Co., Pittsburgh. PA
	financier - director, Dime Savings Bank of Brooklyn (later, Dime Savings Bank of New York; now, The Dime)

Marriage(s):   Mollie Richards Howe (d. 1934)

Address: South Country Road, West Islip
Name of estate: *Sequatogue Farm*
Year of construction:
Style of architecture: Shingle
Architect(s):
Landscape architect(s):
House extant: no
Historical notes:

The house was built by _____ Bergen.

In 1880, it was purchased by Henry Havemeyer, Sr., who called it *Sequatogue Farm*.

The house was subsequently owned by Hubbs, who continued to call it *Sequatogue Farm*.

The *Brooklyn Blue Book and Long Island Society Register, 1918* lists Charles Francis and Mollie R. Howe Hubbs as residing at *Sequatogue Farm* in Babylon [West Islip].

Mollie Richards Howe Hubbs was the daughter of Henry H. and Mary Angel Howe.

By 1929 the Hubbses had relocated to Hegeman's Lane in Old Brookville.

Charles Francis and Mollie Richards Howe Hubbs' daughter Dorothy, who married Richard C. Kettles, inherited her parents' Old Brookville estate. The Kettles called it *Orchard Corners*. The Hubbses' daughter Marjorie, who married George A. Anderson, resided in Old Brookville on adjacent property.

front facade, c. 1903

Huber, Frederick Max, Sr. (d. 1917)

Occupation(s):   industrialist -   partner, Otto Huber Brewing, Brooklyn*
                                    restaurateur -   owned several taverns

Marriage(s):   1901-1917 – Harriet Louise Bossert (b. 1873)

Address: 48 South Clinton Avenue, Bay Shore
Name of estate:
Year of construction:
Style of architecture: Victorian
Architect(s):
Landscape architect(s):
House extant: no; garage complex is extant
Historical notes:

side / front facade

    Frederick Max Huber, Sr. was the son of Otto and Emilie Meyer Huber, Jr. of Brooklyn.

    Harriet Louise Bossert Huber was the daughter of Louis Bossert of *The Oaks* in West Bay Shore. Her brother John married Mary A. Jones and resided in Garden City. Her sister Biene married Carroll Trowbridge Cooney, the son of John J. Cooney of Brooklyn and Plandome. Her brother Charles married Natalie Taylor and resided in Sayville. Her sister Josephine married Dr. Henry Moser of Brooklyn.

    Frederick Max and Harriet Louise Bossert Huber, Sr.'s son Otto was paralyzed in both arms and legs while playing football for St. Paul's School in Garden City. He died a year later at the age of seventeen as a result of his injuries. [Liz Howell, *Continuity: Biography 1819-1934* (Sister Bay, WI: The Dragonsbreath Press, 1993), pp. 320-24.] Their daughter Evelyn married Carl Linn. Their son Frederick Max Huber, Jr. married Louise Draper. Their daughter Elizabeth married Carleton Bell Howell, the son of James F. and Adele Widdifield Howell, Sr.

    *During Prohibition, the Huber family sold the brewery to Edward Hittleman. Its name was changed to Hittleman–Goldenrod Brewery, which used illustrations of the Katzenjammer Kids, from a popular comic strip, on its bottle caps. In 1946, the company's name was changed to Edlebrau. The brewery closed in 1951 shortly after Hittleman's death.

Hulse, The Reverend William Warren (1838-1929)

Occupation(s):   real estate agent
                                  politician -   member, Suffolk County Board of Supervisors;
                                              Superintendent of the Poor, Suffolk County;
                                            assessor, Town of Islip
                                clergy -   disciple of Swedenborg, Church of the New Jerusalem
Civic Activism: trustee, Long Island Chautaqua Assembly (promoted religion, science,
                              art, and "innocent recreation");
                         president, Board of Education, Bay Shore

Marriage(s):   1867-1911 – Josephine Worth (1841-1911)

Address: South Country Road, Bay Shore
Name of estate: *Elysian Views*
Year of construction:
Style of architecture: Modified Victorian
Architect(s):
Landscape architect(s):
House extant: no
Historical notes:

front facade, c. 1903

    During the Civil War, Hulse was known as the "Christian Soldier" because of his practice of praying as he entered battle. [*The New York Times* June 24, 1929, p. 16.]

    He was the son of David Overton and Sarah Hallock Hulse.

Hutchins, Francis Sessions (1877-1924)

Occupation(s):   attorney -   partner, Baldwin, Hutchins, and Todd ;
                                 financier -   vice-president, Commonwealth Trust Co.;
                                             director, Railway Securities Co.;
                                           director, Registration Trust Co.

Marriage(s):   M/1 – 1903 – Margaret G. Noyes (d. 1909)
                           M/2 – 1914-1924 – Sarah H. Crane

Address: Great River Road, Great River
Name of estate:
Year of construction: 1899
Style of architecture: Tudor
Architect(s):   Charles C. Thain designed
                           the house (for R. S. White)
Landscape architect(s):
House extant: no
Historical notes:

The house was built by Raymond S. White.

It was later owned by Hutchins.

The *Long Island Society Register, 1929* lists Francis S. and Sarah Crane Hutchins as residing in Great River.

He was the son of The Reverend R. Grosvenor and Mrs. Harriet James Hutchins.

Sarah H. Crane Hutchins had previously been married to Raymond S. White.

Margaret Noyes Hutchins was the daughter of Dr. Henry D. and Mrs. Anna Grant Noyes.

The house was subsequently owned by Dr. George David Stewart, who called it *Appin House*.

front facade, c. 1910

Hutton, Edward Francis (1877-1962)

Occupation(s):	financier - founder, E. F. Hutton and Co. (investment banking firm)
	industrialist - chairman of board, General Foods Corp.;
	chairman of board, Zonite Products Corp.;
	director, Chrysler Corp. (now, Daimler–Chrysler Corp.);
	director, The Coca–Cola Co.
Civic Activism:	founder, Freedoms Foundation (dedicated to preserving the "freedoms"
	in the Constitution and the Bill of Rights)
Marriage(s):	M/1 – 1900-1918 – Blanche Horton (d. 1918)
	M/2 – 1920-div. 1935 – Marjorie Merriweather Post (1877-1962)
	- industrialist - director, General Foods Corp.
	Civic Activism: woman's suffrage - member, suffragist delegation
	that consulted with President Wilson in 1917;
	equipped a 2,000 bed hospital in France during
	World War I;
	vice-chairman, Emergency Unemployment Drive,
	NYC;
	vice-president, National Symphony Orchestra,
	Washington, DC;
	board member, Good Samaritan Hospital, NYC;
	member, arts education committee, National Cultural
	Center, Washington, DC
	M/3 – 1936-1962 – Dorothy Dear

Address:	Saxon Avenue, Bay Shore
Name of estate:	
Year of construction:	c. 1880
Style of architecture:	Victorian
Architect(s):	
Landscape architect(s):	
House extant:	no; demolished in 1932
Historical notes:	

The house was built by Daniel D. Conover.

It was inherited by his son Augustus Whitlock Conover, Sr.

In 1912, the house was purchased by Franklyn Laws Hutton, who later sold it to his brother Edward Francis Hutton. They were the sons of James Laws Hutton of New York.

In 1920, Edward Francis and Blanch Horton Hutton's eighteen-year-old son Halcourt was killed at the Bay Shore estate when his horse's saddle loosened, throwing Halcourt forward and upside down. Halcourt's head hit the cobblestone pavement resulting in his death a day or two later. [Nancy Rubin, *American Empress: The Life and Times of Marjorie Merriweather Post* (New York: Villard Books, 1995), p. 108.]

Marjorie Merriweather Post Hutton was the daughter of Charles William and Ella Letitia Merriweather Post of Battle Creek, MI. Marjorie's father Charles was the founder of Postum Cereal Co., which later became General Foods Corp. She had previously been married to Edward Bennett Close. After her divorce from Hutton, she married Joseph Edward Davies and, subsequently, Herbert Arthur May.

Edward Francis and Marjorie Merriweather Post Hutton's daughter Nedenia (aka Dina Merrill) married Stanley Maddox Rumbough, Jr. was the son of Stanley and Elizabeth J. Colgate Rumbough, Sr., who resided at *Elston Oaks* in Lloyd Harbor. Stanley Maddox and Nedenia M. Hutton Rumbough, Jr.'s twenty-three-year-old son David drowned in a boating mishap. Their daughter Nedenia married Charles Stiffer Craig of Birmingham, MI. Ms. Merrill subsequently married actor Cliff Robertson.

[See following entry for additional family information.]

In 1921, the house was purchased from E. F. Hutton by Philip Balch Weld.

In 1930, it was purchased from Weld by Cecil Sharp, who demolished the house and built a new house on the site.

Hutton, Franklyn Laws (1877-1940)

Occupation(s):   financier -   partner, E. F. Hutton and Co. (investment banking firm)

Marriage(s):   M/1 – 1907-1917 – Edna Woolworth (1884-1917)*
                        M/2 – 1926-1940 – Irene Curley (d. 1965)

Address: Saxon Avenue, Bay Shore
Name of estate:
Year of construction: c. 1880
Style of architecture: Victorian
Architect(s):
Landscape architect(s):
House extant: no; demolished in 1932
Historical notes:

The house was built by Daniel D. Conover.
It was inherited by his son Augustus Whitlock Conover, Sr.
In 1912, Franklyn Laws Hutton purchased the house.
He was the son of James Laws Hutton of New York.
Edna Woolworth Hutton was the daughter of Frank Winfield and Jennie Creighton Woolworth, who resided at *Winfield Hall* in Glen Cove. Her sister Helena married Charles Francis McCann and resided at *Sunken Orchard* in Oyster Bay Cove. Her sister Jessie married James Paul Donahue, Sr. and resided at *Wooldron Manor* in Southampton.
Franklyn Laws and Edna Woolworth Hutton's daughter Barbara married Prince Alexis Mdivani, Count Kurt von Haugwitz–Reventlow of Denmark, actor Cary Grant, Prince Igor Troubertzkoy of Lithuania, Porfirio Rubirosa, and, subsequently, Baron Gottfied von Cramm.
*In 1917, Edna Woolworth Hutton, dressed in a white charmesues evening gown, committed suicide in her room at the Hotel Plaza in Manhattan with an overdose of strychnine crystals. [C. David Heymann, *Poor Little Rich Girl: The Life and Legend of Barbara Hutton* (Secaucus, NJ: Lyle Stuart, Inc., 1984), p. 15.]
Irene Curley had previously been married to _____ Bodde. She subsequently married James A. Moffett.
[See previous entry for additional family information.]
Franklyn Laws Hutton sold it to his brother Edward Francis Hutton.
In 1921, the house was purchased from E. F. Hutton by Philip Balch Weld.
In 1930, it was purchased from Weld by Cecil Sharp, who demolished the house and built a new house on the site.

front facade, c. 1903

Hyde, Henry Baldwin, II (1915-1997)

Occupation(s):	attorney - partner, Goldstein, Shames, and Hyde
	intelligence agent*
Civic Activism:	director, French Institute Alliance Fund;
	trustee, Hospital for Special Surgery, NYC;
	director, William J. Donovan Foundation

Marriage(s):   M/1 – 1941 – Marie de LaGrange (1919-1983)
                                 - journalist -   editor, French division of War Information
                                                          during World War II
                           M/2 – 1961-1997 – Elizabeth Prokoff Piper

Address: Fire Island
Name of estate:
Year of construction:
Style of architecture:
Architect(s):
Landscape architect(s):
House extant: unconfirmed
Historical notes:

   Henry Baldwin Hyde II was the son of James Hazen and Marthe Leishman Hyde, who resided at *The Oaks* in West Bay Shore.
   Marie de LaGrange Hyde was the daughter of Amcury and Emily Sloane de LaGrange of France.
   Henry Baldwin and Marie de LaGrange Hyde II's daughter Lorna married Baron Hubert de Wangen of Geroldseck. Their daughter Isabel married Jerome J. Jasinowki and resides in Washington, DC.
   Henry Baldwin Hyde II's cousin Annah Ripley, whose parents Sidney Dillon and Mary Hyde Ripley, Sr. resided at *The Crossroads* in Uniondale, married Count Pierre de Viel Castel and resided in Normandy, France. During World War II the de Viel Castels' house was occupied by the German army. Because of her impeccable French, the Germans never suspected that Annah was an American. She was able to eavesdrop on the German conversations and pass the information on to the French resistance in a basket of eggs that she took to the local village for sale. [Patricia Beard, *After the Ball: Gilded Age Secrets, Boardroom Betrayals, and the Party That Ignited the Great Wall Street Scandal of 1905* (New York: Harper Collins Publishers, 2003), p. 345.]
   *Henry Baldwin Hyde II was the chief of the Office of Strategic Services (OSS) in France and, later, in Switzerland, during World War II.
   [See entries for Henry Baldwin Hyde, Sr. and James Hazen Hyde for additional family information.]

Henry Baldwin Hyde, Sr.'s, estate, The Oaks

Hyde, Henry Baldwin, Sr. (1834-1899)

Occupation(s):	financier -	president, Equitable Life Assurance Society of the United States;
		director, Mercantile Safe Deposit Co.;
		director, Mercantile Trust Co.
	capitalist -	director, Union Pacific Railway Co.;
		director, Western Union Telegraph Co.;
		director, Westinghouse Electric Co.;
		director, Coney Island and Brooklyn Railroad, Co.;
		director, Brooklyn City and Newtown Railroad Co.
Civic Activism:	president, Alliance Francaise	
Marriage(s):	1864-1899 – Annie Fitch (d. 1922)	
Address:	South Country Road, West Bay Shore	
Name of estate:	*The Oaks*	
Year of construction:	1874-1876	
Style of architecture:	Stick-style	
Architect(s):	Calvert Vaux designed the house (for H. B. Hyde, Sr.)	
Landscape architect(s):	Olmstead, with Jacob Weidenman (for H. B. Hyde, Sr.)*	
House extant: yes**		
Historical notes:		

The forty-room house, originally named *Marquetux* and later renamed *The Oaks*, was built by Henry Baldwin Hyde, Sr.

He was the son of Henry Hazen and Mary Baldwin Hyde. His unmarried sister Lucy was institutionalized in Bloomingdale's Insane Asylum. [Patricia Beard, *After the Ball: Gilded Age Secrets, Boardroom Betrayals, and the Party That Ignited the Great Wall Street Scandal of 1905* (New York: Harper Collins Publishers, 2003), p. 31.]

Henry Baldwin and Annie Fitch Hyde, Sr.'s daughter Mary married Sidney Dillon Ripley, Sr. and resided at *The Crossroads* in Uniondale. She subsequently married Charles R. Scott, with whom she continued to reside at *The Crossroads*. Their son Henry and daughter Annie died before attaining adulthood. Their son James Hazen Hyde, who inherited *The Oaks*, married Marthe Leishman, Helen Walker, and, subsequently, Marthe Dervaux.

[See entries for Henry Baldwin Hyde II and James Hazen Hyde for additional family information.]

In c. 1900, James Hazen Hyde remodeled the house, eliminating some of its High Victorian elements. He also added a bachelor's annex and squash court.

In 1901, Louis Bossert purchased the four-hundred-acre estate and most of its furniture from James Hazen Hyde.

*Weidenman's landscape design was awarded special honor at the 1876 Centennial Exhibition in Philadelphia, PA.

**The house, which has been extensively modified, is now the clubhouse of the Southward Ho Country Club.

The Oaks, c. 1923

Hyde, James Hazen (1876-1959)

Occupation(s):	writer - "Impressions of the Front, the Valiant Army of the Vosges" (articles)
	financier - vice-president, Equitable Life Assurance Society of the U. S.;
	vice-president, National Bank of Commerce
	capitalist - vice-president, Coney Island & Brooklyn Railroad Co.
Civic Activism:	director, Alliance Francaise;
	trustee, *Academie de Sciences Morales et Politiques*;
	trustee, Metropolitan Opera Co., NYC;
	chairman of board, French Institute of Washington Aid, American Red Cross in Paris, France, during World War I;
	member, American Committee on Public Information in France during WWI
Marriage(s):	M/1 – 1913-1918 – Marthe Leishman (d. 1944)
	M/2 – 1930-1931 – Helen Ella Walker (1875-1959)
	- Civic Activism: donated her villa in Italy and $2 million to the Rockefeller Foundation
	M/3 – Marthe Dervaux (d. 1948)
	- Civic Activism: established a school for Catholic scouts on the grounds of her estate near Paris, France
Address:	South Country Road, West Bay Shore
Name of estate:	*The Oaks*
Year of construction:	1874-1876
Style of architecture:	Stick-style
Architect(s):	Calvert Vaux designed the house (for H. B. Hyde, Sr.)
Landscape architect(s):	Olmstead, with Jacob Weidenman (for H. B. Hyde, Sr.)*
House extant: yes**	
Historical notes:	

The forty-room house, originally named *Marquetux* and later renamed *The Oaks*, was built by Henry Baldwin Hyde, Sr. It was inherited by his son James Hazen Hyde, who continued to call it *The Oaks*.

Marthe Leishman Hyde was the daughter of John G. A. Leishman, who foiled the plot to kill Henry Clay Frick and later became president of Carnegie Steel. Marthe had previously been married to Count Louis de Gontaut–Biron of France, who died of syphilis. As a condition to their marriage, Hyde insisted that she had to be examined by a doctor. Her sister Nancy married Duke de Croy of Germany. Marthe's intense and vocal pro-German position during World War I was one of the primary causes of the Hydes' divorce. [Patricia Beard, *After the Ball: Gilded Age Secrets, Boardroom Betrayals, and the Party That Ignited the Great Wall Street Scandal of 1905* (New York: Harper Collins Publishers, 2003), pp. 314-15.] James Hazen and Marthe Leishman Hyde's son Henry Baldwin Hyde II, who married Marie de LaGrange and, subsequently, Elizabeth Prokoff Piper, resided on Fire Island.

Helen Ella Walker was the daughter of Franklin H. Walker of Detroit, MI. Her grandfather owned Hiram Walker Distilling Co., of Canada [Canadian Club whiskey]. Helen had previously been married to Manfred Matuschka, the Baron of von Toppolczan and Apaaetgen, who was an officer in Kaiser Wilhelm's Bodyguard Regiment. She later married Prince Alexander von Thur and Taxis, the First Prince Della Torre E. Tasso of Italy. During World War II, *Serbelloni*, her Italian villa, was requisitioned by the German army.

Marthe Dervaux Hyde had previously been married to _____ Thom.

[See previous Hyde entries for additional family information.]

The Long Island Museum of American Art, History and Carriages in Stony Brook has James Hazen Hyde's coach on display.

Edwin Hawley of Babylon purchased James Hazen Hyde's private railroad car *Bay Shore*.

In c. 1900, James Hazen Hyde remodeled the house, eliminating some of its High Victorian elements. He also added a bachelor's annex and squash court.

In 1901, Louis Bossert purchased the 400-acre estate and most of its furniture from James Hazen Hyde.

*Weidenman's landscape design was awarded special honor at the 1876 Centennial Exhibition in Philadelphia, PA.

**The house, extensively modified, is now the clubhouse of the Southward Ho Country Club.

Hyde, James R. (1885-1950)

Occupation(s):   capitalist -   director and manager, Madison Square Garden Co.

Marriage(s):

Address: South Country Road, Bay Shore
Name of estate:
Year of construction: 1895
Style of architecture: Shingle
Architect(s):   Clarence K. Birdsall designed
                      the golf course's clubhouse,
                      1899 (for Richard Hyde)*

Landscape architect(s):
House extant: no
Historical notes:

    The house was built by Richard Hyde.
    It was subsequently owned by his son James R. Hyde.
    The *Long Island Society Register, 1929* lists James R. Hyde as residing on South Country Road in Bay
Shore.
    [See following Hyde entries for family information.]
    *The clubhouse for the estate's nine-hole golf course survives as a private residence.

Hyde, Richard (1856-1912)

Occupation(s):   capitalist -   partner, with Louis C. Behman, Sr., Hyde and Behman
                                 Amusement Co., which owned and operated
                                 Volks Garden, Brooklyn; Park Bijou, Brooklyn;
                                 Amphion Theatre, Brooklyn; Folly Theatre,
                                 Brooklyn; Grand Opera House, Brooklyn; Gaiety
                                 Theatre, Brooklyn; and Newark Theatre, Newark, NJ

Marriage(s):
Address: South Country Road, Bay Shore
Name of estate:
Year of construction: 1895
Style of architecture: Shingle
Architect(s):   Clarence K. Birdsall designed
                      the golf course's clubhouse,
                      1899 (for Richard Hyde)*

Landscape architect(s):
House extant: no
Historical notes:

front facade, c. 1903

    The house was built by Richard Hyde.
    His daughter Lillian married Quentin Field Feitner, the son of Thomas L. and Mary C. Moore Feitner of
Manhattan, and, subsequently, George Barnard Wagstaff, with whom she resided in Bay Shore. His daughter
Lulu married V. B. Hubbell, Sr. and, subsequently, Howard Drummond, with whom she resided at *Little
House* in Bay Shore. Both Lillian and Lulu died when their car was struck by a Long Island Railroad train at
a Brentwood crossing. Hyde's son William married Grace M. Riopel and resided at *White Cottage* in Bay
Shore. His son James R. Hyde inherited the house.
    *The clubhouse for the estate's nine-hole golf course survives as a private residence.

Hyde, William J.

Occupation(s):   capitalist -   president, Hyde and Behman Amusement Co., which owned
                                         and operated Volks Garden, Brooklyn; Park Bijou,
                                         Brooklyn; Amphion Theatre, Brooklyn; Folly Theatre,
                                         Brooklyn; Grand Opera House, Brooklyn; Gaiety
                                         Theatre, Brooklyn; and Newark Theatre, Newark, NJ

Marriage(s):   1916-div. 1930 – Grace M. Riopel
                            - entertainers and related professions -   motion picture actress, star
                                                              of Vitagraph Pictures

Address: South Country Road, Bay Shore

Name of estate: *White Cottage*
Year of construction:
Style of architecture:
Architect(s):
Landscape architect(s):
House extant: unconfirmed
Historical notes:

     William J. Hyde was the son of Richard Hyde of Bay Shore.
     Grace M. Riopel had previously been married to James M. Blakeley, an English comedian, who was killed in 1915 during a German zeppelin attack on England.
     [See Richard Hyde entry for additional family information.]

Ireland, John Busteed (b. 1823)

Occupation(s):   attorney
                            capitalist -   building contractor*;
                                         owned Manhattan real estate
                            writer - *Wall Street to Cashmere*

Marriage(s):   1863 – Adelia Duane Pell (1837-1915)

Address: South Country Road, West Islip
Name of estate:
Year of construction:
Style of architecture:
Architect(s):
Landscape architect(s):
House extant: unconfirmed
Historical notes:

     John Busteed Ireland was the son of John L. and Mary Floyd Ireland.
     Adelia Duane Pell Ireland was the daughter of Robert Livingston Pell.
     John Busteed and Adelia Duane Pell Ireland's son John married Elizabeth Gallatin, the daughter of James Gallatin of Manhattan. Their daughter Adelia married Dr. Montgomery Hunt Sicard, the son of Rear Admiral Montgomery Sicard. Their son Robert married Kate B. Hanna and resided at *Pebble Hill Plantation* in Thomasville, GA. Their daughter Maria married The Reverend Easter Earl Maderia, the rector of Christ Church, Waterloo, IA.
     *In 1895, Ireland was censured by a Grand Jury for delinquency in the collapse of the Ireland Building at Third Street and West Broadway in Manhattan. Fifteen construction workers were killed in the accident. [*The New York Times* August 22, 1895, p. 12; August 28, 1895, p. 14; August 30, 1895, p. 9; and October 5, 1895, p. 9.]

Ireland, Rufus J., Sr. (1875-1936)

Occupation(s):   industrialist -   director, Gebo Coal Co.*;
                                                                president, Owl Creek Coal Co.
                               capitalist -   president, Brunswick Home, Amityville;
                                                 director, Westport Sanitarium, Westport, CT
                               financier -   director, Amityville Bond & Mortgage Co.

Marriage(s):   Grace E. Myton

Address: 39 Ocean Avenue, Amityville
Name of estate:
Year of construction: 1897
Style of architecture: Victorian
Architect(s):
Landscape architect(s):
House extant: yes
Historical notes:

front facade, 2005

    The *Long Island Society Register, 1929* lists Rufus J. and Grace E. Myton Ireland [Sr.] as residing at 39 Ocean Avenue, Amityville.
    Their son Rufus J. Ireland, Jr. married Elizabeth Terrell, the daughter of Eugene Terrell of Manhattan.
    *In 1909, Ireland was charged with allegedly conspiring to defraud the federal government out of thousands of acres of coal lands in Wyoming. [*The New York Times* May 22, 1903, p. 16.]

Isbrandtsen, Hans J. (1893-1953)

Occupation(s):   capitalist -   president, Western Operating Co. (largest American-owned
                                                   whaling company);
                                              president, Pan-American Wharfage Co.
                               shipping* -   president, Isbrandtsen–Moller Co., Inc. (shipping line to Gulf,
                                               Pacific Coast, and Far Eastern Ports);
                                             president, Isbrandtsen Co., Inc. (steamship freighter firm)

Marriage(s):   Gertrude Mirus (1898-1959)
               - Civic Activism: president, Long Island College Hospital Guild;
                                          regent, Long Island College Hospital

Address: South Country Road, West Bay Shore
Name of estate:
Year of construction:
Style of architecture:
Architect(s):
Landscape architect(s):
House extant: unconfirmed
Historical notes:

    Hans J. and Gertrude Mirus Isbrandtsen's son Walter married Evelyn Elizabeth Kelley, the daughter of The Reverend Harold H. Kelley of Manhattan and resided in Fair Haven, CT. Their daughter Niel married Albert E. Rising, Jr. of Kew Gardens, NY, and resided in Glen Cove. Their son Jacob married Patricia Cotten of Brooklyn and resided in Riverside, CT.
    *Known as the "lone wolf," Isbrandtsen, who was one of the largest independent ship owners in the country, staunchly believed in the freedom of the seas. He refused to participate in conferences that regulated shipping rates and imposed cargo rules. Rejecting government subsidies, Isbrandtsen was famous for undercutting the rates of his competitors. In 1950, several of his ships were damaged by gun fire while "running" the Nationalist Chinese blockage of Communist China. [*The New York Times* May 14, 1953, pp.6 and 29.]

Johnson, Aymar (1884-1942)

Occupation(s):   financier -   partner, Johnson and Wood (stock brokerage firm)
                                       intelligence agent -   Naval Intelligence during World War II
Civic Activism: trustee, Cathedral of St. John the Divine, NYC;
                                       chairman, Suffolk County Work Relief Committee during 1930s

Marriage(s):   1924-1942 – Marion K. Hoffman

Address: Suffolk Lane, East Islip
Name of estate: *Woodland*
Year of construction: 1909
Style of architecture: Modified Neo-Federal
Architect(s):   Isaac Henry Green II designed
                                the second 1909 house
                                (for Bradish Johnson, Jr.)
Landscape architect(s): Olmsted, 1915
                                (for Bradish Johnson, Jr.)
House extant: first house on the site was destroyed by fire, 1905;
                      second (1909) house and gatehouse on site are extant
Historical notes:

   The first house on the site was built by James Boorman Johnston.
   In 1880, it was purchased from Johnston by Charles T. Harbeck.
   In 1882, Bradish Johnson, Jr. purchased the house from Harbeck and called it *Woodland*. After it was destroyed by fire, Johnson built a second house on the site, which he also called *Woodland*.
   The estate was subsequently inherited by his son Aymar Johnson, who continued to call it *Woodland*.
   Marion K. Hoffman Johnson was the daughter of Charles Frederick Hoffman of Manhattan, Newport, RI, and *Blicking Hall* in Norfolk, England.
   Aymar and Marion K. Hoffman Johnson's daughter Moira married Eugene Minton Moore, the son of William Minton Moore.
   [See following Johnson entries for additional family information.]
   In 1946, Mrs. Aymar Johnson sold the estate to the Hewlett School of East Islip.
   In 2006, the school sold the estate to a developer. The main residence and gatehouse are extant as private residences but the estate property was subdivided for a housing development.

side / rear facade, 2005

Johnson, Bradish, Jr. (1853-1918)

Occupation(s):   capitalist -   Bradish Johnson & Co. (Louisiana real estate holding company)
industrialist -   director, American Cotton Oil Co.
financier -   director, Commonwealth Insurance Co.;
director, Equitable Trust Co.;
director, Equitable Life Assurance Society of the United States;
director, Greenwich Savings Bank;
president, State Investing Co.;
director, Lincoln Trust Co.

Marriage(s):   1877-1918 – Amiee Gaillard (d. 1929)

Address: Suffolk Lane, East Islip
Name of estate: *Woodland*
Year of construction: 1909
Style of architecture: Modified Neo-Federal
Architect(s):   Isaac Henry Green II designed the second 1909 house (for Bradish Johnson, Jr.)
Landscape architect(s):   Olmsted, 1915 (for Bradish Johnson, Jr.)
House extant: first house on the site was destroyed by fire, 1905; second (1909) house and gatehouse on site are extant
Historical notes:

The first house on the site was built by James Boorman Johnston.

In 1880, it was purchased from Johnston by Charles T. Harbeck.

In 1882, Bradish Johnson, Jr. purchased the house from Harbeck and called it *Woodland*. After it was destroyed by fire, Johnson built a second house on the site, which he also called *Woodland*.

He was the son of Bradish and Louise Anna Lawrance Johnson, Sr., who resided at *Sans Souci* in West Bay Shore.

Bradish and Amiee Gaillard Johnson, Jr.'s son Bradish Gaillard Johnson, Sr. married Emma M. Grima and resided in Islip. Their son Enfin also resided in Islip. Their daughter Marie married William Hamilton Russell, Jr. and resided in Islip. She subsequently married Gordon Crother. Their son Aymar, who married Marion K. Hoffman, inherited *Woodland*.

[See other Johnson entries for additional family information.]

In 1946, Mrs. Aymar Johnson sold the estate to the Hewlett School of East Islip.

In 2006, the school sold the estate to a developer. The main residence and gatehouse are extant as private residences but the estate property was subdivided for a housing development.

Woodland, gate house, 2005

Johnson, Bradish, Sr. (1811-1892)

Occupation(s):	attorney
	industrialist - partner, with his father William M. Johnson,
	William M. Johnson & Sons (later, Johnson
	and Lazarus) (distillery and sugar refinery);
	partner, Johnson and Lazarus (distillery and sugar refinery)
	capitalist - president, Bradish Johnson & Co. (Louisiana real estate
	holding company)*
	financier - director, Chemical National Bank
Marriage(s):	1836-1870 – Louisa Anna Lawrance (1817-1870)
Address:	South Country Road, West Bay Shore
Name of estate:	*Sans Souci*
Year of construction:	c. 1860
Style of architecture:	High Victorian Gothic
Architect(s):	
Landscape architect(s):	
House extant:	no
Historical notes:	

The house, originally named *Sans Souci*, was built by Bradish Johnson, Sr.

He was the son of William M. and Sarah Rich Johnson. William M. Johnson was a native of Nova Scotia, Canada, who relocated to Manhattan and made his fortune in the distilling industry and in real estate. The senior Johnson had extensive real estate holdings in New York City and in the New Orleans area of Louisiana. The latter included *Woodland Plantation*, where Bradish Johnson, Sr. was born. Bradish Johnson, Sr.'s brother John Dean Johnson married Helen Maria Wederstrandt and resided in Islip. His brother Edwin Augustus Johnson, Sr. married Ellen Woodruff and resided in East Islip and, later at *Deer Range Farm*, also in East Islip.

Louisa Anna Lawrance Johnson was the daughter of Thomas and Margaret Ireland Lawrance. Her sister Cornelia married George G. Wilmerding and resided in West Bay Shore. Her brother William married Mary Helen Crandell.

Bradish and Louisa Anna Lawrance Johnson, Sr.'s daughter Lucy married Dr. Alfred Ludlow Carroll and resided in Bay Shore. Their daughter Helena married Schuyler Livingston Parsons, Sr. and resided at *Whileaway* in Islip. Their son Effingham married Amy Rowan Scott and resided in Bay Shore. Their daughter Louisa married Robert Cooper Townsend. Their son Bradish Johnson, Jr. married Amiee Gaillard and resided at *Woodland* in East Islip. Their daughter Louise married Stephen Whitney. Their son Henry Meyer Johnson, who married Grace Baldwin, inherited *Sans Souci*.

[See other Johnson entries for additional family information.]

*According to the 1860 Federal Census, Bradish Johnson owned 214 slaves and 2,800 acres of land in Plaquemines Parish, LA. [Joseph Karl Menn, *The Large Slaveholders of Louisiana – 1860* (New Orleans: Pelican Publishing Co., 1964), pp. 310-311.] Both of Johnson's Louisiana plantations still exist. *Woodland* was restored in 1998 and is open to the public as a nine-room country inn. *Whitney Plantation* is privately owned and not open to the public. Johnson's New Orleans house at 2343 Prytania Street, in the Garden District of the city, became a college preparatory school for girls in 1912 and is still operated as Louise S. McGehee School. His Manhattan house, located at the corner of Fifth Avenue and Twenty-first Street, was purchased by the Lotos Club.

Prior to President Lincoln's proclamation to free slaves, Johnson offered to free his Louisiana slaves and pay for their return to Africa. The slaves refused, preferring to remain as his freed employees. During the Union Army's attack on New Orleans, Johnson raised the American flag on his *Woodland Plantation*. [*The New York Times* April 27, 1933, p. 17.]

front facade, c. 1903

Johnson, Bradish Gaillard, Sr. (1851-1944)

Occupation(s):   capitalist -   secretary and treasurer, Bradish Johnson & Co.
                                       (Louisiana real estate holding company)

Marriage(s):   1911-1944 – Emma M. Grima
                 - Civic Activism: member of board, Coordinating Council for
                                     French Relief Societies

Address: St. Mark's Lane, Islip
Name of estate:
Year of construction:
Style of architecture:
Architect(s):
Landscape architect(s):
House extant: unconfirmed
Historical notes:

The *Long Island Society Register, 1929* lists Bradish G. and Emma M. Grima Johnson [Sr.] as residing in Islip.

He was the son of Bradish and Amiee Gaillard Johnson, Jr., who resided at *Woodland* in East Islip.

Bradish Gaillard and Emma M. Grima Johnson, Sr.'s son Alfred Grima Johnson married Francine Buffet, the daughter of Andre and Simone Querenet Buffet of France.

In 1937, their twenty-three-year-old son Bradish Gaillard Johnson, Jr., a war correspondent for *Spur* magazine, was killed covering the Spanish Civil War. [*The New York Times* January 1, 1938, p. 4.]

[See other Johnson entries for additional family information.]

Johnson, Edwin Augustus, Sr.

Occupation(s):   capitalist -   real estate developer in Town of Islip

Marriage(s):   Ellen A. Woodruff (d. 1872)

Address: Suffolk Lane, East Islip
Name of estate:
Year of construction: c. 1840's
Style of architecture:
Architect(s):
Landscape architect(s):
House extant: unconfirmed
Historical notes:

The house was built by Edwin Augustus Johnson, Sr. The Johnsons resided here from 1846 to 1851 prior to building *Deer Range Farm* which was also located in East Islip.

He was the son of William M. and Sarah Rich Johnson.

Edwin Augustus and Ellen A. Woodruff Johnson, Sr.'s son Lee married Fanny Nicoll and resided in East Islip and Garden City. Their daughter Helen married Charles Fiske Bound and resided in Manhattan. Their son Edwin Augustus Johnson, Jr. remained a bachelor.

[See other Johnson entries for additional family information.]

Johnson, Edwin Augustus, Sr.

Occupation(s):   capitalist - real estate developer in Town of Islip

Marriage(s):   Ellen A. Woodruff (d. 1872)

Address: Heckscher Parkway, East Islip
Name of estate: *Deer Range Farm*
Year of construction: c. 1850s
Style of architecture: Eclectic
Architect(s):
Landscape architect(s):
House extant: no*
Historical notes:

   The house, originally named *Deer Range Farm*, was built by Edwin Augustus Johnson, Sr.
He was the son of William M. and Sarah Rich Johnson.
   Edwin Augustus and Ellen Woodruff Johnson, Sr.'s son Lee married Fanny Nicoll and resided in East Islip
and Garden City. Their daughter Helen married Charles Fiske Bound and resided in Manhattan. Their son
Edwin Augustus Johnson, Jr. remained a bachelor.
   [See other Johnson entries for additional family information.]
   In 1872, the estate was purchased by Sarah Ives Plumb. Upon her death, it was inherited by her husband
James Neale Plumb and, subsequently, by their son James Ives Plumb. The Plumbs continued to call it *Deer
Range Farm*.
   In 1884, alterations were made to the house by James Neale Plumb.
   In 1903, James Ives Plumb sold the estate to George Campbell Taylor and relocated to Islip.
   The estate remained in the Taylor / Pyne family corporation until 1924 when it was confiscated by Robert
Moses and became part of Heckscher State Park. [Harry W. Havemeyer, *Along the Great South Bay From Oakdale to
Babylon: The Story of a Summer Spa 1840 to 1940* (Mattituck, NY: Amereon House, 1996), p. 135.]
   *The house was demolished by Moses' Long Island State Park Commission. Portions of the house were
salvaged, moved, and relocated into buildings in the Islip area.

Johnson, Effingham Lawrance (d.1897)

Occupation(s):

Marriage(s):   1890-1897 – Amy Rowan Scott (1865-1953)

Address: South Country Road and Penataquit Avenue, Bay Shore
Name of estate:
Year of construction:
Style of architecture:
Architect(s):
Landscape architect(s):
House extant: unconfirmed
Historical notes:

   Effingham Lawrance Johnson was the son of Bradish and Louisa Anna Lawrance Johnson, Sr., who
resided at *Sans Souci* in West Bay Shore.
   Johnson's fortune, at the time of his death, was valued at $10 million. [*The New York Times* April 14, 1897, p. 1.]
   Amy Rowan Scott Johnson was the daughter of James Rowan Scott. She subsequently married General
William Graves Bates, with whom she resided in Bay Shore.
   Effingham Lawrance and Amy Rowan Scott Johnson's daughter Amy married Herbert Groesbeck, Jr. and
resided in Manhattan.
   [See other Johnson entries for additional family information.]

Johnson, Enfin

Occupation(s):

Marriage(s):

Address: St. Mark's Lane, Islip
Name of estate:
Year of construction:
Style of architecture:
Architect(s):
Landscape architect(s):
House extant: unconfirmed
Historical notes:

    Enfin Johnson was the son of Bradish and Amiee Gaillard Johnson, Jr., who resided at *Woodland* in East Islip.
    [See other Johnson entries for additional family information.]
    The house was purchased by Joseph Lovering.

Johnson, Henry Meyer (1865-1907)

Occupation(s):

Marriage(s):   M/1 – 1890 – Sarah K. Baldwin (d. 1902)
                                  M/2 – 1902-1907 – Grace Baldwin (d. 1930)

Address: South Country Road, West Bay Shore
Name of estate: *Sans Souci*
Year of construction: c. 1860
Style of architecture: High Victorian Gothic
Architect(s):
Landscape architect(s):
House extant: unconfirmed
Historical notes:

    The house, originally named *Sans Souci*, was built by Bradish Johnson, Sr.
    It was inherited by his son Henry Meyer Johnson, who continued to call it *Sans Souci*.
    Both Sarah and Grace Baldwin Johnson were the daughters of Harvey Baldwin, the first mayor of Syracuse, NY. Their brother Townsend Burnet Baldwin married _____ Dillon and resided at *Gable Hall* in Edgewater, NJ.
    Sarah Baldwin Johnson had previously been married to Cornelius W. Olliffee.
    Grace Baldwin Johnson had previously been married to James F. Ruggles. James F. and Grace Baldwin Ruggles' daughter Grace married George Lane of Troy, NY. Their son Burnet R. Ruggles married Natalie E. Smith and resided at *Ox Ridge Farm* in Darien, CT.

Johnson, John Dean (1815-1861)

Occupation(s):   capitalist -   owned Louisiana sugar plantation

Marriage(s):   Helen Maria Wederstrandt (d. 1888)

Address: St. Mark's Lane, Islip
Name of estate:
Year of construction: c. 1840s
Style of architecture:
Architect(s):
Landscape architect(s):
House extant: unconfirmed
Historical notes:

Wanderer

    The house was built by John Dean Johnson.
    He was the son of William M. and Sarah Rich Johnson.
    John Dean Johnson's yacht *Wanderer* was built in 1857 by Joseph Rowland of Setauket. After Johnson sold the yacht, it was used as a slave trade ship. It eventually ran aground on the eastern tip of Cuba.
    [See other Johnson entries for additional family information.]
    In 1886, the house was purchased by Henry Hutchinson Hollister, Sr., who remodeled and expanded it.

Johnson, Lee (1845-1895)

Occupation(s):   capitalist -   subdivided property in the Town of Islip for development; built and rented houses in the Town of Islip

Marriage(s):   Fanny Nicoll

Address: Suffolk Lane, East Islip
Name of estate:
Year of construction:
Style of architecture: Shingle
Architect(s):
Landscape architect(s):
House extant: no; demolished in 1952*
Historical notes:

front facade

    He was the son of Edwin Augustus and Ellen A. Woodruff Johnson, Sr., who resided in East Islip and, later, at *Deer Range Farm*, also in East Islip.
    [See other Johnson entries for additional family information.]
    In 1885, Johnson sold the house to Henry Rieman Duval and relocated to Garden City. Duval called it *Farmouth*.
    *The house was severely damaged by fire during World War II.

Johnson, Parmenus

Occupation(s):   capitalist -   extensive real estate and rental holdings in Brooklyn; director, New York Brooklyn Ferry Co.

Marriage(s):   c. 1815 – _____ Joralemon

Address: St. Mark's Lane, Islip
Name of estate:
Year of construction:
Style of architecture:
Architect(s):
Landscape architect(s):
House extant: unconfirmed
Historical notes:

The house was built by Parmenus Johnson.
In 1880, it was purchased by E. B. Spaulding, who expanded and modernized the house.
In 1886, it was purchased by Robert Cambridge Livingston III and was, subsequently, owned by his daughter Maude and son-in-law Henry Worthington Bull.

Johnston, James Boorman (1823-1887)

Occupation(s):   capitalist -   director, Metropolitan Railroad, NYC

Marriage(s):

Address: Suffolk Lane, East Islip
Name of estate:
Year of construction:
Style of architecture:
Architect(s):   Isaac Henry Green II designed the 1909 house (for Bradish Johnson, Jr.)
Landscape architect(s):   Olmsted, 1915 (for Bradish Johnson Jr.)
House extant: first house on the site was destroyed by fire in 1905; second (1909) house and gatehouse on the site are extant
Historical notes:

The first house on the site was built by James Boorman Johnston.
In 1880, it was purchased from Johnston by Charles T. Harbeck.
In 1882, Bradish Johnson, Jr. purchased the house from Harbeck and called it *Woodland*. After it was destroyed by fire, Johnson built a second house on the site, which he also called *Woodland*.
The estate was subsequently inherited by his son Aymar Johnson, who continued to call it *Woodland*.
In 1946, Mrs. Aymar Johnson sold the estate to the Hewlett School of East Islip.
In 2006, the school sold the estate to a developer. The main residence and gatehouse are extant as private residences but the estate property was subdivided for a housing development.

Jones, Frank Smith (1847-1927)

Occupation(s):	merchant - a founder and president, Jones Brothers Tea Co., Scranton, PA;
	president, Grand Union Tea Co. (Grand Union Supermarkets)
Civic Activism:	trustee, Wesleyan University, Middletown, CT;
	trustee, Brooklyn Institute of Arts and Sciences
Marriage(s):	1879-1927 – Mary Louise Granbery (d. 1927)
Address:	Handsome Avenue, Sayville
Name of estate:	*Beechwold*
Year of construction:	1903
Style of architecture:	Shingle
Architect(s):	Isaac Henry Green II designed the main residence, gatehouse, and 1905 playhouse. The latter included a bowling alley and billiard room (for F. S. Jones)

Landscape architect(s):
House extant: no; destroyed by fire in 1957*
Historical notes:

The house, originally named *Beechwold*, was built by Frank Smith Jones.

He was the son of Isaac Smith and Frances Weed Jones of Stanford, CT.

Mary Louise Granbery Jones was the daughter of Henry A. T. and Prudence Nimmo Granberry of Norfolk, VA. Her sister Mabel married Roland Whitney Betts and resided at *Sunneholm* in Sayville. Mabel subsequently married Charles Edward Spratt.

Frank Smith and Mary Louise Granbery Jones' daughter Henrietta married William Robinson Simonds and resided at *Wyndemoor* in Sayville. Their daughter Maude, who married Clarence Frederick Westin, Sr. and, subsequently, David J. Shea, inherited *Beechwold*. The Sheas resided in the estate's gatehouse.

In 1945, the house was purchased by Elwell Palmer, who sold it to Dr. Daniel McLaughlin in 1949.

*The gatehouse and playhouse are extant. The gatehouse is located at 254 Handsome Avenue and the playhouse is at 96 Benson Avenue.

Beechwold

Kalbfleisch, Franklin H.

Occupation(s):   industrialist -   president and treasurer, Franklin H. Kalbfleisch Co.
                                                 (chemical manufacturer with plants in Erie, PA,
                                                 Waterbury, CT, Elizabeth, NJ, and Brooklyn, NY)

Marriage(s):   Sarah Perine Schenck (d. 1921)

Address: 24 Crescent Avenue, Babylon
Name of estate: *Larklawn*
Year of construction: c. 1881
Style of architecture: Modified Dutch Colonial
Architect(s):
Landscape architect(s):
House extant: yes
Historical notes:

The house was built by Franklin H. Kalbfleisch.
The *Long Island Society Register, 1929* lists Mr. Franklin H. Kalbfleisch as residing at *Larklawn*,
24 Crescent Avenue, Babylon.
He was the son of Brooklyn mayor and congressman Martin Kalbfleisch.
Franklin H. and Sarah Perine Schenck Kalbfleisch's daughter Augusta, who resided at *Blyenbeck* in
Huntington, remained unmarried.

side / front facade, 2006

Keith, Minor C. (1848-1929)

Occupation(s):   engineer
          capitalist - president and chairman of board, International Railways of Central
                   America;
                president, Guatemala and Salvador Railway;
                president, St. Andrew's Bay Lumber Co.;
                extensive property holdings in several states and foreign countries
          industrialist - a founder, with Andrew W. Preston, and vice-president, United
                   Fruit Co.;
                president, Polochic Banana Co.;
                president, Abangarez Gold Fields, Costa Rica;
                vice-president, Premier Gold Mining Co., British Columbia,
                   Canada;
                director, International Food Products Corp.;
                director, General Lead Batteries Co.
          financier - director, Empire Trust Co.

Civic Activism: bequeathed his gold coin collection to the American Museum of Natural History,
          NYC

Marriage(s):   1883-1929 – Cristina Castro (1862-1944)

Address: South Country Road, West Islip
Name of estate:
Year of construction:
Style of architecture:
Architect(s):
Landscape architect(s):
House extant: unconfirmed
Historical notes:

  Minor C. Keith was the son of Minor Hubbell and Emily Meiggs Keith of Brooklyn.
  Cristina Castro Keith was the daughter of Jose Maria Castro, the President of the Republic of Costa Rica.
  After selling the house to William P. Clyde, the Keiths relocated to Babylon. [Harry W. Havemeyer, *Along the Great South Bay From Oakdale to Babylon: The Story of a Summer Spa 1840 to 1940* (Mattituck, NY: Amereon House, 1996), p. 179 and *The New York Times* March 16, 1944, p. 19.]

Keith, Minor C. R., II

Occupation(s):

Marriage(s):   Clara Turnbull (d. 1939)

Address: South Country Road, West Islip
Name of estate:
Year of construction:
Style of architecture:
Architect(s):
Landscape architect(s):
House extant: unconfirmed
Historical notes:

  Minor C. R. Keith II was the grand-nephew of Minor C. Keith.
  Clara Turnbull Keith was the daughter of George R. and Clara Jenkins Turnbull, who resided at *The Pines* in West Islip. Clara bequeathed $50,000 for the care of her dogs and only $20,000 to her husband Minor. [*The New York Times* July 29, 1939, p. 20.]

Kelly, James P.

Occupation(s):   financier -   vice-president, West End Bank of Brooklyn
                                capitalist -   president, Kingsway Realty Corp.

Marriage(s):   Cecelia Rafter (d. 1937)

Address: 117 Awixa Avenue, Bay Shore
Name of estate: *Awixaway*
Year of construction:
Style of architecture: Shingle
Architect(s):
Landscape architect(s):
House extant: unconfirmed
Historical notes:

    The house was built by Rudolph Oelsner, who by 1906 had relocated to Long Island's North Shore.
It was later owned by George W. Hodges, Sr., who sold it to Kelly in 1923. Kelly called the house
Awixaway.

Kempster, James H.

Occupation(s):   publisher -   president, James H. Kempster Printing Co.

Marriage(s):

Address: Saxon Avenue, Bay Shore
Name of estate: *Westbeach*
Year of construction:
Style of architecture: Second Empire
Architect(s):
Landscape architect(s):
House extant: no
Historical notes:

front / side facade, c. 1903

King, Dr. George Suttie (1878-1966)

Occupation(s):

physician
capitalist -   founder, Dr. King's Hospital, 11 Maple Avenue,
                   Bay Shore, 1918
writer - *Doctor on a Bicycle*, 1958 (autobiography);
                   *The Last Slaver**

Civic Activism: **

Marriage(s):   M/1 – Elizabeth Marie Graham (d. 1941)
                             M/2 – Ruth Kahler

Address: 32 Maple Avenue, Bay Shore
Name of estate:
Year of construction:
Style of architecture: Victorian
Architect(s):
Landscape architect(s):
House extant: yes
Historical notes:

   Dr. George Suttie King was the son of Ellen Suttie King of Patchogue. His sister Lotta married ___ Smith and resided in Patchogue. His sister Aida remained unmarried.
   Dr. George Suttie and Mrs. Elizabeth Marie Graham King's daughter Elinor married Cornelius Furgueson III and resided in Brightwaters. Their daughter Virginia married Joseph Salkeld Rider and resided in Brightwaters.
   In 1963, Dr. King's Hospital became the South Bay Manor Rest Home. It was demolished in c. 2005.
   *King's book *The Last Slaver* was adapted into the 1937 motion picture "Slave Ship." The script was written by William Faulkner and the film starred Tay Garnett, Warner Baxter, Wallace Beery, Elizabeth Allan, Mickey Rooney, George Sanders, Jane Darwell, and Joseph Schildkraut.
   **Known for his generosity to the poor, his hospital ledgers had the notation C. T. G., "Charge To God," next to many of his patients' names.
   Bay Shore's Dr. George S. King Park is named in his honor.

side / front facade, 2006

Kingsland, George Lovett, Sr. (1827-1892)

Occupation(s):	capitalist - president, George Creek Railroad
	industrialist - director, George Creek and Cumberland Coal Co.

Marriage(s):   Helen S. Welles (d. 1911)

Address: South Country Road, West Islip
Name of estate:
Year of construction:
Style of architecture:
Architect(s):
Landscape architect(s):
House extant: unconfirmed
Historical notes:

George Lovett Kingsland Sr. was the son of New York City Mayor Ambrose C. Kingsland.
Helen S. Welles Kingsland was the daughter of Benjamin Sumner and Catherine Schermerhorn Welles, Sr. of Islip. Her brother Benjamin Sumner Welles, Jr. married Frances Swan and resided at *Welles House* in Islip. Her sister Harriet remained unmarried.
The Kingslands rented the West Islip house.

Kleinman, David E.

Occupation(s):   attorney

Marriage(s):

Address: South Country Road, Bay Shore
Name of estate:
Year of construction:
Style of architecture:
Architect(s):
Landscape architect(s):
House extant: unconfirmed
Historical notes:

In 1950, Kleinman purchased the house from Howard Drummond.

Knapp, Edward Spring, Sr. (1852-1895)

Occupation(s):	capitalist - manager, Greenport Ferry; president, Thirty-fourth Street Ferry
	financier - president, Queens County Bank

Marriage(s): 1878-1895 – Margaret Ireland Lawrance

Address: 52 Saxon Avenue, Bay Shore
Name of estate: *Awixa Lawn*
Year of construction: 1880
Style of architecture: Colonial Revival
Architect(s): Isaac Henry Green II designed
    the 1889 southwestern wing
    addition of a living room,
    and four bedrooms
    (for E. S. Knapp, Sr.)
Landscape architect(s):
House extant: no
Historical notes:

    The house, originally named *Awixa Lawn*, was built by Edward Spring Knapp, Sr.
He was the son of Gideon Lee and Augusta Murray Spring Knapp.
    Margaret Ireland Lawrance Knapp was the daughter of William R. and Mary Helen Crandell Lawrance.
    Edward Spring and Margaret Ireland Lawrance Knapp, Sr.'s son Edward Spring Knapp, Jr. married Rosalie Moran, the daughter of Amedee Depau Moran of East Islip, and relocated to Long Island's North Shore. Their daughter Margaret married Dr. Lee Hollister Ferguson of New York and Delaware, OH.
    [See other Knapp entries for additional family information.]
    In 1896, after Edward's death, Margaret decided to rent *Awixa Lawn* and build a second house in which to reside. The second house, which is presently located at 52 Saxon Avenue, was subsequently owned by Julius Oppenheimer.
    In 1915, Mrs. Knapp sold *Awixa Lawn* to August Belmont III.
    In 1923, Mrs. Belmont sold the estate, which at that time consisted of a twenty-five-room main residence on nine acres with six hundred feet of shoreline on Awixa Creek, stables, and a five-car garage to John Allen Dillon, Sr.

52 Saxon Avenue, front facade, 2006

Knapp, Harry Kearsarge, II (1890-1943)

Occupation(s):

Marriage(s):   M/1 – 1911-1920 – Phebe Schoonhoven Thorne
                                  M/2 – 1921 – Elizabeth Marshall Mann

Address: Meadow Farm Road, East Islip
Name of estate: *Creekside*
Year of construction: 1929
Style of architecture: Neo-Federal
Architect(s):   William Hamilton Russell, Jr.
                          designed the house
                          (for H. K. Knapp II)
Landscape architect(s):   Charles Wellford Leavitt
                          and Sons (for H. K. Knapp II)
House extant: yes
Historical notes:

The house, originally named *Creekside*, was built by Harry Kearsarge Knapp II.
He was the son of Harry Kearsarge and Caroline Burr Knapp, Sr., who resided at *Brookwood* in East Islip.
Phebe Schoonhoven Thorne Knapp was the daughter of Edwin and Phebe Ketchum Thorne II, who resided at *Okonok* in West Islip. She subsequently married John Tucker. Her brother Landon married Julia Atterbury Loomis and resided at *Thornham* in West Islip. Her brother Francis, who married Evelyn Brown and, subsequently, Hildegarde Kobbe, resided at *Brookwood* in East Islip. Her sister Anna married Robert Titus and resided in West Islip.
Elizabeth Marshall Mann Knapp was the daughter of Francis Norton Mann of Troy, NY. She subsequently married Walter Russell Herrick and resided at *Ivy Cottage* in Watch Hill, RI.
Harry Kearsarge and Elizabeth Marshall Mann Knapp II's daughter Theodosia married Duer McLanahan, Jr. of *Windvale* in Watch Hill, RI.
[See other Knapp entries for additional family information.]
In 1939, the house was purchased by William Hamilton Gregory, Jr., who continued to call it *Creekside*.

rear facade

145

Knapp, Harry Kearsarge, Sr. (1865-1926)

Occupation(s):   capitalist -   general manager, Union Ferry
                                    financier -   director, Corn Exchange Bank;
                                                        director, Queens City Bank;
                                                        director, Kings County Trust Co.

Marriage(s):   Caroline Burr (d. 1928)

Address: South Country Road, East Islip
Name of estate: *Brookwood**
Year of construction: 1902
Style of architecture: Neo-Georgian
Architect(s):
Landscape architect(s):
House extant: yes
Historical notes:

    The house, originally named *Brookwood*, was built by Harry Kearsarge Knapp, Sr.
    He was the son of Gideon Lee and Augusta Murray Spring Knapp, Sr.
    *The *Long Island Society Register, 1929* lists Caroline Burr Knapp as residing at *Brookwood* in East Islip.
Harry Kearsarge and Caroline Burr Knapp, Sr.'s son Harry Kearsarge Knapp II, who married Phebe
Schoonhoven Thorne and, subsequently, Elizabeth Marshall Mann, resided at *Creekside* in East Islip. Their
daughter Caroline married Charles Kintzing Post, the son of Waldron Kintzing and Mary Lawrence Perkins
Post of *Strandhome* in Bayport. Their son Theodore, who inherited *Brookwood*, married Gladys Quarre.
    [See other Knapp entries for additional family information.]
    In 1929, Theodore sold the estate to Francis Burritt Thorne, Sr.
    In 1942, the house was owned by the Orphan Asylum Society of Brooklyn.
    In 1965, the Society sold it to Alfred and Fred Wimmer, who sold the house to the Town of Islip in 1967. It
is currently the site of The Islip Art Museum, a leading exhibit space for contemporary art.
    The Empire State Carousel, now located in Binghamton, NY, was built in the carriage house of
Brookwood. The carriage house is currently the Long Island Center for Experimental Art.

front facade, 2005

entrance hall

sitting room

side facade, 2005

Knapp Lake, c. 1939

carriage house, 2005

Knapp, Shepherd, Sr. (1846-1902)

Occupation(s):   attorney

capitalist -   director, New York and Erie Railroad;
                director, Greenport Ferry Co.

financier -   director, New York Equitable Insurance Co.;
                director, Queens County Bank, Long Island City

Civic Activism: committee member, Riot Fund (for policemen wounded in street riots);
trustee, Washington Monument Association, NYC

Marriage(s):   Catherine Kumble

Address: South Country Road, West Islip
Name of estate:
Year of construction:
Style of architecture:
Architect(s):
Landscape architect(s):
House extant: unconfirmed
Historical notes:

Shepherd Knapp, Sr. was the son of Gideon Lee and Augusta Murray Spring Knapp, Sr.

Shepherd and Catherine Kumble Knapp, Sr.'s son William married Maria Meserole and resided in Islip. Their daughter Elsie married Manhattan attorney Wilson M. Powell, Jr. Their son Shepherd Knapp, Jr. was a clergyman.

[See other Knapp entries for additional family information.]

Knapp, Theodore J., Sr. (1892-1947)

Occupation(s):   financier -   partner, Montgomery, Scott and Co. (stock brokerage firm)

capitalist -   president, Jockey Club (owned and operated Aqueduct Race Track)

Civic Activism: member, board of managers, New York Society for the Ruptured and Crippled

Marriage(s):   1947-1947 – Gladys Quarre

Address: South Country Road, East Islip
Name of estate: *Brookwood*
Year of construction: 1902
Style of architecture: Neo-Georgian
Architect(s):
Landscape architect(s):
House extant: yes
Historical notes:

The house, originally named *Brookwood*, was built by Harry Kearsarge Knapp, Sr.

It was inherited by his son Theodore J. Knapp, Sr. He died of a self-inflicted wound from a twenty-eight-gauge shotgun in his three-room suite at the Southside Sportsman's Club in Oakdale. [*The New York Times* May 8, 1947, p. 52.]

Gladys Quarre Knapp was the daughter of Emil Quarre of San Francisco, CA, and Brussels, Belgium. She had previously been married to Frederick Peabody of Troy, NY.

[See other Knapp entries for additional family information.]

In 1929, Theodore sold the estate to Francis Burritt Thorne, Sr.

In 1942, the house was owned by the Orphan Asylum Society of Brooklyn.

In 1965, the Society sold it to Alfred and Fred Wimmer, who sold the house to the Town of Islip in 1967. It is currently the site of The Islip Art Museum, a leading exhibit space for contemporary art.

The carriage house is currently the Long Island Center for Experimental Art.

Knapp, William K. (1828-1877)

Occupation(s):

Marriage(s):   Maria Meserole (1828-1904)

Address: St. Mark's Lane, Islip
Name of estate:
Year of construction:
Style of architecture:
Architect(s):
Landscape architect(s):
House extant: unconfirmed
Historical notes:

    William K. Knapp was the son of Shepherd and Catherine Kumble Knapp, Sr., who resided in West Bay Shore.
    William K. and Maria Meserole Knapp's daughter Maria remained unmarried. Their daughter Evelina married Harry Bowly Hollins, Sr. and resided at *Meadow Farm* in East Islip.
    [See other Knapp entries for additional family information.]

Kobbe, George Christian (1852-1923)

Occupation(s):   attorney -   partner, Roosevelt and Kobbe
                      industrialist -   a founder and director, Standard Beet Sugar Co.
                      capitalist -   director, Brooklyn Bridge Freezing & Cold Storage Co.;
                                      director, Harrison Street Cold Storage Co.;
                      financier -   director, U. S. Casualty Co.

Marriage(s):   Alice Leavitt

Address: *[unable to determine street address]*, Bayport
Name of estate:
Year of construction:
Style of architecture:
Architect(s):
Landscape architect(s):
House extant: no
Historical notes:

    George Christian Kobbe was the son of the New York Consul General of the Duchy of Nassau, William Augustus Kobbe and Mrs. Sarah Lord Sistare Kobbe.
    Alice Leavitt Kobbe was the daughter of Henry S. Leavitt of New York.
    George Christian and Alice Leavitt Kobbe's daughter Louise married Peter E. Farnum. Their daughter Alice married _____ Rand. Their daughter Martha remained unmarried. Their son Walter married Florence Smith.

Kobbe, Gustave (1857-1918)

Occupation(s):   journalist -   music critic, *New York Herald;* editor, *Musical Review*
                                          writer -   a novel and several reference books about music and the
theater, including *The Complete Opera Book*, 1919

Marriage(s):   1892-1918 – Carolyn Wheeler (d. c. 1953)

Address: South Country Road, Bay Shore
Name of estate:
Year of construction:
Style of architecture:
Architect(s):
Landscape architect(s):
House extant: no
Historical notes:

    Gustave Kobbe was the son of Wilhelm Ludwig and Sarah Lord Sistare Kobbe.
    Gustave was killed while sailing on the Great South Bay when the mast of his boat was struck by an
airplane. [Harry W. Havemeyer, *Along the Great South Bay From Oakdale to Babylon: The Story of a Summer Spa 1840 to 1940*
(Mattituck, NY: Amereon House, 1996), p. 322.]
    Carolyn Wheeler Kobbe was the daughter of George Minor Wheeler of Scarsdale, NY.
    Gustave and Carolyn Wheeler Kobbe's daughter Beatrice married Raymond D. Little, the son of Joseph J.
Little. Their daughter Hildegarde married Joseph H. Stevenson, the son of Richard W. Stevenson of
Cedarhurst, and, later, Francis Burritt Thorne, Sr., with whom she resided at *Brookwood* in East Islip. Their
daughter Carol married Robert Woodward Morgan, Sr., the son of Charles Morgan and resided in East Islip.
Carol subsequently married George Palen Snow of Syosset. Their son George married Marjorie W. Goss.
Their daughter Virginia married Gerald Vanderbilt Hollins, Sr., with whom she resided at *The Hawks* in East
Islip, and, subsequently, Henry Morgan.
    After Gustave's death, his wife Carolyn relocated to Islip.

Koehler, Robert H. (1880-1962)

Occupation(s):   attorney -   member, Strong and Cadwalader;
                                                    general council and director, Fifth Avenue Association;
                                                        attorney for New York Furniture Exchange
                    industrialist -   director, Atlantic Carton Corp.
                    financier -   director, Roselle Park Building & Loan Association
                    capitalist -   president, Fenimore Building Corp.
Civic Activism: director, Nassau County Bar Association

Marriage(s):   M/1 – 1905-1927 – Harriet Bischoff (d. 1927)
                        M/2 – 1929 – Ruth Allen Young

Address: Ocean Avenue, Bayport
Name of estate:
Year of construction:
Style of architecture:
Architect(s):
Landscape architect(s):
House extant: unconfirmed
Historical notes:

    The *Long Island Society Register, 1929* lists Robert H. Koehler as residing in Brooklyn and Bayport.
    He was the son of Henry and Bertha Russell Koehler.
    At the time of death, Robert was residing at 158 Brixton Road, Garden City.

Lawrance, Charles Lanier (1882-1950)

Occupation(s):	industrialist -	a founder, president, and chief engineer, Lawrance Aero Engine Co. (formerly, S. S. Pierce Aeroplane; later, Wright Aeronautical Corp.)
		president, Wright Aeronautical Corp., Paterson, NJ;
		vice-president, Curtiss–Wright Corp.;
		chairman of board, Montreal Aircraft Industries, Ltd.
	capitalist -	president, O–Co–Nee (Bay Shore land development company);
		president, C. L. Lawrance (Bay Shore land development company);
		president, Islip Airport;
		president, Plain Speaker Corp.;
		president, Voice of the Sky Corp.;
		director, Transcontinental Air Transport, Inc.;
		director, Fuel Air Motor Corp.;
		a founder and vice-president, National Air Transport (later, United Aircraft Corp.);
		a founder, president, and chairman of board, Lawrance Engineering & Research Corp., Linden, NJ;
		director, Lawrance Park Properties, Bronxville, NY
	inventor -	Lanier–Lawrance airplane wing design*;
		Wright Whirlwind air-cooled airplane engine**

Civic Activism: treasurer, Emergency Shelter Inc., NYC;
director, Aeronautical Chamber of Commerce of America;
director, Southside Hospital, Bay Shore

Marriage(s):   1910 – Emily Margaret Gordon Dix

Address: South Country Road, Bay Shore
Name of estate: *Manatuck Farm*
Year of construction:
Style of architecture:
Architect(s):
Landscape architect(s):
House extant: unconfirmed
Historical notes:

   Charles Lanier Lawrance was the son of Francis Cooper and Sarah Egleston Lanier Lawrance, Jr. of Bay Shore.
   He inherited the estate from his grandfather Francis Cooper Lawrance, Sr.
   Emily Margaret Gordon Dix Lawrance was the daughter of The Reverend Morgan Dix, the rector of Trinity Parish in Manhattan.
   Charles Lanier and Emily Margaret Gordon Dix Lawrance's daughter Margaret married Drayton Cochran of Centre Island and, subsequently, Winston Frost. The Lawrances' daughter Emily married Joseph Sherman Frelinghuysen, Jr. of NJ. Their son Francis Cooper Lawrance III married Priscilla C. Howe and resided in East Islip.
   In 1925, the Lawrances relocated to East Islip.
   [See other Lawrance entries for additional family information.]
   *Lawrance's airplane wing design was used by Great Britain and Germany during World War I.
   **His air-cooled airplane engine was used by the New York Militia during World War I, by Admiral Richard Byrd on his North Pole and Antarctica expeditions, and by Charles Lindbergh in his solo flight across the Atlantic in the *Spirit of St. Louis*.

151

Lawrance, Charles Lanier (1882-1950)

Occupation(s):   *[See previous entry.]*

Marriage(s):   1910 – Emily Margaret Gordon Dix

Address: Hollins Lane, East Islip
Name of estate:
Year of construction:
Style of architecture:
Architect(s):
Landscape architect(s):
House extant: unconfirmed
Historical notes:

    In 1925, Charles Lanier Lawrance relocated from Bay Shore to a portion of the Harry Bowly Hollins, Sr. estate *Meadow Farm* in East Islip.
    He was the son of Francis Cooper and Sarah Egleston Lanier Lawrance, Jr. of Bay Shore.
    [See other Lawrance entries for additional family information.]

Lawrance, Francis Cooper, Jr. (d. 1904)

Occupation(s):

Marriage(s):   M/1 – Sarah Egleston Lanier (d. 1892)
                            M/2 – 1897-1904 – Susan Willing (d. 1933)

Address: South Country Road, Bay Shore
Name of estate: *Manatuck Farm*
Year of construction:
Year of construction:
Style of architecture:
Architect(s):
Landscape architect(s):
House extant: unconfirmed
Historical notes:

    Francis Cooper Lawrance, Jr. was the son of Francis Cooper and Frances Garner Lawrance, Sr., who also resided at *Manatuck Farm*.
    Sarah Egleston Lanier Lawrance was the daughter of Charles Lanier of New York.
    Francis Cooper Sarah Egleston Lanier Lawrance, Jr.'s son Charles Lanier Lawrance, who married Emily Margaret Gordon Dix, inherited *Manatuck Farm*. In 1925, Charles relocated to East Islip. The Lawrances' daughter Katharine married William Averell Harriman, who resided in Sands Point and Old Westbury. Katharine later married Dr. Eugene Hillhouse Pool, with whom she resided in Lattingtown, and, subsequently, Stanley G. Mortimer, with whom she resided in Manhattan and Westchester, NY.
    Susan Willing Lawrance was the daughter of Edward S. Willing of Philadelphia, PA. Her sister Ava married John Jacob Astor IV.
    Francis Cooper and Alice Willing Lawrance, Jr.'s daughter Frances married Prince Andre Poniatowski of Poland and resided in France.
    [See other Lawrance entries for additional family information.]

Lawrance, Francis Cooper, Sr. (1829-1911)

Occupation(s):   capitalist -   Manhattan real estate

Marriage(s):   Frances Garner (d. 1908)

Address: South Country Road, Bay Shore
Name of estate: *Manatuck Farm*
Year of construction:
Style of architecture:
Architect(s):
Landscape architect(s):
House extant: unconfirmed
Historical notes:

    Frances Garner Lawrance was the daughter of Thomas and Frances M. Thorn Garner, Sr. of Bay Shore. Her brother Thomas Garner, Jr. married Harriet H. Amory and resided in Bay Shore. Her brother William married Macellite Thorne and also resided in Bay Shore. Her sister Annie remained unmarried.
    Francis Cooper and Frances Garner Lawrance, Sr.'s daughter Fanny married George William Henry Veron, the Seventh Baron Veron of *Sudbury Hall* in Derbyshire, Great Britain. She was the first of the South Shore daughters to marry a member of the British nobility. [Harry W. Havemeyer, *Along the Great South Bay From Oakdale to Babylon: The Story of a Summer Spa 1840 to 1940* (Mattituck, NY: Amereon House, 1996), p. 208.] Their son Francis Cooper Lawrance, Jr., who married Sarah Egleston Lanier, and, subsequently, Susan Willing, also resided at *Manatuck Farm*. Their son Thomas died while a student at Yale University.
    [See other Lawrance entries for additional family information.]

Lawrance, John I. (d. 1895)

Occupation(s):

Marriage(s):   Anna Stanton (d. 1909)

Address: South Country Road, West Bay Shore
Name of estate:
Year of construction:
Style of architecture:
Architect(s):
Landscape architect(s):
House extant: unconfirmed
Historical notes:

    Anna Stanton was the daughter of George W. Stanton of Albany, NY.
    John I. and Anna Stanton Lawrance's daughter Sara, who remained unmarried, inherited the house.
    [See other Lawrance entries for additional family information.]

Lawrence, Chester B. (b. 1845)

Occupation(s):   capitalist -   partner, Lawrence & Gerrish (Brooklyn warehouses)
                                 politician -   Brooklyn Fire Commissioner (Schieren administration);
                                             member, executive committee, Brooklyn Young
                                           Republican Club, 1884-1894

Marriage(s):   Kate Covell (1845-1922)

Address: Ocean Avenue, Bay Shore
Name of estate:
Year of construction:
Style of architecture:
Architect(s):
Landscape architect(s):
House extant: unconfirmed
Historical notes:

Lazare, Andrew (1880-1930)

Occupation(s):   capitalist -   founder, Lazare Employment Agency, NYC

Marriage(s):

Address: South Country Road, Islip
Name of estate:
Year of construction:
Style of architecture:
Architect(s):
Landscape architect(s):
House extant: unconfirmed
Historical notes:

    In 1924, Lazare purchased the Joseph Byron Creamer, Sr. house and its twelve surrounding acres from Mrs. Creamer. Lazare later relocated to Woodmere.
    His son married Daphne Sangree, the daughter of Dr. T. Chalmers Sangree of Bayport.

Lemmerman, Fred C. (1894-1947)

Occupation(s):   capitalist -   partner, Gross & Lemmerman, Inc., Queens County, NY
                                            (construction firm)
                            politician -   County Clerk of New York City;
                                            member, Triborough Bridge Authority, 1933
                            financier -   vice-president, Ridgewood Savings Bank

Civic Activism: president, Queens County Chamber of Commerce;
trustee, Wyckoff Heights Hospital, Brooklyn;
member, Queens County War Ration Board during World War II

Marriage(s):   Mabel _____

Address: 32 Awixa Avenue, Bay Shore
Name of estate:
Year of construction: c. 1890
Style of architecture: Shingle
Architect(s):   William H. Wray designed his own house
Landscape architect(s):
House extant: yes
Historical notes:

front facade, c. 1903

The house, originally named *Whileaway*, was built by William H. Wray.
It was later owned by Lemmerman and, subsequently, by William Kemble Clarkson.
In 2003, the house was purchased by Dr. Mark Foehr.

Lester, Joseph Huntington (b. circa 1856)

Occupation(s):   capitalist -   tea importer
                            financier -   *
Civic Activism: director, The Tea Association of New York (tea merchants)

Marriage(s):   Henrietta Frances Maxwell

Address: South Country Road and Awixa Avenue, Bay Shore
Name of estate: *Lestaley*
Year of construction: c. 1903
Style of architecture:
Architect(s):
Landscape architect(s):
House extant: no
Historical notes:

The house was built by Joseph Huntington Lester. [*Brooklyn Daily Eagle* November 22, 1902, p. 11.]

The *Long Island Society Register, 1929* lists Mrs. Joseph Lester as residing at *Lestaley* in Bay Shore.

Her brother Henry W. Maxwell also resided in Bay Shore. Her brother John Rogers Maxwell, Sr. married Louise Washburn and resided at *Maxwelton* in Glen Cove.

At the age of twenty-four, while married to Henrietta, Joseph Huntington Lester allegedly married a sixteen-year-old girl in a scandalous elopement. No charges were pressed; no punishment resulted. [*Brooklyn Daily Eagle* August 9, 1880, p.4.]

*Lester was part of a syndicate that purchased massive amounts of wheat on the commodities market in an attempt to "corner" the cereal market. [*Brooklyn Daily Eagle* December 19, 1897, p. 4.]

Joseph Huntington and Henrietta Frances Maxwell Lester's son Maxwell Lester, Sr. married L. Norma Hegeman and resided at *Four Hedges* in Bay Shore.

[See other Lester and Maxwell entries for additional family information.]

Lester, Maxwell, Jr. (1904-1979)

Occupation(s):   financier -   member, James H. Oliphant and Co. (later, Hornblower, Weekes,
                                             Spencer, and Trask) (stock brokerage firm)
                              politician -   councilman and mayor, Summit, NJ;
                                             commissioner, New Jersey State Turnpike Authority
Civic Activism: director, Summit, NJ, Civil Defense, 1941-1977

Marriage(s):   M/1 – S. Katharine Libby (d. 1957)
                             M/2 – Emily Baldwin (d. 1973)

Address: *[unable to determine street address]*, Bay Shore
Name of estate:
Year of construction:
Style of architecture:
Architect(s):
Landscape architect(s):
House extant: unconfirmed
Historical notes:

    The *Long Island Society Register, 1929* lists the Lesters as residing in Bay Shore.
    He was the son of Maxwell and L. Norma Hegeman Lester, Sr., who resided at *Four Hedges* in Bay Shore.
    S. Katharine Libby Maxwell was the daughter of Walter Gillette Libby of Summit, NJ, and Brooklyn. Her brother Walter Gillette Libby, Jr. resided in Urbanna, VA. Her sister Elizabeth married Paul Wiser and, subsequently, Ruford Davis Franklin of New York.
    Maxwell and S. Katharine Libby Maxwell, Jr.'s son Maxwell Lester III married Mary Randolph Pennywitt, the daughter of John Pennywitt.
    Emily Baldwin Lester had previously been married to ____ Reach.
    [See other Lester and Maxwell entries for additional family information.]

Lester, Maxwell, Sr. (d. 1920)

Occupation(s):   industrialist -   director, Atlas Portland Cement Co.
Civic Activism: secretary, Long Island College Hospital, Brooklyn

Marriage(s):   1902-1920 – L. Norma Hegeman (d. 1967)
                          - Civic Activism: vice-president, Long Island College Hospital Guild,
                                           Brooklyn

Address: *[unable to determine street address]*, Bay Shore
Name of estate: *Four Hedges*
Year of construction:
Style of architecture:
Architect(s):
Landscape architect(s):
House extant: unconfirmed
Historical notes:

    The *Long Island Society Register, 1929* lists only Mrs. Lester, Sr. as residing at *Four Hedges* in Bay Shore.
    Maxwell Lester, Sr. was the son of Joseph Huntington and Henrietta Frances Maxwell Lester, who resided at *Lestaley* in Bay Shore.
    Norma Hegeman Lester was the daughter of Peter Augustus and Lavinia Edna Speir Hegeman of Brooklyn. Her sister Florence married John Fowler Pound.
    Maxwell and Norma Hegeman Lester, Sr.'s son Maxwell Lester, Jr., who married S. Katharine Libby and, subsequently, Emily Baldwin, resided in Bay Shore and Summit, NJ.
    [See other Lester and Maxwell entries for additional family information.]

Liebman, Julius (1867-1957)

Occupation(s): industrialist - president and chairman of board, S. Liebman and Sons, Brooklyn (later, Rheingold Beer; then, C. Schmidt & Sons of Philadelphia, PA)

Marriage(s): Sarah ____
- Civic Activism: member, Organization for National Prohibition Reform (for repeal of Prohibition Laws)

Address: Suydam Lane, Bayport
Name of estate:
Year of construction: c. 1855
Style of architecture: Italianate
Architect(s):
Landscape architect(s):
House extant: no; demolished in 1987
Historical notes:

The house, originally named *Edgewater*, was built by John R. Suydam, Sr.

It was inherited by his son John R. Suydam, Jr., who continued to call it *Edgewater*.

In 1922, the house was purchased by Herbert and Grace Whiting Seaman, who immediately sold it to Julius Liebman.

He was the son of Charles Liebman.

Julius and Sarah Liebman's daughter Catherine married Dr. Morris Rakieten of New Haven, CT. The Rakietens relocated to Bay Shore, where Dr. Rakieten opened a medical clinic. Their son Dr. James Liebman, who inherited his parent's Bayport house, married Winfred Bronson, the daughter of Miles Bronson of Yonkers, NY. James changed his surname to Leland. [Harry W. Havemeyer, *East on the Great South Bay: Sayville and Bayport 1860-1960* (Mattituck, NY: Amereon House, 2001), pp. 199-200.]

The estate was inherited by James' daughter Anne, who sold it to Ira Rubenstein in 1987. Rubenstein demolished the house and built a new one on the site, which he called *Cheap John's Estate*.

front facade

Livingston, Henry Beekman, Jr. (1855-1931)

Occupation(s):   financier -   partner, Maxwell and Co. (stock brokerage firm);
                                         member, Munds and Winslow (stock brokerage firm)

Marriage(s):   M/1 – 1876 – Stephanie Fox
                        M/2 – 1880 – Frances Redmond
                        M/3 – 1918 – Mrs. Leonie Duffard de la Claire

Address: Saxon Avenue, Bay Shore
Name of estate:
Year of construction: 1893
Style of architecture: Shingle
Architect(s):
Landscape architect(s):
House extant: unconfirmed
Historical notes:

front facade, c. 1909

    Henry Beekman Livingston, Jr. was the son of Henry Beekman and Mary Lawrence Livingston, Sr.
    Henry Beekman and Stephanie Fox Livingston, Jr.'s daughter Angelica remained unmarried.
    Frances Redmond Livingston was the daughter of William Redmond of Manhattan. Her brother Roland married Helen C. Bukley and rented a summer residence in Islip.
    Henry Beekman and Frances Redmond Livingston, Jr.'s daughter Lilias married Harry Bowly Hollins, Jr. and resided at *Crickholly* in East Islip.

Livingston, Robert Cambridge, III (1847-1895)

Occupation(s):   capitalist -   treasurer, National Express Co.

Marriage(s):   Maria Whitney

Address: St. Mark's Lane, Islip
Name of estate:
Year of construction:
Style of architecture:
Architect(s):
Landscape architect(s):
House extant: unconfirmed
Historical notes:

    The house was built by Parmenus Johnson.
    In 1880, it was purchased by E. B. Spaulding, who enlarged and modernized the house.
    In 1886, it was purchased by Livingston.
    Robert Cambridge Livingston III was the son of Cambridge and Maria B. Murray Livingston of Manhattan.
    Maria Whitney Livingston was the daughter of Stephen Whitney of Islip.
    Robert Cambridge and Maria Whitney Livingston III's daughter Eloise married James L. Kernochan. Their son John married Clara M. Dudley and resided in Lawrence. Their son Henry remained a bachelor. Their son Johnston married Natalie Havemeyer. Their son Louis married Catherine Murphy and resided in Manhattan. Their daughter Caroline married Maxwell Stevenson.
    The house was subsequently owned by their daughter Maude and son-in-law Henry Worthington Bull.

Lorillard, Dr. George L. (1843-1886)

Occupation(s):   physician
                              industrialist -   president, Pierre and G. L. Lorillard (tobacco firm)

Marriage(s):   Maria Louise Ewing

Address: South Country Road, Great River
Name of estate: *Westbrook Farm*
Year of construction: c. 1860s
Style of architecture: Neo-Tudor
Architect(s):
Landscape architect(s):
House extant: no; demolished in c. 1900*
Historical notes:

    The house, originally named *Westbrook Farm*, was built by Robert L. Maitland.
    In 1873, Mrs. Maitland sold it to Lorillard.
    Dr. George L. Lorillard was the son of Peter A. and Catherine Griswold Lorillard.
    Maria Louise Ewing Lorillard was the daughter of August Ewing of St. Louis, MO. She had previously been married to Edward Wright. After Lorillard's death, she married Count Casa de Agreda.
    The Lorillards were childless.
    The estate was later owned by Robert Fulton Cutting and, subsequently, by his brother William Bayard Cutting, Sr.
    *After the Spanish American War the house was used by the federal government as a convalescent home for returning servicemen and then demolished. [Harry W. Havemeyer, *Along the Great South Bay From Oakdale to Babylon: The Story of a Summer Spa 1840 to 1940* (Mattituck, NY: Amereon House, 1996), p. 148.]

Lovering, Joseph Sears, Jr. (1909-1962)

Occupation(s):

Marriage(s):   M/1 – 1929 – Carol Stevenson
                              M/2 – 1945-1962 – Anne Valentine (d. 1983)

Address: St. Mark's Lane, Islip
Name of estate:
Year of construction:
Style of architecture:
Architect(s):
Landscape architect(s):
House extant: unconfirmed
Historical notes:

    Joseph Sears Lovering, Jr. purchased the Enfin Johnson house.
    He was the son of Joseph Sears Lovering, Sr. of *Sunny Ridge* in Hewlett. His brother William was killed in World War II. His brother Charles married Margaret Murray, the daughter of Herman S. and Susanne E. Warren Murray, who resided at *Our House* in Woodmere.
    Carol Stevenson Lovering was the daughter of Joseph H. and Hildegarde Kobbe Stevenson. Carol subsequently married M. Stuart Roesler of Cos Cob, CT. Her sister Hildegarde married Fredrick Bourne Hard of West Sayville.
    Joseph Sears and Carol Stevenson Lovering, Jr.'s daughter Elsie married William Hamilton Gregory III and, later, Eugene Morris Cheston, Jr.
    Joseph Sears and Anne Valentine Lovering, Jr.'s daughter Alis married George M. Fern.

Low, Chauncey E.

Occupation(s):   merchant -   member, A. A. Low & Brother (tea importer
                                                        and merchant)
Civic Activism: director, Brooklyn Philharmonic Society

Marriage(s):   Mary T. Frothingham

Address: Penataquit Avenue, Bay Shore
Name of estate: *Seaward*
Year of construction: c. 1880
Style of architecture: Queen Anne
Architect(s):
Landscape architect(s):
House extant: unconfirmed
Historical notes:

    The house, originally named *Seaward*, was built by Chauncey E. Low.
    The *Brooklyn Blue Book and Long Island Society Register, 1918* lists Chauncey E. and Mary T. Frothingham Low as residing in Bay Shore.
    He was the son of A. A. Low, Sr.

    Mary T. Frothingham Low was the daughter of John W. Frothingham of Brooklyn.
    Chauncey E. and Mary T. Frothingham Low's daughter Mary married The Reverend Roger S. Forbes of Dedham, MA. Their son Josiah married Dorothy Lewis, the daughter of Theodore J. Lewis of Philadelphia, PA. Their daughter Nathalie married James McFarlan Baker and resided in Brooklyn. The Lows' other son died at eleven months of age.
    The house was subsequently owned by Michael Quinn.

Seaward, c. 1903

Ludlow, William Handy, Sr. (1822-1890)

Occupation(s):   politician -   member, New York State Assembly
                                  financier -   president, American Tontine Life Insurance Co.

Marriage(s):   Frances Louisa Nicholl (1822-1887)

Address: South Country Road, Oakdale
Name of estate:
Year of construction:
Style of architecture:
Architect(s):
Landscape architect(s):
House extant: unconfirmed
Historical notes:

    Frances Louisa Nicholl Ludlow was the daughter of William and Sarah Greenly Nicholl.
    The estate was purchased by Frederick Gilbert Bourne.

Macconnell, John B. (1829-1895)

Occupation(s):   financier -   auditor, New York Life Insurance Co.

Marriage(s):   Margaret Macdonald (1832-1892)

Address: Middle Road and McConnell Avenue, Bayport
Name of estate:
Year of construction: c. 1873
Style of architecture:
Architect(s):
Landscape architect(s):
House extant: yes
Historical notes:

    The house was built by John B. Macconnell.
    John B. and Margaret Macdonald Macconnell's daughter Jennie married Frank Melville, Jr. and resided at *Sunwood* in Old Field.
    In 1875, the house became the first rectory of St. Ann's Episcopal Church of Sayville.

MacLeod, Thomas Woodward, Sr. (1899-1974)

Occupation(s):   merchant -   president and chairman of board, Stern Brothers Department Store,
                                               1950-58 (which merged into Allied Stores Corp., 1951; Allied
                                               Stores Corp. merged into Federated Department Stores in 1992);
                                               president, S. H. Kress & Co. ("five and dime" retail store chain);
                                               president, retail division, Cluett, Peabody & Co., Inc., Chicago
                                               (national department store chain originating in Troy, NY);
                                               merchandise manager, Best & Co.
            financier -   member, advisory board, Fifth Avenue office, Manufacturers
                                             Trust Co.
Civic Activism: president and chairman of board, New York City Convention and Visitors Center;
                      director, New York Better Business Bureau;
                      trustee, National Jewish Hospital, Denver, CO;
                      president, press and promotion committee, New York Arthritis and Rheumatism
                          Foundation, 1954-1955;
                      chairman, employee fund raising committee, Greater New York Fund, 1954

Marriage(s):   M/1 – Henrietta Dobie (d. 1967)
                       M/2 – Josephine M. _____ (d. 1976)

Address: *[unable to determine street address]*, Bay Shore
Name of estate:
Year of construction:
Style of architecture:
Architect(s):
Landscape architect(s):
House extant: unconfirmed
Historical notes:

    Henrietta Dobie MacLeod subsequently married Trevett C. Chase and resided in Bayside.
    Thomas Woodward and Henrietta Dobie MacLeod, Sr.'s son Donald married Marion Norton, the daughter of Thomas J. Norton of Provo, UT. Their son Thomas Woodward MacLeod, Jr. married Jeanne Carolyn Buss, the daughter of Henry C. Buss of Ridgewood, NJ.
    Josephine M. MacLeod had previously been married to Leon A. Swirbul, who resided in Brightwaters and, later, Brookville.

Macy, George Henry (1859-1918)

Occupation(s):   capitalist -   president, Carter, Macy & Co. (tea importer)*;
                                                president, George H. Macy & Co. (tea importer);
                                                director, St. Louis, Southwestern Railway;
                                                director, Union Pacific Tea Co.
                financier -   vice-president, Seaman's Savings Bank, NYC;
                                                director, Atlantic Mutual Insurance Co.;
                                                director, Commonwealth Insurance Co.
                industrialist -   director, Sterling Salt Co.

Marriage(s):   Kate Louise Carter

Address: Penataquit Avenue, Bay Shore
Name of estate:
Year of construction:
Style of architecture:
Architect(s):
Landscape architect(s):
House extant: unconfirmed
Historical notes:

   George Henry Macy was the son of Silvanus J. and Caroline Ridgeway Macy, Sr. of Manhattan. His sister Margaret married Charles W. Pestalozzi, the son of W. Pestalozzi of Zurich, Switzerland.

   George Henry and Kate Louise Carter Macy's son Oliver married Martha J. Law, the daughter of Walter W. Law of Scarborough, NY. Their son William Kingsland Macy, Sr. married Julia A. H. Dick and resided in Islip. Their son Thomas married Mary Louise Pugh.

   [See following entry for additional family information.]

   *Carter, Macy and Company was one of the largest importers of tea in the country.

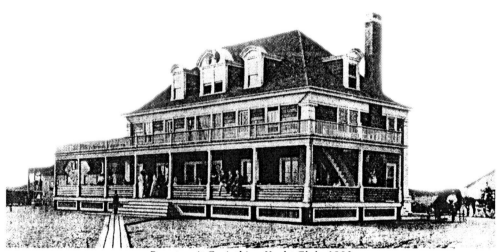

Penataquit Corinthian Yacht Club, 1903

Macy, William Kingsland, Sr. (1889-1961)

Occupation(s):
 financier - chairman of board, Franklin National Bank, Franklin Square, NY;
  trustee, Seaman's Bank for Savings, NYC;
  director, Norwich [England] Union Fire Insurance Society;
  partner, Abbott, Hoppin and Co. (stock brokerage firm)
 capitalist - chairman of board, Suffolk Broadcasting Corp.;
  chairman of board, Suffolk Consolidated Press Co.;
  director, Eagle Fire Co., NYC;
  chairman of board, Great River Reality Corp.
 politician - chairman, New York State Republican Committee, 1926-1951*;
  member, New York State Senate, 1944;
  member, United States Congress representing 1st Congressional
   District, 1946-1950;
  chairman, Town of Islip Planning Board, 1926-1951

Civic Activism: member, New York State Board of Regents, 1940-1952;
 member, United States Food Administration during World War I

Marriage(s): 1912-1961 – Julia A. H. Dick (1891-1977)

Address: 385 Ocean Avenue, Islip
Name of estate:
Year of construction:
Style of architecture: Modified Neo-Georgian
Architect(s):
Landscape architect(s):
House extant: yes
Historical notes:

 William Kingsland Macy, Sr. was the son of George Henry and Kate Louise Carter Macy of Bay Shore.
 *Known as Suffolk County's "Little King," no political decision of any significance in the county was made without Macy's approval.
 Julia A. H. Dick Macy was the daughter of John Henry and Julia Theodora Mollenhauer Dick, who resided at *Allen Winden Farm* in Islip. Her brother William, who married Madeline Force and, subsequently, Virginia K. Conner, resided in Islip. Her sister Doris married Horace Havemeyer, Sr. and resided at *Olympic Point* in Bay Shore. Her brother Adolph remained a bachelor.
 William Kingsland and Julia A. H. Dick Macy, Sr.'s son John Henry Dick Macy married Elizabeth B. Bacon, the daughter of William S. Bacon. Their daughter Julia married W. Cary Potter, Charles Henschel Thieriot II, who resided in Matinecock, and, subsequently, William Thompson, with whom she resided in Tucson, AZ. Their son William Kingsland Macy, Jr. married Margarette Hanes Old, the daughter of William Thomas Old of Jamestown Crescent, VA.
 [See previous entry for additional family information.]
 The estate is currently the convent of the Daughters of Wisdom.

rear facade, 1992

Magoun, Francis Peabody

Occupation(s):   financier -   partner, with his brother George, Magoun Brothers and Co.
                                          (stock brokerage firm)
                        industrialist -   director, Acme Ball Bearing Co.

Marriage(s):   South Country Road, West Islip

Address:
Name of estate:
Year of construction:
Style of architecture:
Architect(s):
Landscape architect(s):
House extant: unconfirmed
Historical notes:

   In 1905, Francis Peabody Magoun was arrested for grand larceny after he allegedly failed to account for
$20,000 worth of a client's stocks. [*The New York Times* March 25, 1905, p. 1.]
   [See other Magoun entries for additional family information.]
   In 1901, the house was purchased by Julien Townsend Davies, Sr., who called it *Casa Rosa*.

Magoun, George B. (c. 1869-1902)

Occupation(s):   financier -   partner, with his brother Francis, Magoun Brothers and Co.
                                          (stock brokerage firm)
                        industrialist -   director, American Sugar Refining Co.;
                                          director, Acme Ball Bearing Co.

Occupation(s):   Katharine Jordon

Marriage(s):   Magoun Road, West Islip

Address:
Name of estate:
Year of construction:
Style of architecture:
Architect(s):
Landscape architect(s):
House extant: unconfirmed
Historical notes:

   In 1880, George B. Magoun purchased the Udall farm for use as his summer residence. [Harry W. Havemeyer,
Along the Great South Bay From Oakdale to Babylon: The Story of a Summer Spa 1840 to 1940 (Mattituck, NY: Amereon House,
1996), p. 179.]
   The *Social Register, 1907* lists Katharine Jordon Magoun as residing in Babylon [West Islip].
   [See other Magoun entries for additional family information.]

Magoun, Kinsley (c. 1869-1898)

Occupation(s):   financier -   partner, Baring, Magoun and Co. (stock brokerage firm)

Marriage(s):   1894-1898 – Jessie Torrence

Address: South Country Road, West Islip
Name of estate:
Year of construction:
Style of architecture:
Architect(s):
Landscape architect(s):
House extant: unconfirmed
Historical notes:

    While returning to his Westbury estate *Oasis* from a polo game at the Rockaway Hunt Club, Magoun was thrown from his carriage and killed when his head struck the macadam surface of the road. [*The New York Times* July 11, 1898, p. 7.]
    His brother George married Katharine Jordon and resided on adjoining property, as did his brother Francis.
    The *Social Register, 1907* lists Jessie Torrence Magoun as residing at *Oasis* in Westbury [Old Westbury]. She was the daughter of General Joseph T. Torrence of Chicago, IL.
    In 1902, Jessie sued her brother-in-law George B. Magoun for failure to provide account of her husband's estate, which George was administrating. [*The New York Times* April 26, 1902, p. 1.]
    [See other Magoun entries for additional family information.]

Maitland, Robert L. (1817-1870)

Occupation(s):   merchant -   president, Robert L. Maitland & Co., NYC
                             (tobacco merchant)

Marriage(s):

Address: South Country Road, Great River
Name of estate: *Westbrook Farm*
Year of construction: c. 1860s
Style of architecture: Neo-Tudor
Architect(s):
Landscape architect(s):
House extant: no; demolished in c. 1900*
Historical notes:

    The house, originally named *Westbrook Farm*, was built by Robert L. Maitland.
    In 1873, Mrs. Maitland sold it to Dr. George L. Lorillard.
    The estate was later owned by Robert Fulton Cutting and, subsequently, by his brother William Bayard Cutting, Sr.
    *After the Spanish American War the house was used by the federal government as a convalescent home for returning servicemen and then demolished. [Harry W. Havemeyer, *Along the Great South Bay From Oakdale to Babylon: The Story of a Summer Spa 1840 to 1940* (Mattituck, NY: Amereon House, 1996), p. 148.]

side facade

Manton, Martin Thomas (1880-1946)

Occupation(s):   attorney -   judge, United States District Court for the Southern
                                                District of New York, 1916-1918;
                                             judge, United States Court of Appeals for the Second
                                                Circuit Court, 1918-1939*

Marriage(s):   1907 – Eva M. Morier
                             - Civic Activism: committee member, Woman's Organization
                                                for National Prohibition Reform (for
                                                (repeal of Prohibition laws)

Address: Fairview Avenue, Bayport
Name of estate:
Year of construction: 1888
Style of architecture:
Architect(s):   Isaac Henry Green II designed
                             the house (for C. F. Stoppani, Sr.)

Landscape architect(s):
House extant: no
Historical notes:

The house, originally named *Arcadia*, was built by Charles F. Stoppani, Sr.

It was inherited by his daughter Jennie, who married Stephen Perry Cox. The Coxes continued to call it *Arcadia*.

In 1919, Cox sold the house to John J. O'Connor, who defaulted on its property taxes.

The house was purchased by Manton at a sheriff's sale. Manton thus owned both Stoppani houses, *Liberty Hall* and *Arcadia*. In 1939, Manton lost the house for failure to pay its property taxes.

He was the son of Michael and Catherine Mullen Manton of Bayside.

*Manton, who was mentioned as a possible United States Supreme Court candidate, was convicted in 1939 of accepting $186,000 in bribes from both sides in the cases brought before him. After his release from prison in 1941 "Preying Manton," as he was known, relocated to Fayetteville, NY, where he was residing at the time of his death. [*The New York Times* November 18, 1946, p. 21 and David Pietrusza, *Rothstein: The Life, Times and Murder of the Criminal Genius Who Fixed the 1919 World Series* (New York: Carroll & Graf Publishers, 2003), p. 370.]

Arcadia

Liberty Hall, front facade, 2005

Maxwell, Henry W. (1850-1902)

Occupation(s): financier - partner, Maxwell and Graves (investment banking firm);
director, American Exchange Bank;
trustee, Caledonia Insurance Co. of Edinburgh, Scotland;
trustee, Union Trust Co.;
vice-president, Liberty National Bank;
director, Hamilton Avenue Bank, Brooklyn;
director, Brooklyn Trust Co.

industrialist - vice-president, Ashcroft Manufacturing Co.;
director, Atlas Portland Cement Co.*

capitalist - director, Garwood Land and Improvement Co.;
director, New York and Long Branch Railroad;
director, Long Island Rail Road;
director, Long Island Elevated Railroad;
director, Jersey Central Railroad;
director, Elmira, Cortland and Northern Railroad;
vice-president, Lehigh Valley Railroad;
director, Marine Railway Co.

Civic Activism: director, Brooklyn Art Museum;
director, Brooklyn Academy of Music;
member, visiting committee, Bay Shore High School;
member, Brooklyn Board of Education;
president, board of regents, Long Island College Hospital, Brooklyn;
donor, Maxwell House, Brooklyn, as memorial to his brother Eugene;
donor, Gertrude Lefferts Vanderbilt Industrial School, Ellery Street, Brooklyn, to
   the Brooklyn Industrial Association;
funded a dormitory building at Long Island College Hospital, Brooklyn;
benefactor, Brooklyn Guild;
established full scholarships at Adelphi College, Brooklyn, for 5 students per year;
treasurer, Polhemus Clinic, Brooklyn;
director, Brooklyn Free Kindergarten Society;
paid the pharmaceutical bills of the poor at all drug stores in the vicinity of his
   Brooklyn home;
reputed to have donated $300,000-per-year to charity

Marriage(s): Clara Alexander

Address: South Country Road, Bay Shore
Name of estate: *Scrub Oaks*
Year of construction:
Style of architecture: Neo-Georgian
Architect(s):
Landscape architect(s):
House extant: unconfirmed
Historical notes:

front facade, c. 1903

Henry W. Maxwell was a business associate of Austin Corbin in the Long Island Rail Road, Long Island Elevated Railroad, Marine Railway Company, Lehigh Valley Railroad, and Marine Railway Company. Unlike Corbin, Maxwell's chief interest was not in the accumulation of wealth but rather philanthropy. [*Brooklyn Daily Eagle* May 12, 1902, p. 2 and *The New York Times* May 13, 1902, p. 9.]

On several occasions Maxwell had decline nominations for New York City Controller and the state's United States Senatorial and Congressional positions.

His sister Henrietta married Joseph Huntington Lester and resided at *Lestaley* in Bay Shore. His brother John Roger Maxwell, Sr. married Marie Louise Washburn and resided at *Maxwelton* in Glen Cove.

*The Atlas Portland Cement Company provided the cement for the Panama Canal.

McBurney, Dr. Malcolm

Occupation(s):	physician
	financier - partner, Markoe, Morgan and Co. (stock brokerage firm)
Marriage(s):	1912 – Helen Dorothy Moran
Address:	Bayview Avenue, East Islip
Name of estate:	
Year of construction:	c. 1915
Style of architecture:	New-French Manorial
Architect(s):	Delano and Aldrich designed
	the house (for McBurney)
Landscape architect(s):	
House extant: no; destroyed by fire in 1976	
Historical notes:	

The house was built by Dr. Malcolm McBurney.

The *Brooklyn Blue Book and Long Island Society Register, 1921* lists Dr. and Mrs. Malcolm McBurney as residing in East Islip.

He was the son of Dr. Charles Heber McBurney, who resided at *Cherry Hill* in Stockbridge, MA. His sister Alice married Dr. Austin Riggs and resided in Stockbridge, MA.

His father Dr. Charles Heber McBurney was the consulting physician who attended President William McKinley immediately after the president had been shot. He devised a muscle splitting surgical entry procedure employed in appendectomy. It is still known as the "McBurney's incision" but often called "gridiron."

Helen Dorothy Moran McBurney was the daughter of Amedee Depau Moran of East Islip. She subsequently married Daniel Raymond Noyes, with whom she continued to reside in the former McBurney East Islip house. Her sister Rosalie married Edward Spring Knapp, Jr. and resided on Long Island's North Shore. Her brother Charles married Martha Adams. Her sister Mollie married Edwin Chase Hoyt and resided in Brentwood.

Malcolm and Helen Dorothy Moran McBurney's daughter Bridget married Charles S. Sargent, Jr., whose parents Charles S. and Dagmar Wetmore Sargent, Sr. resided in Cedarhurst. Their daughter Nora married _____ Tooker and, subsequently, _____ Kolczynski.

In 1949, the house was purchased by the Tesoro family.

rear facade

168

McClure, William (d. 1916)

Occupation(s):   financier -   chairman of board and secretary, New York Stock
                                              Exchange

Civic Activism: trustee, School District #1, Town of Islip

Marriage(s):   Ella Crane

Address: Oak Neck Lane, West Islip
Name of estate: *Clurella*
Year of construction:
Style of architecture: Shingle
Architect(s):
Landscape architect(s):
House extant: no
Historical notes:

William McClure was born in Carlisle, PA.

Clurella, c. 1903

Mc Kee, Henry Sellers, II

Occupation(s):   financier -   stockbroker

Marriage(s):   1916 – Alice M. Davies (d. 1970)

Address: 9 Montrose Avenue, Babylon
Name of estate:
Year of construction:
Style of architecture:
Architect(s):
Landscape architect(s):
House extant: unconfirmed
Historical notes:

The *Long Island Society Register, 1929* lists Henry Sellers and Alice M. Davies Mc Kee [II] as residing at 9 Montrose Avenue, Babylon.

He was the son of Wood Mc Kee of Woodmere.

Alice M. Davies Mc Kee was the daughter of Julien Townsend and Marie Rose de Garmendia Davies, Sr. of *Casa Rosa* in West Islip. Alice's sister Phebe married Walter J. Sutherland, Jr. Her brother Julien Townsend Davies, Jr., who resided in Flower Hill, married Faith de Moss Robinson, Marie O'Connor Quinn, and, subsequently, Ida Pasquali.

Henry Sellers and Alice M. Davies Mc Kee II's daughter Marie married Richard George Yates, Sr., the son of Herbert John and Petra Antonsen Yates, Sr. of *Onsufarm* in West Islip. Marie later married Joseph S. Bynum, the son of Samuel Bynum of Paducah, KY, and, subsequently, Ronald S. Correll, the son of Charles D. Correll. Their son Richard married Suzanne Eddy, the daughter of Harrison Prescott Eddy, Jr. of Cohasset, MA.

Mc Kee, John (1852-1915)

Occupation(s):   industrialist -   Brooklyn manufacturer of iceboxes

Marriage(s):

Address: Bayport Avenue, Bayport
Name of estate:
Year of construction:
Style of architecture: Victorian
Architect(s):
Landscape architect(s):
House extant: no
Historical notes:

In 1887, Mc Kee purchased the Frank Seaman
house. The Mc Kee family continued to reside at
this address until the 1920s. [Harry W. Havemeyer,
East on the Great South Bay: Sayville and Bayport 1860-1960
(Mattituck, NY: Amereon House, 2001), p.90.]

front facade, c. 1902

Mc Kee, William L. (d. 1937)

Occupation(s):   financier -   vice-president, National City Co.;
                                          assistant head, bond department, National City Bank;
                                          vice-president, Chase Securities Corp. (which merged
                                              with Harris, Forbes, & Co.);
                                          director, Harris, Forbes, & Co.
                            industrialist -   director, Idaho Cooper Co.

Marriage(s):   Annie V____

Address: Oak Neck Road, West Islip
Name of estate:
Year of construction:
Style of architecture:
Architect(s):
Landscape architect(s):
House extant: unconfirmed
Historical notes:

The *Long Island Society Register, 1929* lists Mr. and Mrs. William L. Mc Kee as residing on Oak Neck
Road, Babylon [West Islip].

Their daughter Valeria married Monroe Edwards Smith, the son of Floyd M. Smith of Omaha, NE. Their
son William Francis Mc Kee married June Harrah and, subsequently, Joan Armitage, the daughter of John
Foster Armitage of Manhattan.

In 1932, John Suddueth, a thirty-two-year-old local resident, was arrested for sending William L. Mc Kee a
threatening note stating that Mc Kee would be physically injured and his family scandalized if Mc Kee didn't
pay him $25,000. [*The New York Times* August 18, 1932, p. 15.]

McLaughlin, Dr. Daniel

Occupation(s):   physician

Marriage(s):

Address: Handsome Avenue, Sayville
Name of estate:
Year of construction: 1903
Style of architecture: Shingle
Architect(s):   Isaac Henry Green II designed
                          the main residence, gatehouse,
                          and 1905 playhouse. The latter
                          included a bowling alley and
                          billiard room (for F. S. Jones)
Landscape architect(s):
House extant: no; destroyed by fire in 1957*
Historical notes:

 The house, originally named *Beechwold*, was built by Frank Smith Jones.
 It was inherited by his daughter Maude and son-in-law David J. Shea. The Sheas chose to reside in the estate's gatehouse.
 In 1945, the main residence was purchased by Elwell Palmer, who sold it to McLaughlin in 1949.
 *The gatehouse and playhouse are extant. The gatehouse is located at 254 Handsome Avenue and the playhouse is at 96 Benson Avenue.

gatehouse, 2006

McNamee, John (1842-1914)

Occupation(s):
     financier -   trustee, Kings County Trust Co.;
                           trustee, Brooklyn Trust Co.;
                           trustee, Brevoort Savings Co.
     civil engineer
     capitalist -   president, Eagle Warehouse and Storage Co., Brooklyn;
                           director, a Manhattan sanitation company;
                           trustee, National Water Meter Co.;
                           partner, with Frederick L. and Walter Cranford, Cranford
                              & McNamee*

Civic Activism:
     chairman, building committee, Brooklyn Board of Education;
     member, Brooklyn Board of Education (21 years);
     member, New York State Prison Commission (3 years)

Marriage(s):   1885 – Mary Burnett

Address: South Country Road, Islip
Name of estate:
Year of construction:
Style of architecture:
Architect(s):
Landscape architect(s):
House extant: unconfirmed
Historical notes:

    *McNamee, with a succession of partners, was involved in building the foundations of the elevated railroads in Brooklyn, Portsmouth and Suffolk Water Works in Virginia, the Montclair Water Works, part of Brooklyn's Interborough subway, and a section of the Centre Street subway loop in Brooklyn. [*The New York Times* April 9, 1914, p. 11.]

    Mary Burnett McNamee was the daughter of William Burnett, who was one of the original members of the New York Produce Exchange.

    John and Mary Burnett McNamee's daughter Marie married Dr. Raymond Peter Sullivan, Sr. and lived in Bay Shore. Marie's twin sister Esther died at the age of ten.

Meeks, Edward B.

Occupation(s):

Marriage(s):

Address: South Country Road, Islip
Name of estate:
Year of construction:
Style of architecture: Colonial Revival
Architect(s):
Landscape architect(s):
House extant: no
Historical notes:

    In 1869, Joseph W. Meeks, Sr. purchased *Champlin House* and renovated it into his country residence.

    The house was inherited by his son Edward B. Meeks and subsequently owned by James Ives Plumb, who called it *Shadowbrook*.

    Edward B. Meeks' daughter Edna married John E. Carpenter of Nyack, NY.
[See other Meeks entries for additional family information.]

Meeks, Joseph W., Jr. (d. 1897)

Occupation(s):

Marriage(s):   Catherine T. ____

Address: 22 South Ocean Avenue, Bayport
Name of estate:
Year of construction: 1881
Style of architecture: Neo-Italianate
Architect(s):
Landscape architect(s):
House extant: yes
Historical notes:

front / side facade, 2005

   The house was built by Joseph W. Meeks, Jr.
He was the son of Joseph W. Meeks, Sr. of Islip.
*[See other Meeks entries for additional family
information.]*
   In 1916, Mrs. Meeks sold the house to George
W. Dahl.

Meeks, Joseph W., Sr. (1805-1878)

Occupation(s):   capitalist -   Big Cottonwood Mine (silver mine)
                         industrialist -   manufacturer of "high end" furniture

Marriage(s):

Address: South Country Road, Islip
Name of estate:
Year of construction:
Style of architecture: Colonial Revival
Architect(s):
Landscape architect(s):
House extant: no
Historical notes:

front facade, c. 1906

   In 1869, Meeks purchased *Champlin House*
and renovated it into his country residence.
   *[See other Meeks entries for additional family
information.]*
   The house was inherited by his son Edward B.
Meeks and subsequently owned by James Ives
Plumb, who called it *Shadowbrook*.

Melville, Frank, Jr. (1860-1935)

Occupation(s):   merchant -   founder and chairman of board, John Ward
                                        (a twelve-store shoe chain);
                                 founder and chairman of board, Rival Stores
                                        (a seventeen-store shoe chain);
                                 founder, president, and chairman of board, Melville Shoe
                                        Corp. (holding company);
                                 founder and chairman of board, Thom McAn Shoe Co.
                                        (a 565-store shoe chain)
                       capitalist -   president, Suffolk Improvement Co. (built residential
                                        housing in Old Field);
                                   president, R–W Realty Co.

Marriage(s):   1886-1935 – Jennie Florence Macconnell (1857-1939)

Address: *[unable to determine street address]*, Bayport
Name of estate:
Year of construction:
Style of architecture:
Architect(s):
Landscape architect(s):
House extant: unconfirmed
Historical notes:

   Melville later relocated to Old Field. The *Brooklyn Blue Book and Long Island Society Register, 1921* lists Frank [Francis] and Jennie Florence Macconnell Melville, Jr. as residing at *Sunwood* in Setauket [Old Field].
   He was the son of Francis and Mary Bamman Melville, Sr. of Bayport.
   Jennie Florence Macconnell Melville was the daughter of John B. and Margaret Macdonald Macconnell, who resided in Bayport.
   Frank and Jennie Florence Macconnell Melville, Jr.'s son Ward married Dorothy Bigelow and resided at *Wide Water* in Old Field.

Mildeberger, Elwood (d. 1943)

Occupation(s):   capitalist -   Manhattan real estate

Marriage(s):   Mollie Drumm

Address: 47 Awixa Avenue, Bay Shore
Name of estate: *Oakelwood*
Year of construction: c. 1900
Style of architecture: Shingle
Architect(s):
Landscape architect(s):
House extant: yes
Historical notes:

   The *Long Island Society Register, 1928* lists Elwood and Mollie Drumm Mildeberger as residing at *Oakelwood* in Bay Shore.

Oakelwood

174

Moffitt, William Henry

Occupation(s):   capitalist - president, W. H. Moffitt Realty Corp. (residential real
                                        estate developer, Towns of Islip and Hempstead,
                                        Staten Island, and New Jersey)*
                        publisher - owner, *Bay Shore Independent*
Civic Activism: president, New York State Realty Dealers Association

Marriage(s):

Address: South Country Road, Islip
Name of estate: *Beautiful Shore*
Year of construction: 1910
Style of architecture: Modified Mediterranean
Architect(s):
Landscape architect(s):
House extant: no
Historical notes: *Beautiful Shore*

   The twenty-one-room house, originally named *Beautiful Shore*, was built by William Henry Moffitt.
His daughter Ellen married Joseph Byron Creamer, Sr. and resided in Islip.
   In 1915, the house was purchased by Walter George Oakman, Sr.
   In 1918, the Oakmans sold it to George Scott Graham of Philadelphia, PA. Graham renamed the estate
Lohgrame.
   *Moffitt relocated to San Jose, CA. While there, he was indicted by a New York Grand Jury for grand
larceny in connection with his New York real estate transactions. [*The New York Times* January 24, 1920, p. 3 and
February 24, 1920, p. 3.]

Mollenhauer, John (1827-1904)

Occupation(s):   industrialist - a founder, Mollenhauer Sugar Refining Co. (later,
                                          The National Sugar Refining Co.)
                        financier - president, Dime Savings Bank of Williamsburg;
                                      director, Manufacturers Bank of Williamsburg

Marriage(s):   1854-1904 – Doris Siems (1830-1915)

Address: 60 Awixa Avenue, Bay Shore
Name of estate:
Year of construction: 1893
Style of architecture: Shingle
Architect(s):
Landscape architect(s):
House extant: yes
Historical notes:

   The house was built by John Mollenhauer.
   John and Doris Siems Mollenhauer's son John Adolph
married Anna Margaretta Dick and resided at *Homeport* in Bay
Shore. Their son J. Eldred died before attaining adulthood.
Their son Frederick married May Craig. Their daughter Julia
married John Henry Dick and resided at *Allen Winden Farm* in
Islip. Their son Henry married Sarah W. Howe.
   [See other Mollenhauer entries for additional family information.]
   The house was subsequently owned by Dr. Raymond Peter Sullivan, Sr.

front facade, c. 1903

Mollenhauer, John Adolph (1857-1926)

Occupation(s):	industrialist - vice-president, Mollenhauer Sugar Refining Co.;
	director, Cuban–American Sugar Co.;
	director, The National Sugar Refining Co.;
	director, St. Regis Paper Co.
	financier - trustee, Brooklyn Trust Co.;
	president, Allied Mutual Liability Insurance Co.;
	director, Manufacturers National Bank;
	trustee, German Savings Bank;
	trustee, Title Guarantee & Trust Co.
	shipping - director, Consolidated Shipping Corp.
Civic Activism:	member, board of managers, and trustee, Southside Hospital, Bay Shore;
	director, Home of St. Giles the Cripple;
	donated land on Main Street in Bay Shore for Soldiers and Sailors
	Memorial Building;
	trustee, Brooklyn Bureau of Charities;
	trustee, Brooklyn Hospital & Dispensary;
	director, Brooklyn Academy of Music;
	director, Brooklyn Institute of Arts and Sciences
Marriage(s):	1882-1926 – Anna Margaretha Dick (1861-1935)
	- Civic Activism: chairman, Tiny Tim Society of the Home of St. Giles the Cripple;
	chairman, Visiting Nurse Association of Brooklyn;
	president, Suffolk County Y.W.C.A.;
	president, Brooklyn Y.W.C.A.;
	member, National Board of Y.W.C.A.;
	president, Moravian School for Girls, Bethlehem, PA

Address:	Awixa Avenue, Bay Shore
Name of estate:	*Homeport*
Year of construction:	1898-1899
Style of architecture:	Modified Shingle
Architect(s):	Alfred Hopkins designed the farm complex, 1913 (for J. A. Mollenhauer)
Landscape architect(s):	Nathan F. Barrett (for J. A. Mollenhauer)
House extant: yes	
Historical notes:	

The house, originally named *Homeport*, was built by John Adolph Mollenhauer.

He was the son of John and Doris Siems Mollenhauer of Bay Shore.

Anna Margaretha Dick Mollenhauer was the daughter of William and Anna Maria Vagts Dick, who resided at *Allen Winden Farm* in Islip.

John Adolph and Anna Margaretha Dick Mollenhauer did not have children.

The house was subsequently owned by their nephew Adolph Mollenhauer Dick, who sold it in 1936 without ever having resided at the estate. [Harry W. Havemeyer, *Along the Great South Bay From Oakdale to Babylon: The Story of a Summer Spa 1840 to 1940* (Mattituck, NY: Amereon House, 1996), p. 239.]

rear facade, c. 1903

Montgomery, Richard H.

Occupation(s):   capitalist -   real estate builder and broker

Marriage(s):

Address: Montgomery Avenue, Bay Shore
Name of estate:
Year of construction: 1884
Style of architecture: Queen Anne
Architect(s):
Landscape architect(s):
House extant: no
Historical notes:

    The house was built by Richard H. Montgomery.
    It was subsequently owned by Robert Allan Pinkerton, Sr.

Moore, Dr. David Dodge (1900-1972)

Occupation(s):   physician -   president, Southside Hospital, Bay Shore
Civic Activism: medical consultant, Central Islip State Hospital;
                                    medical consultant, Mental Health Board of Suffolk County;
                                    medical consultant, Planned Parenthood Association

Marriage(s):   1928-1972 – Margaret Leighton Hatch (d. 1981)

Address: 137 West Bayberry Road, Islip
Name of estate:
Year of construction: 1899-1900
Style of architecture: Moorish
Architect(s):   Grosvenor Atterbury designed the house
                        (for H. O. Havemeyer)*
Landscape architect(s):   Nathan F. Barrett
                        (for H. O. Havemeyer)**
House extant: yes; but substantially altered
Historical notes:

front / side facade, 2006

    The house, originally named *Bayberry Point*, was built by Henry Osborne Havemeyer as his own residence in his "Modern Venice" development.
    It was later owned by Frank Gulden, Sr. and, subsequently, by Moore.
    Moore's sister Carol married Adlai Stevenson Hardin, the son of The Reverend Martin D. Hardin, pastor of the First Presbyterian Church of Ithaca, NY. His sister Amy married Dr. Anson Phelps Stokes Hoyt and resided in Pasadena, CA.
    Margaret Leighton Hatch Moore was the daughter of Harold Ames and Margaret L. Milliken Hatch of Manhattan and Sharon, CT.
    Margaret's sister Barbara married Dr. James T. Emert and resided in Manhattan.
    Dr. David Dodge and Mrs. Margaret Leighton Hatch Moore's daughter Barbara married Melville Ezra Ingalls IV of Babylon. Their daughter Joyce married John Bruce Maclay of Gettysburg, PA. Their daughter Margaret married John Gerard Dempsey, the son of Joseph Francis and May E. Dempsey, Sr. of Great River.
    *The sales brochure for "Modern Venice" states that the Moorish-style architecture was suggested by Louis Comfort Tiffany.
    **The sales brochure also states that "Modern Venice" would be devoid of trees and vegetation and that Nathan F. Barrett was the landscape architect.

Moran, Amedee Depau (1852-1915)

Occupation(s):   financier -   partner, Moran Brothers (investment banking firm)
                 capitalist - director, Detroit & Mackinac Railway Co.;
                               treasurer, Nevada, California & Oregon Railway

Marriage(s):   _____ Morgan

Address: Suffolk Lane, East Islip
Name of estate:
Year of construction:
Style of architecture: Italian Renaissance
Architect(s):
Landscape architect(s):
House extant: unconfirmed
Historical notes:

rear facade

Amedee Depau Moran rented the Lucius Kellogg Wilmerding house on a ten-year lease.
He was the son of Charles and Arabella Adams Moran of Manhattan.
His daughter Helen, who resided in East Islip, married Dr. Malcolm McBurney and, subsequently, Daniel Raymond Noyes. His daughter Rosalie married Edward Spring Knapp, Jr. and resided on Long Island's North Shore. His son Charles married Martha Adams. His daughter Mollie married Edwin Chase Hoyt and resided in Brentwood.

Moran, Eugene Francis, Jr. (1903-1971)

Occupation: shipping -   vice-president, Moran Towing and Transportation Co.
Civic Activism: president, Friendly Sons of St. Patrick;
                  director, Brooklyn Chamber of Commerce

Marriage(s):   1936 – Marie Josephine Staudt

Address: 235 Lakeview Avenue West,
                     Brightwaters
Name of estate: *Shadow Lawn*
Year of construction:
Style of architecture: Shingle
Architect(s):
Landscape architect(s):
House extant: yes
Historical notes:

side / front facade, 2006

Eugene Francis Moran, Jr. was the son of Eugene Frances and Julia Claire Browne Moran, Sr. of Brooklyn. His sister Helen married Harry Lee Warren and resided in Bay Shore. His sister Claira married Harold B. Epp and resided in Bay Shore. His sister Eugenia married Thomas S. Dwyer and resided in Pelham Manor, NY. His sister Marion married William Brendan Mattimore and resided in Brightwaters. His brother Joseph H. Moran II married Pauline Cotter, the daughter of Richard J. Cotter of Cambridge and Duxbury, MA.

Marie Josephine Staudt Moran was the daughter of John Staudt of Brightwaters. Marie's sister Christine married George Lane Maurer, the son of Edmund John Maurer, and, subsequently, Harry A. Fisher, with whom she resided in Manhattan.

Eugene Francis and Marie Josephine Staudt Moran, Jr.'s son Michael married Margaret Mary Stuberfield, the daughter of William Francis Stuberfield, and resided in Garden City. Their daughter Marie Ann remained unmarried.

Morgan, Charles, Sr. (b. 1869)

Occupation(s): industrialist -   Morgan Mineral Water Co.*

Marriage(s):

Address: Morgan Lane, Bayport**
Name of estate:
Year of construction:
Style of architecture:
Architect(s):
Landscape architect(s):
House extant: yes
Historical notes:

Charles Morgan, Sr. was the son of John and Sarah Elizabeth Oakley Morgan, who resided at *Idle Hour* in Bayport.

His son Charles Morgan, Jr. married Ethel Cowdin, the daughter of John E. Cowdin.

[See John Morgan surname entry for additional family information.]

*After the Morgan family sold the Morgan Mineral Water Company, it became White Rock Soda.

**Morgan resided at the former John A. Hicks house. Originally located on Middle Road, the house was moved to its present location on the west side of Morgan Lane in 1946.

Morgan, Henry (1883-1943)

Occupation(s): financier -   partner, Henry Morgan and Co. (stock brokerage firm)

Marriage(s): 1937-1943 – Virginia Kobbe (1890-1948)

Address: Suffolk Lane, East Islip
Name of estate: *The Stables*
Year of construction:
Style of architecture:
Architect(s):
Landscape architect(s):
House extant: yes
Historical notes:

The house, originally named *The Stables*, was a stables remodeled into a residence.

Born in Bordentown, NJ, and raised in Pau, France, Henry Morgan was the son of Charles and Clara Woodward Morgan, Sr.

Virginia Kobbe Morgan was the daughter of Gustave and Caroline Wheeler Kobbe of Bay Shore. She had previously been married to Gerald Vanderbilt Hollins, Sr., with whom she resided at *The Hawks* in East Islip. Her sister Hildegarde married Joseph H. Stevenson and, subsequently, Francis Burritt Thorne, Sr., with whom she resided at *Brookwood* in East Islip. Her sister Carol married Henry's brother Robert Woodward Morgan, Sr. and also resided in East Islip.

Morgan, John (1837-1915)

Occupation(s):   industrialist -   founder, Morgan Mineral Water Co.*

Marriage(s):   1861-1915 – Sarah Elizabeth Oakley (1843-1934)

Address: 78 South Ocean Avenue, Bayport
Name of estate: *Idle Hour*
Year of construction: c. 1879
Style of architecture: Queen Anne
Architect(s):   Isaac Henry Green II
         designed the alterations
         (for John Morgan)

Landscape architect(s):
House extant: yes
Historical notes:

front facade, 2005

The house, originally named *Idle Hour*, was built by John Morgan.
Sarah Elizabeth Oakley Morgan was the daughter of Henry Stannard Oakley.
John and Sarah Elizabeth Oakley Morgan's son Charles resided in Bayport. Their daughter Gertrude married James Sherwood. Their daughter Sarah remained unmarried. Their son Edward resided in Alaska.
[See Charles Morgan, Sr. surname entry for additional family information.]
*After the Morgan family sold the Morgan Mineral Water Company, it became White Rock Soda.

Morgan, Robert Woodward, Sr. (1888-1960)

Occupation(s):   financier -   partner, Stillman, Maynard and Co. (stock brokerage firm);
         vice-president, Mohawk Valley Investing Co., Utica, NY

Marriage(s):   1921-1960 – Carol Kobbe (1893-1976)

Address: Meadow Farm Road, East Islip
Name of estate:
Year of construction: 1927
Style of architecture: Colonial Revival
Architect(s):   Philip Cusak designed the
         house (for R. W. Morgan, Sr.)

Landscape architect(s):
House extant: yes
Historical notes:

The house was built by Robert Woodward Morgan, Sr.
He was the son of Charles and Clara Woodward Morgan, Sr.
Carol Kobbe Morgan was the daughter of Gustave and Carolyn Wheeler Kobbe of Bay Shore. She subsequently married George Palen Snow of Syosset. Her sister Virginia married Gerald Vanderbilt Hollins, Sr., with whom she resided at *The Hawks* in East Islip, and, subsequently, Robert's brother Henry also of East Islip. Her brother George married Marjorie W. Goss. Her sister Hildegarde married Joseph H. Stevenson and, subsequently, Francis Burritt Thorne, Sr., with whom she resided at *Brookwood* in East Islip.
Robert Woodward and Carol Kobbe Morgan, Sr.'s son Matthew, who resides in Oyster Bay, married Rosetta Ghibrera and, subsequently, Rosalinda Rosales. Their son Robert Woodward Morgan, Jr. married Dorothea Alexander.
The house was later owned by Robert Allan Pinkerton II and, subsequently, by Robert Entenmann.

Morris, Stuyvesant Fish, III (1901-1948)

Occupation(s):   financier -   member, New York Produce Exchange

Marriage(s):   1925 – Madeleine White

Address: 179 Fire Island Avenue, Babylon
Name of estate:
Year of construction:
Style of architecture:
Architect(s):
Landscape architect(s):
House extant: unconfirmed
Historical notes:

The *Long Island Society Register, 1929* lists Stuyvesant Fish and Madeleine White Morris as residing on Fire Island Avenue in Babylon.

He was the son of Stuyvesant Fish and Elizabeth Hilles Wynkoop Morris, Jr. of Hewlett and the great-grandson of President Martin Van Buren. His sister Hilles married Louis Gordon Hamersly, Sr., with whom she resided at *The Moorings* in Sands Point. She subsequently married George Leslie Bartlett and resided in Tuxedo Park, NY. His brother Martin Van Buren Morris married Helen Sloan and resided at *Longacre* in Quogue.

Madeleine White Morris was the daughter of William Towle White of Lowell, MA. She had previously been married to Spencer Kennard, Sr.

Morrison, George Alexander (1867-1931)

Occupation(s):   politician -   Brooklyn alderman, prior to its incorporation into New York City
                               capitalist -   real estate developer, specializing in the construction of apartment
                                                buildings;
                                                owner, Cedarshore Hotel, Sayville*
                               financier -   a founder and president, Greenport National Bank, Brooklyn

Marriage(s):   1893-1931 – Jessie Rae Dickson (1868-1941)

Address: Handsome Avenue, Sayville
Name of estate:
Year of construction: c. 1888
Style of architecture: Queen Anne
Architect(s):
Landscape architect(s):
House extant: no; destroyed by fire in 1916
Historical notes:

The house, originally named *Cedarshore*, was built by David B. Powell and his son Leander Treadwell Powell.

The estate was inherited by Leander's wife Rebecca. In 1912, Rebecca Powell sold it to Morrison, who subdivided its property for a housing development and to build the Cedarshore Hotel.

The *Long Island Society Register, 1929* lists Mr. and Mrs. George A. Morrison as residing on Handsome Avenue in Sayville.

George Alexander and Jessie Rae Dickson Morrison's son George Elliot Morrison married Dorothy Nash and resided in Sayville.

*In 1917, the Cedarshore Hotel was destroyed by fire. In 1924, the hotel was rebuilt by Morrison.

In 1942, the hotel was purchased by the Herald Tribune Fresh Air Fund.

In 1959, after going through several ownerships, the hotel, renamed the Bayview Plaza, was destroyed by fire.

Morse, William Otis

Occupation(s):   capitalist -   Formosan tea importer

Marriage(s):   c. 1907 – Harriet Burr Harmon (1882-1937)

Address: Fire Island Avenue, Babylon
Name of estate:
Year of construction:
Style of architecture:
Architect(s):
Landscape architect(s):
House extant: unconfirmed
Historical notes:

   The *Long Island Society Register, 1929* lists Harriet Burr Harmon Morse as residing on Fire Island Avenue in Babylon.
   William Otis Morse was the son of William Morse of Manhattan.
   Harriet Burr Harmon Morse was the daughter of Frank Harmon, a granddaughter of Aaron Burr, and a niece of William Havemeyer. Her sister Marie married Guernsey Curran and, subsequently, Walworth Pierce, with whom she resided in Boston, MA.
   William Otis and Harriet Burr Harmon Morse's son Franklin married Victoria Sartori, the daughter of Mrs. Frederick Janssen Bloempot of Babylon. Their son William Harmon Morse married Louise Foster Dodd, the daughter of Frank N. Dodd of *Millfield* in Babylon.

Moses, Robert (1888-1981)

Occupation(s):   politician -   president, Long Island State Parks Commission, 1924-1963;
                                             chairman, New York State Council of Parks, 1924-1963;
                                             Commissioner of Parks, NYC, 1934-1960;
                                             chairman, New York State Power Authority, 1954-1963;
                                             chairman, Triborough Bridge and Tunnel Authority, 1954-1963;
                                             New York Secretary of State, 1927-1928;
                                             unsuccessful candidate for governor of New York State, 1934
                              writer -   *Theory and Practice of Politics*, 1939;
                                             Tomorrow's Cars and Roads;
                                             articles in numerous periodicals

Marriage(s):   M/1 – 1915-1966 – Mary Louise Sims (d. 1966)
                              M/2 – 1966-1981 – Mary Grady (1916-1993)

Address: Thompson Avenue, Babylon
Name of estate:
Year of construction:
Style of architecture: Victorian
Architect(s):
Landscape architect(s):
House extant: destroyed by arson*
Historical notes:

   Robert Moses was the son of Emanuel and Bella Cohen Moses.
   Between 1924 and 1964, Robert Moses, known as "New York State's master builder," supervised the construction of eleven bridges, 481 miles of highways, 658 playgrounds, and seventy-five state parks for a total cost to New York State of $27 billion.
   Moses later rented houses at Oak Beach and Gilgo.
   *The arsonist was a local youth.

Murdock, Uriel Atwood, II (d. 1927)

Occupation(s):

Marriage(s):   Reta Nicholas (1886-1930)

Address: 49 Fire Island Avenue, Babylon
Name of estate:
Year of construction:
Style of architecture:
Architect(s):
Landscape architect(s):
House extant: unconfirmed
Historical notes:

Uriel Atwood Murdock II was the son of Lewis Champlin and May M. Shiland Murdock and a descendant of Francis Lewis, a signer of the Declaration of Independence.

Reta Nicholas Murdock was the daughter of Harry Ingersoll and Alice M. Hollins Nicholas, Sr. of Babylon. Her sister Evelyn married Alexander Duncan Cameron Arnold of West Islip, and, subsequently, Joseph H. Stevenson of Hewlett. Her brother Harry Ingersoll Nicholas II married Dorothy Snow and resided at *Rolling Farm* in Muttontown. Her sister Beatrice married Edward Nicholl Townsend, Jr. of Manhattan. Her sister Daisy married Grosvenor Nichol and resided in Old Westbury. Her sister Elsie married Alonzo Potter and resided at *Harbor House* in St. James.

Uriel Atwood and Reta Nicholas Murdock II's daughter Frances married John F. T. Langley of Leicester, England. Their daughter Margaret married E. Cecil Hoar of Kent, England.

Myers, Nathaniel

Occupation(s):

Marriage(s):

Address: Montgomery Avenue, Bay Shore
Name of estate:
Year of construction: 1899
Style of architecture: Neo-Dutch Colonial
Architect(s):   Clarence K. Birdsall designed
                        the house (for Meyers)
Landscape architect(s):
House extant: unconfirmed
Historical notes:

The house was built by Nathaniel Myers.
It was subsequently owned by John H. Eastwood.

rear facade

Nicholas, George S., Sr. (d. 1922)

Occupation(s):   capitalist -   president, George S. Nicholas & Co., (wine and liquor importers)

Marriage(s):   Elizabeth Teackle Purdy (1843-1921)

Address: South Country Road, West Islip
Name of estate:
Year of construction:
Style of architecture: Colonial Revival
Architect(s):
Landscape architect(s):
House extant: unconfirmed
Historical notes:

    George S. Nicholas, Sr.'s brother Harry married Alice M. Hollins and resided at *Virginia Farm* in North Babylon.
    Elizabeth Teackle Purdy Nicholas was the daughter of John S. and Virginia Teackle Purdy.
    George S. and Elizabeth Teackle Purdy Nicholas, Sr.'s daughters Elizabeth and Virginia remained unmarried. Their son Grosvenor, who married Daisy H. Nicholas and resided in Old Westbury, was disinherited by his father's will because of Grosvenor's alleged "unfilial attitude." Grosvenor contested the will claiming that his father was mentally incompetent when he signed it. Grosvenor's position was upheld by the Grand Jury but overturned by the judge who stated that the Grand Jury's decision wasn't binding. [*The New York Times* January 16, 1924, p. 11 and February 26, 1924, p. 21.]
    [See following entry for additional family information.]

Nicholas, Harry Ingersoll, Sr. (1846-1901)

Occupation(s):   financier -   member, New York Stock Exchange
                                    capitalist -   director, Mobile and Ohio Railroad Co.

Marriage(s):   Alice M. Hollins (1849-1917)

Address: Deer Park Avenue, North Babylon
Name of estate: *Virginia Farm*
Year of construction:
Style of architecture:
Architect(s):
Landscape architect(s):
House extant: unconfirmed
Historical notes:

    Harry Ingersoll Nicholas, Sr.'s brother George married Elizabeth Teackle Purdy and resided in West Islip.
    Alice M. Hollins Nicholas' brother Harry Bowly Hollins, Sr. married Evelina Meserole Knapp and resided at *Meadow Farm* in East Islip.
    Harry Ingersoll and Alice M. Hollins Nicholas, Sr.'s son Harry Ingersoll Nicholas II married Dorothy Snow, the daughter of Frederick A. and Mary Palen Snow of *Gardenside* in Southampton. Their daughter Beatrice married Edward Nicoll Townsend, Jr. of Manhattan. Their daughter Reta married Uriel Atwood Murdock II and resided in Babylon. Their daughter Daisy married Grosvenor Nicholas and resided in Old Westbury. Their daughter Elsie married Alonzo Potter and resided at *Harbor House* in St. James. Their daughter Evelyn married Alexander Duncan Cameron Arnold, Sr. of West Islip and, subsequently, Joseph H. Stevenson of Hewlett.
    In 1896, the Nicholas family became incensed when the memorial chapel, which they had donated to Christ Episcopal Church in West Islip was rented by its rector, The Reverend Samuel Moran, to Mrs. James Duffin for use as a pickling and preserving establishment. [*The New York Times* July 4, 1896, p. 1.]
    [See previous entry for additional family information.]

Nicoll, William (1820-1900)

Occupation(s): politician - unsuccessful Republican candidate for the New
York State Senate;
Commissioner of Highways, Town of Islip, 1846;
Suffolk County delegate to New York State
Constitutional Convention, 1886;
Overseer of Highways, Town of Islip, 1843, 1848,
1850-1859;
supervisor, Town of Islip, 1852-1853

Civic Activism: Inspector of Schools, Town of Islip, 1841-1842;
School Commissioner, 1843-1860;
a founder, Emmanuel Episcopal Church, Great River

Marriage(s): 1844-1900 – Sarah Augusta Nicoll (1823-1910)

Address: Heckscher State Parkway, East Islip
Name of estate:
Year of construction:
Style of architecture: Colonial Revival
Architect(s):
Landscape architect(s):
House extant: no
Historical notes:

Islip Grange, the Nicoll ancestral property, was a large land grant given to the family by Queen Anne of Great Britain. The house was located in what is now Heckscher State Park.

William Nicoll was the son of William and Sarah Greenly Nicoll. His sister Frances married William Ludlow.

William and Sarah Augusta Nicoll's daughter Mary married Coryton Woodbury. Their son Edward married Ella Lattling. Their son William Greenly Nicoll, who married Phoebe Disbrow, and, subsequently, Kate Cornwall, resided in Babylon. Their son Henry married Augusta Maltby and resided in Virginia. Their daughter Sarah married Silas R. Corwith and resided in Bridgehampton. Their daughter Frances married Lee Johnson, the son of Edwin A. Johnson of East Islip, and resided in East Islip and, later, in Garden City.

Nicoll Homestead

Oakman, Walter George, Sr. (1845-1922)

Occupation(s):	financier -	chairman of board, Guaranty Trust Co. of New York; Morristown Trust Co.; Mutual Trust Co. of Westchester County; director, National Bank of Commerce
	capitalist -	vice-president, Central Railroad of New Jersey; president, Richmond & Virginia & Georgia Railroad Co.; vice-president, Hudson & Manhattan Railroad Co.; director, Brooklyn Heights Railroad Co.; director, Brooklyn Rapid Transit Co.; director, Interborough Rapid Transit Co.; director, Long Island Rail Road; director, Long Island Electrical Companies; director, Buffalo, Rochester, Pittsburgh Railway Co.; director, Greeley Square Realty Co.; director, Hudson Companies; director, Hudson Improvement Co.; director, Interboro Metropolitan Co.; director, New York & Queens Co.; director, Kings County & Fulton Elevated Railroad Co.; director, Reynoldsville & Falls Creek Railroad; director, New Jersey Dock & Improvement Co.; director, Rapid Transit Subway Construction Co; director, Subway Reality Co.
	industrialist -	director, Jefferson & Clearfield Coal & Iron Co.; director, American Car & Foundry Co.; director, Rogers Locomotive Works; director, Sloss–Sheffield Steel & Iron Co.

Marriage(s): 1879-1922 – Elizabeth Conkling (1856-1931)

Address: South Country Road, Islip
Name of estate:
Year of construction: 1910
Style of architecture: Modified Mediterranean
Architect(s):
Landscape architect(s):
House extant: no
Historical notes:

The twenty-one-room house, originally named *Beautiful Shore*, was built by William Henry Moffitt. In 1915, the house was purchased by Oakman.

Elizabeth Conkling Oakman was the daughter of United States Senator and boss of New York's Republican party machine Roscoe Conkling.

George Walter and Elizabeth Conkling Oakman, Sr.'s daughter Helen married Buchan Liddell and resided at *Ashford* in Ludlow, England. Their son George Walter Oakman, Jr. was severely wounded during World War I while serving with Britain's Coldstream Guard. Their daughter Katharine married John Hammond.

rear facade

In 1918, the Oakmans sold their Islip residence to George Scott Graham of Philadelphia, PA, and relocated to a new estate in Roslyn, which they named *Oakdene*. Graham called the Islip estate *Lohgrame*.

Ockers, Jacob (1847-1918)

Occupation(s):   capitalist -   president, Blue Point Oyster Co. [Bluepoints Oyster
                                               Co.], West Sayville;
                                               director, Live Fish Co., Islip;
                                               president, Jacob Ockers Oyster Co., Greenport and
                                               Glenwood Landing
                        financier -   director, Oystermen's National Bank of Sayville;
                                               trustee, Union Savings Bank, Patchogue

Marriage(s):

Address: South Country Road, Oakdale
Name of estate:
Year of construction:
Style of architecture: Colonial Revival
Architect(s):
Landscape architect(s):
House extant: yes
Historical notes: *front facade, 2005*

Known as "The Oyster King," Ockers was reputedly the largest individual oyster grower and shipper in the country and the first United States exporter of oysters to Europe. His export business alone amounted to 30,000 barrels-a-year. [*The New York Times* December 5, 1918, p. 13.]

The Ockers' house, owned by the Town of Islip, formerly housed the Vanderbilt Historical Society until the house and the research library it contained were damaged by arson in 1991. Much of the society's collection, recovered from the fire, was relocated to Dowling College.

O'Donohue, Charles A. (1859-1935)

Occupation(s):   merchant -   John O'Donohue's Sons
                        financier -   director, Kings County Trust;
                                           trustee, East River Savings Institution;
                                           director, Long Island Safe Deposit Co.
                        capitalist -   director, Union Ferry
                        industrialist -   director, Analomink Paper Co.;
                                           director, Knickerbocker Mills
Civic Activism: trustee, Brooklyn Central Dispensary

Marriage(s):   1891-1935 – Olive A. Scoville (d. 1951)

Address: Clinton Avenue, Bay Shore
Name of estate: *The Moorings*
Year of construction:
Style of architecture: Modified Shingle
Architect(s):
Landscape architect(s):
House extant: no
Historical notes: *front facade, c. 1903*

The *Brooklyn Blue Book and Long Island Society Register, 1918* and *1921* lists Charles A. and Olive A. Scoville O'Donohue as residing at *The Moorings* in Bay Shore. The *Long Island Society Register, 1929* lists the O'Donohues as residing on Shore Road in Huntington [Huntington Bay].

He was the son of Peter J. and Emma M. Bachus O'Donohue.

Oelsner, Rudolph

Occupation(s):   capitalist -   beer importer
                        restaurateur -   president and secretary, Germania Catering Co.
                                          (a holding company for Café New York, NYC,
                                          which was formerly the Kaiserhof Restaurant);
                                          president, German Restaurant Co. (a holding
                                          company for Stadtkeller Restaurant)

Marriage(s):

Address: 117 Awixa Avenue, Bay Shore
Name of estate:
Year of construction:
Style of architecture: Shingle
Architect(s):
Landscape architect(s):
House extant: unconfirmed
Historical notes:

   The house was built by Rudolph Oelsner.
   By 1906 he had relocated to Long Island's North Shore, having purchased the three-hundred-acre Thayer estate in the Roslyn area of the Island.
   In 1918, Oelsner was indicted for allegedly hoarding in excess of five tons of sugar in violation of World War I rationing legislation. [*The New York Times* August 6, 1918, p. 11.]
   His Bay Shore residence was later owned by George W. Hodges, Sr.
   In 1923, Hodges sold the house to James P. Kelly, who called it *Awixaway*.

front facade

Oppenheimer, Julius (1891-1937)

Occupation(s):   capitalist -   partner, Rothfeld, Stern & Co. (importers of men's suit linings);
                                        director, Metal and Thermit Corp.;
                                        director, Hanseatic Corp.

Civic Activism: trustee, Ethical Culture Society;
                       trustee, Hudson Guild

Marriage(s):   1903-1931 – Ella Friedman (1869-1931)
                  - artist;
                    educator -   art instructor, Barnard College, NYC

Address: 52 Saxon Avenue, Bay Shore
Name of estate:
Year of construction: c. 1896
Style of architecture: Colonial Revival
Architect(s):
Landscape architect(s):
House extant: yes
Historical notes:

front facade, 2006

The house was built by Mrs. Edward Spring Knapp, Sr.

Julius Oppenheimer purchased the house in 1916 from Mrs. Knapp.

He was the son of Benjamin Pinhas Oppenheimer of Hanau, Germany.

Both of Julius and Ella Friedman Oppenheimer's sons Julius Robert [aka Robert] and Frank were noted scientists, who worked on the Manhattan Project during World War II to develop the atomic bomb. Julius Robert, known as the "Father of the Atomic Bomb" was the director of the project while Frank worked at government installations at Berkeley, CA, Oak Ridge, TN, and Los Alamos, NM. Both Julius Robert and Frank were later accused of being Communist agents and stripped of their security clearance. While Julius Robert steadfastly denied his involvement with the Communist Party, Frank eventually admitted that he and his wife Jacquenette were members of the party prior to the war.

Otto, Thomas N. (1873-1949)

Occupation(s):   merchant -   president, T. N. Otto Coal & Oil Co.;
                              owner, chain of meat markets along Suffolk County's
                                    South Shore

Marriage(s):   Julia ____ (1882-1950)
                - Civic Activism: a founder, District Nursing Association;
                                  chairman, National Defense Council of Sayville
                                  during World War II

Address: 72 Saxton Avenue, Sayville
Name of estate:
Year of construction:
Style of architecture: Colonial Revival
Architect(s):
Landscape architect(s):
House extant: unconfirmed
Historical notes:

front facade, 2006

Thomas N. Otto was the son of John and Cornelia Otto of West Sayville.

Thomas N. and Julia Otto's daughter Virginia married Jeweth Holt Smith and resided in Sayville. Their daughter Julia married ____Wallace and resided in Amityville.

Owens, Joseph Eugene, Sr.

Occupation(s):   attorney
                                        financier -   trustee, Brooklyn Trust Co.

Marriage(s):   ____ Carey

Address: Saxon Avenue, Bay Shore
Name of estate:
Year of construction:
Style of architecture:
Architect(s):
Landscape architect(s):
House extant: unconfirmed
Historical notes:

Mrs. Owens was the daughter of Dr. George F. and Mrs. Maria F. Carey of Brooklyn.

The Owenses' son Joseph Eugene Owens, Jr. married Beatrice Cronin, the daughter of John L. Cronin of Manhattan, and resided in Brooklyn. Their daughter Edith Carey remained unmarried. Their daughter Olive married Dr. Austin Kilbourn of Hartford, CT.

Packer, Frederick Little (1886-1956)

Occupation(s):   artist -   member, art staff, *Los Angeles Examiner*, 1906;
                                                member, art staff, *San Francisco Call* (which became the
                                                      Call-Post), 1907;
                                          art director, *Call-Post*, 1913-1918;
                                          cartoonist, *New York American*, 1932;
                                          editorial cartoonist, *New York Daily Mirror*, 1932-1956*;
                                          commercial artist;
                                          book and magazine illustrator
Civic Activism: vice-president, Victory Builders (prepared war posters), 1941-1946**;
                                a founder and first president, South Shore Arts Association of Long Island

Marriage(s):   M/1 – Ruth ____
                               M/2 – 1941-1956 – Lillian Pabst (1902-1985)

Address: 216 Lakeview Avenue East, Brightwaters
Name of estate:
Year of construction:
Style of architecture: Mediterranean
Architect(s):
Landscape architect(s):
House extant: yes
Historical notes:

front facade, 2006

Frederick Little Packer was the son of Jacob W. and Elizabeth Little Packer of Los Angeles, CA.

Lillian Pabst Packer was the daughter of William and Grace Ross Pabst of NYC. Lillian had previously been married to William Paul Wilson of Paris, TX.

*In 1952, Packer won the Pulitzer Prize for his editorial cartoon that depicted President Harry S Truman addressing members of the press. The cartoon's caption read "Your Editors Ought to Have More Sense Than to Print What I Say!"

**He received citations from the Department of Treasury and the War Production Board for his World War II cartoons and war posters.

In 1956, he received the Newspaper Guild's award for watercolor. In 1957, he was the recipient of the Freedom Award by the Freedoms Foundation.

Frederick Little Packer's Pulitzer Prize-winning cartoon

Page, Walter Hines, Sr. (1855-1918)

Occupation(s):	journalist -	editor, *Age*;
		editor, *Daily Gazette*, St. Louis, MO;
		literary editor, *New York World*;
		managing editor, *Forum*;
		editor, *Atlantic Monthly*
	writer -	*The Autobiography of a Southerner* [under pseudonym Nicholas Worth]
	publisher -	a founder, *State Chronicle*, Raleigh, NC;
		a founder, with Frank Nelson Doubleday, Doubleday, Page & Co., Garden City (which became Doubleday & Co., Inc.)
	diplomat -	United States Ambassador to the Court of St. James in Wilson administration
Civic Activism:		trustee, Peabody Fund;
		member, Southern Education Board;
		member, General Education Board
Marriage(s):		1880 – Willa Alice Wilson
Address:		Ocean Avenue, Bay Shore
Name of estate:		
Year of construction:		
Style of architecture:		Shingle
Architect(s):		
Landscape architect(s):		
House extant: unconfirmed		
Historical notes:		

Walter Hines Page, Sr. rented the Harry M. Brewster house prior to relocating to Garden City.

He was the son of Allison Francis and Catherine Raboteau Page.

Willa Alice Wilson Page was the daughter of Dr. William Wilson of Michigan.

Walter Hines and Willa Alice Wilson Page, Sr.'s daughter Katherine married Charles G. Loring of Boston, MA. Both King George and Queen Mary of Great Britain attended their wedding. [*The New York Times* June 28, 1915, p. 9.] Their son Arthur married Mollie W. Hall and resided at *County Line Farm* in West Hills.

Palmer, Elwell

Occupation(s):	attorney - Sayville-based practice
	capitalist - owned large tracts of land in Town of Islip
Marriage(s):	M/1 – Marjorie Cleaveland (1888-1951)
	- educator - Brooklyn and Manhattan Public Schools
	M/2 – 1955 – Jeanett Morrison
Address:	71 Benson Avenue, Sayville
Name of estate:	
Year of construction:	c. 1910
Style of architecture:	Modified Colonial Revival
Architect(s):	Isaac Henry Green II
	designed the house
	(for W. R. Simonds)
Landscape architect(s):	
House extant: yes	
Historical notes:	

The house, originally named *Wyndemoor*, was built by Frank Smith Jones as a present for his daughter Henrietta and son-in-law William Robinson Simonds.

The house was later owned by David J. Shea, who continued to call it *Wyndemoor*, and, subsequently, by Palmer, who moved it to Benson Avenue.

Elwell and Marjorie Cleaveland Palmer's son George married Mary Jane Dowd, the daughter of Benjamin S. Down of Rockville Centre. He subsequently married Althea Trochelman, the daughter of Everett Trochelman of Bayport. Althea had previously been married to George N. Henrich. Their son James married Elizabeth Therese Lewis, the daughter of Oscar Mayo Lewis of Cincinnati, OH. Their daughter Nancy married Thomas Paton Knapp, Jr. of Blue Point.

Jeanett Morrison was the daughter of Alexander Morrison of Sayville. She had previously been married to Walter Francis Livingston.

front facade, 2005

Palmer, Elwell

Occupation(s):	attorney - Sayville-based practice
	capitalist - owned large tracts of land in Town of Islip

Marriage(s): M/1 – Marjorie Cleaveland (1888-1951)
                     - educator - Brooklyn and Manhattan Public Schools
            M/2 – 1955 – Jeanett Morrison

Address: Handsome Avenue, Sayville
Name of estate:
Year of construction: 1903
Style of architecture: Shingle
Architect(s): Isaac Henry Green II designed
          the main residence, gatehouse,
          and 1905 playhouse. The latter
          included a bowling alley and
          billiard room (for F. S. Jones)

stables, c. 1912

Landscape architect(s):
House extant: no; destroyed by fire in 1957*
Historical notes:

The house, originally named *Beechwold*, was built by Frank Smith Jones.

It was inherited by his daughter Maude and son-in-law David J. Shea. The Sheas chose to reside in the estate's gatehouse.

In 1945, it was purchased by Palmer, who sold it to Dr. Daniel McLaughlin in 1949.

[See previous entry for additional family information.]

*The gatehouse and playhouse are extant. The gatehouse is located at 254 Handsome Avenue and the playhouse is at 96 Benson Avenue.

Pardee, Dwight W. (1852-1920)

Occupation(s): capitalist - director and secretary, New York Central Railway Co.;
                       director, Raquette Lake Railway Co.

Marriage(s): Mary _____ (d. 1937)

Address: South Country Road, Brightwaters
Name of estate:
Year of construction:
Style of architecture:
Architect(s):
Landscape architect(s):
House extant: unconfirmed
Historical notes:

In 1910, Dwight W. and Mary Pardee's nineteen-year-old daughter Elsa eloped with their chauffeur Kenneth Lee Collins. Their son Roy, who married Lillian H. Beasley and, subsequently, Mae A. Lawler, resided in Islip.

[See following entry for additional family information.]

Pardee, Roy Edmund (1888-1969)

Occupation(s):   capitalist -   one of Long Island's largest breeders of ducks
                        politician -   Town of Islip Clerk

Marriage(s):   M/1 – div. 1909 – Lillian H. Beasley
                        - entertainer - actress
          M/2 – Mae A. Lawler

Address: South Country Road, Islip
Name of estate:
Year of construction:
Style of architecture:
Architect(s):
Landscape architect(s):
House extant: unconfirmed
Historical notes:

    The *Long Island Society Register, 1929* lists Roy E. and Mae A. Lawler Pardee as residing on South Country Road in Islip.
    He was the son of Dwight W. and Mary Pardee of Brightwaters.
    Roy's daughter Maureen married Richard G. Saunders, the son of Charles C. Saunders of Sag Harbor. His son Dwight resided in Greensboro, NC. His daughter Joan married _____ Rydell.
    [See previous entry for additional family information.]

Parkinson, Thomas Ignatius, Jr.

Occupation(s):   attorney -   partner, Milbank, Tweed, Hope, and Hadley, NYC
Civic Activism: vice-president, New York War Fund, 1944;
                        director, Foreign Policy Association, 1951;
                        vice-president, New York State Charities Aid Association

Marriage(s):   1937 – Geralda Moore

Address: Lakeview Avenue, Brightwaters
Name of estate:
Year of construction:
Style of architecture: Colonial Revival
Architect(s):
Landscape architect(s):
House extant: yes
Historical notes:

    Geralda Moore Parkinson was the daughter of Edward C. Moore of Brooklyn.
    Thomas Ignatius and Geralda Moore Parkinson, Jr.'s son Geoffrey married Elizabeth Shirley Pidgeon, the daughter of William Arthur Pidgeon of Greenwich, CT. Their daughter Cynthia married Francisco Zuniga Pena, the son of Manuel Zuniga Pena of Santander, Spain.
    [See following entry for additional family information.]

Parkinson, Thomas Ignatius, Sr. (1881-1959)

Occupation(s):	attorney	
	capitalist -	director, Long Island Rail Road Co.;
		director, American Telephone & Telegraph Co.
	educator -	professor of legislation, Columbia University Law School, NYC;
		dean, law school faculty, Columbia University Law School, NYC
	financier -	president and chairman of board, Equitable Life Assurance Society of the United States;
		trustee, Atlantic Mutual Insurance Co.;
		director, Niagara Fire Insurance Co.;
		director, Centennial Insurance Co.;
		director, Chase National Bank;
		trustee, Emigrant Industrial Savings Bank

Civic Activism: trustee, general education board, Rockefeller Foundation;
trustee, Columbia University, NYC;
trustee, University of Pennsylvania, Philadelphia, PA;
president, New York State Chamber of Commerce;
chairman, Greater New York Fund campaign;
chairman, United Negro College Fund campaign;
trustee, Sailor's Snug Harbor, NYC;
legal council, Bureau of War Risks Insurance, 1919*;
legislative council, United States Senate Commissions, 1919-1920**

Marriage(s):   1912-1959 – Georgia Childs Weed (d. 1962)

Address: South Country Road, West Islip
Name of estate:
Year of construction:
Style of architecture:
Architect(s):
Landscape architect(s):
House extant: no
Historical notes:

The *Long Island Society Register, 1929* lists Thomas I. Parkinson [Sr.] as residing on South Country Road, Babylon [West Islip].

He was the son of John Henry and Rose Fleming Parkinson of Philadelphia, PA.

Thomas Ignatius and Georgia Childs Weed Parkinson, Sr.'s son Thomas Ignatius Parkinson, Jr. married Geralda Moore, the daughter of Edward C. Moore of Brooklyn, and resided in Brightwaters.

[See previous entry for additional family information.]

*Parkinson assisted in drafting War Risks Insurance Act.

**He also assisted in drafting Railroad Transportation Act.

Parsons, Schuyler Livingston, Jr. (1892-1967)

Occupation(s): financier - sugar broker
writer - *Untold Friendships*, 1955

Civic Activism: member, Voluntary Ambulance Service of the American Red Cross in France during World War I

Marriage(s): 1920-div. 1923 – Elizabeth Pierson

Address: St. Mark's Lane, Islip
Name of estate: *Pleasure Island*
Year of construction: 1924
Style of architecture: Ranch
Architect(s):
Landscape architect(s):
House extant: no; demolished in the 1980s
Historical notes:

Pleasure Island

The house, originally named *Pleasure Island*, was built by Schuyler Livingston Parsons, Jr.

The *Long Island Society Register, 1929* lists Schuyler Livingston Parsons [Jr.] as residing at *Pleasure Island* on St. Mark's Lane in Islip.

He was the son of Schuyler Livingston and Helena Johnson Parsons, Sr., who resided at *Whileaway* in Islip.

Elizabeth Pierson Parsons was the daughter of J. Frederick Pierson, Jr. of Newport, RI.

Schuyler Livingston Parsons, Jr. relocated to Newport, RI, Aikens, SC, Palm Beach, FL, and, subsequently, to Torrington, CT.

The Islip house was then owned by Schuyler Livingston Parsons, Jr.'s niece Marion and her husband Gerard Hallock III, who enlarged the house after moving it to the mainland.

[See following entry for additional family information.]

Parsons, Schuyler Livingston, Sr. (1852-1917)

Occupation(s): merchant - president, Parsons & Peter (wholesale chemical dealers)

Marriage(s): 1877-1897 – Helena Johnson (1856-1897)

Address: St. Mark's Lane, Islip
Name of estate: *Whileaway*
Year of construction: c. 1881
Style of architecture: Shingle
Architect(s):
Landscape architect(s):
House extant: no
Historical notes:

front facade

The house, originally named *Whileaway*, was built by Schuyler Livingston Parsons, Sr.

He was the son of William Barclay and Eliza Livingston Parsons, Sr. of Manhattan. His brother William married Anna D. Reed and resided in Manhattan.

Helena Johnson Parsons was the daughter of Bradish and Louisa Anna Lawrance Johnson, Sr. of *Sans Souci* in West Bay Shore.

[See Johnson entries for additional family information.]

Schuyler Livingston and Helena Johnson Parsons, Sr.'s. daughter Evelyn married Amor Hollingsworth of Boston, MA. Their son Schuyler Livingston Parsons, Jr. married Elizabeth Pierson and resided at *Pleasure Island* in Islip. Their daughter Helena, who inherited *Whileaway*, married Richard Wharton.

[See previous entry for additional Parsons family information.]

Parsons, William Decatur (1856-1930)

Occupation(s):   attorney

Civic Activism: donated a Gilbert Stuart portrait of Commodore Stephen Decatur
to the National Art Gallery, Washington, DC;
donated Commodore Decatur's dress uniform sword to the United
States Naval Academy, Annapolis, MD

Marriage(s):   Christine Hilsendegen

Address: 91 Ocean Avenue, Bay Shore

Name of estate: *Restina Cottage*

Year of construction:

Style of architecture: Modified Colonial Revival

Architect(s):

Landscape architect(s):

House extant: yes

Historical notes:

    The *Long Island Society Register, 1929* lists
William Decatur and Christine Hilsendegen Parsons
as residing at *Restina Cottage*, 91 Ocean Avenue,
Bay Shore.

    He was the son of William H. and Anna Pine
Parsons and the great-grandnephew of Commodore
Stephen Decatur.

front facade, 2006

Pasternack, Dr. Richard

Occupation(s):   physician

Marriage(s):

Address: St. Mark's Lane, Islip

Name of estate:

Year of construction: c. 1920

Style of architecture: Neo-French Manorial

Architect(s):

Landscape architect(s):

House extant: yes

Historical notes:

    The Pasternack's son Justus married Elizabeth Rowe, the daughter of Edward Comstock Rowe of
Hamilton, NY.

Payne, Albert (1835-1909)

Occupation(s):   capitalist -   real estate developer and builder

Marriage(s):

Address: 80 Seaman's Avenue, Bayport
Name of estate:
Year of construction: c. 1874
Style of architecture: Queen Anne
Architect(s):   Howard Payne designed the house
                          (for his father Albert Payne)
Landscape architect(s):
House extant: yes
Historical notes:

The house was build by Albert Payne.

front facade, 2005

Peck, William L. (1831-1902)

Occupation(s):   industrialist -   manufacturer

Marriage(s):

Address: Clinton Avenue, Bay Shore
Name of estate:
Year of construction:
Style of architecture: Shingle
Architect(s):
Landscape architect(s):
House extant: unconfirmed
Historical notes:

front facade, 1903

198

Perkins, Richard Sturgis, Sr. (1910-2003)

Occupation(s):	capitalist -	trustee, Consolidated Edison, NYC (utility company);
		director, International Telephone & Telegraph Co.;
		director, Astor Hotel, Inc., NYC;
		director, Carlton House, NYC
	financier -	president and chairman of board, City Bank Farmers Trust
		Co. (later, First National City Bank);
		chairman of board, First National City Bank;
		partner, Harris Upham and Co. (investment banking firm);
		director, Prudential Insurance Company of Great Britain;
		director, Liverpool, London & Globe Insurance Co.;
		director, New York Life Insurance Co.;
		director, British & Foreign Marine Insurance Co.;
		director, Thames & Mersey Marine Insurance Co.
	industrialist -	director, Phelps Dodge Corp.;
		director, Allied Chemical Corp.

Civic Activism: trustee, Metropolitan Museum of Art, NYC;
chairman, Y.M.C.A. of Greater New York;
trustee, Boys' Club of America;
president, New York State Bankers Association

Marriage(s): 1935-div. c. 1976 – Adaline Havemeyer (1913-1998)

Address: 126 East Bayberry Road, Islip
Name of estate:
Year of construction: 1899-1900
Style of architecture: Moorish
Architect(s): Grosvenor Atterbury designed the house
  (for H. O. Havemeyer)*
Landscape architect(s): Nathan F. Barrett (for H. O. Havemeyer)**
House extant: yes
Historical notes:

The house was built by Henry Osborne Havemeyer as part of his "Modern Venice" development.

It was purchased in 1936 by Perkins, who subsequently relocated to a 1948 Colonial Revival house which was built by Horace Havemeyer, Sr. on his *Olympic Point* estate.

He was the son of James Handasyd Perkins of Boston, MA. His sister Eleanor married Franklin E. Parker, Jr. and resided in Greenwich, CT.

Adaline Havemeyer Perkins was the daughter Horace and Doris Anna Dick Havemeyer, Sr., who resided at *Olympic Point* in Bay Shore and the granddaughter of Henry Osborne Havemeyer. She subsequently married Laurance B. Rand of Southport, CT. Her sister Doris married Dr. Daniel Catlin, Sr. and resided in Bay Shore. Her brother Harry married Eugenie Aiguier, the daughter of Dr. James E. Aiguier, and resides on the *Olympic Point* property in Bay Shore. Her brother Horace Havemeyer, Jr. married Rosalind Everdell, the daughter of William and Rosalind Romeyn Everdell of Manhasset, and resided in Islip and Dix Hills.

Richard Sturgis and Adaline Havemeyer Perkins, Sr.'s son Richard Sturgis Perkins, Jr. married Mildred Duer Baxter, the daughter of Richard S. Baxter of Southampton. Their son Thomas married Bonnie Campbell, the daughter of James Gordon Campbell of Princeton, NJ. After his divorce, Thomas relocated to Solvang, CA. Their daughter Sarah married William Moir, the son of James Tweed Moir of Edinburgh, Scotland. After the Moirs' divorce, Sarah relocated to Concord, MA. Their daughter Judith also resides in Concord, MA.

*The sales brochure for "Modern Venice" states that the Moorish-style architecture was suggested by Louis Comfort Tiffany.

**The sales brochure also states that "Modern Venice" would be devoid of trees and vegetation and that Nathan F. Barrett was the landscape architect.

The house was subsequently owned by Anson McCook Beard, Jr.

Peters, Harry Twyford, Sr. (1881-1948)

Occupation(s):	merchant - president, Williams and Peters (wholesale coal);
	director, Peabody Coal Co.
	writer - *Just Hunting*, 1935;
	Currier and Ives: Printmakers To the American People, 1929*
Civic Activism:	chairman, New York State Coal Conservation Committee during World War I

Marriage(s):	1905-1948 – Natalie Wells (1882-1976)
	- Civic Activism: president, Garden Club of America

Address:	St. Mark's Lane, Islip
Name of estate:	*Nearholme*
Year of construction:	c. 1910
Style of architecture:	Modified Shingle
Architect(s):	
Landscape architect(s):	
House extant: no	
Historical notes:	

rear facade

The house, originally named *Nearholme*, was built by Harry Twyford Peters, Sr.

He was the son of Samuel Twyford and Adaline Mapes Elder Peters, who resided at *Windholme Farm* in Islip.

Natalie Wells Peters was the daughter of W. Storrs Wells of *Chelwoda* in Newport, RI.

Harry Twyford and Natalie Wells Peters, Sr.'s daughter Natalie married Charles D. Webster and resided at *Twyford* in Islip. Their son Harry Twyford Peters, Jr. remained a bachelor and resided at *Windholme Farm* in Orange, VA.

*Harry Twyford Peters, Sr. was a noted collector, author, and authority on Currier and Ives prints.

[See Samuel Twyford Peters entry for additional family information.]

Peters, Harry Twyford, Sr. (1881-1948)

Occupation(s):	*[See previous entry.]*

Marriage(s):	1905-1948 – Natalie Wells (1882-1976)
	- Civic Activism: president, Garden Club of America

Address:	St. Mark's Lane, Islip
Name of estate:	*Windholme Farm*
Year of construction:	c. 1850
Style of architecture:	Shingle
Architect(s):	Alfred Hopkins designed
	the c. 1910 farm and garage
	complex (for S. T. Peters)*
Landscape architect(s):	Ellen Biddle Shipman
	(for H. T. Peters, Sr.)
House extant: no; demolished in c. 1950	
Historical notes:	

farm complex, 1912

The house was built by John Dyneley Prince II.

It was purchased by Samuel Twyford Peters, who enlarged the house and called it *Windholme Farm*.

The estate was subsequently owned by his son Harry Twyford Peters, Sr., who continued to call it *Windholme Farm*.

[See other Peters entries for additional family information.]

*The barn complex still exists. It was converted into a residence by Mrs. Harry Twyford Peters.

Peters, Samuel Twyford (1854-1921)

Occupation(s):   merchant -   partner, with Richard H. Williams, Williams and Peters
                                               (wholesale coal)
                                financier -   director, Hanover Bank

Civic Activism: trustee, Metropolitan Museum of Art, NYC*

Marriage(s):   c. 1879-1921 – Adaline Mapes Elder (1857-1943)

Address: St. Mark's Lane, Islip
Name of estate: *Windholme Farm*
Year of construction: c. 1850
Style of architecture: Shingle
Architect(s):   Alfred Hopkins designed
                        the c. 1910 farm and garage
                        complex (for S. T. Peters)**

Landscape architect(s): Ellen Biddle Shipman
                        (for H. T. Peters, Sr.)
House extant: no; demolished in c. 1950
Historical notes:

Windholme Farm

    The house was built by John Dyneley Prince II.
    It was purchased by Peters, who enlarged the house and called it *Windholme Farm.*
    Adaline Mapes Elder Peters was the daughter of George William and Mathilda Adelaide Waldron Elder. Her brother George married Therese Cadwell and resided in Bay Shore. Her sister Anne married Henry Norcross Munn. Her sister Louisine married Henry Osborne Havemeyer and resided at *Bayberry Point* in Islip.
    Samuel Twyford and Adaline Mapes Elder Peters' daughter Louisine married Harold Hathaway Weekes and resided in *Wereholme* in Islip. Louisine subsequently married Alexander Tcherepin and continued to reside at *Wereholme.* Their son Harry Twyford Peters, Sr., who married Natalie Wells and resided at *Nearholme* in Islip, inherited *Windholme Farm.*
    [See other Peters entries for additional family information.]
    *Samuel Twyford Peters donated over four hundred Oriental pieces of jade to the Metropolitan Museum of Art.
    **The barn complex still exists. It was converted into a residence by Mrs. Harry Twyford Peters.

Phelps, Charles E. (1865-1918)

Occupation(s):   financier -   treasurer, Equitable Life Assurance Society
                                           of the United States;

Marriage(s):   Laura W. ____

Address: North Windsor Avenue, Brightwaters
Name of estate: *Brightwaters*
Year of construction: c. 1915
Style of architecture: Shingle
Architect(s):
Landscape architect(s):
House extant: unconfirmed
Historical notes:

Brightwaters

Pinkerton, Allan, II (1876-1930)

Occupation(s):   capitalist -   president, Pinkerton National Detective Agency

Marriage(s):   Franc Woolworth (d. 1945)

Address: Saxon Avenue, Bay Shore
Name of estate:
Year of construction: Colonial Revival
Style of architecture:
Architect(s):
Landscape architect(s):
House extant: no; demolished in c. 1950
Historical notes:

front facade

    The *Long Island Society Register, 1929* lists Allan and Franc Woolworth Pinkerton [II] as residing on Saxon Avenue in Islip [Bay Shore].
    He was the son of Robert Allan and Anna E. Hughes Pinkerton, Sr., who resided at *Dearwood* in Bay Shore.
    Allan and Franc Woolworth Pinkerton II's son Robert Allan Pinkerton II married Louise Eliot Cutter and resided in the caretaker's cottage on his parents' estate, prior to relocating to East Islip.
    [See other Pinkerton entries for additional family information.]

Pinkerton, Robert Allan, II (1904-1967)

Occupation(s):   capitalist -   president and chairman of board, Pinkerton National
                                         Detective Agency
                         financier -   stockbroker

Marriage(s):   1930-1967 – Louise Eliot Cutter

Address: Meadow Farm Road, East Islip
Name of estate:
Year of construction: 1927
Style of architecture: Colonial Revival
Architect(s):   Philip Cusack designed the house
                        (for R. W. Morgan, Sr.)
Landscape architect(s):
House extant: yes
Historical notes:

    The house was built by Robert Woodward Morgan, Sr.
    It was later owned by Pinkerton.
    Robert Allan Pinkerton II was the son of Allan and Franc Woolworth Pinkerton II, who resided in Bay Shore.
    Louise Eliot Cutter Pinkerton was the daughter of Eliot and Anna Louise McBride Cutter of *Minnebama* in Westhampton. Louise subsequently married John Hunt Marshall of Dedham, MA, with whom she resided in East Islip.
    The house was subsequently owned by Robert Entenmann.

Pinkerton, Robert Allan, Sr. (1848-1907)

Occupation(s):   capitalist -   president, Pinkerton National Detective Agency

Marriage(s):   1873-1907 – Anna E. Hughes (d. 1933)

Address: 116 Penataquit Avenue, Bay Shore
Name of estate: *Dearwood*
Year of construction: 1884
Style of architecture: Queen Anne
Architect(s):
Landscape architect(s):
House extant: no
Historical notes:

    The house was built by Richard H. Montgomery.
    In 1899, it was purchased by Pinkerton, who called it *Dearwood*.
    He was the son of Allan and Joan Carfrae Pinkerton, Sr.
    The *Long Island Society Register, 1929* lists Anna E. Hughes Pinkerton as residing at *Dearwood* on Montgomery Avenue, Bay Shore.
    Robert Allan and Anna E. Hughes Pinkerton's daughter Mary married Jay Freeborn Carlisle, Sr. and resided at *Rosemary* in East Islip. Their daughter Anna married Lewis Mills Gibb, Sr. and resided at *Cedarholme* in Bay Shore. Their son Allan Pinkerton II married Franc Woolworth and resided in the caretaker's cottage on his parents' estate, prior to relocating to East Islip.
    [See other Pinkerton entries for additional family information.]

Pless, John Anthony, Jr. (b. 1930)

Occupation(s):   educator -   teacher, Hewlett School of East Islip
Civic Activism: president, Suffolk Hearing and Speech Center, Bay Shore;
                        trustee, United Counseling;
                        member, advisory board, Southside Hospital, Bay Shore

Marriage(s):   1966 – Helena Parsons Hallock (b. 1942)
                        - Civic Activism: president, South Shore Garden Club

Address: St. Mark's Lane, Islip
Name of estate:
Year of construction:
Style of architecture: ranch
Architect(s):
Landscape architect(s):
House extant: no; demolished in 1980s
Historical notes:

    John Anthony and Helena Parsons Hallock Pless, Jr. resided in the former chauffeur's cottage of the Parsons' estate *Whileaway*, which in the 1970s had been converted into a ranch-style house.
    He was the son of John Anthony and Madeline Sichel Pless, Sr. of Holland and France.
    Helena Parsons Hallock Pless was the daughter of Gerard and Marion Wharton Hallock III of Islip.
    John Anthony and Helena Parsons Hallock Pless, Jr.'s daughter Elizabeth married Christopher Kirk of Darian, CT, and resides in Southwest Harbor, ME. Their daughter Katriena married Michael Devlin of Annapolis, MD, and resides in Darian, CT. Their son John Anthony Pless III married Lindley Tilghman of Greenwich, CT, and resides in Manhattan.

Plumb, James Ives

Occupation(s):

Marriage(s):   1885 – Frances Anna Parsons Burton (d. 1933)

Address: Heckscher Parkway, East Islip
Name of estate: *Deer Range Farm*
Year of construction: c. 1850s
Style of architecture: Eclectic
Architect(s):
Landscape architect(s):
House extant: no*
Historical notes:

Deer Range Farm

The house, originally named *Deer Range Farm*, was built by Edwin Augustus Johnson, Sr.

In 1872, the estate was purchased by Sarah Ives Plumb. Upon her death, it was inherited by her husband James Neale Plumb, who made alterations to the house in 1884. It was subsequently owned by their son James Ives Plumb. The Plumbs continued to call it *Deer Range Farm*.

Frances Anna Parsons Burton Plumb was the daughter of Dr. Matthew H. Burton of Troy, NY.

James Ives and Frances Anna Parsons Burton Plumb's son Burton married Marguerite de B. Taylor, the daughter of George W. Taylor of Norfolk, VA, and, subsequently, Louise Everett, the widow of Joseph de Tours Lentilhon of Terrytown, NY.

[See other Plumb entries for additional family information.]

In 1903, James Ives Plumb sold the estate to George Campbell Taylor and relocated to Islip.

The estate remained in the Taylor / Pyne family corporation until 1924 when it was confiscated by Robert Moses and became part of Heckscher State Park. [Harry W. Havemeyer, *Along the Great South Bay From Oakdale to Babylon: The Story of a Summer Spa 1840 to 1940* (Mattituck, NY: Amereon House, 1996), p. 135.]

*The house was demolished by Moses' Long Island State Park Commission. Portions of the house were salvaged, moved, and relocated into buildings in the Islip area.

Plumb, James Ives

Occupation(s):

Marriage(s):   1885 – Frances Anna Parsons Burton (d. 1933)

Address: South Country Road, Islip
Name of estate: *Shadowbrook*
Year of construction:
Style of architecture: Colonial Revival
Architect(s):
Landscape architect(s):
House extant: no
Historical notes:

front facade, c. 1906

In 1869, Josepth W. Meeks, Sr.purchased *Champlin House* and renovated it into his country residence.

The house was inherited by his son Edward B. Meeks and subsequently owned by Plumb, who called it *Shadowbrook*.

The *Long Island Society Register, 1929* lists J. Ives and Anna Burton Plumb as residing at *Shadowbrook* on Main Street [South Country Road], Islip.

He was the son of James Neale and Sarah Ives Plumb, who resided at *Deer Range Farm* in East Islip.

Frances Anna Parsons Burton Plumb was the daughter of Dr. Matthew H. Burton of Troy, NY.

[See other Plumb entries for additional family information.]

Plumb, Sarah Ives (d. 1877)

Marriage(s):   1861-1877 – James Neale Plumb (1834-1899)
                             - professional gambler*

Address: Heckscher Parkway, East Islip
Name of estate: *Deer Range Farm*
Year of construction: c. 1850s
Style of architecture: Eclectic
Architect(s):
Landscape architect(s):
House extant: no**
Historical notes:

The house, originally named *Deer Range Farm*, was built by Edwin Augustus Johnson, Sr.

In 1872, the estate was purchased by Sarah Ives Plumb. Upon her death, it was inherited by her husband James Neale Plumb, who made alterations to the house in 1884.

*After Sarah's death, the Plumbs' daughters Marie and Lenita sued James; Marie for an accounting of his expenses and Lenita, who was a minor at the time, to have him removed as her guardian. In 1899, Plumb murdered Alexander Masterton, the seventy-two-year-old trustee of his wife's trust. Plumb's animosity toward Masterton was long-standing, stemming, in part, from Masterton's opposition to Plumb's marriage to Sarah because of Plumb's gambling activities. As the years had passed, Plumb had come to blame Masterton for his alienation from his wife Sarah and their children. Further complicating matters was Plumb's opposition to the marriage of his son James to Frances Anna Parsons Burton. While awaiting trial in New York City's Tombs, Plumb contracted erysipelas, a severe inflammatory condition caused by a hemolytic streptococcus infection. He was removed to Bellevue Hospital. His face and the underlying tissue of the head were initially affected and, despite warnings that the infection could reach the brain, Plumb refused all medication and died. [*The New York Times* June 27, 1895, p. 8; May 4, 1899, p. 1; May 7, 1899, p. 2; and June 6, 1899, p. 14.]

The estate was subsequently owned by their son James Ives Plumb, who continued to call it *Deer Range Farm*.

[See other Plumb entries for additional family information.]

In 1903, James Ives Plumb sold the estate to George Campbell Taylor and relocated to Islip.

The estate remained in the Taylor / Pyne family corporation until 1924 when it was confiscated by Robert Moses and became part of Heckscher State Park. [Harry W. Havemeyer, *Along the Great South Bay From Oakdale to Babylon: The Story of a Summer Spa 1840 to 1940* (Mattituck, NY: Amereon House, 1996), p. 135.]

**The house was demolished by Moses' Long Island State Park Commission. Portions of the house were salvaged, moved, and relocated into buildings in the Islip area.

Deer Range Farm

205

Poillon, John Edward (1848-1927)

Occupation(s):   industrialist -   partner, C. & R. Poillon Co. (Brooklyn shipyard which
also operated under the names Poillon Brothers and
C. & R. Poillon Steamboat Co.)*

Marriage(s):

Address: Clinton Avenue, Bay Shore
Name of estate:
Year of construction:
Style of architecture: Queen Anne
Architect(s):
Landscape architect(s):
House extant: unconfirmed
Historical notes:

   John Edward Poillon was the son of Cornelius Poillon, the co-founder of C. & R. Poillon, Company.
   John's daughter Gladys married Francis Guerrlich of Shippan Point, CT. His son Arthur married Winifred
Robinson of Colorado Springs, CO.
   *The company, formed in the early 19th century, was a major Brooklyn employer, employing, at one point,
over three hundred workers in its two Brooklyn shipyards. Before its demise in c. 1904, its records note
construction of over 175 yachts, steamships, transports, ferries, and Civil War gun boats. [Nannette Poillon.
"C & R Poillon: 19th Century Brooklyn Shipbuilders." By-The-Sea: The On-Line Boating Magazine, 2002.]

front facade, c. 1903

206

Post, Charles Alfred (1844-1921)

Occupation(s):   attorney
Civic Activism: fellow, Royal Astronomical Society, Great Britain

Marriage(s):   Marie Caroline de Trobriand (1845-1926)
                        - writer - *The Life and Memoirs of General Count de Trobriand*;
                             The Post Family, 1905

Address: Ocean Avenue, Bayport
Name of estate: *Strandhome*
Year of construction: 1880
Style of architecture: Shingle
Architect(s):   Isaac Henry Green II designed
                   the house (for W. R. Foster, Jr.)
                George Browne Post designed the
                 alterations (for C. A. Post)
Landscape architect(s):
House extant: no; demolished in 1950s
Historical notes:

    The house, originally named *Strandhome*, was built by William R. Foster, Jr.
    In 1888, *Strandhome* was purchased at public auction by the Produce Exchange Gratuity Fund which sold it in 1890 to Charles Alfred Post. Post continued to call the estate *Strandhome*.
    He was the son of Joel Browne Post of Manhattan. His brother, the noted architect George Browne Post, married Alice Stone. George Browne Post was on Ward McAllister's "Four Hundred" list, but Charles and Marie were omitted.
    Marie Caroline de Trobriand Post was the daughter of Baron Philippe Regis Denis de Keredern and Mary Mason Jones de Trobriand. Marie had previously been married to Albert Kintzing Post.
    Charles Alfred and Marie Caroline de Trobriand Post's daughter Beatrice married Duncan W. Candler. Their daughter Edith married Goelet Gallatin and resided in Blue Point.
    [See other Post entries for additional family information.]
    The estate was subsequently owned by Waldron Kintzing Post, who continued to call it *Strandhome*.
    Bernard Mannes Baruch, Sr. rented the house during the summers of 1915 and 1916.

Strandhome

Post, Charles Kintzing (d. 1974)

Occupation(s):   military -   lieutenant commander in command of a five-vessel task
                                                          force in the Fourth Fleet
                                        intelligence agent -   officer, Naval Intelligence during World War II

Marriage(s):   1918 – Caroline Knapp

Address: Ocean Avenue, Bayport
Name of estate: *Strandhome*
Year of construction: 1880
Style of architecture: Shingle
Architect(s):   Isaac Henry Green II designed
                                              the house (for W. R. Foster, Jr.)
                                        George Browne Post designed the
                                              alterations (for C. A. Post)
Landscape architect(s):
House extant: no; demolished in 1950s
Historical notes:

   The house, originally named *Strandhome*, was built by William R. Foster, Jr.
   In 1888, *Strandhome* was purchased at public auction by the Produce Exchange Gratuity Fund which sold it in 1890 to Charles Alfred Post. Post continued to call the estate *Strandhome*.
    It was subsequently owned by Waldron Kintzing Post, who also continued to call it *Strandhome*.
   After World War II, Charles Kintzing Post returned to Bayport and resided with his father Waldron at *Strandhome*.
   [See other Post entries for additional family information.]
   Caroline Knapp Post was the daughter of Harry Kearsarge and Caroline Burr Knapp, Sr., who resided at *Brookwood* in East Islip. Her brother Harry Kearsarge Knapp, Jr. married Elizabeth M. Mann and resided at *Creekside* in East Islip. Her brother Theodore inherited *Brookwood*.
   Bernard Mannes Baruch, Sr. rented *Strandhome* during the summers of 1915 and 1916.

Post, Henry

Occupation(s):   merchant -   iron

Marriage(s):   Caroline McLean

Address: Park Avenue, Babylon
Name of estate: *Postholme*
Year of construction: 1874
Style of architecture:
Architect(s):   George Browne Post designed
                                              the house (for H. Post)
Landscape architect(s):
House extant: no
Historical notes:

   The house, originally named *Postholme*, was built by Henry Post.
   The *Brooklyn Blue Book and Long Island Society Register, 1921* lists Henry Post as residing on Park Avenue in Babylon.
   Henry and Caroline McLean Post's daughter Caroline married Regis Henri Post, Sr. and resided at *Littlewood* in Bayport.

Post, Regis Henri, Sr. (1870-1944)

Occupation(s):	capitalist -	built and rented houses in Bayport area
	politician -	member, New York State Assembly, 1899-1900; chairman, Suffolk County Progressive Party
	diplomat -	auditor, Territory of Puerto Rico, 1903; secretary to the Governor of Puerto Rico, 1904; governor, Territory of Puerto Rico, 1907
	financier -	director, Oystermans National Bank, Sayville

Civic Activism: member, Volunteer American Ambulance Corp in France and Italy
during World War I;
secretary, American Society for Relief of French War Orphans,
1917-1918;
chief, Bayport Fire Department, 1900-1903;
president, Bayport School Board, 1898-1903

Marriage(s):   M/1 – 1895-div. 1922 – Caroline Beatrice Post (b. 1876)
M/2 – 1926-1931 – Leila Ellis McBirney (d. 1931)
M/3 – 1933-1944 – Marguerite Denys (d. 1963)

Address: Gillette Avenue, Bayport
Name of estate: *Littlewood*
Year of construction: 1896
Style of architecture: Shingle
Architect(s):   George Browne Post designed
the house (for R. H. Post, Sr.)
Landscape architect(s):
House extant: yes
Historical notes:

    The house, originally named *Littlewood*, was built by Regis Henri Post, Sr.
    He was the son of Albert Kintzing and Marie Caroline de Trobriand Post.
    Caroline Beatrice Post was the daughter of Henry and Caroline McLean Post, who resided at *Postholme* in Babylon.
    Regis Henri and Caroline Beatrice Post, Sr.'s son Regis Henri Post, Jr. married Julester H. Shrady, the daughter of Henry M. Shrady of Elmsford, NY.
    Marguerite Denys Post had previously been married to ____ Delagarde.
    [See other Post entries for additional family information.]
    The house was subsequently owned by John Pierre Zerega, Sr., who continued to call it *Littlewood*.

Littlewood

Post, Regis Henri, Sr. (1870-1944)

Occupation(s):	capitalist -	built and rented houses in Bayport area
	politician -	member, New York State Assembly, 1899-1900; chairman, Suffolk County Progressive Party
	diplomat -	auditor, Territory of Puerto Rico, 1903; secretary to the Governor of Puerto Rico, 1904; governor, Territory of Puerto Rico, 1907
	financier -	director, Oystermans National Bank, Sayville

Civic Activism: member, Volunteer American Ambulance Corp in France and Italy during World War I;
secretary, American Society for Relief of French War Orphans, 1917-1918;
chief, Bayport Fire Department, 1900-1903;
president, Bayport School Board, 1898-1903

Marriage(s): M/1 – 1895-div. 1922 – Caroline Beatrice Post (b. 1876)
M/2 – 1926-1931 – Leila Ellis McBirney (d. 1931)
M/3 – 1933-1944 – Marguerite Denys (d. 1963)

Address: Fairview Avenue, Bayport
Name of estate:
Year of construction: 1881
Style of architecture: Modified Second Empire
Architect(s):
Landscape architect(s):
House extant: no; destroyed by fire in 1940s
Historical notes:

The house, originally named *White House*, was built by Edward Edwards.
In 1883, it was purchased by John R. Ely.
Cyrus E. Staples purchased the house in 1890.
In 1902, Staples sold it to William Kintzing Post and his brother Regis H. Post, Sr., who, in turn, sold it to James H. Snedecor in 1925.
[See previous entry for additional family information.]

front facade

Post, Waldron Kintzing (1858-1955)

Occupation(s):	attorney - partner, Ward, Hayden, and Satterlee
	industrialist - director, Bigelow–Sanford Carpet Co.
	writer - *Harvard Stories*, 1893;
	Smith Brunt, 1899
Civic Activism:	a founder and president, Volunteer Fireman's Assoc. of Suffolk County;
	member, Bayport Fire Commission
Marriage(s):	1894-1939 – Mary Lawrence Perkins (1870-1939)
	- Civic Activism: chairman, Bayport Red Cross;
	chairman, Suffolk County Red Cross;
	secretary, Samaritan Home for the Aged

Address:	Ocean Avenue, Bayport
Name of estate:	*Strandhome*
Year of construction:	1880
Style of architecture:	Shingle
Architect(s):	Isaac Henry Green II designed
	the house (for W. R. Foster, Jr.)
	George Browne Post designed the
	alterations (for C. A. Post)

Landscape architect(s):
House extant: no; demolished in 1950s
Historical notes:

The house, originally named *Strandhome*, was built by William R. Foster, Jr.

In 1888, *Strandhome* was purchased at public auction by the Produce Exchange Gratuity Fund which sold it in 1890 to Charles Alfred Post. Post continued to call the estate *Strandhome*.

It was subsequently owned by Waldron Kintzing Post, who also continued to call it *Strandhome*.

Waldron Kintzing Post was the son of Albert Kintzing and Marie Caroline de Trobriand Post.

Mary Lawrence Perkins Post was the daughter of Charles L. and Elizabeth W. Perkins of Summit, NJ.

Waldron Kintzing and Mary Lawrence Perkins Post's daughter Mary married Viscount Gerard Vernon Wallop of Portsmouth, England, and, subsequently, John Howe of London, England. Their daughter Elizabeth married Kiliaen Van Rensselaer. Their son Charles married Caroline Knapp, the daughter of Harry Kearsarge and Caroline Burr Knapp, Sr., who resided at *Brookwood* in East Islip. Their son Robert married Margaret Lapsley of Pomfret, CT, and resided in Washington, DC. Their son Waldron, married Matilda Jellinghaus and resided in Westport, CT. Their son Landon married Janet Kirby and resided in Westport, CT. Their daughter Lina died at the age of twelve.

[See other Post entries for additional family information.]

Bernard Mannes Baruch, Sr. rented *Strandhome* during the summers of 1915 and 1916.

interior, c. 1950s

Post, William Kintzing

Occupation(s):

Marriage(s):

Address: Fairview Avenue, Bayport
Name of estate:
Year of construction: 1881
Style of architecture: Modified Second Empire
Architect(s):
Landscape architect(s):
House extant: no; destroyed by fire in 1940s
Historical notes:

    The house, originally named *White House*, was built by Edward Edwards.
    In 1883, it was purchased by John R. Ely.
    Cyrus E. Staples purchased the house in 1890.
    In 1902, Staples sold it to William Kintzing Post and his brother Regis H. Post, Sr., who, in turn, sold it to James H. Snedecor in 1925.

Powell, David B. (1821-1904)

Occupation(s):   financier -   president, National City Bank of Brooklyn;
                                     director, Phenix Insurance Company of Brooklyn;
                                     director, National Bank Deposit, NYC
            industrialist -   director, Consolidated Fireworks, Co.;
                                     director, Empire Sawmill Co.
            capitalist -   director, New York and New Jersey Telephone Co.

Marriage(s):

Address: Handsome Avenue, Sayville
Name of estate: *Cedarshore*
Year of construction: c. 1888
Style of architecture: Queen Anne
Architect(s):
Landscape architect(s):
House extant: no; destroyed by fire in 1916
Historical notes:

Cedarshore

    The house, originally named *Cedarshore*, was built by David B. Powell and his son Leander Treadwell Powell.
    David B. Powell was the son of David P. Powell.
    He correctly predicted that he would die on the seventeenth, which was the date his wife had died. [*The New York Times* September 18, 1904, p. 7.]
    [See following entry for additional Powell family information.]
    The estate was inherited by Leander's wife Rebecca. In 1912, Rebecca Powell sold it to George Alexander Morrison, who subdivided its property for a housing development and to build the Cedarshore Hotel.
    *In 1917, the Cedarshore Hotel was destroyed by fire. In 1924, the hotel was rebuilt by Morrison.
    In 1942, the hotel was purchased by the Herald Tribune Fresh Air Fund.
    In 1959, after going through several ownerships, the hotel, renamed the Bayview Plaza, was destroyed by fire.

Powell, Leander Treadwell (d. 1894)

Occupation(s):   attorney -   partner, Powell and Campbell

Marriage(s):   Rebecca Francis (1850-1929)

Address: Handsome Avenue, Sayville
Name of estate: *Cedarshore*
Year of construction: c. 1888
Style of architecture: Queen Anne
Architect(s):
Landscape architect(s):
House extant: no; destroyed by fire in 1916
Historical notes:

The house, originally named *Cedarshore*, was built by David B. Powell and his son Leander Treadwell Powell.

Leander and Rebecca Francis Powell's daughter Isabella married Dr. Clarence Sumner Elebash of Manhattan. Their daughter Ethel married Louis H. Delamater and relocated to Long Island's North Shore.
[See previous entry for additional family information and a history of the estate's ownership.]

Prince, John Dyneley, II (c. 1843-1883)

Occupation(s):   financier -   governor, New York Stock Exchange, 1871-1875;
                                partner, Prince and Whiteley (stock brokerage firm)

Marriage(s):   Anna Maria Morris
                - Civic Activism: member, board of governors, Trinity Sea Side Home,
                                      Great River (formerly, Sea Side Hospital for
                                      Sick Children)

Address: South Bay Avenue, Islip
Name of estate:
Year of construction: c. 1850
Style of architecture: Shingle
Architect(s):   Alfred Hopkins designed the
                     c. 1910 farm and garage
                     complex (for S. T. Peters, Sr.)*
Landscape architect(s):   Ellen Biddle Shipman
                     (for H. T. Peters, Sr.)
House extant: no; demolished in c. 1950
Historical notes:

The house was built by John Dyneley Prince II.
He was the son of John Dyneley and Mary Travers Prince, Sr.
Anna Maria Morris Prince was the daughter of Thomas H. Morris of Baltimore, MD.
John Dyneley and Anna Maria Morris Prince II's son John Dyneley Prince III married Adeline Loomis, the daughter of Dr. Alfred L. Loomis of Manhattan.
The estate was purchased by Samuel Twyford Peters, who enlarged the house and called it *Windholm Farm.*
It was inherited by his son Harry Twyford Peters, Sr., who continued to call it *Windholm Farm.*
*The barn complex still exists. It was converted into a residence by Mrs. Harry Twyford Peters.

Proctor, Cecil W.

Occupation(s):   politician - member, New York State Assembly

Marriage(s):

Address: 240 Green Avenue, Sayville
Name of estate:
Year of construction: c. 1919
Style of architecture:
Architect(s):
Landscape architect(s):
House extant: yes
Historical notes:

The *Long Island Society Register, 1929* lists Cecil W. Proctor as residing at 240 Green Avenue, Sayville.
His daughter Jane married George J. Schlehr, Jr. of Morrisville, NY.
The house was subsequently owned by the West Sayville automobile dealer P. J. Grady.

front facade, 2006

Purdy, Charles Robert (1859-1922)

Occupation(s):   capitalist - Manhattan real estate

Marriage(s):   Abbie Wilkinson (1866-1954)

Address: South Country Road, Bayport
Name of estate: *Edgemere*
Year of construction: c. 1883
Style of architecture: Shingle
Architect(s):
Landscape architect(s):
House extant: yes*
Historical notes:

The house, originally named *Edgemere*, was built by Charles Robert Purdy.
Abbie Wilkinson Purdy was the daughter of Dr. Wilkinson of Jersey City, NJ.
Charles Robert and Abbie Wilkinson Purdy's son Kenneth married Dorothy Cambern of Bayport.
Abbie Wilkinson Purdy sold the house to Robert H. Koehler.
*Koehler subdivided the estate's property for a housing development and cut the main house in half. The two halves of the house survive as numbers 78 and 94 Connetquot Road, Bayport, to which they were moved by Koehler.

front facade

Puzo, Mario (1920-1999)

Occupation(s):   writer - *The Dark Arena*, 1955;
                                  The Fortunate Pilgrim, 1965;
                                  The Godfather, 1969*;
                                  The Runaway Summer of Davie Shaw, 1966;
                                  The Godfather Papers and Other Confessions, 1971;
                                  The Sicilian, 1984;
                                  The Last Don, 1996;
                                  Omerta, 2000 (published posthumously)

Marriage(s):   1946-1978 – Erika Lina Broske (1921-1978)
                                  Carol Gino

Address: Manor Lane, West Bay Shore
Name of estate:
Year of construction:
Style of architecture:
Architect(s):
Landscape architect(s):
House extant: unconfirmed
Historical notes:

    Mario Puzo was born in NYC. His family lived above the railway yards, in the area known as "Hell's Kitchen." He was the son of a railway trackman and one of six children born to the immigrant family. Mario moved to Bay Shore in 1968.
    Mario and Erika Lina Broske Puzo had five children. Their daughter Dorothy Ann Puzo wrote and directed the 1987 film *Cold Steel*.
    Mario Puzo died in Bay Shore, where he had continued to live with Carol, his companion of twenty years.
    *He sold the motion picture rights for *The Godfather* to Paramount Pictures for $85,000. He and Francis Ford Coppola worked on the motion picture's script but, after a fifth rewrite, Puzo withdrew from the project because of differences of opinion with Coppola. Puzo and Coppola later collaborated on the motion picture scripts for *Godfather, Part II* and *Godfather, Part III*. Puzo was a collaborator on the scripts for *Earthquake*, *Superman I*, and, the sequel, *Superman II*.

Quinn, Michael

Occupation(s):

Marriage(s):

Address: Penataquit Avenue, Bay Shore
Name of estate:
Year of construction: c. 1880
Style of architecture: Queen Anne
Architect(s):
Landscape architect(s):
House extant: unconfirmed
Historical notes:

    The house, originally named *Seward*, was built by Chauncey E. Low.
    It was subsequently owned by Quinn.

Seaward, c. 1903

Ranft, Richard, Jr.

Occupation(s):   industrialist -   partner, Richard Ranft (manufacturer of piano
                                                supplies)

Marriage(s):   M/1 – Emma Kapp (d. 1899)
                       M/2 – 1900 – Hermine T. Krieg (d. 1958)

Address: South Country Road and Penataquit Avenue, Bay Shore
Name of estate:
Year of construction: c. 1900
Style of architecture: Mediterranean
Architect(s):
Landscape architect(s):
House extant: yes
Historical notes:

The house was built by Richard Ranft, Jr.

He was the son of Richard Ranft, Sr. of Treben, Germany. His sister Elizabeth married William Steinway, an heir to the Steinway piano fortune. His sister Martha married Major Canzler of the German Army.

Richard and Hermine T. Krief Ranft, Jr.'s daughter Herma married Robert Frasse Whitlock and, subsequently, ____ Schuck. Their daughter Ella M. married ____ Bartner.

In 2006, the house was converted into The Villas condominium complex.

side / front facade, 2006

Redmond, Roland (1845-1894)

Occupation(s):   capitalist -   William Redmond & Sons (importer)

Marriage(s):   1880-1894 – Helen C. Bulkey

Address: Ocean Avenue, Islip
Name of estate:
Year of construction:
Style of architecture:
Architect(s):
Landscape architect(s):
House extant: unconfirmed
Historical notes:

Roland Redmond rented the James Harvey Doxsee house.

He was the son of William Redmond of Manhattan. His sister Frances married Henry Beekman Livingston, Jr. and resided in Bay Shore.

Helen C. Bulkey Redmond was the daughter of Edward H. Bulkey, Sr. Her brother Edward H. Bulkey, Jr. married his nurse Margaret Stewart of St. Johns, New Brunswick, Canada. Helen's sister Katharine married Prescott Lawrence.

Reid, John Robert (1836-1902)

Occupation(s):   attorney - judge - Suffolk County
                            publisher - *Suffolk Democrat*, Babylon

Civic Activism: trustee, Babylon Common School;
                            a founder and president of board, Babylon Union Free School District;
                            a founder and member of board, State Normal School, Jamaica, NY

Marriage(s):   1857 – Angeline Davis

Address: Reid Avenue, Babylon
Name of estate: *The Towers*
Year of construction:
Style of architecture: Queen Anne
Architect(s):
Landscape architect(s):
House extant: unconfirmed
Historical notes:

front facade, c. 1941

    John Robert Reid was the son of James and Alma H. Reid of Middle Island.
    Angeline Davis Reid was from Poughkeepsie, NY.
    Judge John Robert and Mrs. Angeline Davis Reid's daughter M. Loreign Reid remained unmarried. Their son Willard, who married Ada Emeline Ketching, inherited the house.
    [See following entry for additional family information.]

Reid, Willard Placide (1862-1925)

Occupation(s):   attorney -   partner, Fishel and Reid, Babylon;
                                      partner, with Jacob Neu, in Brooklyn law firm
                       financier -   president, Terminal Bank;
                                          vice-president, Williamsburgh Trust Co.;
                                        second vice-president, Empire State Surety Co.
                       industrialist - secretary, Edison Portland Cement Co., Orange, NJ;
                                          treasurer, Reid Ice Co.
                       capitalist - director, Babylon & Oak Island Ferry Co.;
                                        director, Metropolitan Fire Proof and Storage Warehouse Co.;
                                        director, The Berry Realty Co.
                       politician - Democratic state committeeman of his assembly district, 1896
Civic Activism: trustee, Babylon Public Library

Marriage(s):   1891 – Ada Emeline Ketching

Address: Reid Avenue, Babylon
Name of estate: *The Towers*
Year of construction:
Style of architecture: Queen Anne
Architect(s):
Landscape architect(s):
House extant: unconfirmed
Historical notes:

    The *Brooklyn Blue Book and Long Island Society Register, 1918* lists Willard Placide and Ada E. Ketching Reid as residing at *The Towers* on Crescent Avenue, Babylon.
    He was the son of Judge John Robert and Mrs. Angeline Davis Reid, from whom he inherited the house.
    Ada Emeline Ketching Reid was the daughter of Jameson D. Ketching of New York.
    [See previous entry for additional family information.]

Remson, Jacob (1856-1901)

Occupation(s): attorney - judge
       politician - member, New York State Assembly, representing the
             18th district, 1900-1904;
             Assessor of Taxes, Brooklyn;
             Deputy Tax Commissioner, Brooklyn;
             deputy tax collector, United States Internal Revenue Service

Marriage(s): Annie P. Hubbard (1847-1926)
       - Civic Activism: anti-suffragist

Address: Little East Neck Road, Babylon
Name of estate: *The Harbor*
Year of construction:
Style of architecture:
Architect(s):
Landscape architect(s):
House extant: unconfirmed
Historical notes:

The *Brooklyn Blue Book and Long Island Society Register, 1918* lists Annie P. Hubbard Remsen as residing at *The Harbor* in Babylon.

Jacob W. Remsen was the son of Teunis Schenck Remsen of Brooklyn. His sister Anna married Jeremiah Rutger Van Brunt and resided in Brooklyn and at *Kitchawan* in Westchester, NY.

Remsen, Phoenix

Occupation(s): attorney

Marriage(s): M/1 – Sarah Louisa Wagstaff (d. 1907)
       M/2 – 1908 – Naomi Clark

Address: South Country Road, West Islip
Name of estate:
Year of construction:
Style of architecture:
Architect(s):
Landscape architect(s):
House extant: unconfirmed
Historical notes:

Sarah Louisa Wagstaff Remsen was the daughter of Dr. Alfred and Mrs. Sarah Platt DuBois Wagstaff, Sr., who resided at *Tahlulah* in West Islip. Her brother Alfred Wagstaff, Jr. married Mary Anderson Barnard and resided at *Opekeeping* in West Islip. Her brother Cornelius married Amy Colt and also resided in West Islip. Her sister Mary married Henry Gribble.

Phoenix and Sarah Louisa Wagstaff Remsen's son Alfred married Frances Condit, the daughter of Goodhall Condit of Jersey City, NJ. Their son The Reverend Henry Rutgers Remsen resided in Huntington. Their daughter Helen married Woodruff Sutton, Jr. of Babylon. Their son Cornelius married Ethel Folger White, the daughter of B. Ogden White.

Richard, Alfred Joseph (1909-2004)

Occupation(s):   merchant -   president and chairman of board, P. C. Richard & Son
                                               (fifty-store appliance and electronics chain, which
                                               now includes The Wiz*

Marriage(s):   Victoria _____ (d. 1997)

Address: 181 Otis Lane, West Bay Shore
Name of estate:
Year of construction:
Style of architecture:
Architect(s):
Landscape architect(s):
House extant: yes
Historical notes:

   *P. C. Richard & Son was founded in 1909 by Alfred's father Peter Christiaan Richard, who immigrated from The Netherlands in 1889 the age of eighteen.
   "A. J.," as Alfred was known, went to work in his father's Bensonhurst hardware store at the age of eight.

Ridgeway, James W. (d. 1910)

Occupation(s):   attorney -   Brooklyn District Attorney

Marriage(s):

Address: Handsome Avenue, Sayville
Name of estate:
Year of construction:
Style of architecture: Shingle
Architect(s):
Landscape architect(s):   Isaac Henry Green II designed
                               the house (for Ridgeway)
House extant: unconfirmed
Historical notes:

   The house was built by James W. Ridgeway.
   In 1897, Ridgeway sold the house to Elward Smith, Sr. Smith's widow married Robert Gibson Smith, with whom she continued to reside in the Sayville house.

front / side facade

Riggio, Frank Vincent (1906-1984)

Occupation(s):   industrialist -   president, Riggio Tobacco Corp.;
                                          director and vice-president, American Tobacco Co.

Marriage(s):   1931-1984 – Margaret Boughton (d. 1988)

Address: Saxon Avenue, Bay Shore
Name of estate: *Riggio House*
Year of construction: 1933
Style of architecture: Tudor
Architect(s):   William Hamilton Russell, Jr. designed
                          the house (for H. C. Sharp)

Landscape architect(s):
House extant: yes
Historical notes:

   The house, originally named *Millcreek*, was built by H. Cecil Sharp.
   In 1944, it was purchased from Mrs. Sharp by Riggio, who called it *Riggio House*.
   He was the son of Vincent and Antoinette Gallo Riggio, Sr. His sister Flavia married Montague Horace Hacket, the son of Horace Hacket of Brightwaters.
   Margaret Boughton Riggio was the daughter of H. Boughton of Manhattan. Mrs. Riggio was residing in the house at the time of her death.
   Frank Vincent and Margaret Boughton Riggio's son Vincent Riggio II married Katherine Penelope Knowlton, the daughter of James A. F. Knowlton of Babylon.
   In 1991, 9.68 acres and the 8,000-square-foot, nineteen-room house, with a seven-car garage, horse stable, guest cottage, and windmill, were for sale.

Robb, James (1871-1937)

Occupation(s):   industrialist -   vice-president, American Telephone and Telegraph Co.
                        military -   general, New York National Guard
Civic Activism: member, Emergency Relief Bureau, NYC (LaGuardia administration);
                        trustee, Berkeley Institute;
                        trustee, Veterans Association of 23rd Regiment

Marriage(s):   Elizabeth Donovan

Address: *[unable to determine street address]*, Sayville
Name of estate:
Year of construction:
Style of architecture:
Architect(s):
Landscape architect(s):
House extant: unconfirmed
Historical notes:

   The *Long Island Society Register, 1929* lists General James and Mrs. Elizabeth Donovan Robb as residing in Sayville.
   His sisters, Mrs. Helen Crawford and Mrs. John Ross, both resided in Scotland.
   James and Elizabeth Donovan Robb's daughter Helen married John Bernsee Catlin, the son of Rufus Olmstead Catlin of Brooklyn. John and Helen Catlin also resided in Brooklyn.

Robbins, Josiah

Occupation(s):   financier -   trustee, Patchogue Savings Bank
                                  politician -   unsuccessful Republican candidate for supervisor,
                                                        Town of Islip

Marriage(s):   Ella Blydenburgh

Address: South Country Road, Bay Shore
Name of estate:
Year of construction:
Style of architecture: Modified Victorian
Architect(s):
Landscape architect(s):
House extant: unconfirmed
Historical notes:

front facade, c. 1903

   In 1915, Robbins was accused of allegedly destroying ballots in a congressional election. [*The New York Times* December 30, 1915, p. 6.]
   Josiah and Ella Blydenburgh Robbins' son William married Martha Brewster and also resided in Bay Shore.

Robbins, William H., Sr. (1877-1943)

Occupation(s):   attorney -   partner, Robbins, Wells, and Walser
                                  financier -   a founder, president and chairman of board, First
                                                  National Bank & Trust Co. of Bay Shore;
                                                  director, Southside Bank of Bay Shore
Civic Activism: trustee, Southside Hospital, Bay Shore;
                                  member, Bay Shore School Board

Marriage(s):   Marietta Brewster (1876-1937)

Address: 69 Lawrence Lane, Bay Shore
Name of estate:
Year of construction: c. 1928
Style of architecture: Tudor
Architect(s):   Hart and Shape designed
                                  the house (for Robbins)
Landscape architect(s):
House extant: yes
Historical notes:

   The house was built by William H. Robbins, Sr.
   He was the son of Josiah and Ella Blydenburg Robbins of Bay Shore.
   Marietta Brewster Robbins was the daughter of Henry Brewster.
   William H. and Marietta Brewster Robbins, Sr.'s. daughter Eleanor married John A. Barringer.

Robert, Christopher Rhinelander, Jr. (1830-1898)

Occupation(s):   capitalist -   builder and owner La Rochelle, 57th Street, NYC
                                                   (apartment building)

Marriage(s):   M/1 – 1872-div. 1875 – *[unable to determine name of first wife]*
                                  M/2 – Julia Remington (d. 1924)

Address: south of Montauk Highway, Oakdale
Name of estate: *Peperidge Hall*
Year of construction: c. 1890
Style of architecture: French Chateau
Architect(s):   H. Edward Ficken designed
                                    and reassembled the house
                                    (for C. R. Robert, Jr.)*
Landscape architect(s):
House extant: no; demolished in 1940
Historical notes:

   The house, originally named *Peperidge Hall*, was built by Christopher Rhinelander Robert, Jr.
He was the son of Christopher Rhinelander and Anna Maria Shaw Robert, Sr. of Mastic.
Julia Remington Robert had previously been married to New England banker Charles Morgan.
   According to Julia, Robert's behavior in the last few days of his life was that of an "insane man." The
circumstances surrounding his death, in the Roberts' La Rochelle apartment, were, to say the least,
questionable. Julia testified that she was in the bathroom when she heard a shot and that she sent her maid to
notify the apartment manager, who entered Robert's room and found him dead with a pistol shot in the
temple and a pistol in his hand. The police were summoned with the statement that Mr. Robert had
committed suicide. The coroner accepted it as a suicide even though there were no powder burns on Robert's
temple, no autopsy was done, and there wasn't any record of Robert ever buying or owning a pistol. The
authorities seemed to be unconcerned that Robert had just signed a will a few months before his death
bequeathing his fortune to his wife. Robert's brother Frederick, who learned of Christopher's death in a
newspaper article, publicly called for an in-depth and rigorous investigation. The police ignored Frederick's
pleas and simply declared the death a suicide without ever performing an investigation. *[The New York Times
January 4, 1898, p. 4; January 29, 1898, p. 3; and January 30, 1898, p. 5.]*
   After Robert's death, Julia Remington Robert relocated to France, where she resided until her death.
   In 1896, Robert had sold *Peperidge Hall* to W. K. Aston, who unsuccessfully attempted to subdivide the
estate's property for a housing development in 1907.
   *The house's interior was from a chateau in Normandy, France, which Robert had brought to Long Island
and had had reassembled in his country house.

Peperidge Hall

Peperidge Hall interior

Peperidge Hall interior

Rolston, Roswell, G.

Occupation(s):   financier -   president, Farmer's Loan and Trust Co.
Civic Activism: trustee, American Museum of National History, NYC

Marriage(s):   Sarah E. Littell

Address: Deer Park Avenue, North Babylon
Name of estate: *Armagh*
Year of construction:
Style of architecture:
Architect(s):
Landscape architect(s):
House extant: unconfirmed
Historical notes:

   While riding on the Long Island Rail Road, Rolston suffered a stroke which left him paralyzed on his right side. [*The New York Times* April 4, 1897, p. 5.]
   Roswell G. and Sarah E. Littell Rolston's son Louis was a Manhattan attorney and partner in the firm of Turner, McClure, and Rolston. Their son William was a partner in the Manhattan stock brokerage firm of Rolston and Bass.

Roosevelt, John Ellis (1853-1939)

Occupation(s):   attorney - partner, Roosevelt and Henry;
                                           partner, Jones, Roosevelt, and Carley;
                                           partner, Roosevelt and Kobbe
                       capitalist - director, Broadway Improvement Co.

Marriage(s):   M/1 – 1879-1912 – Nannie Mitchell Vance (1860-1912)
                       M/2 – 1914-div. 1916* – Edith Hamersly (c. 1884-1943)

Address: South Country Road, Sayville
Name of estate: *Meadow Croft*
Year of Construction: 1891
Style of architecture: Colonial Revival
Architect(s):   Isaac Henry Green II designed
                       the c. 1891 alterations of the
                       19th century farmhouse
                       (for J. E. Roosevelt)

Landscape architect(s):
House extant: yes
Historical notes:

front facade, 2005

In 1890, John Ellis Roosevelt purchased the Woodward farm and combined its two farmhouses into one which became Roosevelt's country residence.

He was the son of Robert Barnwell and Elizabeth Ellis Roosevelt, Sr., who resided at *Lotos Lake*, Bayport.

Nannie Mitchell Vance Roosevelt was the daughter of New York City Acting-Mayor Samuel H. B. Vance. Nannie died of typhoid.

John Ellis and Nannie Mitchell Vance Roosevelt's daughter Anita, institutionalized for schizophrenia, never married. Their daughter Gladys married Fairman Rogers Dick and resided at *Apple Tree Hill* in Old Brookville. Gladys died when her horse stumbled at a fence during a competition at the Meadow Brook Hunt Club. Their daughter Jean married Philip James Roosevelt, Sr., the son of William Emlen and Christine Griffin Kean Roosevelt of *Yellowbanks* in Cove Neck, and resided at *Dolonar* in Cove Neck. Philip drowned when his dinghy capsized in Oyster Bay. Philip's wife Jean found his body on the beach near *Dolonar*.

Edith Hamersly Roosevelt was the daughter of Louis Randolph and Mary Palmer Hamersly, Sr. She had previously been married to United States Navy Paymaster Henry E. Biscoe. Her sister Lilie married Robert Barnwell Roosevelt, Jr. and, then, Rear Admiral Charles Edward Courtney. Her brother Louis H. Hamersly, Jr. married May Harris, the daughter of Mrs. Stephen Perry Cox of Bayport. Her sister May married Roland I. Curtin and, subsequently, Thorwald A. Solberg.

*The notorious Roosevelt divorce trial was a very public affair. Edith was the first to file for divorce, alleging that John had, on several occasions, struck her, grabbed her about the neck, threatened her with violence, and used insulting epithets when referring to her. John unsuccessfully countered by filing for an annulment, claiming the marriage had never been consummated. Tearfully, John testified about his happy first marriage. He sobbed as he stated that he still loved Edith. John's brother Robert Barnwell Roosevelt, Jr. testified that John had told him that he was content with his marriage to Edith. Robert further testified that he was present during an occasion when John had verbally abused Edith. John countered by testifying that Robert's testimony about John's contented marriage to Edith was a lie, that Robert had a weak character, was under the domination of his strong-willed wife Lilie, and financially supported virtually the entire Hamersly family. John was exonerated by the court of all charges against him and won the divorce case. [*The Washington Post* October 31, 1915, p. 4; November 13, 1915, p. 3; February 16, 1916, p. 4; March 12, 1916, p. 5; and March 31, 1916, p. 4; *The New York Times* November 13, 1915, p. 14; March 12, 1916, p. 20; June 7, 1916, p. 9; June 8, 1916, p. 10; and June 27, 1916, p. 11.] Edith never remarried.

[See other Roosevelt entries for additional family information.]

The estate was inherited by Roosevelt's daughter Jean, who sold it to Suffolk County.

The house, which has been conscientiously restored by the county, Sayville Historical Society, and the Bayport Heritage Association, is on the National Register of Historic Places and is open to the public as the Sans Souci Lakes County Nature Preserve.

Roosevelt, Robert Barnwell, Jr. (1866-1929)

Occupation(s):   capitalist -   owned a Sayville yacht basin and marine supply
                                     company*;
                                   extensive real estate investments

Marriage(s):   M/1 – 1890-1894 – Grace Guernsey Woodhouse (1867-1894)
                   M/2 – 1898-1929 – Lilie Hamersly (b. 1887)

Address: off South Country Road, Sayville
Name of estate: *The Lilacs*
Year of construction: c. 1899
Style of architecture: Modified Shingle
Architect(s):   Isaac Henry Green II
                     designed the house for
                     (R. B. Roosevelt, Jr.)
Landscape architect(s):
House extant: no: demolished in c. 1954
Historical notes:

   The house, originally named *The Lilacs*, was built by Robert Barnwell Roosevelt, Jr.
   He was the son of Robert Barnwell and Elizabeth Ellis Roosevelt, Sr., who resided at *Lotos Lake* in
Bayport.
   Grace Guernsey Woodhouse Roosevelt was the daughter of Lorenzo G. and Emma Arrowsmith
Woodhouse.
   Robert Barnwell and Grace Guernsey Woodhouse Roosevelt, Jr.'s daughter Olga married Dr. Breckenridge
Baye and, subsequently, Sidney Graves, with whom she resided in Washington, DC.
   Lilie Hamersly Roosevelt was the daughter of Louis Randolph and Mary Palmer Hamersly, Sr. Lilie
subsequently married Rear Admiral Charles Edward Courtney. Her brother Louis married May Harris, the
daughter of Mrs. Stephen Perry Cox of Bayport. Her sister Edith married Henry E. Biscoe and, subsequently,
John Ellis Roosevelt, with whom she resided at *Meadow Croft* in Sayville. Her sister May married Roland I.
Curtin, and, subsequently, Thorwald A. Solberg.
   Robert Barnwell and Lilie Hamersly Roosevelt, Jr.'s daughter Lilie eloped with James Lee, the son of
James S. Lee of Boston, MA, and resided in Washington, DC. She later married Hugh O'Donnell and,
subsequently, the first secretary of the British Embassy in Washington, DC, Christopher Bramwell, the son of
Frederick Charles Bramwell, the Clerk of The Journals in the British House of Commons. Robert and Lilie
Roosevelt's son Robert Barnwell Roosevelt III died at the age of twenty-two, when he was struck by a bus.
He had married Virginia Lee Minor, the daughter of George A. and Jennie Prince Minor. Robert and
Virginia's son Robert Barnwell Roosevelt IV was killed in 1944 when his plane crashed into the China Sea.
Virginia subsequently married Arthur Percy Jones.
   Robert Barnwell Roosevelt, Jr. was estranged from his brother John Ellis Roosevelt, despite the fact that
they were married to sisters. A tall "spite" fence topped with jagged pieces of broken glass and barbed wire
separated their adjoining estates. [Stephen Birmingham, *America's Secret Aristocracy* (Boston: Little Brown & Co., 1987),
p 124.] The animosity between Robert and John stemmed from Robert's attempt to suppress a codicil in their
father's will, which had been given to John on their father's deathbed. The relationship further deteriorated
with the friction generated between Robert and John's first wife and John's testimony at Robert's divorce
trial. [*The New York Times* February 16, 1916, p. 22 and March 12, 1916, p. 20.]
   [See other Roosevelt entries for additional family information.]
   The estate was inherited by Roosevelt's daughter Lilie, who sold it to a real estate developer in 1954. The
developer demolished the house.
   *Roosevelt's Sayville yacht basin and marine supply company was later owned by John Pierre Zerega, Sr.
of Bayport. [*The New York Times* May 31, 1936, p. S5.]

Roosevelt, Robert Barnwell, Sr. (1829-1906)

Occupation(s):   attorney

publisher -   owner and editor, *New York Citizen* (a political newspaper)

capitalist -   trustee, Brooklyn Bridge

politician -   congressman from Manhattan, 1871-1873;

a founder and president, New York Fisheries (which became New York State Department of Environmental Conservation)

diplomat -   United States Ambassador to The Netherlands

writer -   *Game Fish of the Northern States of America*, 1862; *The Game Birds of the Coast and Lakes of the Northern States of America*; *The Striped Bass, Trout, and Black Bass of the Northern States*, 1866; *Superior Fishing*, 1865; *The South Bay of Long Island*; *Game Fish of the Northern States of America and the British Provinces*; *Love and Luck: The Story of a Summer's Loitering On The Great South Bay*, 1887

Civic Activism: president, New York Association for the Protection of Game;

advocate, organic gardening;

advocate, protection of wildlife;

president, Founders and Patriots;

president, Holland Society

Marriage(s):   M/1 – 1850-1887 – Elizabeth Thorn Ellis (1830-1887)

M/2 – 1888-1902 – Marion Theresa O'Shea (1849-1902)

(aka Mrs. Marion T. Fortescue)*

Lotos Lake, sketch by Henry N. Betemann, 1958

Address: McConnell Avenue, Bayport

Name of estate: *Lotos Lake*

Year of construction: c. 1873

Style of architecture: Eclectic with Italianate elements

Architect(s):

Landscape architect(s):

House extant: no destroyed by fire in 1958**

Historical notes:

In 1873, Robert Barnwell Roosevelt, Sr. purchased the two-hundred-acre farm of Daniel Lane and remodeled the farmhouse into his country residence *Lotos Lake*.

He was the son of Cornelius Van Shaach and Margaret Barnhill Roosevelt, Sr. of Manhattan. His brother Theodore, the father of President Theodore Roosevelt, married Martha Bullock and resided at *Tranquility* in Oyster Bay Cove. His brother Silas married Mary West. His brother James married Elizabeth Norris Emlen. His brother Cornelius Van Shaach Roosevelt, Jr. married Laura Horton Porter.

Elizabeth Thorn Ellis Roosevelt was the daughter of John French and Elizabeth Glen Thorn Ellis of Manhattan.

Robert Barnwell and Elizabeth Thorn Ellis Roosevelt, Sr.'s son Robert Barnwell Roosevelt, Jr., who resided at *The Lilacs* in Sayville, married Grace Guernsey Woodhouse and, subsequently, Lilie Hamersly. Their son John Ellis Roosevelt, who married Nannie Mitchell Vance and, subsequently, Edith Hamersly, resided at *Meadow Croft* in Sayville. Their daughter Margaret married August Van Horne Kimberly and resided in Chicago, IL.

[See Fortescue entry for information about Roosevelt's concurrent family.]

Roosevelt purchased garish green gloves for his numerous mistresses at A. T. Stewart Department Store in Manhattan. His friends made a point of looking for the gloves while strolling Fifth Avenue and Central Park.

*The estate was subsequently owned by Roosevelt's illegitimate son Granville Roland Fortescue, who called it *Wildholme*.

In 1953, the house and its furnishings were severely vandalized.

**In 1954, it was sold to real estate developer Maurice Babash. While Babash was demolishing the house, it was destroyed by fire.

Rothschild, Simon Frank (1861-1936)

Occupation(s):   financier -   member, F. and A. Rothschild (private investment banking firm founded by his father)

                                   merchant -   president and chairman of board, Abraham & Straus Department Store (which merged into Federated Department Stores, Inc.); president, Federated Department Stores, Inc.

Civic Activism: director, Brooklyn Academy of Music;
vice-president, Brooklyn Federation of Jewish Charities;
a founder and chairman of board, Downtown Brooklyn Association;
director, Better Business Bureau of Brooklyn;
president, Hebrew Education Society;
director, Hebrew Orphan Asylum of Brooklyn;
director, Society for the Prevention of Cruelty to Children of Brooklyn

Marriage(s):   1890-1927 – Lillian Abraham (d. 1927)

Address: Saxon Avenue, Bay Shore
Name of estate:
Year of construction: 1903
Style of architecture: Mediterranean
Architect(s):
Landscape architect(s):
House extant: no
Historical notes:

    The house was built by Simon Frank Rothschild.

    The *Brooklyn Blue Book and Long Island Society Register, 1918* lists Simon Frank and Lillian Abraham Rothschild as residing in Bay Shore. The *Brooklyn Blue Book and Long Island Society Register, 1921* lists the Rothschilds as residing at *The Hummocks* in Larchmont, NY.

    He was the son of Frank and Amanda B. Rothschild of Brooklyn.

    Lillian Abraham Rothschild was the daughter of the co-founder of Abraham and Straus Department Store, Abraham Abraham. Her sister Edith married Percy S. Straus and resided in Red Bank, NJ. Her sister Florence married Edward Charles Blum and resided at *Shore Acres* in Bay Shore.

    Simon Frank and Lillian Abraham Rothschild's son Walter married Carola Therese Warburg, the daughter of Felix M. and Frieda Schiff Warburg of Manhattan. Carola's brother Gerald Felix Warburg resided at *Box Hill Farm* in Brookville.

front facade

Rubinstein, Ira

Occupation(s):   merchant - president, Cheap John's (discount store chain)

Marriage(s):   Denise ____

Address: Suydam Lane, Bayport
Name of estate: *Cheap John's Estate*
Year of construction: 1992
Style of architecture: 20th century Contemporary
Architect(s):
Landscape architect(s):
House extant: yes
Historical notes:

   The house, originally named *Cheap John's Estate*, was built by Ira Rubinstein.
   In 1987, Rubinstein purchased the former Suydam / Liebman estate *Edgewater*, demolished the house, and build a new house on the site.
   In 1998, the nineteen-room, 13,000-square-foot house, with a pool house and three-car garage on 2.9 acres, was for sale. The asking price was $2 million; the annual taxes were $37,072.

Russell, William Hamilton, Jr. (1896-1958)

Occupation(s):   architect - partner, with George W. Clinton, Clinton and Russell
                                         [See appendix for South Shore commissions.]
Civic Activism: president, Municipal Art Society of New York City, 1952

Marriage(s):   M/1 – 1918 – Marie G. Johnson (1896-1977)
                            M/2 – 1937 – Emma Muller

Address: off Maple Avenue, Islip
Name of estate:
Year of construction: 1928
Style of architecture: Modified Mediterranean
Architect(s):   William Hamilton Russell, Jr.
                               designed his own house
Landscape architect(s):
House extant: yes
Historical notes:

   The house was built by William Hamilton Russell, Jr.
   Marie G. Johnson Russell was the daughter of Bradish and Amiee E. J. Gaillard Johnson, Jr. of *Woodland* in East Islip. Her brother Aymar, who inherited *Woodland*, married Marion K. Hoffman. Her brother Bradish Gaillard Johnson, Sr. married Emma M. Grima and resided in Islip. Her brother Enfin also resided in Islip. Marie subsequently married Gordon Crothers, with whom she resided at *La Casetta* in Islip.
   William Hamilton and Marie G. Johnson Russell, Jr.'s daughter Amiee married Don Cino Tomaso Corsini, the eldest son of Don Emmanuele and Donna Maria Carolina Corsini of Florence, Italy. Their daughter Joan married Malcolm Scollary Low, the son of Benjamin R. C. Low of Manhattan. Their son The Reverend William Hamilton Russell III married Joan Schildhauer, the daughter of Clarence Henry Schildhauer of *White Oak* in Owings Mills, MD, Diane Sawyer Fenton, and, subsequently, Elizabeth Buck Truslow, the daughter of Francis Adams and Elizabeth Auchincloss Jennings Truslow of *The Point* in Laurel Hollow.
   Emma Muller Russell had previously been married to ____ Wartman.
   In 1954, William Hamilton and Emma Muller Russell, Jr. were residing at The Piping Rock Club in Lattingtown.

Ryan, John T. (1871-1901)

Occupation(s):	capitalist - builder
	politician - unsuccessful Democratic candidate for New York State Assembly

Marriage(s): 1895-1901 – Helen M. Oldner

Address: South Country Road, Bay Shore
Name of estate:
Year of construction:
Style of architecture: Shingle
Architect(s):
Landscape architect(s):
House extant: unconfirmed
Historical notes:

He was the son John F. Ryan.

front facade, c. 1903

Schieren, Charles Adolph, Sr. (1842-1915)

Occupation(s):	politician - mayor, Brooklyn, 1894-1895 (prior to its incorporation into NYC)
	industrialist - a founder and president, Charles A. Schieren & Co. (one of the country's largest leather tanneries/belting manufacturers); trustee, Holstein Extract Co.; trustee, Dixie Tanning Co.
	financier - a founder, Leather National Bank, Brooklyn; president, Germania Bank of Brooklyn; trustee, Nassau National Bank
Civic Activism:	president, Brooklyn Academy of Music; member, advisory board, Brooklyn Y. M. C. A.; trustee, Union for Christian Work; director, Society for the Prevention of Cruelty to Children; vice-president, Brooklyn Institute of Arts and Sciences

Marriage(s): 1865-1915 – Marie Louise Bramm (1842-1915)*

Address: Ocean Avenue, Islip
Name of estate: *Mapleton*
Year of construction: c. 1890
Style of architecture: Shingle
Architect(s): Isaac Henry Green II designed the house (for C. A. Schieren, Sr.)
Landscape architect(s): Olmstead
House extant: no; demolished in 1979**
Historical notes:

west facade, c. 1908

The house, originally named *Mapleton*, was built by Charles Adolph Schieren, Sr.

Charles Adolph and Marie Louise Bramm Schieren, Sr.'s son Harrie married Alice Unkles and resided in Montclair, NJ. Their daughter married A. T. Mathews. Their son George married Blanche Mabelle Barker and resided at *Beachleigh* in Kings Point.

*Mrs. Schieren was the principle beneficiary of her husband's will. Because she died one day after Charles, his bequest was subject to a second inheritance tax at her death. [*The New York Times* March 18, 1915, p. 20.]

The house was purchased in 1926 by Kimball Chase Atwood, Jr., who continued to call it *Mapleton*.

**The garage, stable, and caretaker's apartment are extant and are currently private residences. The estate's carriage house is also extant. It was moved to Frederic Lawrence Atwood's property.

Scully, Charles B. (1896-1959)

Occupation(s):   capitalist -   owner, camp for boys, East Otis, MA

Civic Activism: chairman of recreation, Town of Islip;
director, first aid, water safety, and accident prevention, New York
         Chapter of American Red Cross;
trustee, National Board of Campfire Girls

Marriage(s):   Adeline Hathaway Weekes (d. 1984)
  - Civic Activism: *

Address: South Bay Avenue, Islip

Name of estate: *Wereholme*

Year of construction: c. 1917

Style of architecture: Neo-French Manor

Architect(s):   Grosvenor Atterbury designed the house
   (for H. H. Weekes)

Landscape architect(s):

House extant: yes

Historical notes:

    The house, originally named *Wereholme*, was built by Harold Hathaway Weekes.

    His wife, the former Louisine Peters, subsequently married Alexander Tcherepnin, with whom she continued to reside at *Wereholme*.

    Harold Hathaway and Louisine Peters Weekes' daughter Adaline, who inherited *Wereholme*, married Charles B. Scully and resided at the estate. Adaline subsequently married Count Philip Orssich of Denkendorf bei Stuttgart, Germany.

    *In 1984, Mrs. Scully, who had divorced the count and reverted to the surname Scully, bequeathed the house to the National Audubon Society.

    In 2004, the estate was purchased by Suffolk County and is now the county's Environmental Interpretive Center.

rear facade, 1991

Seaman, Frank

Occupation(s):   industrialist -   Brooklyn distiller

Marriage(s):

Address: Bayport Avenue, Bayport
Name of estate:
Year of construction:
Style of architecture: Victorian
Architect(s):
Landscape architect(s):
House extant: no
Historical notes:

    In 1887, Seaman sold the house to John McKee.

Sharp, H. Cecil (1895-1944)

Occupation(s):   capitalist -   member, Automatic Electric Co.

Marriage(s):   1929-1944 – Ruth Lawrence Carroll

Address: Saxon Avenue, Bay Shore
Name of estate: *Millcreek*
Year of construction: 1933
Style of architecture: Tudor
Architect(s):   William Hamilton Russell, Jr. designed
                          the house (for H. C. Sharp)
Landscape architect(s):
House extant: yes
Historical notes:

    Sharp demolished the Daniel D. Conover house and built a new house on the site, which he called *Millcreek*.

    The *Social Register, Summer 1937* lists H. Cecil and Ruth L. Carroll Sharp as residing at *Millcreek* in Islip [Bay Shore].

    He was the son of Hamlet C. Sharp of Maysville, NY.

    Ruth Lawrence Carroll Sharp was the daughter of Anson Carroll. She had previously been married to Eben S. Draper of Massachusetts. After Cecil's death, Mrs. Sharp relocated to Connecticut.

    In 1944, the house was purchased by Frank Vincent Riggio, who called it *Riggio House*.

    In 1991, 9.68 acres and the 8,000-square-foot, nineteen-room house, with a seven-car garage, horse stable, guest cottage, and windmill, were for sale.

rear facade, 2005

Shea, David J.

Occupation(s):   industrialist -   salesman for cash register company

Marriage(s):   1928 – Maude Virginia Jones (1885-1977)

Address: 71 Benson Avenue, Sayville
Name of estate: *Wyndemoor*
Year of construction: c. 1910
Style of architecture: Modified Colonial Revival
Architect(s):   Isaac Henry Green II
                              designed the house
                              (for W. R. Simonds)
Landscape architect(s):
House extant: yes
Historical notes:

front facade, 2005

    The house, originally named *Wyndemoor*, was built by Frank Smith Jones for his daughter Henrietta and son-in-law William Robinson Simonds.
    Henrietta later sold the house to her sister Maude Virginia Jones Westin, who subsequently married Shea. The Sheas continued to call it *Wyndemoor*.
    The house was then purchased by Elwell Palmer, who moved it to Benson Avenue.

Shea, David J.

Occupation(s):   industrialist -   salesman for cash register company

Marriage(s):   1928 – Maude Virginia Jones (1885-1977)

Address: Handsome Avenue, Sayville
Name of estate: *Beechwold*
Year of construction: 1903
Style of architecture: Shingle
Architect(s):   Isaac Henry Green II designed
                              the main residence, gatehouse,
                              and 1905 playhouse. The latter
                              included a bowling alley and
                              billiard room (for F. S. Jones)
Landscape architect(s):
House extant: no; destroyed by fire in 1957*
Historical notes:

gatehouse, c. 1908

    The house, originally named *Beechwold*, was built by Frank Smith Jones.
    It was inherited by his daughter Maude, who married Clarence Frederick Westin, Sr. and, subsequently, David J. Shea. The Sheas resided in the estate's gatehouse.
    In 1945, the estate was purchased by Elwell Palmer, who sold it to Dr. Daniel McLaughlin in 1949.
    *The gatehouse and playhouse are extant. The gatehouse is located at 254 Handsome Avenue and the playhouse is at 96 Benson Avenue.

232

Shea, Timothy J., Sr. (1887-1933)

Occupation(s):   attorney -   New York State Assistant Attorney General, in charge
                                of the state's Anti-Stock Fraud Bureau;
                                member, Dykman, Oeland and Kuhn;
                                member, Cullen and Dykman
                merchant - chairman of board, National Bellas Hess & Co.* (mail
                                order clothing firm which merged with National
                                Coat and Suit Co.)

Marriage(s):   Gertrude Scanlan (d. 1956)

Address: Garner Avenue, Bay Shore
Name of estate: *O'Conee*
Year of construction: c. 1930
Style of architecture: Tudor
Architect(s):   James Dwight Baum designed
                      the house (for T. J. Shea, Sr.)

Landscape architect(s):
House extant: yes
Historical notes:

The house, originally named *O'Conee*, was built by
Timothy J. Shea, Sr.
*National Bellas Hess & Co. was founded by Harry
Bellas Hess, who lived at *The Cedars* on New York
Avenue, Huntington Station. Hess' firm was the third
largest mail order company in the country.

front facade, c. 1931

Shortland, Thomas Francis (1856-1918)

Occupation(s):

Marriage(s):   Anita Ketcham (d. 1923)

Address: 55 Crescent Avenue, Babylon
Name of estate:
Year of construction   c. 1905
Style of architecture: Modified Queen Anne
Architect(s):
Landscape architect(s):
House extant: yes
Historical notes:

Thomas Francis Shortland was the son of Thomas S. and
Charlotte A. Luff Shortland of Brooklyn. His sister Maude
married Albert H. Lugalla of Brooklyn. His sister Florence
married Isaac O. Horton, Jr. of Brooklyn.
Anita Ketcham Shortland was the daughter of E. B. and
Mary C. Ketcham.
Thomas Francis and Anita Ketcham Shortland's daughter
Hazel died at the age of twenty-eight.

front facade, 2006

233

Simonds, William Robinson (1878-1933)

Occupation(s):	financier - member, Robert P. Marshall (stock brokerage firm); partner, Blagden and Simonds (stock brokerage firm)
Marriage(s):	1903-1933 – Henrietta Louise Jones (d. 1936)

Address: 71 Benson Avenue, Sayville
Name of estate: *Wyndemoor*
Year of construction: c. 1910
Style of architecture: Modified Colonial Revival
Architect(s):   Isaac Henry Green II
                       designed the house
                       (for W. R. Simonds)
Landscape architect(s):
House extant: yes
Historical notes:

Wyndemoor

    The house, originally named *Wyndemoor*, was built by Frank Smith Jones for his daughter Henrietta and son-in-law William Robinson Simonds.

    The *Long Island Society Register, 1929* lists William Robinson and Henrietta Louise Jones Simonds as residing in Southampton.

    The Simondses' daughter Marjorie married William M. Duryea, the son of Walter B. Duryea of Manhattan.

    Henrietta later sold the house to her sister Maude Virginia Jones Westin, who subsequently married David J. Shea. The Sheas continued to call it *Wyndemoor*.

    The house was then purchased by Elwell Palmer, who moved it to Benson Avenue.

Slote, Alonzo (1829-1901)

Occupation(s):   merchant - partner, Tredwell & Slote (clothing firm)
                               financier - director, Firemen's Insurance Co.;
                                             vice-president, Wallabout Bank;
                                             trustee, People's Trust Co.;
                                           director, Brooklyn Life Insurance Co.;
                                         director, National Shoe and Leather Bank
                               capitalist - director, Brooklyn City Railroad

Marriage(s):

Address: Saxon Avenue, Bay Shore
Name of estate:
Year of construction:
Style of architecture:
Architect(s):
Landscape architect(s):
House extant: unconfirmed
Historical notes:

    Alonzo Slote was the son of Daniel and Anna Slote, Sr. of Brooklyn and the first cousin of Duchess de Arcos. His brother Daniel also resided on Saxon Avenue.

    [See following entry for additional family information.]

Slote, Daniel, Jr. (d. 1882)

Occupation(s):	publisher - president, Slote, Woodman & Co.; president, Daniel Slote & Co.
Civic Activism:	member, New York Board of Education
Marriage(s):	c. 1867-1882 – ____ Griffiths
Address:	Saxon Avenue, Bay Shore
Name of estate:	
Year of construction:	
Style of architecture:	
Architect(s):	
Landscape architect(s):	
House extant: unconfirmed	
Historical notes:	

Daniel Slote, Jr. is reputed to have been the model for the character "Dan" in Mark Twain's *Innocents Abroad*. [*The New York Times* February 14, 1882, p. 5.] His sister Sarah married John F. Wood and resided in Huntington.

Slote's wife was the daughter of Alderman James Griffiths.

[See previous entry for additional family information.]

Smith, Charles Robinson (1855-1930)

Occupation(s):	attorney - partner, Smith and Martin
	industrialist - a founder and vice president, General Chemical Co. (later, Allied Chemical & Dye Co.); director, Pitnam Sewing Co.
	capitalist - director, Wilhelms Realty Co.; director, Sackett & Wilhelms Lithographing & Printing Co.; director, Timmis Lithographing Co.; director, U. S. Aluminum Printing Plate Co.
	writer - magazine articles on World War I and its aftermath
Civic Activism:	director, Austin Fox Riggs Foundation (for treatment of psychoneurotic patients)
Marriage(s):	1889-1930 – Jeannie Porter Steele

Address:	80 Montgomery Avenue, Bay Shore	
Name of estate:		
Year of construction:	c. 1890	
Style of architecture:	Modified Shingle	
Architect(s):		
Landscape architect(s):		
House extant: yes		
Historical notes:		*side / front facade, c. 1894*

The house was built by Charles Robinson Smith.

The *Brooklyn Blue Book and Long Island Society Register, 1918* lists the Smiths as residing in Manhattan. He was the son of Edwin and Jane Townsend Mather Smith.

Jennie Porter Steele Smith was the daughter of William Porter Steele of Manhattan.

Charles Robinson and Jennie Porter Steele Smith's daughter Gertrude remained unmarried. Their daughter Hilda married Lyman Beecher Stowe, the grandson of Harriet Beecher Stow.

The house was subsequently owned by Edward Gordon.

The fifteen-room house, with nine bedrooms, six fireplaces, and five-and-a-half bathrooms, was for sale in 2006. The asking price was $1,490,000; the annual taxes were $18,055.

Smith, Elward, Jr. (1895-1947)

Occupation(s):   capitalist -   real estate
Civic Activism: member, Town of Islip Planning Board

Marriage(s):   1928-1947 – Ella Bailey (1897-1957)

Address: Green Avenue, Sayville
Name of estate:
Year of construction:
Style of architecture:
Architect(s):
Landscape architect(s):
House extant: unconfirmed
Historical notes:

Elward Smith Jr. was the son of Elward and Frances Cairns Smith, Sr. of Sayville.
Ella Bailey Smith was the daughter of Joseph Bailey of Patchogue.
[See following entry for additional family information.]

Smith, Elward, Sr. (1835-1900)

Occupation(s):   architect
                           capitalist -   builder
                           politician -   New York City Fire Commissioner

Marriage(s):   Frances Cairns (1856-1942)

Address: Handsome Avenue, Sayville
Name of estate:
Year of construction:
Style of architecture: Shingle
Architect(s):   Isaac Henry Green II designed
                           the house (for Ridgeway)
Landscape architect(s):
House extant: unconfirmed
Historical notes:

The house was built by James W. Ridgeway.
In 1897, Elward Smith, Sr. purchased the house from Ridgeway.
Frances Cairns Smith subsequently married Robert Gibson Smith, with whom she resided in the Handsome Avenue house.

Elward and Frances Cairns Smith, Sr.'s daughter Marjorie died at the age of twenty-one. Their son Irving was killed in World War I. Their son Elward Smith, Jr. married Ella Bailey and resided in Sayville. Their son Jewett married Virginia Woodhull Otto and also resided in Sayville. Their daughter Frances married Admiral Harry Alexander Baldridge and resided in Sayville. Their daughter Laurie married Andrew Perry de Forest Allgood and also resided in Sayville.

front facade

236

Smith, Fred D. (1866-1953)

Occupation(s):   financier -   director, Oysterman's National Bank of Sayville
                                   naval architect -   designed Great South Bay scooters
Civic Activism: chief, Bayport Volunteer Fire Department

Marriage(s):

Address: Fairview Avenue, Bayport
Name of estate:
Year of construction:
Style of architecture:
Architect(s):
Landscape architect(s):
House extant: unconfirmed
Historical notes:

    His son Hervey Garret Smith resided in Sayville.
    [See following entry for additional family information.]

Smith, Hervey Garret

Occupation(s):   artist
Civic Activism: a founder, Long Island Maritime Museum, West Sayville, 1966

Marriage(s):

Address: 76 Hampton Street, Sayville
Name of estate:
Year of construction:
Style of architecture:
Architect(s):
Landscape architect(s):
House extant: unconfirmed
Historical notes:

    Hervey Garret Smith was the son of Fred D. Smith of Bayport.
    [See previous entry for additional family information.]

Smith, Jewett Holt

Occupation(s):   capitalist -   builder

Marriage(s):   1926 – Virginia Woodhull Otto (1900-1974)
                           - capitalist -   real estate broker
                           publisher -   owner, *Suffolk Citizen*
                           Civic Activism: secretary, Episcopal Diocese of Long Island;
                                                  a founder, Long Island Women's Organization
                                                    of Democratic Party;
                                                a founder, Sayville Historical Society

Address: *[unable to determine street address]*, Sayville
Name of estate:
Year of construction:
Style of architecture:
Architect(s):
Landscape architect(s):
House extant: unconfirmed
Historical notes:

    Jewett Holt Smith was the son of Elward and Frances Cairns Smith, Sr. of Sayville.
    Virginia Woodhull Otto Smith was the daughter of Thomas N. and Julia Otto of Sayville.
    [See Elward Smith, Sr. entry for additional family information.]

Smith, Robert Gibson

Occupation(s):   military -   general, New Jersey National Guard

Marriage(s):   Frances Cairns (1856-1942)

Address: Handsome Avenue, Sayville
Name of estate:
Year of construction:
Style of architecture: Shingle
Architect(s):   Isaac Henry Green II
                         designed the house
                         (for Ridgeway)

Landscape architect(s):
House extant: unconfirmed
Historical notes:

side / front facade

    The house was built by James W. Ridgeway.
    In 1897, it was purchased from Ridgeway by Elward Smith, Sr.
    Frances Cairns Smith had previously been married to Elward Smith, Sr.
    [See Elward Smith, Sr. entry for additional family information.]
    The globe and eagle lawn ornament, visible to the left in the above picture, is from *The New York World*
newspaper building in Manhattan. It was donated by the Smith family to the Village of Sayville as a
memorial to Sayville residents killed during World War I. It currently is located in Sayville Village's
Sparrow Park.

Snedecor, James H. (1887-1964)

Occupation(s):

Marriage(s):   Florence Parker (1887-1966)

Address: Fairview Avenue, Bayport
Name of estate:
Year of construction: 1881
Style of architecture: Modified Second Empire
Architect(s):
Landscape architect(s):
House extant: no; destroyed by fire in 1940s
Historical notes:

front facade

   The house, originally named *White House*, was built by Edward Edwards.
   In 1883, it was purchased by John R. Ely.
   Cyrus E. Staples purchased the house in 1890.
   In 1902, Staples sold it to William Kintzing Post and his brother Regis H. Post, Sr., who, in turn, sold it to Snedecor in 1925.

Snedeker, Charles V. (1894-1951)

Occupation(s):   financier -   partner, Carreau and Snedeker (stock brokerage firm);
                                  president, Charles V. Snedeker and Co. (stock brokerage firm)
Civic Activism: trustee, Village of Babylon;
                          president, Babylon Village Economic Council

Marriage(s):   Marion Olsen (d. 1968)

Address: Little East Neck Road, Babylon
Name of estate:
Year of construction:
Style of architecture: Colonial Revival
Architect(s):
Landscape architect(s):
House extant: unconfirmed
Historical notes:

   Charles V. Snedeker was the son of Alfred M. and Emma Gulden Snedeker of Manhattan.
   The Snedekers' son John married Eve Kinloch, the daughter of Bohun Baker Kinloch of Charleston, SC. Their daughters Emma-Marie and Marianne remained unmarried.
   Charles V. Snedeker died as a result of two self-inflicted gunshot wounds in the chest.

Snow, Frederick B. (1870-1954)

Occupation(s):   capitalist -   president, Jere Johnson, Jr., Co. (Brooklyn real estate
                                      firm)
Civic Activism: chairman, auditing committee, Brooklyn Real Estate Board

Marriage(s):

Address: Garner Lane, Bay Shore
Name of estate:
Year of construction:
Style of architecture:
Architect(s):
Landscape architect(s):
House extant: unconfirmed
Historical notes:

    The *Long Island Society Register, 1929* lists Mr. and Mrs. Frederick B. Snow as residing on Garner Lane in Bay Shore.
    He was the son of Augustus Snow.

Spaulding, E. B.

Occupation(s):   capitalist -   secretary, Wright Universal Electric Co.

Marriage(s):

Address: St. Mark's Lane, Islip
Name of estate:
Year of construction:
Style of architecture:
Architect(s):
Landscape architect(s):
House extant: unconfirmed
Historical notes:

    The house was built by Parmenus Johnson.
    In 1880, it was purchased by E. B. Spaulding, who expanded and modernized the house.
    In 1886, it was purchased by Robert Cambridge Livingston III and was, subsequently, owned by his daughter Maude and son-in-law Henry Worthington Bull.

Stanchfield, John Barry, Sr. (1855-1921)

Occupation(s):   attorney* -   partner, Stanchfield and Levy;
                                        partner, Reynolds, Stanchfield, and Collins;
                                        partner, Hill and Stanchfield;
                                        district attorney, Chemung County, NY, 1880-1885
                          politician** -   mayor, Elmira, NY, 1886-1888;
                                        member, New York State Assembly, 1895-1896;
                                        New York State Assembly Minority Leader, 1896

Marriage(s):   1886-1921 – Clara Spaulding (1860-1935)

Address: Ocean Avenue, Islip
Name of estate: *Afterglow*
Year of construction: c. 1890
Style of architecture: Shingle
Architect(s):
Landscape architect(s):
House extant: no; demolished in c. 1950
Historical notes:

The house, originally named *Afterglow*, was built by John Gibb.
In 1909, it was purchased by Stanchfield.
He was the son of Dr. John K. and Mrs. Glovina S. Barry Stanchfield of Elmira, NY.
Clara Spaulding Stanchfield was the daughter of Henry C. and Clara W. Spaulding of Elmira, NY.
John Barry and Clara Spaulding Stanchfield, Sr.'s son Dr. John Barry Stanchfield, Jr., an endocrinologist, resided in Salt Lake City, UT. Their daughter Alice, who inherited the Islip house, married Dr. Arthur Mullen Wright.
Both the Stanchfields and Wrights continued to call the estate *Afterglow*.
*Stanchfield established the right of non-incrimination based on the Fifth Amendment of the United States Constitution in the case of Forbes vs. Taylor. The 1894 case involved Cornell University sophomores who attempted to disrupt a freshman banquet by releasing chlorine gas. The gas caused the death of a college employee in the next room. Stanchfield advised his client Taylor not to answer any incriminating questions at the Grand Jury hearing which resulted in Taylor being charged with contempt of court. Stanchfield's position was upheld by the United States Supreme Court thus establishing a defendant's right to "Plead the Fifth." [*The National Cyclopaedia of American Biography* (Clifton, NJ: James T. White & Co., 1984), vol. 14, pp. 360-361.] In another famous court case, Stanchfield succeeded in having Harry K. Thaw, the murderer of architect Stanford White, released after Thaw had spent nine years as an inmate in the Matteawan Asylum. [*The New York Times* June 26, 1921, p. 23.]
**In the 1900 election for Governor of New York, Stanchfield, who was the Democratic candidate, lost. In 1901, he lost in the election for United States Senator from New York State.

Afterglow

Staples, Cyrus E. (1842-1903)

Occupation(s):   financier -   investment banker (involved primarily in Brooklyn
                                            corporations)*;
                                         a founder, New York Mutual Title Insurance Co.
                        shipping -   president, New York, Maine and New Brunswick
                                          Steamship Co.

Marriage(s):

Address: Fairview Avenue, Bayport
Name of estate:
Year of construction: 1881
Style of architecture: Modified Second Empire
Architect(s):
Landscape architect(s):
House extant: no; destroyed by fire in 1940s
Historical notes:

   The house, originally named *White House*, was built by Edward Edwards.
   In 1883, it was purchased by John R. Ely.
   Cyrus E. Staples purchased the house in 1890.
   In 1902, Staples sold it to William Kintzing Post and his brother Regis H. Post, Sr., who, in turn, sold it to James H. Snedecor in 1925.
   *As agent for the sale of the Long Island Water Supply Company to the City of Brooklyn, Staples became the center of a political scandal. The water company, a private corporation whose owners included several local and state politicians, including former Senator Alfred Wagstaff, Jr. of West Islip, supplied water to Brooklyn's Twenty-sixth Ward. Staples negotiated a contract whereby the company's $70-a-share stock was sold to the city at the inflated price of $800-a-share. Fortunately for the taxpayers, the sale was declared void by the courts. [*The New York Times* December 20, 1890, p. 9; December 29, 1890, p. 3; January 5, 1891, p. 1; January 31, 1891, p. 8; March 2, 1891, p. 1; May 29, 1891, p. 8; and May 31, 1892, p. 9.]

Stephens, John L. (b. circa 1836)

Occupation(s):   attorney

Marriage(s):   1896 – Julia True (b. circa 1858)

Address: South Country Road, West Islip
Name of estate: *Lone Oak*
Year of construction:
Style of architecture:
Architect(s):
Landscape architect(s):
House extant: unconfirmed
Historical notes:

   The Society Register, 1907 lists John L. and Julia True Stephens as residing at *Lone Oak* in West Islip.
   In the early 1890s, Stephens was severely injured in a railroad accident, which temporarily left him an invalid. [*The New York Times* February 14, 1896, p. 3.] His brother Benjamin resided in West Islip on the south side of South Country Road.
   Julia True Stephens was the daughter of Benjamin K. and Martha True of West Islip.

Stewart, Dr. George David (1862-1933)

Occupation(s):	physician* - chief surgeon, Bellevue Hospital, NYC; president, medical board, St. Vincent's Hospital, NYC educator - professor of anatomy and surgery, Bellevue Hospital, NYC writer - poet
Civic Activism:	chairman, executive committee, Hospital Fund; a founder and president, American College of Surgeons; president, New York Academy of Medicine; president, Robert Burns Society
Marriage(s):	1890-1933 – Ida May Robb
Address:	Great River Road, Great River
Name of estate:	*Appin House*
Year of construction:	1899
Style of architecture:	Tudor
Architect(s):	Charles C. Thain designed the house (for R. S. White)
Landscape architect(s):	
House extant: no	
Historical notes:	

The house was built by Raymond S. White.

After White's death, it was owned by his wife Sarah, who married Francis Sessions Hutchins and continued to reside in the house.

It was later owned by Stewart, who called it *Appin House*.

The *Long Island Society Register, 1929* lists Dr. George David and Mrs. Ida May Robb Stewart as residing at *Appin House* in Great River.

He was the son of Daniel and Mary J. McCallum Stewart of Nova Scotia, Canada.

Ida May Robb Stewart was the daughter of James Finley Robb.

The Stewarts' daughter Jean married Robert Vose White and resided at *Rohallion* in Rumson, NJ. Their daughter Margery married Porter Hoagland and resided at *Appin* in Rumson, NJ. Their daughter Dorothy married Edward Hope Coffey, Jr. Their daughter Mary remained unmarried.

*When New York City Mayor William J. Gaynor, who resided at *Deepwells* in St. James, was shot in an assassination attempt, Stewart was a consulting physician.

Stewart, James

Occupation(s):	
Marriage(s):	
Address:	Great River Road, Great River
Name of estate:	
Year of construction:	
Style of architecture:	Shingle
Architect(s):	
Landscape architect(s):	
House extant: no	
Historical notes:	

side facade

The house, originally named *Questover Lodge*, was built by Frederick C. Truslow.

It was subsequently owned by Stewart.

243

Stillman, Benjamin D. (d. 1901)

Occupation(s):   attorney

Civic Activism: bequeathed $110,000 to Yale University, New Haven, CT;
bequeathed $10,000 to Columbia University, NYC;
member, Grant Monument Committee, NYC

Marriage(s):

Address: South Country Road, West Islip
Name of estate:
Year of construction:
Style of architecture:
Architect(s):
Landscape architect(s):
House extant: unconfirmed
Historical notes:

At the time of his death Benjamin D. Stillman's total wealth was estimated at $1.5 million. [*Brooklyn Daily Eagle* January 29, 1901, p. 1.]

Stillman's sister Laura married ____ Blagden and resided in Washington, DC.

In 1902, the house was purchased by Stillman's niece Miss Caroline S. Taylor. [*Brooklyn Daily Eagle* July 30, 1902, p. 15.]

*Stillman's gift to Columbia University was for the establishment of the William Mitchell Fellowship.

Stoppani, Charles F., Jr. (1867-1941)

Occupation(s):   financier -   partner, Ennis and Stoppani (odd-lot brokers specializing
in grain futures)*;
member, McManamy and Co. (stock brokerage firm)

Marriage(s):   Evelyn Henry

Address: *[unable to determine street address]*, Bayport
Name of estate:
Year of construction:
Style of architecture:
Architect(s):
Landscape architect(s):
House extant: unconfirmed
Historical notes:

Evelyn Henry Stoppani was the daughter of William F. Henry of Berkeley, CA.

Charles F. and Evelyn Henry Stoppani, Jr.'s daughter married Harding T. Mason.

*As a result of alleged irregularities in their 1903, 1909, and 1916 stock transactions, arrest warrants were issued for Charles F. Stoppani and his partner and fellow Bayport resident Thomas A. Ennis. The scandal caused the firm of Ennis and Stoppani to declare bankruptcy. [Harry W. Havemeyer, *East on the Great South Bay: Sayville and Bayport 1860-1960* (Mattituck, NY: Amereon House, 2001), p. 82 and *The New York Times* November 8, 1903, p. 20; April 14, 1909, p. 1; April 16, 1909, p. 5; April 22, 1909, p. 5; April 28, 1909, p. 18; May 5, 1909, p. 7; and May 22, 1909, p. 1.]

[See following Stoppani entries for additional family information.]

Stoppani, Charles F. , Sr. (1832-1892)

Occupation(s):

Marriage(s):   Eliza J. _____

Address: Fairview Avenue, Bayport
Name of estate: *Arcadia*
Year of construction: 1888
Style of architecture:
Architect(s):   Isaac Henry Green II
                               designed the house
                               (for C. F. Stoppani, Sr.)
Landscape architect(s):
House extant: no
Historical notes:

     The house, originally named *Arcadia*, was built by Charles F. Stoppani, Sr.
     The *Brooklyn Blue Book and Long Island Society Register, 1918* lists Eliza J. Stoppani as residing in Manhattan.
     Charles F, and Eliza J. Stoppani, Sr.'s son Charles F. Stoppani, Jr. married Evelyn Henry, the daughter of William F. Henry of Berkeley, CA, and resided in Bayport. Their son Joseph married Ida Maloney and resided at *Liberty Hall* in Bayport.
     The estate was inherited by Charles' daughter Jane, who married Stephen Perry Cox. The Coxes continued to call it *Arcadia*.
     [See other Stoppani entries for additional family information.]
     In 1919, Cox sold the house to John J. O'Connor, who defaulted on its property taxes.
     The house was purchased by Judge Martin Thomas Manton at a sheriff's sale, thereby giving Manton ownership of both Stoppani houses, *Liberty Hall* and *Arcadia*. In 1939, Manton, who was convicted of accepting $186,000 in bribes, lost the house for failure to pay its property taxes.

Arcadia

Stoppani, Joseph H. (1870-1938)

Occupation(s):   capitalist -   president, Bayport Road Co.
                                  financier -   Stoppani and Hotchkins (odd-lot brokers specializing
                                                          in grain futures)*

Marriage(s):   1898 – Ida Maloney

Address: 133 South Ocean Avenue, Bayport
Name of estate: *Liberty Hall*
Year of construction: 1898
Style of architecture:
Architect(s):   Isaac Henry Green II designed
                               the main house, carriage
                               house, and gardener's cottage
                               (for J. H. Stoppani)

Landscape architect(s):
House extant: yes
Historical notes: *side / front facade, 2006*

The house, originally named *Liberty Hall*, was built by Joseph H. Stoppani.
He was the son of Charles F. and Eliza J. Stoppani, Sr., who resided at *Arcadia* in Bayport.
*Joseph and his brother Charles F. Stoppani, Jr. were known locally as "the noodle kings of Bayport."
In 1916, Joseph's firm entered bankruptcy as a result of his overextension in grain speculation. Charged with alleged misappropriation of a client's funds, Joseph was convicted and received a four-year jail sentence in Sing Sing. After serving eighteen months, Stoppani was released from prison. [Harry W. Havemeyer, *East on the Great South Bay: Sayville and Bayport 1860-1960* (Mattituck, NY: Amereon House, 2001), pp. 81-3.]
[See other Stoppani entries for additional family information.]
Liberty Hall was transferred to Joseph's brother-in-law Stephen Perry Cox to keep it out of bankruptcy proceedings.
In 1916, Cox sold the estate to Judge Martin Thomas Manton, who lost in 1939 for failure to pay its property tax.

Strong, James H. S.

Occupation(s):

Marriage(s):   Georgiana Louisa Berryman (d. 1909)

Address: Montrose Avenue, Babylon
Name of estate:
Year of construction:
Style of architecture:
Architect(s):
Landscape architect(s):
House extant: unconfirmed
Historical notes:

Georgiana Louisa Berryman Strong was the daughter of Upschur Berryman.
James H. and Georgiana Louisa Berryman Strong's daughter Silvie married Richard Bailey Post and, subsequently, Henry Chester Hepburn, with whom she resided in Babylon. Their daughter Henrietta married Daniel B. Fearing of Newport, RI.

Strong, Theron George (1846-1924)

Occupation(s):	attorney*
	writer - *Landmarks of a Lawyer's Lifetime*, 1914;
	Joseph H. Choate: New Englander, New Yorker,
	Lawyer, Ambassador, 1917
Civic Activism:	trustee, New York Presbytery;
	president, Alumni Association, University of Rochester,
	Rochester, NY;
	director, New York Juvenile Asylum;
	director, Legal Aid Society of New York;
	director, New York Bible Society
Marriage(s):	1878-1924 – Martha Howard Prentice (d. 1949)
Address:	Penataquit Avenue, Bay Shore
Name of estate:	
Year of construction:	1890
Style of architecture:	
Architect(s):	Romeyn and Stever designed
	the house (for Strong)
Landscape architect(s):	
House extant: no	
Historical notes:	

The house was built by Theron George Strong.

The *Brooklyn Blue Book and Long Island Society Register, 1918* and *1921* lists Theron George and Martha Howard Prentice Strong as residing at *The Dolphins* in East Hampton.

He was the son of Judge Theron Rudd and Mrs. Cornelia Barnes Strong of Palmyra, NY.

Martha Howard Prentice Strong was the daughter of John H. Prentice of Brooklyn.

Theron George and Martha Howard Prentice Strong's son Theron Roundell Strong married Maude Robbins and resided at *Asher House* in Southampton. Their daughter Martha, who inherited *The Dolphins*, married Harold Turner.

*Strong was the author of the 1901 anti-policy provision in the New York State Penal Code.

The house was subsequently owned by John Healey.

Sullivan, Dr. Raymond Peter, Sr. (1882-1963)

Occupation(s):   physician -   chief surgeon and surgical director, St. Vincent's
                                                     Hospital, NYC;
                                              consultant in surgery, Brunswick General Hospital,
                                                     Amityville; Kings Park State Hospital, Kings Park;
                                                     Southside Hospital, Bay Shore; St. Vincent's Hospital,
                                                     Staten Island; Hospital of the Holy Family, Brooklyn;
                                                     Police Department of the City of New York;
                                              chief of surgery, division of Surgeon General's Office
                                 writer -   numerous articles on cancer therapy;
                                              "Some Observations on Hyperthyroidism," 1912;
                                              "Perforated Ulcers of the Stomach and Duodenum," 1916;
                                              "Non-tubercular Kidney Infections," 1922;
                                              "Carcinoma of Stomach in Young People," 1924, 1927;
                                              "Tumors of Carotid Body," 1927

Civic Activism: trustee, St. Patrick's Cathedral, NYC;
                                 trustee, Manhattan College

Marriage(s):   1911-1963 – Marie E. Mc Namee (1886-1972)

Address: Awixa Avenue, Bay Shore
Name of estate:
Year of construction: 1893
Style of architecture: Shingle
Architect(s):
Landscape architect(s):
House extant: yes
Historical notes:

    The house was built by John Mollenhauer.
    It was subsequently owned by Sullivan.
    The *Long Island Society Register, 1929* lists Dr. Raymond P. and Mrs. Marie E. Mc Namee Sullivan [Sr.]
as residing in Bay Shore.
    He was the son of Dr. D. and Mrs. Eleanor Sullivan Sullivan.
    Marie E. Mc Namee Sullivan was the daughter of John and Mary Burnett Mc Namee of Islip. Marie's twin
sister Esther died at the age of ten.
    Dr. Raymond Peter and Mrs. Marie E. Mc Namee Sullivan, Sr.'s daughter Marie remained unmarried.

Their daughter Katherine married Joseph A. Meehan,
the son of Michael J. Meehan, Sr. of Manhattan and
Pinehurst, NC. Their son William married Jean Kay
Simonson, the daughter of Henry J. Simonson of
Southampton. Their son John married Pauline Elaine
Gerli, the daughter of Paolino Gerli of Manhattan and
Longford in Ridgefield, CT. Their son Raymond
Peter Sullivan, Jr. married Catherine McDonnell, the
daughter of James Francis and Anna Murray
McDonnell, Sr., who resided at *East Wickapogue
Cottage* in Southampton. Catherine's sister Ann
married Henry Ford II, the son of Edsel Bryant Ford.

front facade, 2006

248

Sutton, Effingham B., Sr. (1817-1891)

Occupation(s):   shipping - a founder. Sutton Line, 1849 (clipper ships between
                   New York City and California);
                   a founder, Cromwell Steamship Line
            financier - director, Shoe and Leather Bank

Marriage(s):   Mary L. Woodruff (d. 1889)

Address: South Country Road, West Islip
Name of estate: *Effingham Pond*
Year of construction: c. 1870
Style of architecture:
Architect(s):
Landscape architect(s):
House extant: unconfirmed
Historical notes:

  Effingham B. and Mary L. Woodruff Sutton, Sr.'s son Frederick married Olive Brown, whose grandfather was mayor of New York City. The Suttons' nineteen-month-old daughter Pauline died of cholera. Their daughter married Philetus H. Woodruff. Their son Woodruff married Frances Steele and resided in West Islip. Their son James married Julia Gorham Marshall. Their son Theodore married Carrie Fleming. Their daughter Marie remained unmarried.
  Sutton Place in New York City was named for Effingham B. Sutton, Sr. [*The New York Times* February 18, 1957, p. 27.]
  [See other Sutton entries for additional family information.]

Sutton, Frank (1875-1957)

Occupation(s):   engineer
            shipping - member, Cromwell Steamship Line
Civic Activism: trustee, Southside Hospital, Bay Shore

Marriage(s):   Jane Louise Bauman

Address: 94 Martha Court, North Babylon
Name of estate: *North East Farm*
Year of construction: c. 1916
Style of architecture: Tudor
Architect(s):
Landscape architect(s):
House extant: yes
Historical notes:

front facade, 1991

  The house, originally named *North East Farm*, was built by Frank Sutton.
  The *Long Island Society Register, 1929* lists Frank Sutton as residing at *North East Farm* in Babylon.
  He was the son of Woodruff and Frances Steele Sutton, Sr., who resided at *Sutton Park* in West Islip.
  Jane Louise Bauman Sutton had previously been married to William Tyson Hayward, Jr., with whom she resided in Babylon.
  [See other Sutton entries for additional family information.]
  The house has been converted into a condominium complex.

rear facade, 1924

Sutton, Woodruff, Sr. (1851-1896)

Occupation(s):   shipping -   president, Cromwell Steamship Line;
                                  partner, Sutton & Co.

Marriage(s):   Frances Steele

Address: South Country Road, West Islip
Name of estate: *Sutton Park*
Year of construction:
Style of architecture:
Architect(s):
Landscape architect(s):
House extant: unconfirmed
Historical notes:

    Woodruff Sutton, Sr. was the son of Effingham B. and Mary L. Woodruff Sutton, Sr. of *Effingham Pond* in West Islip.

    Woodruff and Frances Steele Sutton, Sr.'s son Woodruff Sutton, Jr. married Helen Remsen, the daughter of Phoenix Remsen of West Islip and, subsequently, Helen Anthes. Their son Frank married Jane Louise Baumann and resided at *North East Farm* in Babylon. Their son Harold married Mary Anthony, the daughter of A. Rowan Anthony of Montrose, PA. Their son David married Mary Anthony's sister Lilly and, subsequently, Dorothy Magie, the widow of Robert B. Whittlesey. Their son William married Muriel Winfred.

[See other Sutton entries for additional family information.]

Suydam, Charles (1818-1882)

Occupation(s):   merchant

Marriage(s):   Ann White Schermerhorn (1818-1886)

Address: *[unable to determine street address]*, Bayport
Name of estate:
Year of construction:
Style of architecture:
Architect(s):
Landscape architect(s):
House extant: unconfirmed
Historical notes:

    Charles Suydam was the son of Ferdinand Suydam.

    Ann White Schermerhorn Suydam was the daughter of Abraham Schermerhorn of Manhattan. Her sister Catherine married Benjamin Sumner Welles, Sr. and resided in Islip. Her sister Caroline ["Mystic Rose"], who married William Blackhouse Astor, was the undisputed arbiter of society's elite "Four Hundred." Benjamin and Catherine Schermerhorn Welles, Sr. were on the elite "Four Hundred" list, that Ward McAllister compiled for Caroline Astor but Charles and Ann Schermerhorn Suydam were omitted.

    Charles and Ann White Schermerhorn Suydam's daughter Helen married Robert Fulton Cutting and resided in Great River. Their son Walter married Jane Meiser Suydam, the daughter of John R. and Anna Middleton Lawrence Suydam, Sr. of Bayport and resided at *Manowtasquott Lodge* in Blue Point.

Suydam, John R., Jr. (1858-1928)

Occupation(s):   engineer

Marriage(s):   1883-1927 – Harriet Penrose Cochran (1859-1927)

Address: Suydam Lane, Bayport
Name of estate: *Edgewater*
Year of construction: c. 1855
Style of architecture: Italianate
Architect(s):
Landscape architect(s):
House extant: no; demolished in 1987
Historical notes:

    The house, originally named *Edgewater*, was built by John R. Suydam, Sr.
    It was inherited by his son John R. Suydam, Jr., who continued to call it *Edgewater*.
    Harriet Penrose Cochran Suydam was the daughter of William and Eliza Penrose Cochran of Philadelphia, PA.
    John R. and Harriet Penrose Cochran Suydam, Jr.'s son John R. Suydam III married Margaret Thayer, the daughter of William Greenough Thayer of Southborough, MA. Their daughter Lisa married Paul Renshaw and resided in Manhattan.
    [See other Suydam entries for additional family information.]
    In 1922, the house was purchased from John R. Suydam, Jr. by Herbert and Grace Whitney Seaman, who immediately sold it to Julius Liebman.
    The estate was inherited by Liebman's son James, who had changed his surname to Leland.
    The house was inherited by James Leland's daughter Anne.
    In 1987, Anne sold it to Ira Rubenstein, who demolished the house the same year and built a new house on the site, which he called *Cheap John's Estate*.

Suydam, John R., Sr. (1807-1882)

Occupation(s):   merchant -   partner, Suydam & York (dry goods)

Marriage(s):   1854-1870 – Ann Middleton Lawrence (1823-1870)

Address: Suydam Lane, Bayport
Name of estate: *Edgewater*
Year of construction: c. 1855
Style of architecture: Italianate
Architect(s):
Landscape architect(s):
House extant: no; demolished in 1987
Historical notes:

front facade

    The house, originally named *Edgewater*, was built by John R. Suydam, Sr.
    He was the son of John and Jane Mesier Suydam.
    Ann Middleton Lawrence Suydam was the daughter of John L. and Sarah Augusta Smith Lawrence of Mastic.
    [See other Suydam entries for additional family information.]
    John R. and Ann Middleton Lawrence Suydam, daughter Jane married her half, second cousin Walter L. Suydam. Their son John R. Suydam, Jr. inherited the estate and continued to call it *Edgewater*.
    [See previous entry for history of estate.]

Swan, Alden S. (1838-1917)

Occupation(s):	politician -	Brooklyn alderman
	capitalist -	trustee, Brooklyn Bridge
	financier -	director, Market and Fulton National Bank

Marriage(s):   Mary Althea Farwell

Address: Ocean Avenue, Islip
Name of estate: *Orowoc*
Year of construction: c. 1893
Style of architecture: Queen Anne
Architect(s):
Landscape architect(s):
House extant: unconfirmed
Historical notes:

Swirbul, Leon A. (1898-1960)

Occupation(s):   industrialist -   a founder, general manager, and president, Grumman Aircraft
                                    Engineering Corp., Bethpage (now, Northrop–Grumman)*
                          capitalist -   director, Republic Pictures Corp.
Civic Activism: president, Long Island Hospital Regional Planning Council;
                          president, Long Island Industrial Hospital Commission;
                          honorary vice-chairman, American Cancer Society;
                          trustee, Nassau Hospital (now, Winthrop University Hospital), Mineola;
                          member, New York State Racing Commission, 1949-1955;
                          co-founder, Long Island Fund;
                          chairman of board, Waldemar Clinic of Cancer Research Foundation, Port
                             Washington;
                          member, Greater Cornell Council;
                          member, Aircraft Industry Advisory Committee of the Munitions Board;
                          trustee, Adelphi College, Garden City, 1958-1960 (now, Adelphi University)**;
                          trustee, Hofstra University, Hempstead

Marriage(s):   M/1 – Josephine M. ____ (d. 1976)
                          M/2 – Estelle Stephens

Address: Plymouth Avenue, Brightwaters
Name of estate:
Year of construction:
Style of architecture:
Architect(s):
Landscape architect(s):
House extant: unconfirmed
Historical notes:

   Leon A. Swirbul was the son of Frederick and Lena Dannenberg Swirbul of Brooklyn and Sag Harbor.
Josephine M. Swirbul subsequently married Thomas Woodward MacLeod, Sr. and resided in Bay Shore.
   Leon A. and Josephine M. Swirbul's son William married Thora Elizabeth Sullivan, the daughter of
Marcus Henry Lewis Sullivan of Brightwaters. Their son Philip married Serene Dorothy Grey, the daughter
of Mason W. Grey of Erie, PA, and resided in Bay Shore. They eventually relocated to Tuxedo, NY.
   *In 1946, Swirbul was awarded the Medal of Merit by President Harry S Truman for Grumman's
production and design excellence during World War II.
   **The library at Adelphi University is named in honor of Swirbul.
   The Swirbuls subsequently relocated to Brookville.

Tappin, Charles L. (1854-1941)

Occupation(s):   capitalist -   partner, Borne Scrymser Co., NYC (oil)

Marriage(s):   1914-1927 – Flora Roberts (d. 1927)

Address: South Country Road, Babylon
Name of estate: *Twin Oaks*
Year of construction: c. 1891
Style of architecture: Shingle
Architect(s):
Landscape architect(s):
House extant: no; destroyed by fire, 1950
Historical notes:

    Charles L Tappin was the son of John C. and Jane Lindsay Tappin of Islip.
[See following entry for additional family information.]

front facade, 1924

Tappin, John C. (1851-1922)

Occupation(s):   financier -   member, Stokes and Hedges Co. (stock brokerage firm)

Marriage(s):   Jane Lindsay

Address: St. Mark's Lane, Islip
Name of estate:
Year of construction: 1888
Style of architecture:
Architect(s):
Landscape architect(s):
House extant: no
Historical notes:

    The house was built by John C. Tappin.
    He was the son of John Tappin.
    John C. and Jane Lindsay Tappin's son Lindsay married Elsie Huntington, the daughter of Charles R. Huntington. Elsie had previously been married to Leopold Francke. Their son Charles married Floria Roberts and resided at *Twin Oaks* in Babylon.
    [See previous entry for additional family information.]

Taylor, George Campbell (1835-1907)

Occupation(s):   diplomat -   member, United States Embassy in Great Britain
                                        (Lincoln administration)

Marriage(s):   common-law-wife – Betsy Head (c. 1847-1907)*

Address: Heckscher Parkway, East Islip
Name of estate: *Deer Range Farm*
Year of construction: c. 1850s
Style of architecture: Eclectic
Architect(s):
Landscape architect(s):
House extant: no**
Historical notes:

    The house, originally named *Deer Range Farm*, was built by Edwin Augustus Johnson, Sr.
    In 1872, the estate was purchased by Sarah Ives Plumb. Upon her death, it was inherited by her husband James Neale Plumb and, subsequently, by their son James Ives Plumb. The Plumbs continued to call it *Deer Range Farm*.
    In 1884, alterations were made to the house by James Neale Plumb.
    In 1903, James Ives Plumb sold the estate to Taylor. The estate remained in the Taylor / Pyne family corporation until 1924 when it was confiscated by Robert Moses and became part of Heckscher State Park.
[Harry W. Havemeyer, *Along the Great South Bay From Oakdale to Babylon: The Story of a Summer Spa 1840 to 1940* (Mattituck, NY: Amereon House, 1996), p. 135.]
    George Campbell Taylor was the son of Moses Taylor of Manhattan, from whom he had inherited an income from a $20 million trust his father had established. [*The New York Times* September 18, 1907, p. 9.] His sister Albertina married Percy Rivington Pyne, Sr.
    *Taylor met Betsy Head in England and engaged her as his housekeeper and private secretary. Betsy's daughter Lena married Taylor's gardener William Bodley and was disinherited by her mother and Taylor. Bodley was later employed as a foreman on William Kissam Vanderbilt, Jr.'s estate *Deepdale* in Lake Success.
    **The house was demolished by Moses' Long Island State Park Commission. The estate property is now part of Heckscher State Park.

Taylor, George Campbell (1835-1907)

Occupation(s):   diplomat -   member, United States Embassy in Great Britain
                                              (Lincoln administration)

Marriage(s):   common-law-wife – Betsy Head (c. 1847-1907)

Address: Heckscher Parkway, East Islip
Name of estate:
Year of construction: 1885
Style of architecture:
Architect(s):
Landscape architect(s):
House extant: no; demolished in 1933*
Historical notes:

    The house and approximately thirty service buildings were built by George Campbell Taylor.
[See previous entry for family information.]
    In 1903, Taylor purchased the adjacent *Deer Range Farm* of James Ives Plumb, thus increasing his estate
holdings to two main residences on approximately 1,500 acres.
    *The house was demolished by Robert Moses' Long Island State Park Commission. The estate property is
now part of Heckscher State Park.

original 1885 house, front facade

front facade, c. 1924, after alterations

255

Tcherepnin, Alexander (1899-1977)

Occupation(s):   entertainers and associated professions -
                                                concert pianist;
                                                composer - *Ol, Ol*, 1934 (opera);
  Piano Sonata in A Minor;
  Ten Bagatelles;
  Arabesques;
  Scherzo in C Minor for Piano;
  Nocturne in G Sharp for Piano;
  Toccata in D Major for Piano

Marriage(s):   1926 – Louisine Peters (c. 1884-1960s)

Address: South Bay Avenue, Islip
Name of estate: *Wereholme*
Year of construction: c. 1917
Style of architecture: Neo-French Manor
Architect(s):   Grosvenor Atterbury designed
                                       the house (for H. H. Weekes)
Landscape architect(s):
House extant: yes
Historical notes:

   The house, originally named *Wereholme*, was built by Harold Hathaway Weekes.

   His wife, the former Louisine Peters, subsequently married Tcherepnin, with whom she continued to reside at *Wereholme*.

   Louisine Peters Tcherepnin was the daughter of Samuel Twyford and Adaline Mapes Elder Peters of *Windholme Farm* in Islip. Her brother Harry Twyford Peters, Sr., who married Natalie Wells and resided at *Nearholme* in Islip, inherited *Windholme Farm*.

   Alexander Tcherepnin was the son of the Russian composer Nikolai Tcherepnin.

   Harold Hathaway and Louisine Peters Weekes' daughter Adaline, who married Charles B. Scully, inherited *Wereholme* and resided at the estate. Adaline subsequently married Count Philip Orssich of Denkendorf bei Stuttgart, Germany.

   In 1984, Mrs. Scully, who had divorced the count and reverted to the surname Scully, bequeathed the house to the National Audubon Society.

   In 2004, the estate was purchased by Suffolk County and is now the county's Environmental Interpretive Center.

Wereholme

Tenney, Charles Henry, Sr. (1911-1994)

Occupation(s):   attorney -   partner, Breed, Abbott, and Morgan;
                                        judge, United States Federal Court, Southern District,
                                            1964-1994
             politician -   deputy mayor, New York City, 1961-1964 (Robert F.
                                            Wagner administration)
             intelligence agent -   Naval intelligence during World War II

Marriage(s):   1938-1994 – Joan Penfold Lusk (d. 1996)

Address: Dover Court, Bay Shore
Name of estate:
Year of construction: 1903
Style of architecture: Shingle
Architect(s):
Landscape architect(s):
House extant: yes
Historical notes:

The house, originally named *Cedarholme*, was built by Lewis Mills Gibb, Sr.
It was later owned by his son Lewis Mills Gibb, Jr., who continued to call it *Cedarholme*.
It was subsequently owned by Tenney.
He was the son of Daniel Gleason and Marguerite Sedgwick Smith Tenney, Sr., who resided on Wheatley Road in Brookville. His brother Daniel Gleason Tenney, Jr. married Constance Lippincott Franchot, the daughter of Douglas Warner Franchot of Baltimore, MD. His sister Frances, who married G. Morgan Brown, Sr., and, subsequently, Laurent Oppenheim, Jr., resided in Manhattan.
Joan Penfold Lusk Tenney was the daughter of The Reverend William B. Lusk, Sr. of Ridgefield, CT.
Charles Henry and Joan Penfold Lusk Tenney, Sr.'s son Charles Henry Tenney, Jr. resided in Elizabethtown, NY. Their daughters Anne and Joan remained unmarried. Their daughter Marguerite married Talton R. Embry.

Thorn, Edward Floyd–Jones, Sr. (d. 1974)

Occupation(s):

Marriage(s):   Marjorie Peirce (d. 1969)

Address: 106 Ocean Avenue, Amityville
Name of estate:
Year of construction:
Style of architecture: Long Island farmhouse
Architect(s):
Landscape architect(s):
House extant: yes
Historical notes:

front facade, 2006

The *Long Island Society Register, 1929* lists Edward F. J. and Marjorie Peirce Thorn [Sr.] as residing at 106 Ocean Avenue, Amityville.
He was the son of Conde Raguet and Louise Akerly Floyd–Jones Thorn of *Tryon Lodge* in Massapequa.
Edward Floyd–Jones and Marjorie Peirce Thorn, Sr.'s son William married Barbara Norton, the daughter of Algernon Sidney Norton of Manhattan. Their daughter Louisa married Paul Hyde Bonner, Jr., the son of Paul Hyde and Lilly M. Stehli Bonner, Sr., who resided on Locust Valley – Bayville Road, Lattingtown.

Thorne, Edwin, II (1861-1935)

Occupation(s):   capitalist -   director, New York Dock Co.
                                  financier -   trustee, Mutual Life Insurance Co.;
                                             director, North American Trust Co.;
                                             trustee, Central Hanover Bank & Trust Co.;
                                             trustee, Bank of America
                                  industrialist -   director, Granby Consolidated Copper Co.;
                                             director, Federal Terra Cotta Co.

Civic Activism: vice-president, New York Society for the Prevention of Cruelty
                                to Children;
                            a founder and trustee, New York Zoological Society;
                            trustee, Northfield Schools

Marriage(s):   1886-1931 – Phebe Ketchum (d. 1931)

Address: 75 Oak Neck Road, West Islip
Name of estate: *Okonok*
Year of construction: 1890
Style of architecture: Shingle
Architect(s):
Landscape architect(s):
House extant: yes
Historical notes:

The house, originally named *Okonok*, was built by Edwin Thorne II.

The *Long Island Society Register, 1929* lists Edwin and Phebe Ketchum Thorne [II] as residing at *Okonok* in Babylon [West Islip].

He was the son of Samuel and Phebe van Schoonhoven Thorne of Millbrook, NY.

Phebe Ketchum Thorne was the daughter of Landon Ketchum of Saugatuck, CT.

Edwin and Phebe Ketchum Thorne II's son Landon married Julia Atterbury Loomis, the daughter of Henry Patterson Loomis, and resided at *Thorneham* in West Bay Shore. Their son Francis, who married Evelyn Brown, and, subsequently, Hildegarde Kobbe, resided in East Islip. Their daughter Anna married Robert Titus and resided in West Islip. Their daughter Phebe, who married Harry Kearsarge Knapp II, the son of Harry Kearsarge and Caroline Burr Knapp, Sr., of *Brookwood* in East Islip, resided at *Creekside* in East Islip. Phebe later married John Tucker.

[See other Thorne entries for additional family information.]

The house is currently called *Gracemore.*

front facade, 2006

258

Thorne, Edwin, III (b. circa 1914)

Occupation(s):	financier -	vice-president, First National Bank of New York (now, Citibank);
		director, Vigilant Insurance Co.;
		director, Putnam Trust Co., Greenwich, CT;
		director, Federated Insurance Co.;
		director, First Boston Corp. (investment banking firm);
		chairman, Advanced Investors Corp. (closed-end investment firm)
	capitalist -	director, Consumers Power Co.;
		director, Michigan Gas Storage Co.
Civic Activism:		trustee, American Museum of Natural History, NYC; trustee, Community Service Society of New York
Marriage(s):		1938-1986 – Helen Grand (d. 1986)
Address:		108 East Bayberry Road, Islip
Name of estate:		
Year of construction:		1899-1900
Style of architecture:		Moorish
Architect(s):		Grosvenor Atterbury designed the house (for H. O. Havemeyer)*
Landscape architect(s):		Nathan F. Barrett (for H. O. Havemeyer)**

House extant: yes
Historical notes:

The house was built by Henry Osborne Havemeyer as part of his "Modern Venice" development.

Edwin Thorne III was the son of Landon Ketchum and Julia Atterbury Loomis Thorne, Sr., who resided at *Thorneham* in West Bay Shore.

Helen Grand Thorne was the daughter of Gordon and Emma Dill Grand, Sr. of Millbrook, NY, and Greenwich, CT. Her brother Gordon Grand, Jr. married Ruth Young, the daughter of William Henry Young of Tuxedo Park, NY, and resided in Greenwich, CT.

Edwin and Helen Grand Thorne III's son Gordon married Lee Kellogg Ammidon, the daughter of Hoyt and Elizabeth Callaway Ammidon, Sr. of Glen Head. Their son Peter married Katherine Gross, the daughter of Sidney and Zenith Gross of New York. Their son Brinkley married Mary Ann Livingston Delafield Cox, the daughter of Howard E. and Ann Finch Cox, Sr. of *Sunswyck* in Westhampton Beach. Their son Edwin

Thorne, Jr. [IV] married Laura Castleman Gary, the daughter of Theodore Sauvinet and Laura Brown Gary of Madeline Island, WI.

*The sales brochure for "Modern Venice" states that the Moorish-style architecture was suggested by Louis Comfort Tiffany.

**The sales brochure also states that "Modern Venice" would be devoid of trees and vegetation and that Nathan F. Barrett was the landscape architect.

The house was subsequently owned by Carleton Bell Howell.

front facade, 2006

Thorne, Francis Burritt, Jr. (b. 1922)

Occupation(s):	financier - stockbroker
	composer* - composed over one hundred pieces, including symphonies, concerti, string quartets, and choral music
Civic Activism:	a founder, president, and chairman of board, American Composers' Orchestra;
	president and treasurer, Thorne Music Fund;
	executive director, Naumburg Foundation;
	executive director, Music Theatre Group;
	executive director, American Composers Alliance;
	director, Composers Recording Inc.;
	director, American Music Center;
	director, Virgil Thomson Foundation
Marriage(s):	1942 – Ann C. Cobb
Address:	19 Lawrence Lane, Bay Shore
Name of estate:	
Year of construction:	
Style of architecture:	Modified Tudor
Architect(s):	
Landscape architect(s):	
House extant: yes	
Historical notes:	

The *Social Register, 1954* lists Francis B. and Ann C. Cobb Thorne [Jr.] as residing at 19 Lawrence Lane in Bay Shore.

He was the son of Francis B. and Hildegarde Kobbe Thorne, Sr. of *Brookwood* in East Islip.

*Thorne studied music with Paul Hindemith at Yale University.

Ann C. Cobb Thorne was the daughter of Boughton Cobb of Manhattan.

Francis Burritt and Ann C. Cobb Thorne, Jr.'s daughter Ann married William Freeman Niles, the son of Nicholas Niles of Menham, NJ. Their daughter Wendy married Willing H. Forsyth, Jr. of Salisbury, CT. Their daughter Candace married Anthony M. Canton, the son of Jess Canton of Poughquag, NY.

front facade, 2006

Thorne, Francis Burritt, Sr. (1892-1950)

Occupation(s):   financier -   partner, Taylor and Thorne (stock brokerage firm);
                                      partner, Lindley and Co. (stock brokerage firm);
                                      partner, F. B. Thorne and Co. (stock brokerage firm)
                        industrialist -   chairman of board, North Central Texas Oil Co.
Civic Activism: director, Society for the Prevention of Cruelty to Children, NYC

Marriage(s):   M/1 – 1915-1917 – Evelyn Brown (d. 1917)
                        M/2 – 1920-1950 – Hildegarde Kobbe (1889-1959)

Address: South Country Road, East Islip
Name of estate: *Brookwood**
Year of construction: 1902
Style of architecture: Neo-Georgian
Architect(s):
Landscape architect(s):
House extant: yes
Historical notes:

The house, originally named *Brookwood,* was built by Harry Kearsarge Knapp, Sr.
It was inherited by his son Theodore J. Knapp, Sr., who sold the estate to Thorne in 1929.
Francis Burritt Thorne, Sr. was the son of Edwin and Phebe Ketchum Thorne II of *Okonok* in West Islip.
Evelyn Brown Thorne was the daughter of James and Adele Quartley Brown.
Hildegarde Kobbe Thorne was the daughter of Gustav and Carolyn Wheeler Kobbe, who resided in Bay Shore. She had previously been married to Joseph H. Stevenson. Joseph H. and Hildegarde Kobbe Stevenson's daughter Carol married Joseph Sears Lovering, Jr. of Islip. Hildegarde's sister Virginia married Gerald Vanderbilt Hollins, Sr. and resided at *The Hawks* in East Islip. Virginia subsequently married Henry Morgan, with whom she resided in East Islip. Hildegarde's sister Carol married Robert Woodward Morgan and also resided in East Islip. Carol subsequently married George Palen Snow of Syosset. Their sister Beatrice married Raymond E. Little.
Francis Burritt and Hildegarde Kobbe Thorne, Sr.'s son Francis Burritt Thorne, Jr. married Ann C. Cobb, the daughter of Boughton Cobb of Manhattan, and resided in Bay Shore. Their daughter Phebe married Joseph Francis Dempsey, Jr. of Great River and resided in Islip. Their daughter Julia married Dennis McCarty. Their son Oakleigh Thorne II, who resided at *Valley Ranch* in Cody, WY, married Peggy N. Schroll and, subsequently, Lisa L. Bellows.
[See other Thorne entries for additional family information.]
*According to Francis Burritt Thorne, Jr., the name of his parents' estate was *Brookwood* and that it was renamed *Brookwood Hall* by a subsequent owner.
In 1942, the house was owned by the Orphan Asylum Society of Brooklyn.
In 1965, the Society sold it to Alfred and Fred Wimmer, who sold the house to the Town of Islip in 1967. It is currently the site of The Islip Art Museum, a leading exhibit space for contemporary art.
The Empire State Carousel, now located in Binghamton, NY, was built in the carriage house of *Brookwood.* The carriage house is currently the Long Island Center for Experimental Art.

front facade, 1992

Thorne, Landon Ketchum, Jr. (1913-1980)

Occupation(s):	publisher - *The Rome Daily American*, Rome, Italy
	financier - vice-president, Bankers Trust Co.;
	director, United Corp. (closed-ended investment firm);
	managing director, Bankers International Corp.;
	managing director, Bankers International Financing Co, Inc.
	industrialist - president, Vorac Co. (chemical coating manufacturer)
	diplomat - United States Economic Minister, Office of Foreign Operations, to Italy;
	United States Economic Minister, Office of Foreign Operations, to Belgium
Civic Activism:	chairman of board, American University, Cairo, Egypt;
	chairman of board, YMCA–YWCA Camping Services of Greater New York;
	trustee, New York Zoological Society;
	trustee, Pierpont Morgan Library, NYC;
	trustee, American Academy, Rome, Italy;
	assistant treasurer, New York Young Republican Club
Marriage(s):	M/1 – 1936-1941 – Veronica Boswell Elliot
	M/2 – 1942 – Alice Hoadley Barry
	M/3 – 1969-1980 – Miriam A. Rose

living room

Address:	Admiral's Drive East, West Bay Shore
Name of estate:	*The Lodge*
Year of construction:	
Style of architecture:	Ranch
Architect(s):	
Landscape architect(s):	
House extant: yes	
Historical notes:	

Landon Ketchum Thorne, Jr. was the son of Landon Ketchum and Julia Atterbury Loomis Thorne, Sr., who resided at *Thorneham* in West Bay Shore. Before moving to West Bay Shore, he had resided on Split Rock Road in Syosset and on Lake Avenue in Greenwich, CT.

Veronica Boswell Elliot Thorne was the daughter of Sir Gilbert and Lady Flournoy Hopkins Elliot of *Wolfelee* in Rorburghshire, Scotland, and a descendant of Samuel Johnson's biographer James Boswell.

Alice Hoadley Barry Thorne was the daughter of David S. and Alice Hoadley Smith Barry of Washington, DC. Her sister Frances married B. Gordon Dickey, the son of Robert B. Dickey of Tuxedo, NY.

Landon Ketchum and Alice Hoadley Barry Thorne, Jr.'s daughter Julia married John Forbes Kerry at the Thorne's ancestral home *Thorneham* in West Bay Shore. Kerry is the United States Senator from Massachusetts and was the unsuccessful Democratic candidate for the presidency of the United States in 2004. Julia subsequently married Richard J. Charlesworth, with whom she resided in Bozeman, MT, until her death in 2006. The Thornes' son Landon Ketchum Thorne III married Sarah Ashton Nuese, the daughter of Robert E. Nuese of *Indian Lane Farm* in Cornwall, CT. Their son David married Rose O'Neil Geer, the daughter of Garrow Throop Geer of Manhattan.

west facade

The *Social Register, Summer 1974* lists Landon K. and Miriam A. Rose Thorne [Jr.] as residing at *The Lodge* on South Country Road in Bay Shore [Admiral's Drive East, West Bay Shore].

Miriam A. Rose Thorne had previously been married to Fulton H. Cahners.

Thorne, Landon Ketchum, Sr. (1888-1964)

Occupation(s):	financier -	president and partner, with brother-in-law Alfred Loomis II, Bonbright and Co. (investment banking firm)*;
		president, Thorne, Loomis & Co. (holding company);
		president, American Superpower Corp. (investment banking firm);
		trustee, United Corp. (closed-ended investment firm)**;
		director, Bankers Trust Co.;
		director, First National Bank of New York (now, Citibank);
		director, Federal Insurance Co.;
		director, Vigilant Insurance Co.
	capitalist -	director, Commonwealth & Southern Corp.;
		director, New York United Corp.;
		director, Niagara Hudson Power Corp.;
		director, Public Service Corporation of New Jersey;
		director, Southern Pacific Co.
	politician -	commissioner, Long Island State Parks Commission

Civic Activism: trustee, New York Zoological Society;
governor, New York Hospital, Inc.;
member, executive committee, New York World Fair Corp., 1963-1964;
founder, with Alfred L Loomis II, Thorne–Loomis Foundation (which became Thorne Foundation)

Marriage(s): 1911-1964 – Julia Atterbury Loomis (d. 1973)

Address: South Country Road, West Bay Shore
Name of estate: *Thorneham*
Year of construction: 1928
Style of architecture: Tudor
Architect(s): William F. Dominick designed the house
  (for L. K. Thorne, Sr.)
Landscape architect(s): Ferruccio Vitalie (for L. K. Thorne, Sr.)
Umberto Innocenti designed the gardens
  (for L. K. Thorne, Sr.)
House extant: no; demolished in 1976
Historical notes:

The house, originally named *Thorneham*, was built by Landon Ketchum Thorne, Sr.
He was the son of Edwin and Phebe Ketchum Thorne II of *Okonok* in West Islip.
Julia Atterbury Loomis Thorne was the daughter of Henry Patterson Loomis.

Landon Ketchum and Julia Atterbury Loomis Thorne, Sr.'s son Landon Ketchum Thorne, Jr., who resided at *The Lodge* in West Bay Shore, married Veronica Boswell Elliot, Alice Hoadley Barry, and Miriam A. Rose. Their son Edwin Thorne III married Helen Grand and resided in Islip prior to relocating to Greenwich, CT.

*Bonbright and Co. is credited with helping shape the country's electrical utility industry. It was known as one of Wall Street's "Big Six" investment banks.

**United Corporation controlled twenty-one percent of the country's electrical production.

front facade

Thorneham

sitting room

side facade, c 1929

garden

side facade

Thurber, Fred C. (1873-1943)

Occupation(s):   capitalist -   owner, Bellport Hotel, Bellport;
                                  owner, Five Mile Look Hotel, Blue Point;
                                  owner, Central Hotel, Patchogue

Marriage(s):   Carrie B. ____

Address: Penataquit Avenue, Bay Shore
Name of estate:
Year of construction:
Style of architecture: Queen Anne
Architect(s):   Henry G. Hardenburg designed
              the house (for Thurber)

Landscape architect(s):
House extant: no
Historical notes:

front facade, c. 1897

    The house was built by Fred C. Thurber.
    It was subsequently owned by Harmanus B. Hubbard, who called it *Oakhurst*.

Timmerman, Henry Gerlard (d. 1925)

Occupation(s):   financier -   partner, Timmerman, Moore, and Schuley
                              (stock brokerage firm)

Marriage(s):   Kate Fry (d. 1933)

Address: Ocean Avenue, Islip
Name of estate: *Breeze Lawn*
Year of construction: c. 1889
Style of architecture: Colonial Revival with Shingle elements
Architect(s):
Landscape architect(s):
House extant: no
Historical notes:

rear facade

    The house was built by Leander Waterbury.
    It was subsequently owned by Howard Gibb, Sr.
    In 1898, Timmerman purchased the house and named it *Breeze Lawn*.
    It was subsequently owned by Timmerman's daughter Grace, who had married Orville Hurd Tobey. Mrs. Tobey continued to call the estate *Breeze Lawn*.

Titus, James Gulden, Sr. (1911-1991)

Occupation(s):   restaurateur -   vice-president, Harry M. Stevens Inc., Cranberry, NJ
                                            (catering firm for Yankee Stadium, New York Mets'
                                            Shea Stadium, Boston Red Sox' Fenway Park,
                                            Brooklyn Dodgers' Ebbets Field, San Francisco Giants'
                                            Candlestick Park, Aqueduct Race Track, Belmont Park
                                            Racetrack, Saratoga Raceway, Gulfstream Park,
                                            Tropical Park, Roosevelt Raceway, Mineola, Yonkers
                                            Raceway, Hialeah Park Racetrack, New York Coliseum,
                                            and Madison Square Garden)*
                        capitalist -   part-owner, Boston Red Sox baseball team
                        military -   member, Squadron A, United States Cavalry Reserve, 1939-1942;
                                              second lieutenant, United States Army, 1942-1946

Civic Activism: member, St. Nicholas Society

Marriage(s):   1942-1991 – Alice Muriel Stevens

Address: 21 Beech Road, Islip
Name of estate:
Year of construction:
Style of architecture: Ranch
Architect(s):
Landscape architect(s):
House extant: yes
Historical note:

   The *Social Register, Summer 1969* lists James G. and Alice M. Stevens Titus [Sr.] as residing at 21 Beech Road, Islip.
   He was the son of Walter Livingston and Margaret Gulden Titus, Sr. of West Islip.
   Alice Muriel Stevens Titus was the daughter of Frank Mozley and Gertrude Honhorst Stevens of Manhattan.
   James Gulden and Alice Muriel Stevens Titus, Sr.'s daughter Stephanie married Dr. William Shain Schley, the son of Dr. Frank Schley, and resides in Manhattan. Their daughter Sandra married Michael McCoy McKinstry, the son of Richard E. McKinstry, and resides in Englewood, CO. Their son James Gulden Titus, Jr. died in 2000.
   [See other Titus entries for additional family information.]
   *Harry M. Stevens Inc. had concession rights to approximately fifty race and harness tracks in the country.

front facade, 2006

Titus, Walter Livingston, Jr. (1906-1969)

Occupation(s):   capitalist -   director, Republic Pictures (which became Republic Corp.)
Civic Activism: member, St. Nicholas Society

Marriage(s):   1933-1969 – Elsa Marcia Yates (1911-1994)

Address: 88 East Bayberry Road, Islip
Name of estate:
Year of construction: 1899-1900
Style of architecture: Moorish
Architect(s):   Grosvenor Atterbury designed the house
                            (for H. O. Havemeyer)*
Landscape architect(s): Nathan F. Barrett (for H. O. Havemeyer)**
House extant: yes
Historical notes:

    The house was built by Henry Osborne Havemeyer as part of his "Modern Venice" development. It was owned by Charles Gulden II and, subsequently, by Titus.
    He was the son of Walter Livingston and Margaret Gulden Titus, Sr. of West Islip.
    Elsa Marcia Yates Titus was the daughter of Herbert John and Petra Antonsen Yates, Sr. of *Onsrufarm* in West Islip.
    Walter Livingston and Elsa Marcia Yates Titus, Jr.'s son Peter married Jill Mennella of Islip. Their son David married Joan Purdy of Englewood, NJ. Their son Walter Livingston Titus III married Louise McCarthy of Bronxville, NY. Their daughter Marcia married Thomas Young of Bay Shore.
    [See other Titus entries for additional family information.]
    *The sales brochure for "Modern Venice" states that the Moorish-style architecture was suggested by Louis Comfort Tiffany.
    **The sales brochure also states that "Modern Venice" would be devoid of trees and vegetation and that Nathan F. Barrett was the landscape architect.

Titus, Walter Livingston, Sr. (1877-1953)

Occupation(s):   merchant -   general store manager, Lord & Taylor Department Store
                              industrialist -   director, Nedick's Orange Drink
Civic Activism: member, St. Nicholas Society

Marriage(s):   Margaret Gulden (d. 1965)

Address: Eaton's Lane, West Islip
Name of estate:
Year of construction:
Style of architecture:
Architect(s):
Landscape architect(s):
House extant: no; demolished c. 1962
Historical notes:

    Walter Livingston Titus, Sr. was the son of James Livingston Titus of Manhattan.
    Margaret Gulden Titus was the daughter of Charles and Mary C. Kellers Gulden, Sr. of *Netherbay* in Bay Shore.
    Walter Livingston and Margaret Gulden Titus, Sr.'s son Walter Livingston Titus, Jr. married Elsa Marcia Yates and resided in Islip. The Tituses' daughter Margaret married Elsa's brother Douglas Thomas Yates, Sr. and resided in Islip. Their son James Gulden Titus married Alice Muriel Stevens and also resided in Islip.
    [See other Titus entries for additional family information.]

Tobey, Orville Hurd (1879-1934)

Occupation(s):   financier -   partner, Lawrence Turnure and Co., NYC (investment
                                   banking firm)

Marriage(s):   M/1 – 1907 – Grace Ethel Timmerman
                    M/2 – Elizabeth Fry

Address: Ocean Avenue, Islip
Name of estate: *Breeze Lawn*
Year of construction: c. 1889
Style of architecture: Colonial Revival with Shingle elements
Architect(s):
Landscape architect(s):
House extant: no
Historical notes:

    The house was built by Leander Waterbury.
    It was subsequently owned by Howard Gibb, Sr.
    In 1898, Henry Gerlard and Kate Fry Timmerman purchased the house and named it *Breeze Lawn*.
    It was subsequently owned by the Timmermans' daughter Grace Ethel Timmerman Tobey. Mrs. Tobey
continued to call the estate *Breeze Lawn*.
    The *Social Register, Summer 1937* lists Mrs. Grace E. T. Tobey as residing at *Breeze Lawn* in Islip.
    Orville Hurd Tobey was the son of Frank Hurd and Katherine Tobey of Manhattan.

Todd, William H. (1864-1932)

Occupation(s):   industrialist -   president, Robbins Dry Dock and Repair Co., Brooklyn, NY;
                                   president, Todd Shipyards Corp. (ship building firm)*

Marriage(s):   1889-1928 – Mary Emma Babcock (d. 1928)

Address: Middle Road and Marina Court, Bayport
Name of estate: *Lenapes Lodge*
Year of construction:
Style of architecture: Colonial Revival
Architect(s):
Landscape architect(s):
House extant: yes
Historical notes:

    In 1911, Todd purchased the William Brown farm and converted the farm house into his country residence
Lenapes Lodge.
    William H. Todd was the son of James and Sarah Elizabeth Moody Todd.
    Mary Emma Babcock Todd was the daughter of Peter J. Babcock of Wilmington, DE.
    William H. and Mary Emma Babcock Todd's son J. Herbert
Todd married Dorothy D. Parker and resided in Brooklyn and
Pinehurst, NC. Their daughter Natalie married Thomas R.
Lilly of Stamford, CT. Their daughter Margaret, who inherited
Lenapes Lodge, married William Henry Smith of Brooklyn
and, subsequently, Herbert Williams Richter, also of Brooklyn.
Margaret sold *Lenapes Lodge* in the 1960s.
    *During World War I Todd Shipyard Corp. had seven
different facilities and was a major contractor for construction
of cruisers for the United States Navy.

front / side facade, 2005

268

True, Benjamin K.

Occupation(s):   capitalist -   secretary, Southside Railroad

Marriage(s):   Martha B. _____ (d. 1893)

Address: Oak Neck Road, West Islip
Name of estate:
Year of construction:
Style of architecture: Colonial Revival
Architect(s):
Landscape architect(s):
House extant: unconfirmed
Historical notes:

front facade

   The house was built by Benjamin K. True.
   Benjamin K. and Martha True's daughter Julia married
William J. Fowler and, subsequently, John L. Stephens
of West Islip.

Truslow, Frederick C. (d. 1920)

Occupation(s):   industrialist -   general manager, Williamsburgh Cork Works
                                   (a division of Armstrong Cork Co.)*

Marriage(s):   Anne Gates Babcock

Address: Great River Road, Great River
Name of estate: *Questover Lodge*
Year of construction:
Style of architecture: Shingle
Architect(s):
Landscape architect(s):
House extant: no
Historical notes:

   The house, originally named *Questover Lodge*, was built by Frederick C. Truslow.
   The *Brooklyn Blue Book and Long Island Society Register, 1918* lists Frederick C. and Anne Gates
Babcock Truslow as residing in Cranford, NJ.
   He was the son of James L. Truslow. His sister married William Newton Adams and resided in Brooklyn.
His other sister married Dr. Henry Conklin and resided in Brooklyn. His brother was president of the
Brooklyn Board of Assessors.
   Anne Gates Babcock Truslow was the daughter of James
A. Babcock. Her brother Edwin married Addie Burgess
Murr and resided in Brooklyn. Her brother Augustus
married Lillian A. Sloan, the daughter of Augustus Kellogg
and Mary Cromwell Sloan, Sr. of Brooklyn.
   Frederick C. and Anne Gates Babcock Truslow's son
Percival married Grace Rhodes.
   *James L. Truslow's wholesale cork companies of
Truslow, Nostrand & Co. and Truslow & Co. were merged
into Armstrong Cork Co. [*Brooklyn Daily Eagle* June 27, 1901, p. 3.]
   The estate was subsequently owned by James Stewart.

front facade

Tucker, Charles A.

Occupation(s):

Marriage(s):

Address: Ocean Avenue, Islip
Name of estate:
Year of construction: c. 1880s
Style of architecture: Victorian
Architect(s):   Isaac Henry Green II designed the
                     c. 1889 alterations (for W. Dick)
                 Alfred Hopkins designed the garage
                     and stables (for John Henry Dick)
Landscape architect(s):
House extant: no; demolished in 1960s*
Historical notes:

front facade, c. 1903

   The house was built by Charles A. Tucker.
   His brother Clarence also resided in Islip.
   The Ocean Avenue home was later owned by William Dick, his son John Henry Dick and, subsequently, by William Karl Dick, all of whom called in *Allen Winden Farm*.
   *Garage and stables are extant.

Tucker, Clarence

Occupation(s):

Marriage(s):

Address: St. Mark's Lane, Islip
Name of estate:
Year of construction: c. 1881
Style of architecture:
Architect(s):
Landscape architect(s):
House extant: unconfirmed
Historical notes:

   The house was built by William Collins Whitney.
   In 1882, Tucker purchased the house from Whitney who, by 1902, had relocated to Old Westbury.
   By 1889 Clarence Tucker was spending his summers in Seabright, NJ.
   In 1893, the house was purchased by Mrs. Richard H. Williams.

Turnbull, George R. (1842-1909)

Occupation(s):   financier -   director, East River National Bank, NYC;
                               director, Market & Fulton National Bank;
                               director, South Brooklyn Savings Institution;
                               director, Guaranty Trust Co.
                 capitalist -   director, Norfolk & Southern Railroad;
                               director, Brooklyn Union Gas Co.;
                               director, Kansas City Gas Co.;
                               director, Galveston City Railroad Co.
                 industrialist -   treasurer, Butler Hard Rubber Co.;
                               director, Central Stamping Co.;
                               director, American Type Founders Co.;
                               trustee, Central Asphalt Co.

Marriage(s):   1873-1909 – Clara Jenkins (d. 1935)

Address: South Country Road, West Islip
Name of estate: *The Pines*
Year of construction: 1889
Style of architecture: Shingle
Architect(s):
Landscape architect(s):
House extant: no
Historical notes:

front facade, c. 1903

The house, originally named *The Pines*, was built by George R. Turnbull.

He was the son of John and Elizabeth Whitehead Turnbull.

The *Long Island Society Register, 1929* lists Clara Jenkins Turnbull as residing at *The Pines* on Main Road [South Country Road] in Bay Shore [West Islip].

She was the daughter of Edward Osland and Henrietta Hodes Jenkins.

George R. and Clara Jenkins Turnbull's daughter Clara married Minor C. R. Keith II and resided in West Islip.

Turnbull, John Gourlay, Jr. (1856-1903)

Occupation(s):

Marriage(s):   Josephine Sherwood

Address: Potter Boulevard, Brightwaters
Name of estate:
Year of construction:
Style of architecture:
Architect(s):
Landscape architect(s):
House extant: unconfirmed
Historical notes:

The *Brooklyn Blue Book and Long Island Society Register, 1918* lists John Gourlay and Josephine Sherwood Turnbull [Jr.] as residing in Brightwaters, prior to their relocation to Garden City.

John Gourlay and Josephine Sherwood Turnbull, Jr.'s son John Gourlay Turnbull III married Hariette Boden Hutchinson and resided on Nassau Boulevard in Garden City.

271

Underhill, Edward Beekman, Sr. (1833-1899)

Occupation(s):	financier - stockbroker
	capitalist - Manhattan and Bay Shore real estate

Marriage(s):   Lydia F. ____

Address: Ocean Avenue, Bay Shore
Name of estate:
Year of construction:
Style of architecture: Eclectic*
Architect(s):
Landscape architect(s):
House extant: unconfirmed
Historical notes:

   *Edward Beekman Underhill, Sr.'s Bay Shore house was built in the style of a lighthouse. [*Brooklyn Daily Eagle* July 3, 1887, p. 4.]
   The Underhill's son Rawson married Grace C. Crowley and resided in Albany, NY. Their son Joseph married Elizabeth Wyman Aldrich, the daughter of William Aldrich.

Valentine, Landon Barrett

Occupation(s):	industrialist - president, Valentine & Co. (manufacturer of paint and Varnish)
Civic Activism:	member, board of managers, Southside Hospital, Bay Shore

Marriage(s):	M/1 – May Harper
	M/2 – 1909 – Louise Hollister (1883-1946)

Address: South Bay Avenue, Islip
Name of estate:
Year of construction:
Style of architecture:
Architect(s):
Landscape architect(s):
House extant: unconfirmed
Historical notes:

   The *Long Island Society Register, 1929* lists Landon Barrett and Louise Hollister Valentine as residing on South Bay Avenue in Islip.
   He was the son of Henry C. Valentine.
   Louise Hollister Valentine was the daughter of Henry Hutchinson Hollister, Sr. of Islip. She had previously been married to Richard E. Forest. Her brother Buell Hollister, Sr. married Louise R. Knowlton and resided in Islip. Her brother Henry Hutchinson Hollister, Jr. married Hope Shepley.
   Landon Barrett and Louise Hollister Valentine's daughter Anne married Joseph Sears Lovering, Jr. of Islip.

Van Anden, Frank (1876-1952)

Occupation(s):   inventor - designed pontoons used on amphibian airplanes into the 1950s; constructed one of the first wind tunnels to test airplane wing stresses

Marriage(s):   M/1 – c. 1897 – Ida Kessberg*
M/2 – Edwina _____ (1885-1924)
M/3 – Nellie R. Dunn

Address: Ocean Avenue, Islip
Name of estate:
Year of construction:
Style of architecture:
Architect(s):
Landscape architect(s):
House extant: unconfirmed
Historical notes:

Frank Van Anden was the son of William M. and Alice H. Frost Van Anden of Islip.

His daughter Mrs. Evelyn Seay resided in Fort Lauderdale, FL. His daughter Mrs. Italia Kingcade resided in Covington, KY. His son William M. Van Anden II resided in Miami, FL.

*While in Berlin, Germany, to improve his German language skills, Van Anden secretly married Ida Kessberg. Upon returning to the United States, he convinced his parents to advertise for a tutor to help him with his German writing skills. Ida answered the advertisement and was engaged by the family to tutor Frank. The Van Andens learned of Frank and Ida's marriage when his father William was congratulated by a friend on the marriage of his son. [*The New York Times* September 26, 1897, p. 8.]

[See following entry for additional family information.]

Van Anden, William M., Sr. (1842-1918)

Occupation(s):   capitalist -   director, American District Telegraph Co.;
president, Eagle Warehouse and Storage Co.
financier -   director, Long Island Safe Deposit Co.;
director, Capital Surplus
publisher -   president, secretary, and treasurer, *Brooklyn Daily Eagle**

Marriage(s):   Alice H. Frost (1851-1933)

Address: Ocean Avenue, Islip
Name of estate:
Year of construction:
Style of architecture:
Architect(s):
Landscape architect(s):
House extant: unconfirmed
Historical notes:

The *Brooklyn Blue Book and Long Island Society Register, 1918* and *1921* list William M. and Alice Frost Van Anden [Sr.] as residing in Islip.

He was the son of William Van Anden of Brooklyn.

*William M. Van Anden, Sr.'s uncle Isaac Van Anden was a founder of *The Brooklyn Daily Eagle*.

Alice H. Frost Van Anden was the daughter of Jacob and Sarah Titus Frost. Her sister Louise married George R. Read of Manhattan. Her brother Newbury H. Frost, a bachelor, resided in Hempstead.

William M. and Alice H. Frost Van Anden, Sr.'s daughter Louise married George S. Frank, the son of Emil H. and Paula Van Glahn Frank of Bay Shore, and resided in New Canaan, CT. Their daughter Estelle married D. Rait Richardson and resided in Manhattan. Their son Frank also lived in Islip. *[See previous entry.]*

Vanderbilt, William Kissam, Sr. (1849-1920)

Occupation(s):   capitalist -   president, New York Central Railroad and its subsidiaries
Civic Activism: built and endowed St. Mark's Episcopal Church, Islip

Marriage(s):   M/1 – 1875-div. 1895 – Alva Erskine Smith (1853-1933)
                          - writer -   *Melinda and Her Sisters* (suffragist opera/with Elsa
                                   Maxwell);
                                   One Month's Log of the Seminole, 1916;
                                   two unpublished autobiographies, 1917, 1933
                      journalist -   numerous newspaper and magazine articles*
                      Civic Activism: woman's suffrage -
                                     founder and president, Political Equality Assoc.;
                                   first president, National Woman's Party**;
                                   purchased building in Washington, DC, for
                                       National Woman's Party Headquarters [now,
                                       known as Sewall–Belmont House];
                               primary benefactor and president of board,
                                     Hempstead Hospital, Hempstead [not the
                                     present-day hospital also named Hempstead
                                     Hospital];
                             established, Brookholt School of Agriculture for
                                     Women at East Meadow estate;
                             built and supported, Sea Side Hospital for Sick
                                     Children, a 200-bed hospital in Great River
                                     (later, Trinity Sea Side Home)
         M/2 – 1903-1920 – Anne Harriman (1860-1940)
                        - Civic Activism: a founder, Franco–American War Museum;
                                       donated $1 million for the establishment of the
                                     East River Home and Hospital, NYC;
                                       a founder and director, American Woman's
                                       Association, NYC;
                                 ***

Address: South County Road, Oakdale
Name of estate: *Idlehour*****
Year of construction: 1878
Style of architecture: Shingle
Architect(s):   Richard Morris Hunt
                       designed the 1878 house
                       (for W. K. Vanderbilt, Sr.)

Landscape architect(s):
House extant: no; 1878 house destroyed by fire in 1899*****
Historical notes:

Idlehour, c. 1895

   The one-hundred-room house, originally named *Idlehour*, was built by William Kissam Vanderbilt, Sr. He was the son of William Henry and Maria Kissam Vanderbilt of Staten Island, NY.
   Alva Erskine Smith Vanderbilt was the daughter of Murray Forbes and Phoebe Desha Smith of Mobile, AL, and Manhattan. Alva subsequently married Oliver Hazard Perry Belmont, with whom she resided at *Marble House* and *Belcourt* in Newport, RI, and *Brookholt* in East Meadow. After Belmont's death in 1908, Alva relocated to *Beacon Towers* in Sands Point and, subsequently, to France, where she was living at the time of her death.
   William Kissam and Alva Erskine Smith Vanderbilt Sr.'s daughter Consuelo married Charles Richard John Spencer–Churchill, the Ninth Duke of Marlborough and, subsequently, Louis Jacques Balsan, with whom she resided at *Old Fields* in East Norwich, in Southampton, and in Palm Beach, FL. Their son William Kissam Vanderbilt, Jr. married Virginia Graham Fair and, subsequently, Rosamund Lancaster and resided at

Deepdale in Lake Success and at *Eagle's Nest* in Centerport. Their son Harold, who inherited the second *Idlehour* house, married Gertrude Lewis Conaway.

Anne Harriman Vanderbilt was the daughter of Oliver and Laura Low Harriman. She had previously been married to Samuel Stevens Sands, Jr. and Lewis Morris Rutherfurd. Samuel Stevens and Anne Harriman Sands, Jr.'s son Samuel Stevens Sands III married Gertrude Sheldon, the daughter of George R. Sheldon of Manhattan. Their son George married Anne Aldridge Gibson, the daughter of John Aldridge Gibson of Leesburg, VA. Both George and his brother Samuel were killed in automobile accidents. Lewis Morris and Anne Harriman Rutherfurd's daughter Barbara married Cyril Hatch and, subsequently, Winfield J. Nichols. Their daughter Margaret married Frederick Leybourne Sprague.

*Mrs. Belmont donated the proceeds from her newspaper and magazine articles to the suffrage movement.

**Alva Belmont's Sands Point estate was the site of the 1920 National Woman's Party Conference.

***Anne Harriman Vanderbilt was the first woman to receive a gold medal from the French Ministry of Foreign Affairs for her service to France.

****According to Vanderbilt's own stationery and the name painted on his private railroad car, *Idlehour* was one word.

*****In 1899, while William Kissam, Jr. and his wife Virginia Graham Fair were spending their honeymoon at the estate, the 1879 house was destroyed by fire.

[See following entry for history of 1900 house.]

Vanderbilt, William Kissam, Sr. (1849-1920)

Occupation(s):	*[See previous entry.]*
Marriage(s):	*[See previous entry.]*
Address:	South Country Road, Oakdale
Name of estate:	*Idlehour*
Year of construction:	1900
Style of architecture: elements	Beaux Arts with Flemish
Architect(s):	Richard Howland Hunt designed the 1900 house (for W. K. Vanderbilt, Sr.) Warren and Wetmore designed the 1903 bachelor annex and indoor tennis court (for W. K. Vanderbilt, Sr.)

Idlehour, 1900 house, 1990

Landscape architect(s):
House extant: yes
Historical notes:

With the destruction of the first *Idlehour* by fire, William Kissam Vanderbilt, Sr. built a second house on the site which he also called *Idlehour*.

The estate, which was inherited by his son Harold, had several subsequent owners including the firm of Edmund G. and Charles F. Burke, Inc., which, in the 1920s, was unsuccessful in its attempt to subdivide the estate's property for a housing development. In 1937, the main residence and the carriage house were acquired by the Fraternity of Master Metaphysicians. In 1947, National Dairy Research Labs, Inc. purchased the main residence, carriage house, and twenty-three acres. In 1963, the National Dairy holdings were acquired by Adelphi University of Garden City for use as its Adelphi Suffolk campus. In 1968, the Oakdale campus became Dowling College.

In 1974, the main residence was the site of a devastating fire. The smoking lounge, main staircase, plaster friezes in the dining room [Hunt Room], woodwork and the ornate ceiling in the living room, and velvet tapestry wallcovering throughout the house were destroyed. Repairs were made to the fire-damaged main residence by the Fortunoff family; historic elements were not restored. Karl Bitter's sculpture, "Diana, the Huntress," in the dining room, was restored by a member of the college's art department.

[See previous entry for family information and a history of the 1878 house.]

275

living room, c. 1903

living room, 1990

section of friezes in Hunt Room (dining room)

front entrance foyer and main staircase, c. 1903

men's smoking lounge, c. 1903

William Kissam Vanderbilt Sr. Estate, *Idlehour [1900]*

main staircase, c. 1903

main staircase, 1990

wallpaper replacement of Hunt Room friezes,
1990

hallway outside men's smoking lounge,
c. 1903

hallway outside men's smoking lounge,
1990

Vander Veer, Dr. Albert, Jr. (d. 1959)*

Occupation(s):   physician -   Roosevelt Hospital, NYC

Marriage(s):   M/1 – 1912-1944 – Sylvia A. deMurias (1888-1944)
                                M/2 – 1951-1959 – Margaret Maxwell Clark

Address: Point of Woods, Fire Island
Name of estate: *Alkmaar Cottage*
Year of construction:
Style of architecture:
Architect(s):
Landscape architect(s):
House extant: unconfirmed
Historical notes:

   The *Long Island Society Register, 1929* lists Dr. Albert and Mrs. Sylvia A. deMurias Vander Veer, Jr. as residing at *Alkmaar Cottage* in Point of Woods.
   He was the son of Dr. Albert and Mrs. Margaret E. Snow Vander Veer, Sr. of Albany, NY.
   Sylvia A. deMurias Vander Veer was the daughter of Ramon and Clara Gardin deMurias of Cuba and Manhattan. Sylvia's brother Fernando resided in Babylon.
   Dr. Albert and Mrs. Sylvia A. deMurias Vander Veer, Jr.'s daughter Margaret married Charles B. Colmore, Jr. and resided in Glen Ridge, NJ. Their daughter Jean married Girardeau Leland, Jr. of McClennanville, SC.
   The *Social Register, Summer 1954* lists Dr. Albert and Mrs. Margaret M. Clark Vander Veer, Jr. as residing at *Gray Shingles* in Point of Woods.
   Margaret Maxwell Clark Vander Veer was the daughter of John Kirkland and Margaret Holbrook Clark of Manhattan.
   *Another branch of the family uses Vanderveer for the spelling of the family surname.

Vanderveer, John (1868-1941)*

Occupation(s):
Civic Activism: philanthropist**

Marriage(s):   Gertrude Van Siclen Lott (d. 1945)

Address: South Country Road, West Islip
Name of estate: *Sunnymead*
Year of construction:
Style of architecture: Shingle
Architect(s):
Landscape architect(s):
House extant: no; demolished c. 1953***
Historical notes:

front facade, 1930s

   John Vanderveer purchased the house in 1904.
   The *Long Island Society Register, 1929* lists John and Gertrude V. S. Lott Vanderveer as residing on South Country Road, Babylon [West Islip].
   Their daughter Cornelia, who married John Joseph Gibson, inherited *Sunnymead*.
   *Another branch of the family uses Vander Veer for the spelling of the family surname.
   **Vanderveer was known for his generosity to those in need in the local community.
   During the 1930s and 1940s a local nursery leased a portion of the estate's property for Dutch bulb cultivation. During World War II German prisoners-of-war were utilized to assist in the bulb cultivation.
[Personal communication from John Vanderveer Gibson]
   In 1958, the sixty-acre estate became the site of Good Samaritan Hospital.
   ***The gardener's cottage, at 175 Beach Drive, is currently the hospital's Office of Hospital Development.

Wagstaff, Alfred, Jr. (1844-1921)

Occupation(s):   attorney -   partner, North, Ward, and Wagstaff
                          politician -   member, New York State Assembly from Manhattan's
                                              5th District, 1867-1873;
                                        member, New York State Senate, 1876-1878;
                                        clerk, Court of Common Pleas, 1892-1895;
                                        clerk, Appellate Division, New York State Supreme
                                          Court;
                                        president, Brooklyn Bridge Commission, 1890-1891
                          capitalist -   president Brooklyn Bridge Co.;
                                          president, Christopher & 10th Street Railroad;
                                        director, Central Crosstown Railroad

Civic Activism: president, American Society for the Prevention of Cruelty to Animals,
                1906;
              president, New York Association for the Protection of Game;
              trustee, Samaritan Home for the Aged;
              president of board, Southside Hospital, Bay Shore

Marriage(s):   1880-1921 – Mary Anderson Barnard (1859-1938)
                - Civic Activism: president, West Islip Board of Education

Address: South Country Road, West Islip
Name of estate: *Opekeepsing**
Year of construction:
Style of architecture: Shingle
Architect(s):
Landscape architect(s):
House extant: no
Historical notes:

    The house, originally named *Opekeepsing*, was built by Alfred Wagstaff, Jr.

    He was the son of Dr. Alfred and Mrs. Sarah Platt DuBois Wagstaff, Sr., who resided at *Tahlulah* in West Islip.

    Mary Anderson Barnard Wagstaff was the daughter of New York Supreme Court Judge George C. and Mrs. Mary Anderson Barnard. [Judge Barnard was a member of New York City's infamous Tweed Ring.]

    Alfred and Mary Anderson Barnard Wagstaff, Jr.'s daughter Margaret married John Fairchild Adams, the son of Horatio M. and Mary Hartwell Carter Adams of *Appledale* in Glen Cove. Margaret subsequently married ____ Singleton and resided in Babylon. Their son George, who married Mary Cutting Cumnock, Dorothy W. Frothingham, and, subsequently, Lillian Hyde, resided in Bay Shore. Their son David married Isabelle Tilford and resided at *Ledgelands* in Tuxedo Park, NY. Their son Samuel, who resided in Syosset, married Pauline French, the daughter of Amos Tucker French, and, subsequently, Cornelia Walker Scranton. Their son Alfred Wagstaff III married Blanch Shoemaker of Philadelphia, PA.

    [See other Wagstaff entries for additional family information.]

    **Opekeepsing* means "safe harbor." [Harry W. Havemeyer, *Along the Great South Bay From Oakdale to Babylon: The Story of a Summer Spa 1840 to 1940* (Mattituck, NY: Amereon House, 1996), p. 252.]

front facade

Wagstaff, Dr. Alfred, Sr. (1804-1878)

Occupation(s):   physician
                           capitalist -   owned real estate in Manhattan

Marriage(s):   Sarah Platt DuBois (1813-1897)

Address: South Country Road, West Islip
Name of estate: *Tahlulah*
Year of construction: c. 1827
Style of architecture: Italianate
Architect(s):
Landscape architect(s):
House extant: no
Historical notes:

   In 1827, Dr. Alfred Wagstaff, Sr. purchased the Bergen farm and built *Tahlulah* as his country residence.
[*The New York Times* June 16, 1938, p. 23.]
   He was the son of Manhattan merchant David Wagstaff. Alfred's sister married William Lowerre. His sister Ann married Benjamin D. K. Craig. Another sister married Henry Maunsell Schieffelin, the son of Henry Hamilton Schieffelin.
   Sarah Platt DuBois Wagstaff was the daughter of Cornelius DuBois.
   Dr. Alfred and Mrs. Sarah Platt DuBois Wagstaff, Sr.'s son Alfred Wagstaff, Jr. married Mary Anderson Barnard and resided at *Opekeepsing* in West Islip. Their son Cornelius married Amy Colt and resided in West Islip. Their daughter Sarah married Phoenix Remsen and also resided in West Islip. Their daughter Mary married Henry Gribble.
   [See other Wagstaff entries for additional family information.]
   In 1904, the estate was sold at public auction. [*Brooklyn Daily Eagle* April 29, 1900, p. 41 and May 10, 1900, p. 13.]

front facade, c. 1925

Wagstaff, Cornelius DuBois (1845-1919)

Occupation(s):

Marriage(s):   Amy Colt (d. 1934)

Address: South Country Road, West Islip
Name of estate:
Year of construction:
Style of architecture:
Architect(s):
Landscape architect(s):
House extant: unconfirmed
Historical notes:

   Cornelius DuBois Wagstaff was the son of Dr. Alfred and Mrs. Sarah Platt DuBois Wagstaff, Sr. of *Tahlulah* in West Islip.
   Amy Colt Wagstaff was the daughter of Robert Oliver and Adelaide Colt, who resided in West Bay Shore.
   [See other Wagstaff entries for additional family information.]

Wagstaff, George Barnard (1886-1964)

Occupation(s):	financier - partner, E. F. Hutton and Co. (investment banking firm)
Civic Activism:	member, New York Stock Exchange committee to aid refugees from The Netherlands during World War II

Marriage(s):	M/1 – 1914 – Mary Cutting Cumnock
	M/2 – 1921 – Dorothy W. Frothingham
	M/3 – 1940-1964 – Lillian Hyde

Address:	57 Lawrence Lane, Bay Shore
Name of estate:	
Year of construction:	
Style of architecture:	Modified Colonial
Architect(s):	
Landscape architect(s):	
House extant:	yes
Historical notes:	

   George Barnard Wagstaff was the son of Alfred and Mary Anderson Barnard Wagstaff, Jr., who resided at *Opekeepsing* in West Islip.
   Mary Cutting Cumnock Wagstaff was the daughter of Arthur J. and Mary Cutting Cumnock of Manhattan.
   Dorothy W. Frothingham Wagstaff had previously been married to ____ Arnold. She subsequently married the Honorable Lionel Forbes–Sempill, with whom she resided in London, England. The death of Lord Sempill, the 10th Baronet of Forbes of Rux, in 1965 initiated an unprecedented and bizarre succession situation which centered on whether Lord Sempill's brother Ewan was the legitimate heir to the baronetcy. A physician, who practiced medicine under the name Elizabeth Forbes–Sempill until the age of forty, Dr. Forbes–Sempill was registered at birth as female but changed his name to Ewan Forbes–Sempill and his birth registration from female to male in 1952. A three-year private court case ensued during which extensive medical evidence was presented. Based on the court proceedings, the Home Secretary declared Ewan the 11th Baronet. It was not until 1997 that court records, which allegedly declared Ewan a true hermaphrodite, but male, became available. [Dr. Angus Campbell, "The Forbes–Sempill Case." The 6th International Congress on Sex and Gender Diversity: Reflecting Gender. The School of Law, Manchester Metropolitan University September 10th to 12th, 2004; *The New York Times* December 31, 1963, pp. 3, 23 and December 3, 1968, p. 13.]
   George Barnard and Dorothy W. Frothingham Wagstaff's daughter Beatrice married David Wagstaff, Jr. of *Ledgeland* in Tuxedo Park, NY, and, subsequently, Henri A. Luebermann. Their daughter Dorothy married Louis Rose Ripley, the son of Baillie Ripley of Litchfield, CT.
   Lillian Hyde Wagstaff was the daughter of Richard Hyde of Bay Shore. She had previously been married to Quentin Field Feitner, the son of Thomas L. and Mary C. Moore Feitner of Manhattan. Lillian's sister Lulu married V. B. Hubbell, Sr. and, subsequently, Howard Drummond, with whom she resided at *Little House* in Bay Shore. Her brother William married Grace M. Riopel and resided at *White Cottage* in Bay Shore.

front facade, 2006

Walbridge, Ernest A. (1892-1940)

Occupation(s):   financier -   member, Mackay and Company (stock brokerage firm)

Marriage(s):   Blanche Gifford Wandel

Address: 3 Reid Avenue, Babylon
Name of estate:
Year of construction:
Style of architecture: Victorian farmhouse
Architect(s):
Landscape architect(s):
House extant: yes
Historical notes:

The *Long Island Society Register, 1929* lists Ernest A. Walbridge as residing at 3 Reid Avenue, Babylon. At the time of his death, he was residing at 102 Crescent Avenue, Babylon.

He was the son of August C. and Katherine Clarke Walbridge. His sister Helen remained unmarried. His sister Anna married E. H. Peck and resided in Manhattan. His sister Ethel married ____ McCully and resided in Bronxville, NY.

Ernest A. and Blanche Gifford Wandel Walbridge's son John married Michelle Kelley, the daughter of Leon Kelley of Babylon.

front / side facade, 2006

Walbridge, George Hicks (1869-1936)

Occupation(s):   engineer
                         capitalist -   president, Colorado Power Co. (in charge of construction and management of hydro-electric plants);
                                       vice-president, J. G. White & Co. (engineering firm);
                                       member, L. P. Hammond (public utility and industrial management firm);
                                       chairman of board, Royalties Management Corp.
                         financier -   vice-president, Bonbright and Company (investment banking firm)

Marriage(s):   1900 – Mary Gilley Taylor

Address: Crescent Avenue, Babylon
Name of estate:
Year of construction:
Style of architecture:
Architect(s):
Landscape architect(s):
House extant: unconfirmed
Historical notes:

George Hicks Walbridge was the son of James Hicks and Delia M. Perry Walbridge.

Ward. Edwin Carrington

Occupation(s):   attorney
Civic Activism: director, Brooklyn Academy of Music

Marriage(s):   1895 – Marion Louette Matson

Address: Penataquit Avenue, Bay Shore
Name of estate: *Wake Robin*
Year of construction:
Style of architecture:
Architect(s):
Landscape architect(s):
House extant: unconfirmed
Historical notes:

    The *Brooklyn Blue Book and Long Island Society Register, 1918* lists Marion Louette Matson Ward as residing at *Wake Robin* in Bay Shore.
    Edwin Carrington and Marion Louette Matson Ward's son Kenneth married Barbara Wey, the daughter of H. F. G. Wey, who resided at *The Birches* in Rye, NY. Their daughter Winifred married Walter Talbot Spalding and resided in Bronxville, NY.

Waterbury, Leander (d. 1889)

Occupation(s):   politician -   Brooklyn Parks Commissioner

Marriage(s):

Address: Ocean Avenue, Islip
Name of estate:
Year of construction: c. 1889
Style of architecture: Colonial Revival with Shingle elements
Architect(s):
Landscape architect(s):
House extant: no
Historical notes:

    The house was built by Leander Waterbury.
    It was later owned by Howard Gibb, Sr.
    In 1898, the house was purchased by Henry Gerlard Timmerman. It was later owned by Timmerman's daughter Grace, who married Orville Hurd Tobey. Both the Timmermans and the Tobeys called the house *Breeze Lawn*.

rear facade

Watt, Dr. James, Sr.

Occupation(s):   physician

Marriage(s):   M/1 – Maude ____
                        M/2 – Roberta Bach

Address: Handsome Avenue, Sayville
Name of estate:
Year of construction: c. 1890
Style of architecture:
Architect(s):
Landscape architect(s):
House extant: unconfirmed
Historical notes:

The house was built by Dr. James Watt, Sr.
The *Long Island Society Register, 1929* lists Dr. James and Mrs. Roberta Bach Watt as residing in Sayville.
Watt's son James Watt, Jr. married Marion Kraeger.

Webster, Charles D. (1905-1998)

Occupation(s):
Civic Activism: member, medieval art department visiting committee, Metropolitan
                            Museum of Art, NYC;
                        committee chairman, The Cloisters, NYC;
                        trustee, Society for the Preservation of Fire Island Lighthouse;
                        fellow, Old Westbury Gardens, Old Westbury;
                        ornithological field associate, New York Zoological Society;
                        chairman of board, Seatuck Environmental Association, Islip;
                        trustee, Bayard Cutting Arboretum, Great River;
                        director, National Wild Waterfowl Association, Jamestown, MD;
                        director, Caribbean Conservation Corporation, Tallahasse, FL

Marriage(s):   Natalie Peters (1907-1979)

Address: South Bay Avenue, Islip
Name of estate: *Twyford*
Year of construction: c. 1880s
Style of architecture: Modified Neo-Victorian
Architect(s):
Landscape architect(s):
House extant: no; demolished in 2002*
Historical notes:

front facade

The house was built by Dr. T. S. Ryder.
It was purchased by Samuel Twyford Peters, who used as a guest house on his estate *Windholm Farm*.
The house was later owned by his son Harry Twyford Peters, Sr., who remodeled it and called it *Twyford*.
It was subsequently owned by Harry Twyford Peters, Sr.'s daughter Natalie, who married Webster.
In 1968, the Websters donated the house, to be used for staff offices and as a wildlife study and teaching center, and the surrounding property to the Seatuck National Wildlife Refuge. [*Seatuck* in Algonquian is said to mean "little creek flowing into the sea."] The terms of the gift gave the Websters life tenancy but did not specifically require maintenance or preservation of the house by the Department of the Interior after their deaths.
*The house was demolished in 2002 by the federal government.

Weekes, Harold Hathaway (d. 1950)

Occupation(s): financier - Thomas, Maclay and Co. (stock brokerage firm)

Marriage(s): M/1 – 1906-1926 – Louisine Peters (c. 1884-1960s)
M/2 – 1933-1950 – Frances Stokes (d. 1967)

Address: South Bay Avenue, Islip
Name of estate: *Wereholme*
Year of construction: c. 1917
Style of architecture: Neo-French Manor
Architect(s): Grosvenor Atterbury designed
the house (for H. H. Weekes)
Landscape architect(s):
House extant: yes
Historical notes:

The house, originally named *Wereholme*, was built by Harold Hathaway Weekes.
The *Long Island Society Register, 1929* lists Harold H. Weekes as residing in Oyster Bay.
He was the son of Arthur Delano and Lily Underhill Weekes, Sr., who resided at *The Anchorage* in Oyster Bay Cove. His brother Arthur Delano Weekes, Jr., who inherited *The Anchorage*, married Dorothy Lee Higginson. His sister Edith married John Slade, Sr. and resided at *Underhill House* in Upper Brookville and at *Berry Hill House* in Oyster Bay Cove. Harold Hathaway Weekes subsequently married Frances Stokes and resided at *Valentine Farm* in Old Brookville.
Louisine Peters Weekes was the daughter of Samuel Twyford and Adaline Mapes Elder Peters of *Windholme Farm* in Islip. Her brother Harry Twyford Peters, Sr., who married Natalie Wells and resided at *Nearholme* in Islip, inherited *Windholme Farm*. Louisine subsequently married Alexander Tcherepnin, with whom she continued to reside at *Wereholme*.
Harold Hathaway and Louisine Peters Weekes' daughter Adaline, who inherited *Wereholme*, married Charles B. Scully and resided at the estate. Adaline subsequently married Count Philip Orssich of Denkendorf bei Stuttgart, Germany.
Frances Stokes Weekes had previously been married to Louis Crawford Clark II, with who she resided at *Valentine Farm* in Old Brookville.
*In 1984, Mrs. Scully, who had divorced the count and reverted to the surname Scully, bequeathed the house to the National Audubon Society.
In 2004, the estate was purchased by Suffolk County and is now the county's Environmental Interpretive Center.

front facade, 1991

Weld, Philip Balch (b. 1887)

Occupation(s):	financier - president, New York Cotton Exchange; member, Kidder, Peabody and Co. (stock brokerage firm); partner, Stephen M. Weld and Co.; partner, Weld, Jackson, and Curtis

Marriage(s):   1912 – Katharine Saltonstall

Address: Saxon Avenue, Bay Shore
Name of estate:
Year of construction: c. 1880
Style of architecture: Victorian
Architect(s):
Landscape architect(s):
House extant: no; demolished in 1932
Historical notes:

The house was built by Daniel D. Conover and inherited by his son Augustus W. Conover, Sr.
It was purchased in 1912 by Franklyn Hutton, who later sold it to his brother Edward Francis Hutton.
In 1921, the house was purchased from E. F. Hutton by Weld.
He was the son of General Stephen Minot and Mrs. Eloise Rodman Weld of Dedham, MA.
Katharine Saltonstall Weld was the daughter of Philip L. Saltonstall of Boston, MA.
Philip Balch and Katharine Saltonstall Weld's son Philip Saltonstall Weld married Anne Warren, the daughter of Samuel Dennis Warren of *Rockyhill Farm* in Essex, MA. Their daughter Rose married Ian Baldwin, the son of Joseph Clark Baldwin, Jr. of Mt. Kisco, NY, and resided in Mt. Kisco. Their daughter Adelaide married Robert Bacon Whitney, Sr. and resided in Old Westbury. Adelaide subsequently married James Knott, with whom she continued to reside in Old Westbury.
In 1930, the house was purchased from Weld by H. Cecil Sharp, who demolished it and built a new house on the site.

Welles, Benjamin Sumner, Jr. (d. 1935)

Occupation(s):

Marriage(s):   Frances Wyeth Swan (d. 1911)*

Address: St. Mark's Lane, Islip
Name of estate: *Welles House*
Year of construction:
Style of architecture:
Architect(s):
Landscape architect(s):
House extant: unconfirmed
Historical notes:

The *Long Island Society Register, 1929* lists Benjamin [Sumner] Welles [Jr.] as residing at *Welles House* on St. Mark's Lane in Islip. His Manhattan residence was located at 110 East Fifty-fifth Street.
He was the son of Benjamin Sumner and Catherine Schermerhorn Welles, Sr.
Frances Wyeth Swan Welles was the daughter of Frederick G. and Emily Wyeth Swan of Oyster Bay.
Benjamin Sumner and Frances Wyeth Swan Welles, Jr.'s daughter Emily married Harry Pelham Robbins, the son of Henry Archer Robbins, and resided at *Pelham Farm* in Southampton. Their son Benjamin Sumner Welles III [aka Sumner Welles] inherited the house.
*Mrs. Welles died of a stroke at the Foord Sanatorium in Kerhonkson, NY, where she was being treated for a nervous disorder. [Benjamin Welles, *Sumner Welles: FDR's Global Strategist* (New York: St. Martin's Press, 1999), p. 18.]
[See other Welles entries for additional family information.]

Welles, Benjamin Sumner, Sr. (1823-1904)

Occupation(s):   merchant -   dry goods

Marriage(s):   1850-1858 – Catherine Schermerhorn (1828-1858)

Address: St. Mark's Lane, Islip
 Name of estate:
Year of construction: c. 1850s
Style of architecture:
Architect(s):
Landscape architect(s):
House extant: unconfirmed
Historical notes:

  The house was built by Benjamin Sumner Welles, Sr.
  He was a member of the Patriarchs, an organization of twenty-five men which had been created in 1872 by Ward McAllister to "establish and lead" New York society.
  Catherine Schermerhorn Welles was the daughter of Abraham Schermerhorn of Manhattan. Her sister Ann married Charles Suydam and resided in Bayport. Her sister Caroline ["Mystic Rose"], who married William Blackhouse Astor, was the undisputed arbiter of society's elite "Four Hundred."
  Benjamin Sumner and Catherine Schermerhorn Welles, Sr. were members of society's 'Four Hundred." However, Catherine's sister Ann and brother-in-law Charles Suydam were omitted from the list.
  Their son Benjamin Sumner Welles, Jr. married Frances Wyeth Swan and resided at *Welles House* in Islip. Their daughter Helen married George Lovett Kingsland, Sr. and rented a house in West Islip for their summer residence. Their daughter Harriet remained unmarried.
  [See other Welles entries for additional family information.]

St. Mark's Lane, Islip, c. 1920

Welles, Benjamin Sumner, III (1892-1961)
[aka Sumner Welles]

Occupation(s):	diplomat - secretary, United Sates Embassy in Japan, 1917; United States Ambassador to Cuba, 1933; chief, Latin American Affairs Division, Department of State, 1920
	statesman* - Assistant Secretary of State, 1933; Under Secretary of State, 1937
	writer - *Naboth's Vineyard*, 1928; *The World of Four Freedoms*, 1943; *The Time of Decision*, 1944; *The Ciano Diaries 1939-1943* (introduction by Welles), 1946; *Where Are We Heading?* 1946; *We Need Not Fail*, 1948; *Seven Decision That Shaped History*, 1950

Marriage(s):	M/1 – 1915-1923 – Esther Slater (d. 1951) M/2 – 1925-1949 – Mathilde Scott Townsend (d. 1949) M/3 – 1952-1961 – Harriette Appleton Post (1896-1969)

Address:	St. Mark's Lane, Islip
Name of estate:	*Welles House*
Year of construction:	
Style of architecture:	
Architect(s):	
Landscape architect(s):	
House extant: unconfirmed	
Historical notes:	

Benjamin Sumner Welles III inherited *Welles House* from his parents Benjamin Sumner and Frances Wyeth Swan Wells, Jr.

Esther Slater Welles was the daughter of Horatio and Mabel Hunt Slater. Esther's uncle was the noted architect William Morris Hunt. She subsequently married Joseph J. Kerrigan and resided in Cove Neck.

Benjamin Sumner and Esther Slater Welles III's son Benjamin Sumner Welles IV married Cynthia Monteith. Their son Arnold married Adele Harman, the daughter of Archer Harman of Edgartown, MA, and resided in Savannah, GA.

Mathilde Scott Townsend Welles had previously been married to United States Senator Peter Goelet Gerry of Rhode Island.

Harriette Appleton Post Welles was the daughter of George Browne Post of Bernardsville, NJ, and granddaughter of the noted architect George Browne Post. She had previously been married to R. Thornton Wilson, the son of Marshall Orme Wilson of Manhattan, and to the ardent Austro–Hungarian Nazi sympathizer Baron Emmerich von Jeszenzky.

Benjamin Sumner Welles III's Washington, DC, residence, located at 2121 Massachusetts Avenue, NW, was purchased by the Cosmos Club. His 250-acre estate in Maryland was located at Oxon Hill.

*For a discussion of the personal scandal that led to Welles' fall from political power see Raymond E. Spinzia, "Sumner Welles: Brilliance and Tragedy." *The Freeholder* 9 (Winter 2005):8-9, 22.

Westin, Clarence Frederick, Sr.

Occupation(s):	merchant - president, Jones Brothers Tea Co., Scranton, PA; director, Grand Union Tea Co. (which became Grand Union Supermarket)
	industrialist - director, Anchor Pottery Co.

Marriage(s):   c. 1909 – Maude Virginia Jones (1886-1977)

Address:	Handsome Avenue, Sayville
Name of estate:	*Beechwold*
Year of construction:	1903
Style of architecture:	Shingle
Architect(s):	Isaac Henry Green II designed the main residence, gatehouse, and 1905 playhouse. The latter included a bowling alley and billiard room (for F. S. Jones)

Landscape architect(s):
House extant: no; destroyed by fire in 1957*
Historical notes:

The house, originally named *Beechwold*, was built by Frank Smith Jones.
Clarence Frederick Westin, Sr. was the son of Charles F. Westin of Brooklyn.
Maude Virginia Jones Westin, the daughter of Frank Smith and Mary Louise Granbery Jones, inherited *Beechwold*. Maude, who had married Clarence Frederick Westin, Sr., subsequently married David J. Shea. The Sheas resided in the estate's gatehouse. Her sister Henrietta married William Robinson Simonds and resided at *Wyndemoor* in Sayville. Maude later purchased *Wyndemoor* from her sister.
Clarence Frederick and Maude Virginia Jones Westin, Sr.'s son Gordon died at the age of eight in a horse riding accident. [Harry W. Havemeyer, *East on the Great South Bay: Sayville and Bayport 1860-1960* (Mattituck, NY: Amereon House, 2001), p.154.] Their son Charles married Flora Harris, the daughter of Dr. Raymond Victor Harris of Savannah, GA. Their son Douglas married Florence Saunders, the daughter of Dr. Samuel Saunders, Jr. of Binghamton, NY, and resided in Sayville.
The *Long Island Society Register, 1929* lists Clarence F. Westin [Sr.] as residing on Maple Drive in Great Neck.
In 1945, *Beechwold* was purchased by Elwell Palmer, who sold it to Dr. Daniel McLaughlin in 1949.
*The gatehouse and playhouse are extant. The gatehouse is located at 254 Handsome Avenue and the playhouse is at 96 Benson Avenue.

Beechwold

Wharton, Percival C. (1882-1937)

Occupation(s):

Marriage(s):   Louise Lousdale (d. 1937)

Address: Bayview Avenue, East Islip
Name of estate:
Year of construction:
Style of architecture:
Architect(s):
Landscape architect(s):
House extant: unconfirmed
Historical notes:

Percival C. Wharton was the son of William Fishbourne and Frances T. Fisher Wharton of Philadelphia, PA, who rented a summer residence in Islip.

Despondent over his poor health and financial problems, Percival shot his wife to death then committed suicide at their Cranberry Lake, NY, cabin. [*The New York Times* October 18, 1937, p. 36.]

Louise Lousdale Wharton's sister married Richard Elkins, the son of Stephen B. Elkins, United States Senator from West Virginia.

[See other Wharton entries for additional family information.]

Wharton, Richard (d. 1933)

Occupation(s):   financier -   member, Childs and Co. (stock brokerage firm)

Marriage(s):   1906-1933 – Helena Johnson Parsons (d. 1936)

Address: St. Mark's Lane, Islip
Name of estate: *Whileaway*
Year of construction: c. 1881
Style of architecture: Shingle
Architect(s):
Landscape architect(s):
House extant: no
Historical notes:

The house, originally named *Whileaway*, was built by Schuyler Livingston Parsons, Sr.

It was inherited by his daughter Helena, who had married Richard Wharton and, then, by the Wharton's son Richard T. Wharton, Sr. The Whartons continued to call it *Whileaway*.

The *Long Island Society Register, 1929* lists Richard and Helena Parsons Wharton as residing at *Whileaway* in Islip.

He was the son of William Fishbourne and Frances T. Fisher Wharton of Philadelphia, PA, and Islip. His brother Percival married Louise Lousdale and resided in East Islip.

Helena Johnson Parsons Wharton's brother Schuyler Livingston Parsons, Jr. married Elizabeth Pierson and resided at *Pleasure Island* in Islip. Her sister Evelyn married Amor Hollingsworth of Boston, MA.

Richard and Helena Johnson Parsons Wharton's son Richard T. Wharton, Sr. married Mara di Zoppola and resided at *Whileaway* in Newport, RI, and at *Whileaway* in Islip. Their daughter Marion married Gerald Hallock III of Great Barrington, MA, and Brooklyn, NY.

[See other Wharton entries for additional family information.]

Wharton, Richard T., Sr. (d. 1995)

Occupation(s):   financier -   member, Abbott, Proctor and Paine (stock brokerage firm)

Marriage(s):   1945-1995 – Mara di Zoppola

Address: St. Mark's Lane, Islip
Name of estate: *Whileaway*
Year of construction: c. 1881
Style of architecture: Shingle
Architect(s):
Landscape architect(s):
House extant: no
Historical notes:

     The house, originally named *Whileaway*, was built by Schuyler Livingston Parsons, Sr.
     It was inherited by his daughter Helena, who married Richard Wharton, and, then, by the Whartons' son Richard T. Wharton, Sr. The Whartons continued to call it *Whileaway*.
     Mara di Zoppola Wharton was the daughter of Count Andrea Alexsandro Mario and Countess Edith Mortimer di Zoppola of Mill Neck.
     The *Social Register, Summer 1949* lists Richard T. and Mara di Zoppola Wharton [Sr.] as residing at *Whileaway* in Newport, RI.
     Richard T. and Mara di Zoppola Wharton, Sr.'s daughter Stephanie married Peter M. Holbrook and resided in San Francisco, CA. Their daughter Lucie and their son Richard T. Wharton, Jr. remained unmarried.
     At the time of his death, Richard T. Wharton, Sr. was residing in Pound Ridge, NY.
     [See other Wharton entries for additional family information.]

Wharton, William Fishbourne

Occupation(s):   capitalist -   vice president, Madison Square Garden Co.
                              financier -   member, New York Stock Exchange

Marriage(s):   1871 – Frances T. Fisher

Address: Suffolk Lane, East Islip
Name of estate:
Year of construction:
Style of architecture: Shingle
Architect(s):
Landscape architect(s):
House extant: unconfirmed
Historical notes:

     The *Social Register, 1890* lists William Fishbourne and Fanny T. Fisher Wharton as residing in Islip [East Islip]. They rented this house for use as their summer residence.
     William Fishbourne and Francis T. Fisher Wharton's son Richard married Helena Parsons and resided at *Whileaway* in Islip. Their son Percival married Louise Lousdale and resided in East Islip.
     [See other Wharton entries for additional family information.]

front facade, c. 1913

White, Raymond S. (1873-1903)

Occupation(s): financier -   partner, Baldwin and White (stock brokerage firm)
industrialist -   director, Union Typewriter Co.
capitalist -   director, General Building & Construction Co.

Marriage(s): Sarah H. Crane

Address: Great River Road, Great River
Name of estate:
Year of construction: 1899
Style of architecture: Tudor
Architect(s): Charles C. Thain designed
   the house (for R. S. White)

Landscape architect(s):
House extant: no
Historical notes:

   The house was built by Raymond S. White.
   Raymond S. and Sarah H. Crane White's daughter Katherine married Herbert G. Garrick, the son of Frederick Garrick and resided in Manhattan.
   Raymond S. White died as a result of an automobile accident in Bay Shore. [*The New York Times* December 22, 1903, p. 9.]
   Sarah subsequently married Francis Sessions Hutchins, with whom she continued to reside in the Great River residence.
   The house was subsequently owned by Dr. George David Stewart, who called it *Appin House*.

front facade, c. 1910

Whitney, William Collins (1841-1904)

Occupation(s):

attorney -   corporate council for the City of New York
industrialist -   partner, Standard Oil Co. (which became Exxon Corp.)
capitalist -   Metropolitan Street Railroad Co.
statesman -   Secretary of the Navy in the Cleveland and Benjamin
                        Harrison administrations

Marriage(s):

M/1 – 1869-1893 – Flora Payne (1842-1893)
M/2 – 1896-1899 – Edith Sybil May (c. 1859-1899)

Address: St. Mark's Lane, Islip
Name of estate:
Year of construction: c. 1881
Style of architecture:
Architect(s):
Landscape architect(s):
House extant: unconfirmed
Historical notes:

The house was built by William Collins Whitney.

He is reported to have been the largest property owner in the Commonwealth of Massachusetts. [Jerry E. Patterson, *The First Four Hundred: Mrs. Astor's New York in the Gilded Age* (New York: Rizzoli International Publ., Inc., 2000), p. 136.]

Born in Conway, MA, William Collins Whitney was the son of Brigadier General James Scollay and Laurenda Collins Whitney. His sister Lillian married Charles Tracy Barney and resided in Old Westbury.

Flora Payne Whitney was the daughter of Senator Henry B. Payne of Ohio.

William Collins and Flora Payne Whitney were on Ward McAllister's "Four Hundred" list.

Their daughter Dorothy married William Dickerman Straight and, then, Leonard Knight Elmhirst. She resided at *Elmhurst,* later called *Applegreen,* in Old Westbury. Their son Henry [aka Harry Payne Whitney] married Gertrude Vanderbilt, the daughter of Cornelius and Alice Claypoole Gwynne Vanderbilt.

Whitney's second wife was the former Edith Sybil May Randolph, who, with her first husband English Captain Arthur Randolph, had resided in Douglaston, Queens. Her husband had died when their daughter Adelaide was thirteen and their son Arthur, known as Bertie, was eleven. Edith's father Dr. J. Frederick May was the physician who identified the body of John Wilkes Booth.

In 1882, Clarence Tucker purchased the house from Whitney who, by 1902, had relocated to Old Westbury. The Whitney's Old Westbury estate was inherited by Whitney's son Harry. It was to this estate that Gertrude brought Gloria Laura Vanderbilt ("Little Gloria"), the daughter of her brother Reginald Claypoole Vanderbilt and Gloria Laura Mercedes Morgan Vanderbilt, during the vicious and much-publicized trial for custody of Little Gloria.

In 1893, Whitney's Islip house was purchased by Mrs. Richard H. Williams.

Whitney's Old Westbury estate,
rear facade

Wilbur, Edward Russell, Sr. (1849-1905)

Occupation(s):   industrialist -   partner, William & Hastings (stationery manufacturer)
                               publisher -   a founder, *Forest and Stream*, 1873

Marriage(s):

Address: Handsome Avenue, Sayville
Name of estate: *Beach Grove*
Year of construction:
Style of architecture:
Architect(s):
Landscape architect(s):
House extant: unconfirmed
Historical notes:

    In 1875, Edward Russell Wilbur, Sr. purchased the Manly farm and converted the house into his summer residence.
    His son Edward Russell Wilbur, Jr. married Lydia Whiteside of Ashville, NC, and resided in Scarsdale, NY.
    In 1902, the senior Wilbur sold the house to Frank Smith Jones and relocated to Oyster Bay.

Williams, Percy G. (1857-1923)

Occupation(s):   entertainers and related professions -   comedian
                               capitalist -   partner, with Thomas Adams, Jr., real estate development,
                                        Bergen Beach, Brooklyn;
                                        constructed and owned a casino in Brooklyn, 1896;
                                        manager, Brooklyn Music Hall, Brooklyn;
                                        owner, Novelty Theater, Brooklyn;
                                        builder and owner, Orpheum Theater, Brooklyn;
                                        owner, Circle Theater, NYC;
                                        owner, Colonial Theater, NYC
Civic Activism: established Percy G. Williams Home, East Islip*

Marriage(s):   Ida E. _____

Address: Suffolk Lane, East Islip
Name of estate: *Pine Acres*
Year of construction: 1911
Style of architecture: Modified Shingle
Architect(s):
Landscape architect(s):
House extant: no; demolished in c. 1975
Historical notes:

front facade

    The house, originally named *Pine Acres*, was built by Percy G. Williams.
    The *Brooklyn Blue Book and Long Island Society Register, 1921* lists Percy G. Williams as residing in East Islip.
    He was the son of Dr. John B. Williams.
    Percy's wife Ida began to manifest signs of mental problems after the death of their son Victor.
    *Williams' will stated that upon the death of his wife, *Pine Acres* would become the Percy G. Williams Home for Aged, Indigent and Infirm Actors. It remained a retirement home until after World War II. [Harry W. Havemeyer, *Along the Great South Bay From Oakdale to Babylon: The Story of a Summer Spa 1840 to 1940* (Mattituck, NY: Amereon House, 1996), pp. 314-15; *The New York Times* August 1, 1923, p. 1 and August 2, 1923, p. 16.]

Williams, Richard H., Sr.

Occupation(s): merchant -   partner, with Samuel Twyford Peters, Williams
                                and Peters (wholesale coal)

Marriage(s): Sarah W. Peters (d. 1929)

Address: St. Mark's Lane, Islip
Name of estate:
Year of construction: c. 1881
Style of architecture:
Architect(s):
Landscape architect(s):
House extant: unconfirmed
Historical notes:

The house was built by William Collins Whitney.
In 1882, Clarence Tucker purchased it from Whitney.
In 1893, the house was purchased by Mrs. Richard H. Williams.
Richard H. and Sarah W. Peters Williams, Sr.'s son Richard H. Williams, Jr. married Julia Lorillard Edgar, the daughter of Newbold Edgar, and resided at *Brookrace* in Mendham, NJ.

Wilmerding, George G.

Occupation(s):

Marriage(s): 1851 – Cornelia Lawrance

Address: South Country Road, West Bay Shore
Name of estate:
Year of construction:
Style of architecture:
Architect(s):
Landscape architect(s):
House extant: unconfirmed
Historical notes:

Julia Lawrance Wilmerding was the daughter of Thomas and Margaret Ireland Lawrance. Her brother William married Mary Helen Crandell. Her sister Louisa married Bradish Johnson, Sr. and resided at *Sans Souci* in Bay Shore.

Wilmerding, Lucius Kellogg (1848-1922)

Occupation(s):   merchant -   partner, Wilmerding & Huguet (dry goods importer
                                            and merchant);
                                 partner, Wilmerding & Bissett (dry goods importer
                                          and merchant)
               financier -   partner, Gray and Wilmerding (stock brokerage firm);
                                 trustee, Greenwich Savings Bank

Marriage(s):   1876-1922 – Caroline Murray

Address: Suffolk Lane, East Islip
Name of estate:
Year of construction:
Style of architecture: Italian Renaissance
Architect(s):
Landscape architect(s):
House extant: unconfirmed
Historical notes:

   Lucius Kellogg Wilmerding was the son of Henry
Augustus and Harriet Kellogg Wilmerding.
   The *Long Island Society Register, 1929* lists Caroline
Murray Wilmerding as residing in East Islip.
   Lucius Kellogg and Caroline Murray Wilmerding's
son Lucius married Helen Cutting, the daughter of
Robert Fulton and Helen Suydam Cutting of Great
River, and resided in Far Hills, NJ. Their daughter
Caroline married John B. Trevor, Sr. and resided at
Trevallyn in Paul Smiths, NY.
   The house was rented by Amedee Depau Moran
under a ten-year lease agreement.

rear facade

Wood, Henry Duncan, Jr.

Occupation(s):   financier -   member, William M. Clarke (stock brokerage firm);
                                 member, Frederic H. Hatch and Co. (stock brokerage firm)

Marriage(s):   Effe J. Sauders

Address: *[unable to determine street address]*, Bay Shore
Name of estate:
Year of construction:
Style of architecture:
Architect(s):
Landscape architect(s):
House extant: unconfirmed
Historical notes:

   The *Social Register, 1907* lists Henry Duncan and Effe J. Saunders Wood [Jr.] as residing in Bay Shore.
   He was the son of Henry Duncan and Ellen E. Pulsifer Wood, Sr., who resided at *Ellenwood* in East Islip.
   Henry Duncan and Effe J. Saunders Wood, Jr.'s son Henry Duncan Wood III married Gladys Howell
Peters, the daughter of George Willis Peters.
   [See following entry for additional family information.]

Wood, Henry Duncan, Sr. (1852-1915)

Occupation(s):   financier -   a founder, with Harry Bowly Hollins, Sr., H. B. Hollins
                                               and Co. (stock brokerage firm)
                              capitalist -   director, Madison Square Garden Co.

Marriage(s):   Ellen E. Pulsifer (d. 1926)

Address: Islip Avenue, Islip
Name of estate: *Ellenwood*
Year of construction: 1885
Style of architecture:
Architect(s):
Landscape architect(s):
House extant: unconfirmed
Historical notes:

    In 1885, the house was destroyed by fire. Wood immediately built a new house on the site. [*The New York Times* April 9, 1885, p. 5.]
    He was the son of William and Margaret Lawrence Wood.
    Henry Duncan and Ellen E. Pulsifer Wood, Sr.'s son Henry Duncan Wood, Jr. married Effe J. Saunders and resided in Bay Shore. Their daughter Gertrude married Edward Bell, Jr., the son of Edward and Helen A. Wilmerding Bell, Sr.
    [See previous entry for additional family information.]

Woolley, Dr. James V. S., Sr.

Occupation(s):   physician
Marriage(s):

Address: Awixa Avenue, Bay Shore
Name of estate:
Year of construction:
Style of architecture:
Architect(s):
Landscape architect(s):
House extant: unconfirmed
Historical notes:

    His son James V. S. Woolley, Jr. was an attorney and real estate speculator in Brooklyn and Queens.

front facade, c. 1903

Wray, William H.

Occupation(s):   capitalist -   owned commercial rental property, Brooklyn;
                               builder, built houses in Town of Islip

Marriage(s):

Address: 32 Awixa Avenue, Bay Shore
Name of estate: *Whileaway*
Year of construction: c. 1890
Style of architecture: Shingle
Architect(s):   William H. Wray designed his own house
Landscape architect(s):
House extant: yes
Historical notes:

    The house, originally named *Whileaway*, was built by William
H. Wray.
    It was later owned by Fred C. Lemmerman and, subsequently,
by William Kemble Clarkson.
    In 2003, the house was purchased by Dr. Mark Foehr.

front facade

Wright, Dr. Arthur Mullen (d. 1948)

Occupation(s):   physician -   director of surgery, French Hospital, NYC;
                          member, medical board, French Hospital;
                          president, medical board, Bellevue Hospital, NYC

Marriage(s):   Alice Stanchfield (1856-1941)

Address: Ocean Avenue, Islip
Name of estate: *Afterglow*
Year of construction: c. 1890
Style of architecture: Shingle
Architect(s):
Landscape architect(s):
House extant: no; demolished in c. 1950
Historical notes:

    The house, originally named *Afterglow*, was built by John Gibb.
    In 1909, it was purchased by John Barry Stanchfield, Sr.
    It was inherited by his daughter Alice, who had married Dr. Arthur Mullen Wright. Both the Stanchfields
and Wrights continued to call the estate *Afterglow*.
    Dr. Arthur Mullen and Mrs. Alice Stanchfield Wright's son Richard, who married Adele Carlisle, the
daughter of Floyd Leslie and Edna Rogers Carlisle, Sr. of Lattingtown, resided in Locust Valley prior to
relocating to Ruxton, MD.

Yates, Douglas Thomas, Sr. (b. 1915)

Occupation(s):	financier - partner, White, Weld, and Co. (investment banking firm); chairman of board, Seaboard Association (investment banking firm)
	capitalist - executive vice-president and director, Republic Pictures Corp., 1950-1978
	military - major, United States Army, 1941-1946
Civic Activism:	founding trustee, Episcopal School, NYC;
	trustee, General Theological Seminary;
	chairman of board, United Hospital Fund, NYC;
	chairman of board, Foreign Parishes of the Episcopal Church
	trustee, Buckley, School, NYC;
	trustee, Lenox Hill Hospital, NYC;
	trustee, Hospital Association of New York State
Marriage(s):	1941-2006 – Margaret Louise Titus (1918-2006)
	- Civic Activism: president, Altar Guild, St. James' Episcopal Church, NYC;
	a founder and tutor, East Harlem Neighborhood Study Group
Address:	69 West Bayberry Road, Islip
Name of estate:	
Year of construction:	1899-1900
Style of architecture:	Moorish
Architect(s):	Grosvenor Atterbury designed the house (for H. O. Havemeyer)*
Landscape architect(s):	Nathan F. Barrett (for H. O. Havemeyer)**
House extant: yes	
Historical notes:	

The house was built by Henry Osborne Havemeyer as part of his "Modern Venice" development.

Douglas Thomas Yates, Sr. was the son of Herbert John and Petra Antonsen Yates, Sr., who resided at *Onsru Farm* in West Islip.

Margaret Louise Titus Yates was the daughter of Walter Livingston and Margaret Gulden Titus, Sr. of West Islip.

Douglas Thomas and Margaret Louise Titus Yates, Sr.'s son Douglas Thomas Yates, Jr. married Doris Catlin, the daughter of Dr. Daniel and Mrs. Doris Havemeyer Catlin, Sr. of Bay Shore, and resides in New Haven, CT. Their son Timothy, who resides in Rye, NY, married Dorinda Hoyte Le Maire, the daughter of Edward Le Maire, and, subsequently, Katherine Jurusik, the daughter of Eugene and Jean Jurusik of Elmira, NY. Their son Lawrance Randall Yates married Hope Starr Lloyd, the daughter of Morris Lloyd of Chestnut Hill, PA, and resides in Manhattan. Their daughter Margaret married Nathan Comstock Thorne, the son of Harold Wooster Thorne, Jr. of Oakland, CA, and also resides in Manhattan.

[See other Yates entries for additional family information.]

*The sales brochure for "Modern Venice" states that the Moorish-style architecture was suggested by Louis Comfort Tiffany.

**The sales brochure also states that "Modern Venice" would be devoid of trees and vegetation and that Nathan F. Barrett was the landscape architect.

front facade, 2006

Yates, Herbert John, Sr. (1880-1966)

Occupation(s):	capitalist -	a founder, with his brother George, Republic Film Laboratories, Inc., NYC, 1917 (which became Consolidated Film Industries, Inc.);
		president and chairman of board, Consolidated Film Industries, Inc. (motion picture film developing laboratory and distributor, which became Republic Pictures Corp.);
		president and chairman of board, Republic Pictures Corp. (motion picture studio);
		director, Cinema Patents Co., Inc.
	financier -	director, Liberty National Bank and Trust Co., NYC;
		director, Concord Casualty Insurance Co.
Civic Activism:		director, Motion Pictures Association of New York;
		director, St. Joseph Hospital, Burbank, CA

Marriage(s):   M/1 – 1910-1949 – Petra Antonsen (1882-1949)
                 M/2 – 1952-1966 – Verra Hruba Ralston
                        - entertainers and associated professions -   actress

Address: South Country Road and Snedecor Avenue, West Islip
Name of estate: *Onsrufarm*
Year of construction: c. 1892
Style of architecture: Colonial Revival
Architect(s):
Landscape architect(s):
House extant: no; destroyed by fire, 1967*
Historical notes:

   Herbert John Yates, Sr. was the son of Charles Henry and Emma Worthington Yates of Brooklyn.
   Petra Antonsen Yates was the daughter of Henry Antonsen of Oslo, Norway.
   Herbert John and Petra Antonsen Yates, Sr.'s son Herbert John Yates, Jr. married Jean St. Amand and resided in Great Neck. Their son Douglas married Margaret Titus, the daughter of Walter Livingston and Margaret Gulden Titus, Sr.

Onsrufarm

of West Islip, and resided in Islip. Their daughter Elsa married Walter Livingston Titus, Jr. and resided in Islip. Their son Richard, who resided in Brightwaters, married Marie Rose Mc Kee, the daughter of Henry Sellers and Alice M. Davies Mc Kee II of Babylon, and, subsequently, Roberta Daniel, the daughter of Daniel M. Daniel.
   [See other Yates entries for additional family information.]
   *The tennis house is extant. It has been converted into a private residence.

front facade

Yates, Richard George, Sr. (1919-1992)

Occupation(s):   capitalist -   vice-president and assistant sales director, Republic Pictures;
                                     motion picture producer, *What* [aka *Night is the Phantom*], 1965
                     military -   captain, United States Army, 1943-1947

Marriage(s):   M/1 – 1941-div. 1954 – Marie Rose Mc Kee
                     M/2 – 1958 – Roberta Daniel

Address: 112 South Winsor Avenue, Brightwaters
Name of estate:
Year of construction:
Style of architecture: Shingle with Victorian elements
Architect(s):
Landscape architect(s):
House extant: yes
Historical notes:

    The *Social Register, New York 1948* lists Richard G. and Marie R. Mc Kee Yates [Sr.] as residing on South Country Road, West Islip. The *Social Register, 1952* lists them as residing at 112 Winsor Avenue, Brightwaters.
    He was the son of Herbert John and Petra Antonsen Yates, Sr. of *Onsrufarm* in West Islip.
    Marie Rose Mc Kee Yates was the daughter of Henry Sellers and Alice M. Davies Mc Kee II of Babylon. Marie later married Joseph S. Bynum, the son of Samuel Bynum of Paducah, KY, and, subsequently, Ronald S. Correll, the son of Charles D. Correll.
    Richard George and Marie Rose McKee Yates, Sr.'s son Jeffrey married Lauran Boakes. Their son Richard George Yates, Jr. married Linda Templeton.
    Roberta Daniel Yates was the daughter of Daniel M. Daniel.
    [See other Yates entries for additional family information.]

front facade, 2006

Young, Albert (d. 1895)

Occupation(s):   financier -   stockbroker

Marriage(s):   Minnie E. Arents

Address: Awixa Avenue, Bay Shore
Name of estate: *Awixaway*
Year of construction: c. 1880
Style of architecture: Queen Anne
Architect(s):
Landscape architect(s):
House extant: unconfirmed
Historical notes:

The house, originally named *Awixaway*, was built by Albert Young.

Minnie E. Arents Young's brother George was the treasurer of the American Tobacco Company.

Albert and Minnie E. Arents Young's son Albert M. Young died at the age of twenty-five. Their son Lewis Gunther Young married the actress Leona Anderson (aka Aronson). Their daughter married the millionaire Alfred S. Dietrich, prior to eloping with Harry S. Brenchley, a trainer at Alfred Gwynne Vanderbilt, Sr.'s stables. [*The New York Times* February 17, 1909, p. 2.]

Zerega, John Pierre, Sr. (1865-1958)

Occupation(s):   capitalist -   owned a Sayville yacht basis and marine supply
                      company*

Marriage(s):   Ethel Hill

Address: Gillette Avenue, Bayport
Name of estate: *Littlewood*
Year of construction: 1896
Style of architecture: Shingle
Architect(s):   George Browne Post designed
                      the house (for R. H. Post, Sr.)
Landscape architect(s):
House extant: yes
Historical notes:

The house, originally named *Littlewood*, was built by Regis Henri Post, Sr.

The house was subsequently owned by Zeraga, who continued to call it *Littlewood*.

The Long Island Society Register, 1929 lists John P. and Ethel Hill Zeraga [Sr.] as residing at *Littlewood* on Gillette Avenue, Bayport.

The Zeregas' daughter died of influenza during the Spanish Flu epidemic of 1918-1919. Their son John Pierre Zerega, Jr. married Kathryn Anne Hurst, the daughter of William H. Hurst of *Orchard Hill* in Monroe, CT. Their daughter Arlene married William Joseph Kent, Jr. of Brooklyn and South Norwalk, CT.

*The yacht basis and marine supply company had been previously owned by Robert Barnwell Roosevelt, Jr. [*The New York Times* May 31, 1936, p. 55.]

APPENDICES

Table of Contents for Appendices

Architects 305

Civic Activists 311

Estate Names 314

Golf Courses on Former South Shore Estates. 320

Landscape Architects 321

Maiden Names 323

Occupations 337

Rehabilitative Secondary Uses of Surviving Estate Houses . . . 348

Statesmen and Diplomats Who Resided on Long Island's South Shore . . 350

Village Locations of Estates 352

America's First Age of Fortune: A Selected Bibliography 359

Selected Bibliographic References to Individual
South Shore Estate Owners 366

Biographical Sources Consulted 387

Maps Consulted for Estate Locations 388

Illustration Credits 389

See the surname entry to ascertain if more than one architect was involved in designing the various buildings on an estate. This list reflects their South Shore commissions and includes the original and subsequent owners of the estates. When the owner who contracted with the architect is known, it is indicated by an asterisk.

Grosvenor Atterbury

Baker, William Dunham		Islip
Beard, Anson Mc Cook, Jr.		Islip
Dempsey, Joseph Francis, Jr.		Islip
Egly, Henry Harris		Islip
Garben, Dr. Louis F., Sr.		Islip
Gulden, Charles, II		Islip
Gulden, Frank, Sr.		Islip
* Havemeyer, Henry Osborne	*Bayberry Point*	Islip
Havemeyer, Horace, Jr.		Islip
Havemeyer, Horace, Sr.		Islip
Howell, Carlton Bell		Islip
Moore, Dr. David Dodge		Islip
Perkins, Richard Sturgis, Sr.		Islip
Scully, Charles B.	*Wereholme*	Islip
Tcherepnin, Alexander	*Wereholme*	Islip
Thorne, Edwin, III		Islip
Titus, Walter Livingston, Jr.		Islip
* Weekes, Harold Hathaway	*Wereholme*	Islip
Yates, Douglas Thomas, Sr.		Islip

James Dwight Baum

* Shea, Timothy J., Sr.	*O'Conee*	Bay Shore

Clarence K. Birdsall

* Behman, Louis C., Sr.	*Lindenwalt*	Bayport
Eastwood, John H.		Bay Shore
Hyde, James R.	(golf course clubhouse, 1899)	Bay Shore
* Hyde, Richard	(golf course clubhouse, 1899)	Bay Shore
* Myers, Nathaniel		Bay Shore

Cross and Cross

* Hollins, Harry Bowly, Jr.	*Crickholly*	East Islip

Philip Cusack

Entenmann, Robert		East Islip
* Morgan, Robert Woodward, Sr.		East Islip
Pinkerton, Robert Allan, II		East Islip

Delano and Aldrich

    * McBurney, Dr. Malcolm   East Islip

Adolph M. Dick of Fuller and Dick

    * Dick, Adolph M.   Islip

William F. Dominick

    * Thorne, Landon Ketchum, Sr.   *Thornham*   West Islip

H. Edward Ficken

    Aston, W. K.   *Peperidge Hall*   Oakdale
                                        (reassembled house)

    * Robert, Christopher Rhinelander, Jr.   *Peperidge Hall*   Oakdale
                                        (reassembled house)

Ernest Flagg

    * Bourne, Frederick Gilbert   *Indian Neck Hall*   Oakdale
                                 (main house; alterations, 1907-1908;
                                 garage, c. 1909)

Isaac Henry Green II

    * Allen, Theodore   (alterations)   Bayport

    Atwood, Kimball Chase, Jr.   Islip

    Baruch, Bernard Mannes, Sr.   *Strandhome*   Bayport

    Belmont, August, III   (alteration, 1889)   Bay Shore

    * Bourne, Arthur Keeler, Sr.   *Lake House*   Oakdale

    * Bourne, Frederick Gilbert   *Indian Neck Hall*   Oakdale
                                   (gatehouse, c. 1904;
                                 boathouse, c. 1905;
                                 pumphouse, c. 1913)

    * Childs, Eversley   Sayville

    * Childs, William Hamlin   Sayville

    Cox, Stephen Perry   *Arcadia*   Bayport

    * Cutting, William Bayard   *Westbrook Farm*   Great River
                                   (barns, unconfirmed)
                                   (gatehouse, confirmed)

    Dick, John Henry   *Allen Winden Farm*   Islip
                                   (alterations, c. 1889)

    * Dick, William   *Allen Winden Farm*   Islip
                                   (alterations, c. 1889)

    Dick, William Karl   *Allen Winden Farm*   Islip
                                   (alterations, c. 1889)

    Dillon, John Allen, Sr.   (alterations, 1899)   Bay Shore

    * Foster, Andrew D.   *Greycote*   Sayville

    * Foster, William R., Jr.   *Strandhome*   Bayport

    * Green, Isaac Henry, II   *Brookside*   Sayville

    Harbeck, Charles T.   (1909 house)   East Islip

    * Hard, Anson, Wales, Jr.   *Meadow Edge*   West Sayville
                            (main house and carriage house)

Isaac Henry Green II (cont'd)

*	Hayward, William Tyson, Sr.	*The Anchorage*	Sayville
*	Hollins, Gerald Vanderbilt, Sr.	*The Hawks*	East Islip
	Johnson, Aymar	*Woodland* (1909 house)	East Islip
*	Johnson, Bradish, Jr.	*Woodland* (1909 house)	East Islip
	Johnston, James Boorman	(1909 house)	East Islip
*	Jones, Frank Smith	*Beechwold* (main house, gatehouse, and 1905 playhouse)	Sayville
*	Knapp, Edward Spring, Sr.	*Awixa Lawn* (alterations, 1889)	Bay Shore
	Manton, Martin Thomas		Bayport
	McLaughlin, Dr. Daniel	(main house, gatehouse, and 1905 playhouse)	Bayport
*	Morgan, John	*Idle Hour* (alterations)	Bayport
	Palmer, Elwell		Sayville
	Palmer, Elwell	(main house, gatehouse, and 1905 playhouse)	Bayport
	Post, Charles Alfred	*Strandhome*	Bayport
	Post, Charles Kintzing	*Strandhome*	Bayport
	Post, Waldron Kintzing	*Strandhome*	Bayport
*	Ridgeway, James W.		Sayville
*	Roosevelt, John Ellis	*Meadow Croft* (alterations, c. 1891)	Sayville
*	Roosevelt, Robert Barnwell, Jr.	*The Lilacs*	Sayville
*	Schieren, Charles Adolph, Sr.	*Mapleton*	Islip
	Shea, David J.	*Beechwold* (main house, gatehouse, and 1905 playhouse)	Sayville
	Shea, David J.	*Wyndemoor*	Sayville
*	Simonds, William Robinson	*Wyndemoor*	Sayville
	Smith, Elward, Sr.		Sayville
	Smith, Robert Gibson		Sayville
*	Stoppani, Charles F., Sr.	*Arcadia*	Bayport
*	Stoppani, Joseph H.	*Liberty Hall* (main house, carriage house, and gardener's cottage)	Bayport
	Tucker, Charles A.	(alterations, c. 1889)	Islip
	Westin, Clarence Frederick, Sr.	*Beechwold* (main house, gatehouse, and 1905 playhouse)	Sayville

Rafael Guastavino, Jr.

    * Guastavino, Rafael, Jr.   Bay Shore

    Gulden, Frank, Jr.   Bay Shore

    * Gulden, Frank, Jr.   Islip

Charles Coolidge Haight

    * Cutting, William Bayard, Sr.   *Westbrook Farm*   Great River
                                 (main house and east gate house)

Harry G. Hardenburg

    Hubbard, Harmanus B.   *Oakhurst*   Bay Shore

    * Thurber, Fred C.   Bay Shore

Hart and Shape

    Breese, William Laurence   *Timber Point*   Great River
                                 (alterations)

    Davies, Julien Tappan   *Timber Point*   Great River
                                 (alterations)

    * Robbins, William H., Sr.   Bay Shore

Alfred Hopkins

    * Bourne, Frederick Gilbert   *Indian Neck Hall*   Oakdale
                                (farm complex, c. 1910)

    * Dick, John Henry   *Allen Winden Farm*   Islip
                                (garage and stables)

    Dick, William   *Allen Winden Farm*   Islip
                                (garage and stables)

    Dick, William Karl   *Allen Winden Farm*   Islip
                                (garage and stables)

    * Havemeyer, Horace, Sr.   *Olympic Point*   Bay Shore
                                (farm complex)

    * Mollenhauer, John Adolph   *Homeport*   Bay Shore
                                (farm complex, 1913)

    Peters, Harry Twyford, Sr.   *Windholme Farm*   Islip
                      (c. 1910 garage and farm complex)

    * Peters, Samuel Twyford   *Windholme Farm*   Islip
                      (c. 1910 garage and farm complex)

    Prince, John Dyneley, II   Islip

    Tucker, Charles A.   (garage and stables)   Islip

Richard Howland Hunt

    * Vanderbilt, William Kissam, Sr.   *Idlehour*   Oakdale
                                (1900 house)

Richard Morris Hunt

    * Vanderbilt, William Kissam, Sr.   *Idlehour*   Oakdale
                                (1878 house)

Kirby, Petit and Green

    * Dodson, Robert Bowman   *Kanonsioni*   West Islip

Herbert W. Korber

    * Gibson, John Joseph   Bay Shore

Harrie T. Lindeberg

    * Havemeyer, Horace, Sr.   *Olympic Point*   Bay Shore

Howard Payne

    * Payne, Albert   Bay Shore

George Browne Post

Baruch, Bernard Mannes, Sr.	*Strandhome* (alterations)	Bayport
Foster, William R., Jr.	*Strandhome* (alterations)	Bayport
* Post, Charles Alfred	*Strandhome* (alterations)	Bayport
Post, Charles Kintzing	*Strandhome* (alterations)	Bayport
* Post, Henry	*Postholme*	Babylon
* Post, Regis Henri	*Littlewood*	Bayport
Post, Waldron Kintzing	*Strandhome* (alterations)	Bayport
Zerega, John Pierre, Sr.	*Littlewood*	Bayport

Francis Day Rogers of Rogers and Butler

    * Havemeyer, Harry Waldron   Bay Shore

Romeyn and Stever

    * Strong, Theron George   Bay Shore

William Hamilton Russell, Jr.

Gregory, William Hamilton, Jr.	*Creekside*	East Islip
* Knapp, Harry Kearsarge, II	*Creekside*	East Islip
Riggio, Frank Vincent	*Riggio House*	Bay Shore
* Russell, William Hamilton, Jr.		Islip
* Sharp, H. Cecil	*Millcreek*	Bay Shore

Charles C. Thain

Hutchins, Francis Sessions		Great River
Stewart, Dr. George David	*Appin House*	Great River
* White, Raymond S.		Great River

Trowbridge and Ackerman

    * Carlisle, Jay Freeborn, Sr.   *Rosemary*   East Islip

Calvert Vaux

    Bossert, Louis   *The Oaks*   West Bay Shore

* Hyde, Henry Baldwin, Sr.   *The Oaks*   West Bay Shore

    Hyde, James Hazen   *The Oaks*   West Bay Shore

Warren and Wetmore

* Vanderbilt, William Kissam, Sr.   *Idlehour*   Oakdale
                                       (indoor tennis court and
                                       bachelor annex, 1903)

William H. Wray

    Clarkson, William Kemble   Bay Shore

    Lemmerman, Fred C.   Bay Shore

* Wray, William H.   Bay Shore

Civic Activism

See the surname entry to ascertain specific civic activism information.

Aldrich, Spencer, Sr.

Andrews, William Loring

Arnold, Annie Stuart Cameron

Arnold, Edward William Cameron

Ash, Dr. Charles F.

Atwood, Frederic Lawrence

Atwood, Kimball Chase, Jr.

Baruch, Bernard Mannes, Sr.

Bates, William Graves

Baxter, John Edward

Baxter, Katherine Byrne

Belmont, August, Sr.

Belmont, Perry

Betts, Mabel Granbery

Bigelow, Edward Hicks

Blagden, Crawford, Sr.

Blum, Edward Charles

Blum, Ethel Mildred Halsey

Blum, Florence May Abraham

Blum, Robert Edward

Bohack, Henry C.

Bossert, Louis

Bourne, Alfred Severin, Sr.

Bourne, Arthur Keeler, Sr.

Bourne, Hattie Louise Barnes

Bruce–Brown, Ruth A. Loney

Bull, Henry Worthington

Burchell, George W.

Burke, Charles Felix

Carlisle, Jay Freeborn, Sr.

Carlisle, Mary Pinkerton

Ceballos, Juan Manuel, Sr.

Carroll, Dr. Alfred Ludlow

Childs, Eversley, Sr.

Childs, William Hamlin

Cutting, Olivia Peyton Murray

Cutting, Robert Fulton

Cutting, William Bayard, Sr.

Davies, Julien Tappan

Davies, Julien Townsend, Sr.

deGoicouria, Albert V.

Delaney, Eleanor Gertrude Leary

Delaney, John Hanlon

Dempsey, May E.

Dick, Adolph M.

Dick, William Karl

Dodson, Robert Bowman

Doxsee, Almira S. Jennings

Egly, Henry Harris

Ellis, George Augustus, Jr.

Fairchild, Julian Douglas

Foster, Jay Stanley, II

Frothingham, John Sewell

Garben, Dr. Louis F.

Gibb, John

Gibb, Anna Pinkerton

Gibson, Frederick E.

Gibson, John James

Gibson, John Joseph

Goodrich, Frances Wickes

Goodrich, William W.

Green, Isaac Henry, II

Gregory, William Hamilton, Jr.

Guggenheim, Meyer Robert, Sr.

Gulden, Frank, Sr.

Hallock, Gerard, III

Hallock, Marion Wharton

Havemeyer, Eugenie Aiguier

Havemeyer, Harry Waldron

Havemeyer, Henry Osborne

Havemeyer, Horace, Jr.

Havemeyer, Horace, Sr.

Havemeyer, Louisine Waldron Elder

Hayward, Martha Eugenia Wemple

Hepburn, Henry Charles, Jr.

Hodges, George W., Sr.

Hodges, Maitia Angus Marvin

Hollins, Gerald Vanderbilt, Sr.

Hollins, Harry Bowly, Jr.

Hollister, Buell, Sr.

Hollister, Henry Hutchinson, Sr.

Hoppin, Bayard Cushing

Howell, Elmer Brown

Hubbard, Margaret G. McKay

Hulse, The Reverend William Warren

Hutton, Edward Francis

Hutton, Marjorie Merriweather Post

Hyde, Helen Walker

Hyde, Henry Baldwin, II

Hyde, Henry Baldwin, Sr.

Hyde, James Hazen

Hyde, Marthe Dervaux

Isbrandtsen, Gertrude Mirus

Johnson, Aymar

Johnson, Emma M. Grima

Jones, Frank Smith

Keith, Minor C.

King, Dr. George Suttie

Knapp, Shepherd, Sr.

Knapp, Theodore J., Sr.

Koehler, Robert H.

Lawrance, Charles Lanier

Lemmerman, Fred C.

Lester, Joseph Huntington

Lester, L. Norma Hegeman

Lester, Maxwell, Jr.

Lester, Maxwell, Sr.

Liebman, Sarah

Low, Chauncey E.

MacLeod, Thomas Woodward, Sr.

Macy, William Kingsland, Sr.

Manton, Eva Morier

Maxwell, Henry W.

McClure, William

McNamee, John

Moffitt, William Henry

Mollenhauer, Anna Margaretha Dick

Mollenhauer, John Adolph

Moore, Dr. David Dodge

Moore, Eugene Francis, Jr.

Moran, Eugene Francis, Jr.

Nicoll, William

O'Donohue, Charles A.

Oppenheimer, Julius

Otto, Julia

Packer, Frederick Little

Page, Walter Hines, Sr.

Parkinson, Thomas Ignatius, Jr.

Parkinson, Thomas Ignatius, Sr.

Parsons, Schuyler Livingston, Jr.

Parsons, William Decatur

Perkins, Richard Sturgis, Sr.

Peters, Harry Twyford, Sr.

Peters, Natalie Wells

Peters, Samuel Twyford

Pless, Helena Parsons Hallock

Pless, John Anthony, Jr.

Post, Charles Alfred

Post, Mary Lawrence Perkins

Post, Regis Henri, Sr.

Post, Waldron Kintzing

Prince, Anna Maria Morris

Reid, John Robert

Reid, Willard Placide

Remsen, Annie P. Hubbard

Robb, James

Robbins, William H., Sr.

Rolston, Roswell G.

Roosevelt, Robert Barnwell, Sr.

Rothschild, Simon Frank

Russell, William Hamilton, Jr.

Schieren, Charles Adolph, Sr.

Scully, Adaline Hathaway Weekes

Scully, Charles B.

Slote, Daniel, Jr.

Smith, Charles Robinson

Smith, Elward, Jr.

Smith, Fred D.

Smith, Hervey Garret

Smith, Virginia Woodhull Otto

Snedeker, Charles V.

Snow, Frederick B.

Stewart, Dr. George David

Stillman, Benjamin D.

Strong, Theron George

Sullivan, Dr. Raymond Peter, Sr.

Sutton, Frank

Swirbul, Leon A.

Thorne, Edwin, II

Thorne, Edwin, III

Thorne, Francis Burritt, Jr.

Thorne, Francis Burritt, Sr.

Thorne, Landon Ketchum, Jr.

Thorne, Landon Ketchum, Sr.

Titus, James Gulden, Sr.

Titus, Walter Livingston, Jr.

Titus, Walter Livingston, Sr.

Valentine, Landon Barrett

Vanderbilt, Alva Erskine Smith [*later*, Belmont]

Vanderbilt, Anne Harriman

Vanderbilt, William Kissam, Sr.

Vanderveer, John

Wagstaff, Alfred, Jr.

Wagstaff, George Barnard

Wagstaff, Mary Anderson Barnard

Ward, Edwin Carrington

Webster, Charles D.

Williams, Percy G.

Yates, Douglas Thomas, Sr.

Yates, Herbert John, Sr.

Yates, Margaret Louise Titus

Brook Russell Astor,
chairman of the Astor Foundation and widow of William Vincent Astor,
quipped on the concept of *noblesse oblige:*

"Money is like manure, it should be spread around."

When the owner who contracted with the architect is known, it is indicated by an asterisk. Multiple owners are listed in chronological order of ownership, not alphabetically by surname. Ownership of estates is listed only for those that used that particular estate name. See the surname entry to ascertain names used by other owners of the same estate.

Afterglow	* Gibb, John Stanchfield, John Barry, Sr. Wright, Dr. Arthur Mullen	Islip
Alkmaar Cottage	Vander Veer, Dr. Albert, Jr.	Fire Island
Allen Winden Farm	Dick, William Dick, John Henry Dick, William Karl	Islip
The Anchorage	* Hayward, William Tyson	Sayville
Appin House	Stewart, Dr. George David	Great River
Arcadia	* Stoppani, Charles F. Cox, Stephen Perry	Bayport
Ardmore	* Adams, Thomas, Jr. Ellis, George Augustus, Jr.	West Bay Shore
Armagh	Rolston, Roswell G.	North Babylon
Armory	Havemeyer, Henry, Sr.	West Islip
Awixa Lawn	* Knapp, Edward Spring, Sr.	Bay Shore
Awixaway	* Young, Albert Kelly, James P.	Bay Shore
Bayberry Point	* Havemeyer, Henry Osborne	Islip
Beach Grove	* Wilbur, Edward Russell, Sr.	Sayville
Beautiful Shore	* Moffitt, William Henry	Islip
Beechwold	* Jones, Frank Smith Westin, Clarence Frederick, Sr. Shea, David J.	Sayville
Breeze Lawn	Timmerman, Henry Gerlard Tobey, Orville Hurd	Islip
Brightwaters	Phelps, Charles E.	Brightwaters
Bronhurst	* Bruce–Brown, Ruth A. Loney	Islip
Brookhurst Farm	Ceballos, Juan Manuel, Sr.	Bay Shore
Brookside	* Green, Isaac Henry, II	Sayville

Brookwood	* Knapp, Harry Kearsarge, Sr.	East Islip
	Knapp, Theodore J., Sr.	
	Thorne, Francis Burritt, Sr.	
Casa Rosa	Davies, Julien Townsend, Sr.	West Islip
Cedarholme	* Gibb, Lewis Mills, Sr.	Bay Shore
	Gibb, Lewis Mills, Jr.	
Cedarshore	* Powell, David B.	Sayville
	* Powell, Leander Treadwell	
Cheap John's Estate	* Rubenstein, Ira	Bayport
Clovelly	* Arnold, Annie Stuart Cameron	West Islip
Clurella	McClure, William	West Islip
Creekside	* Knapp, Harry Kearsarge, II	East Islip
	Gregory, William Hamilton, Jr.	
The Crescent	* Arnold, Richard	West Islip
	Arnold, William	
Crickholly	* Hollins, Harry Bowly, Jr.	East Islip
Dearwood	Pinkerton, Robert Allan, Sr.	Bay Shore
Deer Park Farm	* Corbin, Austin	North Babylon
Deer Range Farm	* Johnston, Edwin Augustus, Sr.	East Islip
	Plumb, Sarah Ives	
	Plumb, James Ives	
	Taylor, George Campbell	
Edgemere	* Purdy, Charles Robert	Bayport
Edgewater	* Suydam, John R., Sr.	Bayport
	Suydam, John R., Jr.	
Effingham Pond	Sutton, Effingham B., Sr.	West Islip
Ellenwood	* Wood, Henry Duncan, Sr.	Islip
Elysian Views	Hulse, The Reverend William Warren	Bay Shore
Evergreens	Bates, William Graves	Bay Shore
Evershade	Flint, Sherman	Islip
Farmouth	Duval, Henry Rieman	East Islip
Firenze Farm	Guggenheim, Meyer Robert, Sr.	North Babylon
The Firs	Hepburn, Henry Charles, Jr.	Babylon

Four Hedges	Lester, Maxwell, Sr.	Bay Shore
Greycote	* Foster, Andrew D.	Sayville
The Harbor	Remsen, Jacob	Babylon
The Hawks	* Hollins, Gerald Vanderbilt, Sr.	East Islip
Homeport	* Mollenhauer, John Adolph	Bay Shore
Idle Hour	* Morgan, John	Bayport
Idlehour	* Vanderbilt, William Kissam, Sr.	Oakdale
Indian Neck Hall	* Bourne, Frederick Gilbert	Oakdale
Joy Farm	* Hayward, Frank Earl, Sr.	Sayville
Kanonsioni	* Dodson, Robert Bowman	West Islip
La Casetta	Crothers, Gordon	Islip
Lake House	* Bourne, Arthur Keeler, Sr.	Oakdale
Larklawn	Kalbfleisch, Franklin H.	Babylon
Lestaley	* Lester, Joseph Huntington	Bay Shore
Liberty Hall	* Stoppani, Joseph H.	Bayport
Lenapes Lodge	* Todd, William H.	Bayport
The Lilacs	* Roosevelt, Robert Barnwell, Jr.	Sayville
Lindenwalt	* Behman, Louis C., Sr.	Bayport
Little House	Drummond, Howard	Bay Shore
Littlewood	* Post, Regis Henri, Sr. Zerega, John Pierre, Sr.	Bayport
The Lodge	Thorne, Landon Ketchum, Jr.	West Bay Shore
Lohgrame	Graham, George Scott	Islip
Lone Oak	Stephens, John L.	West Islip
Lotos Lake	* Roosevelt, Robert Barnwell, Sr.	Bayport
Manatuck Farm	Lawrance, Francis Cooper, Sr. Lawrance, Francis Cooper, Jr. Lawrance, Charles Lanier	Bay Shore
Mapleton	* Schieren, Charles Adolph, Sr. Atwood, Kimball Chase, Jr.	Islip

316

Meadow Croft	* Roosevelt, John Ellis	Sayville
Meadow Edge	* Hard, Anson Wales, Jr.	West Sayville
Meadow Farm	* Hollins, Harry Bowly, Sr.	East Islip
Meadow Road Farm	Morgan, Robert Woodward, Sr.	East Islip
Millcreek	* Sharp, H. Cecil	Bay Shore
The Moorings	O'Donohue, Charles A.	Bay Shore
Nearholme	* Peters, Harry Twyford, Sr.	Islip
Netherbay	Gulden, Charles, Sr.	Bay Shore
North East Farm	* Sutton, Frank	North Babylon
Nursery Stud Farm	* Belmont, August, Sr. Belmont, Perry	North Babylon
Oakelwood	Mildeberger, Elwood	Bay Shore
Oakhurst	Hubbard, Harmanus B.	Bay Shore
The Oaks	* Hyde, Henry Baldwin, Sr. Hyde, James Hazen Bossert, Louis	West Bay Shore
O'Conee	* Shea, Timothy J., Sr.	Bay Shore
Oknoke	Arnold, Edward William Cameron [different house from that of Thorne]	West Islip
Oknoke	* Thorne, Edwin, II [different house from that of Arnold]	West Islip
Olympic Point	* Havemeyer, Horace, Sr.	Bay Shore
Onsrufarm	Yates, Herbert John, Sr.	West Islip
Opekeepsing	* Wagstaff, Alfred, Jr.	West Islip
Orowoc	Swan, Alden S.	Islip
Peperidge Hall	* Robert, Christopher Rhinelander, Jr. Aston, W. K.	Oakdale
Pepperidges	Andrews, William Loring	West Islip
Pine Acres	* Williams, Percy G.	East Islip
The Pines	* Turnbull, George R.	West Islip
Pleasure Island	* Parsons, Schuyler Livingston, Jr.	Islip

Postholme	* Post, Henry	Babylon
Questover Lodge	* Truslow, Frederick C.	Great River
Restina Cottage	Parsons, William Decatur	Bay Shore
Riggio House	Riggio, Frank Vincent	Bay Shore
River Croft	* Hobbs, Charles Buxton	Great River
Rosemary	* Carlisle, Jay Freeborn, Sr.	East Islip
Sagtikos Manor	Gardiner, Robert David Lion	West Bay Shore
Sans Souci	* Johnson, Bradish, Sr. Johnson, Henry Meyer	West Bay Shore
Scrub Oaks	Maxwell, Henry W.	Bay Shore
Seaward	* Low, Chauncey E.	Bay Shore
Sequatogue Farm	Havemeyer, Henry, Sr. Hubbs, Charles Francis	West Islip
Shadowbrook	Plumb, James Ives	Islip
Shadow Lawn	Moran, Eugene Francis, Jr.	Brightwaters
Shore Acres	Blum, Edward Charles	Bay Shore
The Stables	Morgan, Henry	East Islip
Strandhome	* Foster, William R., Jr. Post, Charles Alfred Post, Waldron Kintzing Baruch, Bernard Mannes, Sr. [rented]	Bayport
Sunneholm	Betts, Roland Whitney	Sayville
Sunnymead	Vanderveer, John Gibson, Cornelia Lott Vanderveer	West Islip
Sutton Park	Sutton, Woodruff, Sr.	West Islip
The Swamp	Corse, Israel S.	Sayville
Tahlulah	* Wagstaff, Dr. Alfred, Sr.	West Islip
The Towers	Reid, John Robert Reid, Willard Placide	Babylon
Thorneham	* Thorne, Landon Ketchum, Sr.	West Bay Shore
Timber Point	* Breese, William Laurence Davies, Julien Tappan	Great River

Twin Oaks	Tappin, Charles L.	Babylon
Twyford	Webster, Charles D.	Islip
Villa Avalon	* Covell, Charles Heber, Sr.	Bay Shore
Virginia Farm	Nicholas, Harry Ingersoll, Sr.	North Babylon
Wake Robin	Ward. Edwin Carrington	Bay Shore
Welles House	Welles, Benjamin Sumner, Jr. Welles, Benjamin Sumner, III	Islip
Wereholme	* Weekes, Harold Hathaway Tcherepnin, Alexander Scully, Charles B.	Islip
Westbeach	Kempster, James H.	Bay Shore
Westbrook Farm	* Maitland, Robert L. (c. 1860's house) Lorillard, Dr. George L. (c. 1860's house)	Great River
Westbrook Farm	* Cutting, William Bayard, Sr. (1886 house)	Great River
Whileaway	* Parsons, Schuyler Livingston, Sr. Wharton, Richard Wharton, Richard T., Sr.	Islip
Whileaway	* Wray, William H.	Bay Shore
White Cottage	Hyde, William J.	Bay Shore
White House	* Edwards, Edward	Bayport
Wildholme	Fortescue, Granville Roland	Bayport
Willow Close	Brownlie, George	Babylon
The Willows	deCoppet, Andre H.	Islip
Windermere	Aldrich, Spencer, Sr.	Bay Shore
Windholme	Peters, Samuel Twyford, Sr. Peters, Harry Twyford, Sr.	Islip
Woodland	* Johnson, Bradish, Jr. Johnson, Aymar	East Islip
Woodlea	Adams, John Dunbar	Bay Shore
Wyndemoor	* Simonds, William Robinson Shea, David J.	Sayville

South Shore estates that are presently golf courses are identified by the
original owner. For subsequent estate owners, see surname entry.

Southward Ho Country Club, South Country Road, West Bay Shore
    —located on the Henry Baldwin Hyde Sr. estate, *The Oaks*

Suffolk Country West Sayville Golf Course, South Country Road, West Sayville
    —located on the Anson Wales Hard, Jr. estate, *Meadow Edge*

Timber Point Country Club, Great River Road, Great River
    —located on the William Laurence Breese estate, *Timber Point*

The Oaks, main residence, c. 1900

The Oaks, main residence, 2005,
after remodeling by the country club

When the date of landscaping is known, it has been included in brackets. Since, in some instances, more than one landscape architect worked on an estate and, in some rare instances, the architect who designed the house also designed the estate's grounds, the surname entry should be consulted to determine if anyone else was involved in designing the estate grounds. When the estate owner who contracted for landscaping is known, it is indicated by an asterisk. Original and subsequent estate owners are included in the list.

Nathan F. Barrett

Baker, William Dunham		Islip
Beard, Anson Mc Cook, Jr.		Islip
Dempsey, Joseph Francis, Jr.		Islip
Egly, Henry Harris		Islip
Garben, Dr. Louis F., Sr.		Islip
Gulden, Charles, II		Islip
Gulden, Frank, Sr.		Islip
* Havemeyer, Henry Osborne	*Bayberry Point*	Islip
Havemeyer, Horace, Jr.		Islip
Havemeyer, Horace, Sr.		Islip
Howell, Carlton Bell		Islip
* Mollenhauer, John Adolph	*Homeport*	Bay Shore
Moore, Dr. David Dodge		Islip
Perkins, Richard Sturgis, Sr.		Islip
Thorne, Edwin, III		Islip
Titus, Walter Livingston, Jr.		Islip
Yates, Douglas Thomas, Sr.		Islip

Beatrix Jones Farrand

* Cutting, William Bayard, Sr.	*Westbrook Farm* (animal cemetery)	Great River
* Flint, Sherman	*Evershade* (landscape plan not executed)	Islip

Martha Brooks Brown Hutcheson

* Breese, William Laurence	*Timber Point*	Great River
Davies, Julien Tappan	*Timber Point*	Great River

Innocenti and Webel

* Thorne, Landon Ketchum, Sr.	*Thornham* (gardens)	West Islip

Charles Wellford Leavitt and Sons

Gregory, William Hamilton, Jr.	*Creekside*	East Islip
* Hard, Anson Wales, Jr.	*Meadow Edge*	West Sayville
* Knapp, Harry Kearsarge, II	*Creekside*	East Islip

Olmstead

Atwood, Kimball Chase, Jr.	*Mapleton*	Islip
Bossert, Louis	*The Oaks* (designed landscaping, jointly with Jacob Weidenman)	West Bay Shore
* Bourne, Frederick Gilbert	*Indian Neck Hall*	Oakdale
* Cutting, William Bayard, Sr.	*Westbrook Farm* (1887-1894)	Great River
Harbeck, Charles T.	(1915)	East Islip
* Havemeyer, Horace, Sr.	*Olympic Point*	Bay Shore
* Hollins, Harry Bowly, Sr.	*Meadow Farm*	East Islip
* Hyde, Henry Baldwin, Sr.	*The Oaks* (designed landscaping, jointly with Jacob Weidenman)	West Bay Shore
Hyde, James Hazen	*The Oaks* (designed landscaping, jointly with Jacob Weidenman)	West Bay Shore
Johnson, Aymar	*Woodland* (1915)	East Islip
* Johnston, Bradish, Jr.	*Woodland* (1915)	East Islip
Johnston, James Boorman	(1915)	East Islip
Schieren, Charles Adolph, Sr.	*Mapleton*	Islip

Harold Truesdel Patterson

* Dodson, Robert Bowman	*Kanonsioni*	West Islip

Ellen Biddle Shipman

Prince, John Dyneley, II		Islip
* Peters, Harry Twyford, Sr.	*Windholme Farm*	Islip
Peters, Samuel Twyford	*Windholme Farm*	Islip

Vitale, Brinkerhoff and Geiffert

* Carlisle, Jay Freeborn, Sr.	*Rosemary*	East Islip

Ferruccio Vitale

* Thorne, Landon Ketchum, Sr.	*Thornham*	West Islip

Jacob Weidenman

Bossert, Louis	*The Oaks* (designed landscaping, jointly with Olmsted)	West Bay Shore
* Hyde, Henry Baldwin, Sr.	*The Oaks* (designed landscaping, jointly with Olmsted)	West Bay Shore
Hyde, James Hazen	*The Oaks* (designed landscaping, jointly with Olmsted	West Bay Shore

The following list of maiden names of women associated with Long Island South Shore estates was compiled from various biographical sources, social registers, and newspaper obituaries. It should be noted that women occasionally gave surnames from previous marriages to editors, without designating them as such. If there were multiple marriages, husbands are listed in chronological order. Please note that the women included in this list were either the homeowners or spouses of homeowners. Women of subsequent generations are not included unless they assumed ownership of the house.

Abraham, Florence May	*married*	**Blum,** Edward Charles
Abraham, Lillian		**Rothschild,** Simon Frank
Adams, Florence Vance		**Ellis,** George Augustus, Jr.
Aiguier, Eugenie		**Havemeyer,** Harry Waldron
Alexander, Clara		**Maxwell,** Henry W.
Alexandre, Helen Lispenard		**Hoppin,** Bayard Cushing
Amory, Harriet H.		**Garner,** Thomas, Jr.
Antonsen, Petra		**Yates,** Herbert John, Sr.
Arents, Minnie E.		**Young,** Albert
Arnold, ____		**Cameron,** Edward Miller
Babcock, Ann Gates		**Truslow,** Frederick C.
Babcock, Mary Emma		**Todd,** William H.
Bach, Roberta		**Watt,** Dr. James, Sr.
Bailey, Ella		**Smith,** Elward, Jr.
Baldwin, Emily		**Reach,** ____ **Lester,** Maxwell, Jr.
Baldwin, Grace		**Ruggles,** James F. **Johnson,** Henry Meyer
Baldwin, Sarah K.		**Olliffee,** Cornelius W. **Johnson,** Henry Meyer
Balsdon, Harriet		**Gibb,** John
Barclay, Clara W.		**Onativia,** Jose Victor, Jr. **deCoppet,** Andre H. **Boatwright,** John Lord
Barnard, Alice		**Childs,** Eversley, Sr.
Barnard, Mary Anderson		**Wagstaff,** Alfred, Jr.
Barnes, Hattie Louise		**Bourne,** Alfred Severin, Sr.
Barry, Alice Hoadley		**Thorne,** Landon Ketchum, Jr.
Bauman, Jane Louise		**Hayward,** William Tyson, Jr. **Sutton,** Frank
Beasley, Lillian H.		**Pardee,** Roy Edmund
Bell, Grace Hubbard		**Fortescue,** Granville Roland
Benoit, Lulu		**Foster,** William R., Jr.

Bernheimer, Grace L.

Berryman, Georgiana Louisa

Bicar, Pauline

Bischoff, Harriet

Blum, Alice I.

Blydenburgh, Ella

Bolmer, Georgina E.

Boscher, Margaret

Bossert, Harriet Louise

Boughton, Margaret

Bourne, Florence

Bradley, Florence Irene

Bramm, Marie Louise

Brewster, Marietta

Broske, Erika Lina

Bross, Elizabeth

Brown, Ann Eliza

Brown, Evelyn

Brown, Kizze

Brown, Mary Augusta

Bulkey, Helen C.

Bulkley, Mary Faran

Burchell, Susan

Burnett, Mary

Burr, Caroline

Burton, Frances Anna Parsons

Byrne, Katherine

Cadwell, Ellen Therese

Cairns, Frances

Cameron, Annie Stuart

Carey, ____

Guggenheim, Meyer Robert, Sr.
Snellenberg, Martin E.

Strong, James H. S.

Arnold, Richard

Koehler, Robert H.

Bigelow, Edwin Hick
Taliaferro, Eugene Sinclair
Warfield, Ethelbert

Robbins, Josiah

Arnold, Richard

Heins, John Lewis, Sr.

Huber, Frederick Max, Sr.

Riggio, Frank Vincent

Hard, Anson Wales, Jr.
Deans, Robert Barr, Sr.
Thayer, Alexander Dallas

Fairchild, Julian Douglas

Schieren, Charles Adolph, Sr.

Robbins, William H., Sr.

Puzo, Mario

Eaton, James Waterbury, Sr.

Foster, Andrew D.

Thorne, Francis Burritt, Sr.

Howell, Elmer W.

Clarkson, William Kemble

Redmond, Roland

Gulden, Charles, II

Adams, John Dunbar

McNamee, John

Knapp, Harry Kearsarge, Sr.

Plumb, James Ives

Baxter, John Edward

Elder, George Waldron, Sr.

Smith, Elward, Sr.
Smith, Robert Gibson

Arnold, William

Owens, Joseph Eugene, Sr.

Carll, Annie	**Cameron**, Edward Miller
Carroll, Ruth Lawrence	**Draper**, Eben S. **Sharp**, H. Cecil
Carter, Kate Louise	**Macy**, George Henry
Castro, Cristina	**Keith**, Minor C.
Child, Sophia	**Harbeck**, Charles T.
Clark, Margaret Maxwell	**Vander Veer**, Dr. Albert, Jr.
Clark, Naomi	**Remsen**, Phoenix
Clarke, Pauline M.	**Graham**, George Scott
Cleaveland, Marjorie	**Palmer**, Elwell
Cobb, Ann C.	**Thorne**, Francis Burritt, Jr.
Cochran, Harriet Penrose	**Suydam**, John R., Jr.
Colt, Amy	**Wagstaff**, Cornelius DuBois
Conkling, Elizabeth	**Oakman**, Walter George, Sr.
Conner, Virginia Kenniston	**Dick**, William Karl **Moseley**, Frederick S., Jr.
Covell, Kate	**Lawrence**, Chester B.
Cox, Amabel Bancker	**Dahl**, George W.
Crane, Ella	**McClure**, William
Crane, Jane Elizabeth	**Andrews**, William Loring
Crane, Sarah H.	**White**, Raymond S. **Hutchins**, Francis Sessions
Crosby, Alice	**Allison**, William Manwaring, Sr.
Crowley, Edith A.	**Gregory**, William Hamilton, Jr.
Cumnock, Mary Cutting	**Wagstaff**, George Barnard
Curley, Irene	**Bodde**, ____ **Hutton**, Franklyn Laws **Moffett**, James A.
Cushman, Lavonne Jeanette	**Gibson**, John James
Cutter, Louise Eliot	**Pinkerton**, Robert Allan, II **Marshall**, John Hunt
Dall, Hariette Holley	**Aldrich**, Spencer, Sr.
Daniel, Roberta	**Yates**, Richard George, Sr.
Davies, Alice M.	**Mc Kee**, Henry Sellers, II
Davis, Angeline	**Reid**, John Robert
Dear, Dorothy	**Hutton**, Edward Francis
de Garmendia, Marie Rose	**Davies**, Julien Townsend, Sr.

deGoicouria, Alice Wall	**Belmont**, August, III **Wing**, John D.
de LaGrange, Marie	**Hyde**, Henry Baldwin, II
deMurias, Sylvia A.	**Vander Veer**, Dr. Albert, Jr.
Denys, Marguerite	**Delagarde**, ____ **Post**, Regis Henri, Sr.
Dervaux, Marthe	**Thom**, ____ **Hyde**, James Hazen
de Trobriand, Marie Caroline	**Post**, Albert Kintzing **Post**, Charles Alfred
Dick, Anna Margaretha	**Mollenhauer**, John Adolph
Dick, Doris Anna	**Havemeyer**, Horace, Sr.
Dick, Julia A. H.	**Macy**, William Kingsland, Sr.
Dickson, Jessie Rae	**Morrison**, George Alexander
Dix, Emily Margaret Gordon	**Lawrance**, Charles Lanier
di Zoppola, Mara	**Wharton**, Richard T., Sr.
Dobie, Henrietta	**MacLeod**, Thomas Woodward, Sr. **Chase**, C. Trevett
Donovan, Elizabeth	**Robb**, James
Drumm, Mollie	**Mildeberger**, Elwood
DuBois, Sarah Platt	**Wagstaff**, Dr. Alfred, Sr.
Dunn, Nellie R.	**Van Anden**, Frank
Durfey, Lucretia	**Ash**, Dr. Charles F.
Eaton, Elizabeth Bross	**Guggenheim**, Meyer Robert, Sr.
Elder, Adeline Mapes	**Peters**, Samuel Twyford
Elder, Louisine Waldron	**Havemeyer**, Henry Osborne
Elder, Mary Louise	**Havemeyer**, Henry Osborne
Elliott, Veronica Boswell	**Thorne**, Landon Ketchum, Jr.
Ellis, Elizabeth Thorn	**Roosevelt**, Robert Barnwell, Sr.
Epp, Carol Eugenia	**Gibson**, Gregory Martin
Ellis, Emma M.	**Graham**, George Scott
Everdell, Rosalind	**Havemeyer**, Horace, Jr.
Ewing, Maria Louisa	**Wright**, Edward **Lorillard**, Dr. George L. **Casa de Agreda**, Count
Eytinge, Elizabeth Sarah	**Hepburn**, Henry Charles, Jr.
Farrington, Josephine	**Hoff**, Albert D.
Farwell, Mary Althea	**Swan**, Alden S.

Fisher, Frances	**Wharton**, William Fishbourne
Fitch, Annie	**Hyde**, Henry Baldwin, Sr.
Flood, Elizabeth	**Adams**, Thomas, Jr.
Force, Madeleine	**Astor**, John Jacob, IV **Dick**, William Karl **Fiermonte**, Enzo
Fox, Stephanie	**Livingston**, Henry Beekman, Jr.
Francis, Rebecca	**Powell**, Leander Treadwell
Friedman, Ella	**Oppenheimer**, Julius
Frost, Alice H.	**Van Anden**, William M., Sr.
Frothingham, Dorothy W.	**Arnold**, ____ **Wagstaff**, George Barnard **Forbes–Sempill**, Lionel
Frothingham, Mary T.	**Low**, Chauncey E.
Fry, Elizabeth	**Tobey**, Orville Hurd
Fry, Kate	**Timmerman**, Henry Gerlard
Gaillard, Amiee	**Johnson**, Bradish, Jr. **Crother**, Gordon
Garner, Frances	**Lawrance**, Francis Cooper, Sr.
Gilbert, Kathleen	**Hayward**, Frank Earle, Sr. **McCullough**, P.
Gino, Carol (common-law-wife)	**Puzo**, Mario
Girdner, Adela Overton	**Atwood**, Kimball Chase, Jr.
Giusti, Jean	**Gibson**, Frederick E.
Gordon, Anne	**Duval**, Henry Rieman
Grady, Mary	**Moses**, Robert
Graham, Elizabeth Marie	**King**, Dr. George Suttie
Granbery, Mabel	**Betts**, Roland Whitney **Spratt**, Charles Edward
Granbery, Mary Louise	**Jones**, Frank Smith
Grand, Helen	**Thorne**, Edwin, III
Graves, Jeanette	**Ford**, Malcolm W.
Griffen, Annie	**Baruch**, Bernard Mannes, Sr.
Griffiths, ____	**Slote**, Daniel, Jr.
Grima, Emma M.	**Johnson**, Bradish Gaillard, Sr.
Guastavino, Louise	**Gulden**, Frank, Jr.
Gulden, Margaret	**Titus**, Walter Livingston, Sr.
Hallock, Helena Parsons	**Pless**, John Anthony, Jr.

Halsey, Ethel Mildred	**Blum**, Robert Edward
Hamersly, Edith	**Biscoe**, Henry E. **Roosevelt**, John Ellis
Hamersly, Lilie	**Roosevelt**, Robert Barnwell, Jr. **Courtney**, Charles Edward
Harmon, Harriet Burr	**Morse**, William Otis
Harper, May	**Valentine**, Landon Barrett
Harriman, Anne	**Sands**, Samuel Stevens, Jr. **Rutherfurd**, Lewis Morris **Vanderbilt**, William Kissam, Sr.
Hatch, Margaret Leighton	**Moore**, Dr. David Dodge
Hatch, Mary R.	**Gunther**, William Henry, Jr.
Havemeyer, Adeline	**Perkins**, Richard Sturgis, Sr. **Rand**, Laurance B.
Havemeyer, Doris	**Catlin**, Dr. Daniel, Sr.
Haviland, Ellen Rushton	**Burchell**, George W.
Head, Betsey (common-law-wife)	**Taylor**, George Campbell
Hegeman, L. Norma	**Lester**, Maxwell, Sr.
Henes, Augusta	**Gulden**, Frank, Sr.
Henry, Evelyn	**Stoppani**, Charles F., Jr.
Hibbard, Emma Louise	**Green**, Isaac Henry, II
Hill, Emeline Field	**Clyde**, William Pancoast, Sr.
Hill, Ethel	**Zerega**, John Pierre, Sr.
Hilsendegen, Christine	**Parsons**, William Decatur
Hoar, Roseanne	**Beard**, Anson Mc Cook, Jr.
Hoffman, Marion K.	**Johnson**, Aymar
Hollins, Alice M.	**Nicholas**, Harry Ingersoll, Sr.
Hollins, Ethel L.	**Bourne**, Arthur Keeler, Sr.
Hollins, Faith	**Little**, Arthur W. **Gulden**, Charles, II
Hollister, Louise	**Forest**, Richard E. **Valentine**, Landon Barrett
Hopkins, Mary	**Blagden**, Crawford, Sr.
Horton, Blanche	**Hutton**, Edward Francis
Howe, Mollie Richards	**Hubbs**, Charles Francis
Howell, Isabelle	**Hollister**, Henry Hutchinson, Sr.
Hubbard, Annie P.	**Remson**, Jacob
Huber, Elizabeth	**Howell**, Carlton Bell

Hughes, Anna E.	**Pinkerton**, Robert Allan, Sr.
Hughes, Greta	**Howell**, James Frederick, Sr. **Witherspoon**, Herbert
Hyde, Lillian	**Feitner**, Quentin Field **Wagstaff**, George Barnard
Hyde, Lulu	**Hubbell**, Vincent B. **Drummond**, Howard
Isham, Samantha Gaynor	**Gulden**, Charles, II
Ives, Sarah	**Plumb**, James Neale
Jenkins, Clara	**Turnbull**, George R.
Jennings, Almira S.	**Doxsee**, James Harvey, Sr.
Johnson, Eona	**Cox**, George, Jr.
Johnson, Helena	**Parsons**, Schuyler Livingston, Sr.
Johnson, Lucy	**Carroll**, Dr. Alfred Ludlow
Johnson, Marie G.	**Russell**, William Hamilton, Jr. **Crothers**, Gordon
Johnson, Muriel	**Belasco**, Raymond **deCoppet**, Andre H. **Fitch**, George Hopper
Johnston, Eileen	**deCoppet**, Andre H. **Zu Wied**, Prince Wilhelm
Jones, Henrietta Louise	**Simonds**, William Robinson
Jones, Maude Virginia	**Westin**, Clarence Frederick, Sr. **Shea**, David J.
Joralemon, ____	**Johnson**, Parmenus
Jordon, Katharine	**Magoun**, George B.
Kahler, Ruth	**King**, Dr. George Suttie
Kapp, Emma	**Ranft**, Richard
Keeler, Elizabeth B.	**Ballard**, Frederick E., Sr.
Keeler, Emma Sparks	**Bourne**, Frederick Gilbert
Kellers, Mary C.	**Gulden**, Charles, Sr.
Kennedy, Laurette	**Hoppin**, Bayard Cushing
Kent, Katharine	**Frothingham**, John Sewell
Kessberg, Ida	**Van Anden**, Frank
Ketcham, Anita	**Shortland**, Thomas Francis
Ketching, Ada Emeline	**Reid**, Willard Placide
Ketchum, Phebe	**Thorne**, Edwin, II
Knapp, Caroline	**Post**, Charles Kintzing
Knapp, Evelina Meserole	**Hollins**, Harry Bowly, Sr.

Knight, Mary	**Arnold**, Edward William Cameron
Knowles, Estelle	**Foster**, Jay Stanley, II
	Bromell, Alfred Henry
Knowlton, Louise R.	**Hollister**, Buell, Sr.
Kobbe, Carol	**Morgan**, Robert Woodward, Sr.
	Snow, George Palen
Kobbe, Hildegarde	**Stevenson**, Joseph H.
	Thorne, Francis Burritt, Sr.
Kobbe, Virginia	**Hollins**, Gerald Vanderbilt, Sr.
	Morgan, Henry
Krieg, Hermine T.	**Ranft**, Richard, Jr.
Krippendorf, Philippine	**Bossert**, Louis
Kumble, Catherine	**Knapp**, Shepherd, Sr.
Lanier, Sarah Egleston	**Lawrance**, Francis Cooper, Jr.
Lawler, Mae A.	**Pardee**, Roy Edmund
Lawrance, Cornelia	**Wilmerding**, George C.
Lawrance, Louisa Anna	**Johnson**, Bradish, Sr.
Lawrance, Margaret Ireland	**Knapp**, Edward Spring, Sr.
Lawrence, Anna Middleton	**Suydam**, John R., Sr.
Leary, Eleanor Gertrude	**Delaney**, John Hanlon
Leavitt, Alice	**Kobbe**, George Christian
Leishman, Marthe	**de Gontaut–Biron**, Count Louis
	Hyde, James Hazen
Libby, S. Katharine	**Lester**, Maxwell, Jr.
Lindsay, Jane	**Tappin**, John C.
Littell, Sarah E.	**Rolston**, Roswell G.
Livingston, Lilias	**Hollins**, Harry Bowly, Jr.
Livingston, Maria Maude	**Bull**, Henry Worthington
Lockwood, Mary Shubrick	**Childs**, Eversley, Sr.
Loney, Ruth A.	**Bruce–Brown**, George
Loomis, Julia Atterbury	**Thorne**, Landon Ketchum, Sr.
Lott, Gertrude Van Siclen	**Vanderveer**, John
Lousdale, Louise	**Wharton**, Percival C.
Lusk, Joan Penfold	**Tenney**, Charles Henry, Sr.
Macconnell, Jennie Florence	**Melville**, Frank, Jr.
Macdonald, Margaret	**Macconnell**, John B.
Mackay, Sarah D.	**Gibb**, John

MacLeond, Mina E.	**Blagden**, Crawford, Sr.
Maloney, Ida	**Stoppani**, Joseph H.
Mann, Elizabeth Marshall	**Knapp**, Harry Kearsarge, II **Herrick**, Walter Russell
Martin, Alice	**Davies**, Julien Tappan
Marvin, Maita Angus	**Hodges**, George W., Sr.
Matson, Marion Louette	**Ward**, Edwin Carrington
Maxwell, Henrietta Frances	**Lester**, Joseph Huntington
May, Edith Sybil	**Randolph**, Arthur **Whitney**, William Collins
McBirney, Leila Ellis	**Post**, Regis Henri, Sr.
McDermot, Rosalie	**Baldridge**, Harry Alexander, Sr.
McKay, Margaret G.	**Hubbard**, Harmanus B.
Mc Kee, Marie Rose	**Yates**, Richard George, Sr. **Bynum**, Joseph S. **Correll**, Ronald S.
McLean, Caroline	**Post**, Henry
McNamee, Marie E.	**Sullivan**, Dr. Raymond Peter, Sr.
Meredith, Mary R.	**Dana**, Richard Turner
Meserole, Maria	**Knapp**, William K.
Miller, Emily Boxley	**Bourne**, Arthur Keeler, Sr.
Mills, Emma	**Adams**, Thomas, Jr.
Minor, Mary E.	**Hobbs**, Charles Buxton
Mirus, Gertrude	**Isbrandtsen**, Hans J.
Moffit, Ellen Juliette	**Creamer**, Joseph Byron, Sr.
Mollenhauer, Julia Theodora	**Dick**, John Henry
Moller, Mary Jane	**Havemeyer**, Henry, Sr.
Moore, Geralda	**Parkinson**, Thomas Ignatius, Jr.
Moore, Sarlta	**Garben**, Dr. Louis F., Sr.
Moran, Helen Dorothy	**McBurney**, Dr. Malcolm **Noyes**, Daniel Raymond
Morgan, ____	**Moran**, Amedee Depau
Morgan, Jennie Rice	**Foster**, Jay Stanley, II
Morier, Eva M.	**Manton**, Martin Thomas
Morris, Anna Maria	**Prince**, John Dyneley, II
Morrison, Jeanett	**Livingston**, Walter Francis **Palmer**, Elwell

Morse, Elizabeth	**Atwood**, Frederic Lawrence
Murray, Caroline	**Wilmerding**, Lucius Kellogg
Murray, Lulu	**Creamer**, Frank D., Sr.
Murray, Olivia Peyton	**Cutting**, William Bayard, Sr.
Myton, Grace E.	**Ireland**, Rufus J., Sr.
Neger, Elizabeth	**Bossert**, Louis
Newall, Elizabeth	**Drummond**, Howard
Nicholas, Evelyn Hollins	**Arnold**, Alexander Duncan Cameron **Stevenson**, Joseph H.
Nicholas, Reta	**Murdock**, Uriel Atwood, II
Nicholl, Frances Louisa	**Ludlow**, William Handy, Sr.
Nicoll, Fanny	**Johnson**, Lee
Nicoll, Sarah Augusta	**Nicoll**, William
Noyes, Margaret G.	**Hutchins**, Francis Sessions
Oakes, Eunice Bailey	**Gardiner**, Robert David Lion
Oakley, Sarah Elizabeth	**Morgan**, John
Oldner, Helen M.	**Ryan**, John T.
Olsen, Marion	**Snedeker**, Charles V.
O'Shea, Marion Theresa	**Roosevelt**, Robert Barnwell, Sr.
Otto, Virginia Woodhull	**Smith**, Jewett Holt
Pabst, Lillian	**Wilson**, William Paul **Packer**, Frederick Little
Parker, Florence	**Snedecor**, James H.
Parsons, Helena Johnson	**Wharton**, Richard
Parsons, Mary	**Breese**, William Laurence **Higgins**, Henry Vincent
Pasfield, Matilda Anna	**Egly**, Henry Harris
Payne, Flora	**Whitney**, William Collins
Pease, Patty Carroll	**McKinney**, Rigan **Gibb**, Lewis Mills, Jr.
Peirce, Marjorie	**Thorn**, Edward Floyd–Jones, Sr.
Pell, Adelia Duane	**Ireland**, John Busteed
Perkins, Mary Lawrence	**Post**, Waldron Kintzing
Perry, Caroline Slidell	**Belmont**, August, Sr.
Peters, Louisine	**Weekes**, Harold Hathaway **Tcherepnin**, Alexander
Peters, Natalie	**Webster**, Charles D.

Peters, Sarah W.	**Williams**, Richard H., Sr.
Pierson, Elizabeth	**Parsons**, Schuyler Livingston, Jr.
Pinkerton, Anna	**Gibb**, Lewis Mills, Sr.
Pinkerton, Mary	**Carlisle**, Jay Freeborn, Sr.
Piper, Elizabeth Prokoff	**Hyde**, Henry Baldwin, II
Pollard, Rebecca	**Van Lennep**, William, Jr. **Guggenheim**, Meyer Robert, Sr. **Logan**, John A.
Post, Caroline Beatrice	**Post**, Regis Henri, Sr.
Post, Harriette Appleton	**Wilson**, R. Thornton **Von Jeszenzky**, Baron Emmerich **Welles**, Benjamin Sumner, III
Post, Marjorie Merriweather	**Close**, Edward Bennett **Hutton**, Edward Francis **Davies**, Joseph Edward **May**, Herbert Arthur
Potter, Katherine	**Avery**, Joseph W. Hemmersley **Hard**, Anson Wales, Jr. **Wear**, Joseph W.
Prentice, Martha Howard	**Strong**, Theron George
Pulsifer, Ellen E.	**Wood**, Henry Duncan, Sr.
Purdy, Elizabeth Teackle	**Nicholas**, George S., Sr.
Quarre, Gladys	**Peabody**, Frederick **Knapp**, Theodore J., Sr.
Rafter, Cecelia	**Kelly**, James P.
Ralston, Verra Hruba	**Yates**, Herbert John, Sr.
Redmond, Frances	**Livingston**, Henry Beekman, Jr.
Regan, Jean	**Gibb**, Lewis Mills, Jr.
Remington, Julia	**Morgan**, Charles **Robert**, Christopher Rhinelander, Jr.
Rieliey, Mary Teresa	**Bachia**, Richard Augustus, Jr.
Riopel, Grace M.	**Blakeley**, James M. **Hyde**, William J.
Robb, Helen	**Catlin**, John Bernsee, Sr.
Robb, Ida May	**Stewart**, Dr. George David
Robbins, Jessie A.	**Sloane**, Henry T. **Belmont**, Perry
Roberts, Flora	**Tappin**, Charles L.
Rogers, Frances	**Howell**, Elmer Brown
Rose, Miriam A.	**Thorne**, Landon Ketchum, Jr.

Rossiter, Elizabeth	**Gibb**, Howard, Sr.
Saltonstall, Katharine	**Weld**, Philip Balch
Sauders, Effe J.	**Wood**, Henry Duncan, Jr.
Scanlan, Gertrude	**Shea**, Timothy J., Sr.
Schenck, Natalie	**Cutting**, Robert Fulton
Schenck, Sarah Perine	**Kalbfleisch**, Franklin H.
Schermerhorn, Ann White	**Suydam**, Charles
Schermerhorn, Catherine	**Welles**, Benjamin Sumner, Sr.
Scott, Amy Rowan	**Johnson**, Effingham Lawrence **Bates**, William Graves
Scott, Evelyn P.	**Behman**, Louis C., Sr.
Scott, Margaret	**Behman**, Louis C., Sr.
Scoville, Olive A.	**O'Donohue**, Charles A.
Seidel, Elsie	**Guastavino**, Rafael, Jr. **Mann**, Randolph
Sherwood, Josephine	**Turnbull**, John Gourlay, Jr.
Siems, Doris	**Mollenhauer**, John
Sims, Mary Louise	**Moses**, Robert
Slater, Esther	**Welles**, Benjamin Sumner, III **Kerrigan**, Joseph J.
Slocum, Margaret Olivia	**Flint**, Sherman
Smith, ____	**Allen**, Theodore
Smith, Alva Erskine	**Vanderbilt**, William Kissam, Sr. **Belmont**, Oliver Hazard
Smith, Frances Elward	**Baldridge**, Harry Alexander, Sr.
Smith, Laurie	**Allgood**, Andrew Perry de Forest
Spaulding, Clara	**Stanchfield**, John Barry, Sr.
Spence, Margaret	**Eastwood**, John H.
Spencer, Nellie White	**Childs**, William Hamlin
Stanchfield, Alice	**Wright**, Dr. Arthur Mullen
Stanton, Anna	**Lawrance**, John I.
Staudt, Marie Josephine	**Moran**, Eugene Francis, Jr.
Steele, Frances	**Sutton**, Woodruff, Sr.
Steele, Jeannie Porter	**Smith**, Charles Robinson
Steffens, Emma A.	**Bohack**, Henry C.
Stephens, Estelle	**Swirbul**, Leon A.
Stevens, Alice Muriel	**Titus**, James Gulden, Sr.

Stevenson, Carol	**Lovering**, Joseph Sears, Jr.
	Roesler, M. Stuart
Stokes, Frances	**Clark**, Louis Crawford, II
	Weekes, Harold Hathaway
Stoppani, E. Jane	**Harris**, ____
	Cox, Stephen Perry
Strong, Silvie Livingston	**Post**, Richard Bailey
	Hepburn, Henry Chester
Suydam, Helen	**Cutting**, Robert Fulton
Swan, Frances Wyeth	**Welles**, Benjamin Sumner, Jr.
Taylor, Mary Gilley	**Walbridge**, George Hicks
Taylor, Natalie	**Bossert**, Charles Volunteer
Thebaud, Emelia I.	**Heckscher**, Charles Augustus, Jr.
Thompson, Louise	**Baker**, William Dunham
Thorn, Frances M.	**Garner**, Thomas, Sr.
Thorne, Macellite	**Garner**, William Thorn
Thorne, Phebe	**Dempsey**, Joseph Francis, Jr.
Thorne, Phebe Schoonhoven	**Knapp**, Harry Kearsarge, II
	Tucker, John
Timmerman, Grace Ethel	**Tobey**, Orville Hurd
Titus, Margaret Louise	**Yates**, Douglas Thomas, Sr.
Torrence, Jessie	**Magoun**, Kinsley
Townsend, Mathilde Scott	**Gerry**, Peter Goelet
	Welles, Benjamin Sumner, III
Trenchard, Edith Isabelle	**Power**, John Anthony
	Arnold, Edward William Cameron
True, Julia	**Stephens**, John L.
Turnbull, Clara	**Keith**, Minor C. R., II
Vagts, Anna Maria	**Dick**, William
Valentine, Anne	**Lovering**, Joseph Sears, Jr.
Vance, Nannie Mitchell	**Roosevelt**, John Ellis
Vanderveer, Cornelia Lott	**Gibson**, John Joseph
Van Glahn, Paula	**Frank**, Emil H., Sr.
Wagstaff, Sarah Louisa	**Remsen**, Phoenix
Walker, Helen Ella	**Matuschka**, Baron Manfred
	Hyde, James Hazen
	Von Thur and Taxis, Prince Alexander
Wall, Mary Cecelia	**deGoicouria**, Albert V.
Wandel, Blanche Gifford	**Walbridge**, Ernest A.

Washington, Lulu	**Ceballos**, Juan Manuel, Sr.
Wederstrandt, Helen Maria	**Johnson**, John Dean
Weed, Georgia Childs	**Parkinson**, Thomas Ignatius, Sr.
Weekes, Adeline Hathaway	**Scully**, Charles B. **Orssich**, Count Philip
Weeks, Katharine	**Arnold**, Alexander Duncan Cameron
Welles, Helen S.	**Kingsland**, George Lovett, Sr.
Wells, Mary	**Dodson**, Robert Bowman
Wells, Natalie	**Peters**, Harry Twyford, Sr.
Wemple, Martha Eugenia	**Hayward**, William Tyson, Sr.
Weyher, Margaret Gibbs Miller	**Guggenheim**, Meyer Robert, Sr.
Wharton, Marion	**Hallock**, Gerard, III
Wheeler, Carolyn	**Kobbe**, Gustave
Wheeler, Hannah	**Corbin**, Austin
White, Madeleine	**Kennard**, Spencer, Sr. **Morris**, Stuyvesant Fish, III
Whitlock, Catherine E.	**Conover**, Daniel D.
Whitman, ____	**Doxsee**, James Harvey, Sr.
Whitney, Maria	**Livingston**, Robert Cambridge, III
Wickes, Frances	**Goodrich**, William W.
Widdifield, Adele Cornwell	**Howell**, James Frederick, Sr.
Wilkinson, Abbie	**Purdy**, Charles Robert
Willard, Anne	**Hollister**, Henry Hutchinson, Sr.
Willing, Susan	**Lawrance**, Francis Cooper, Jr.
Wilson, Willa Alice	**Page**, Walter Hines, Sr.
Woodhouse, Grace Guernsey	**Roosevelt**, Robert Barnwell, Jr.
Woodrow, Lorena M.	**Burke**, Charles Felix
Woodruff, Ellen A.	**Johnson**, Edwin Augustus, Sr.
Woodruff, Mary L.	**Sutton**, Effingham B., Sr.
Woolworth, Edna	**Hutton**, Franklyn Laws
Woolworth, Franc	**Pinkerton**, Allan, II
Worth, Josephine	**Hulse**, The Reverend William Warren
Yates, Elsa Marcia	**Titus**, Walter Livingston, Jr.
Young, Ruth Allen	**Koehler**, Robert H.
Zundt, Eliza Anna	**Heins**, John Lewis, Sr.

Occupations

See the surname entry to ascertain if an individual is listed under several occupational headings.

ARCHITECTS

Dick, Adolph M.

Green, Isaac Henry, II

Russell, William Hamilton, Jr.

Smith, Elward, Sr.

ARTISTS

Blum, Ethel Mildred Halsey

Oppenheimer, Ella Friedman

Packer, Frederick Little

Smith, Hervey Garret

ATTORNEYS

Aldrich, Spencer, Sr.

Atwood, Frederic Lawrence

Bates, William Graves

Belmont, Perry

Corbin, Austin

Cutting, William Bayard, Sr.

Davies, Julien Tappan

Davies, Julien Townsend, Sr.

Dempsey, Joseph Francis, Jr.

Dempsey, Joseph Francis, Sr.

Fortescue, Kenyon

Foster, Jay Stanley, II

Foster, William R., Jr.

Gibson, John Joseph

Goodrich, William W.

Graham, George Scott

Haff, Albert D.

Hobbs, Charles Buxton

Hubbard, Harmanus B.

Hutchins, Francis Sessions

Hyde, Henry Baldwin, II

Ireland, John Busteed

Johnson, Bradish, Sr.

Kleinman, David E.

Knapp, Shepherd, Sr.

Kobbe, George Christian

Koehler, Robert H.

Manton, Martin Thomas

Owens, Joseph Eugene, Sr.

Palmer, Elwell

Parkinson, Thomas Ignatius, Jr.

Parkinson, Thomas Ignatius, Sr.

Parsons, William Decatur

Post, Charles Alfred

Post, Waldron Kintzing

Powell, Leander Treadwell

Reid, John Robert

Reid, Willard Placide

Remsen, Jacob

Remsen, Phoenix

Ridgeway, James W.

Robbins, William H., Sr.

Roosevelt, John Ellis

Roosevelt, Robert Barnwell, Sr.

Shea, Timothy, J., Sr.

Smith, Charles Robinson

Stanchfield, John Barry, Sr.

Stephens, John L.

Stillman, Benjamin D.

Strong, Theron George

Tenney, Charles Henry, Sr.

Wagstaff, Alfred, Jr.

Ward, Edwin Carrington

Whitney, William Collins

CAPITALISTS

Aldrich, Spencer, Sr.

Allison, William Manwaring, Sr.

Aston, W. K.

Behman, Louis C., Sr.

Belmont, August, III

Blum, Edward Charles

Bohack, Henry C.

Bossert, Charles Volunteer

Bossert, Louis

Bourne, Arthur Keeler, Sr.

Bourne, Frederick Gilbert

Brownlie, George

Burke, Charles Felix

Ceballos, Juan Manuel, Sr.

Childs, Eversley, Sr.

Childs, William Hamlin

Clarkson, William Kemble

Clyde, William Pancoast, Sr.

Colt, Robert Oliver

Conover, Daniel D.

Corbin, Austin

Creamer, Frank D., Sr.

Creamer, Joseph Byron, Sr.

Cutting, Robert Fulton

Cutting, William Bayard, Sr.

Davies, Julien Townsend, Sr.

deCoppet, Andre H.

Dempsey, Joseph Francis, Sr.

Dick, William Karl

Duval, Henry Rieman

Edwards, Edward

Entenmann, Robert

Fairchild, Julian Douglas

Ford, Malcolm W.

Foster, Andrew D.

Frothingham, John Sewell

Gardiner, Robert David Lion

Gibb, John

Gibb, Lewis Mills, Jr.

Gibb, Lewis Mills, Sr.

Gibson, Frederick E.

Gibson, Gregory Martin

Goodrich, William W.

Graham, George Scott

Gregory, William Hamilton, Jr.

Guastavino, Rafael, Jr.

Havemeyer, Henry, Sr.

Havemeyer, Henry Osborne

Havemeyer, Horace, Sr.

Hawley, Edwin

Heckscher, Charles Augustus, Jr.

Heins, John Lewis, Sr.

Hollins, Harry Bowly, Sr.

Hollister, Buell, Sr.

Hoppin, Bayard Cushing

Howell, Carlton Bell

Howell, Elmer Brown

Howell, Elmer W.

Hyde, Henry Baldwin, Sr.

Hyde, James Hazen

Hyde, James R.

Hyde, Richard

Hyde, William J.

Ireland, John Busteed

Ireland, Rufus J., Sr.

Isbrandtsen, Hans J.

Johnson, Bradish, Jr.

Johnson, Bradish, Sr.

Johnson, Bradish Gaillard, Sr.

Johnson, Edwin Augustus, Sr.

Johnson, John Dean

Johnson, Lee

Johnson, Parmenus

CAPITALISTS (cont'd)

Johnston, James Boorman

Keith, Minor C.

Kelly, James P.

King, Dr. George Suttie

Kingsland, George Lovett, Sr.

Knapp, Edward Spring, Sr.

Knapp, Harry Kearsarge, Sr.

Knapp, Shepherd, Sr.

Knapp, Theodore J., Sr.

Kobbe, George Christian

Koehler, Robert H.

Lawrance, Charles Lanier

Lawrance, Francis Cooper, Sr.

Lawrence, Chester B.

Lazare, Andrew

Lemmerman, Fred C.

Lester, Joseph Huntington

Livingston, Robert Cambridge, III

Macy, George Henry

Macy, William Kingsland, Sr.

Maxwell, Henry W.

McNamee, John

Meeks, Joseph W., Sr.

Melville, Frank, Jr.

Mildeberger, Elwood

Moffitt, William Henry

Montgomery, Richard H.

Moran, Amedee Depau

Morrison, George Alexander

Morse, William Otis

Nicholas, George S., Sr.

Nicholas, Harry Ingersoll, Sr.

Oakman, Walter George, Sr.

Ockers, Jacob

O'Donohue, Charles A.

Oelsner, Rudolph

Oppenheimer, Julius

Palmer, Elwell

Pardee, Dwight W.

Pardee, Roy Edmund

Parkinson, Thomas Ignatius, Sr.

Payne, Albert

Perkins, Richard Sturgis, Sr.

Pinkerton, Allan, II

Pinkerton, Robert Allan, II

Pinkerton, Robert Allan, Sr.

Post, Regis Henri, Sr.

Powell, David B.

Purdy, Charles Robert

Redmond, Roland

Reid, Willard Placide

Robert, Christopher Rhinelander, Jr.

Roosevelt, John Ellis

Roosevelt, Robert Barnwell, Jr.

Roosevelt, Robert Barnwell, Sr.

Ryan, John T.

Scully, Charles B.

Sharp, H. Cecil

Slote, Alonzo

Smith, Charles Robinson

Smith Elward, Jr.

Smith Elward, Sr.

Smith, Jewett Holt

Smith, Virginia Woodhull Otto

Snow, Frederick B.

Spaulding, E. B.

Stoppani, Joseph H.

Swan, Alden S.

Swirbul, Leon A.

Tappin, Charles L.

Thorne, Edwin, II

Thorne, Edwin, III

Thorne, Landon Ketchum, Sr.

CAPITALISTS (cont'd)

Thurber, Fred C.

Titus, James Gulden, Sr.

Titus, Walter Livingston, Jr.

True, Benjamin K.

Turnbull, George R.

Underhill, Edward Beekman, Sr.

Van Anden, William M., Sr.

Vanderbilt, William Kissam, Sr.

Wagstaff, Alfred, Jr.

Wagstaff, Dr. Alfred, Sr.

Walbridge, George Hicks

Wharton, William Fishbourne

White, Raymond S.

Whitney, William Collins

Williams, Percy G.

Wood, Henry Duncan, Sr.

Wray, William H.

Yates, Douglas Thomas, Sr.

Yates, Herbert John, Sr.

Yates, Richard George, Sr.

Zerega, John Pierre, Sr.

CLERGY

Hulse, The Reverend William Warren

COMPOSERS

Tcherepnin, Alexander

Thorne, Francis Burritt, Jr.

EDUCATORS

Oppenheimer, Ella Friedman

Palmer, Marjorie Cleaveland

Parkinson, Thomas Ignatius, Sr.

Pless, John Anthony, Jr.

Stewart, Dr. George David

ENTERTAINERS AND ASSOCIATED PROFESSIONS

Behman, Margaret Scott

Hyde, Grace M. Riopel

Pardee, Lillian H. Beasley

Tcherepnin, Alexander

Williams, Percy G.

Yates, Vera Hruba Ralston

FINANCIERS

Andrews, William Loring

Atwood, Kimball Chase, Jr.

Ballard, Frederick E., Sr.

Baruch, Bernard Mannes, Sr.

Baxter, John Edward

Beard, Anson Mc Cook, Jr.

Bedell, Walter Ellwood

Belmont, August, Sr.

Belmont, August, III

Betts, Roland Whitney

Bigelow, Edwin Hicks

Blagden, Crawford, Sr.

Blum, Edward Charles

Blum, Robert Edward

Bohack, Henry C.

Bossert, Louis

Bourne, Frederick Gilbert

Breese, William Laurence

Bull, Henry Worthington

Burchell, George W.

Cameron, Edward Miller

Carlisle, Jay Freeborn, Sr.

FINANCIERS (cont'd)

Catlin, John Bernsee, Sr.

Ceballos, Juan Manuel, Sr.

Corbin, Austin

Cox, George, Jr.

Cutting, Robert Fulton

Cutting, William Bayard, Sr.

Davies, Julien Tappan

deCoppet, Andre H.

de Forest, James G.

deGoicouria, Albert V.

Dempsey, Joseph Francis, Sr.

Dick, John Henry

Dick, William

Dick, William Karl

Dodson, Robert Bowman

Drummond, Howard

Duval, Henry Rieman

Eaton, James Waterbury, Sr.

Egly, Henry Harris

Ellis, George Augustus, Jr.

Ennis, Thomas

Entenmann, Robert

Evers, Cecil C.

Fairchild, Julian Douglas

Flint, Sherman

Foster, Jay Stanley, II

Frank, Emil H., Sr.

Frothingham, John Sewell

Gardiner, Robert David Lion

Gibb, John

Gibson, John James

Gibson, John Joseph

Goodrich, William W.

Gordon, Edward

Graham, George Scott

Green, Isaac Henry, II

Gregory, William Hamilton, Jr.

Guggenheim, Meyer Robert, Sr.

Gulden, Charles, Sr.

Haff, Albert D.

Hallock, Gerard, III

Hard, Anson Wales, Jr.

Havemeyer, Henry Osborne

Havemeyer, Horace, Jr.

Havemeyer, Horace, Sr.

Heins, John Lewis, Sr.

Hepburn, Henry Charles, Jr.

Hepburn, Henry Chester

Hodges, George W., Sr.

Hollins, Gerald Vanderbilt, Sr.

Hollins, Harry Bowly, Jr.

Hollins, Harry Bowly, Sr.

Hollister, Buell, Sr.

Hollister, Henry Hutchinson, Sr.

Hoppin, Bayard Cushing

Howell, Elmer Brown

Hubbs, Charles Francis

Hutchins, Francis Sessions

Hutton, Edward Francis

Hutton, Franklyn Laws

Hyde, Henry Baldwin, Sr.

Hyde, James Hazen

Ireland, Rufus J., Sr.

Johnson, Aymar

Johnson, Bradish, Jr.

Johnson, Bradish, Sr.

Keith, Minor C.

Kelly, James P.

Knapp, Edward Spring, Sr.

Knapp, Harry Kearsarge, Sr.

Knapp, Shepherd, Sr.

Knapp, Theodore J., Sr.

Kobbe, George Christian

FINANCIERS (cont'd)

Koehler, Robert H.	Pinkerton, Robert Allan, II
Lemmerman, Fred C.	Post, Regis Henri, Sr.
Lester, Joseph Huntington	Powell, David B.
Lester, Maxwell, Jr.	Prince, John Dyneley, II
Livingston, Harry Beekman, Jr.	Reid, Willard Placide
Ludlow, William Handy, Sr.	Robbins, Josiah
Macconnell, John B.	Robbins, William H., Sr.
MacLeod, Thomas Woodward, Sr.	Rolston, Roswell G.
Macy, George Henry	Rothschild, Simon Frank
Macy, William Kingsland, Sr.	Schieren, Charles Adolph, Sr.
Magoun, Francis Peabody	Simonds, William Robinson
Magoun, George B.	Slote, Alonzo
Magoun, Kinsley	Smith, Fred D.
Maxwell, Henry W.	Snedeker, Charles V.
McBurney, Dr. Malcolm	Staples, Cyrus E.
McClure, William	Stoppani, Charles F., Jr.
Mc Kee, Henry Sellers, II	Stoppani, Joseph H.
Mc Kee, William L.	Sutton, Effingham B., Sr.
McNamee, John	Swan, Alden S.
Mollenhauer, John	Tappin, John C.
Mollenhauer, John Adolph	Thorne, Edwin, II
Moran, Amedee Depau	Thorne, Edwin, III
Morgan, Henry	Thorne, Francis Burritt, Jr.
Morgan, Robert Woodward, Sr.	Thorne, Francis Burritt, Sr.
Morris, Stuyvesant Fish, III	Thorne, Landon Ketchum, Jr.
Morrison, George Alexander	Thorne, Landon Ketchum, Sr.
Nicholas, Harry Ingersoll, Sr.	Timmerman, Henry Gerlard
Oakman, Walter George, Sr.	Tobey, Orville Hurd
Ockers, Jacob	Turnbull, George R.
O'Donohue, Charles A.	Underhill, Edward Beekman, Sr.
Owens, Joseph Eugene, Sr.	Van Anden, William M., Sr.
Parkinson, Thomas Ignatius, Sr.	Wagstaff, George Barnard
Parsons, Schuyler Livingston, Jr.	Walbridge, Ernest A.
Perkins, Richard Sturgis, Sr.	Walbridge, George Hicks
Peters, Samuel Twyford	Weekes, Harold Hathaway
Phelps, Charles E.	Weld, Philip Balch
	Wharton, Richard

FINANCIERS (cont'd)

Wharton, Richard T., Sr.

Wharton, William Fishbourne

White, Raymond S.

Wilmerding, Lucius Kellogg

Wood, Henry Duncan, Jr.

Wood, Henry Duncan, Sr.

Yates, Douglas Thomas, Sr.

Yates, Herbert John, Sr.

Young, Albert

INDUSTRIALISTS

Adams, John Dunbar

Adams, Thomas, Jr.

Bachia, Richard Augustus, Jr.

Baxter, John Edward

Bossert, Charles Volunteer

Bossert, Louis

Bourne, Arthur Keeler, Sr.

Bourne, Frederick Gilbert

Cameron, Edward Miller

Childs, Eversley, Sr.

Childs, William Hamlin

Clarkson, William Kemble

Corbin, Austin

Crothers, Gordon

deCoppet, Andre H.

Delaney, John Hanlon

Dempsey, Joseph Francis, Sr.

deMurias, Fernando Enrique

Dick, John Henry

Dick, William

Dick, William Karl

Dillon, John Allen, Sr.

Doxsee, James Harvey, Sr.

Duval, Henry Rieman

Eastwood, John H.

Eaton, James Waterbury, Sr.

Elder, George Waldron, Sr.

Ely, John R.

Entenmann, Robert

Fairchild, Julian Douglas

Garner, Thomas, Jr.

Garner, Thomas, Sr.

Garner, William Thorn

Gibson, John Joseph

Graham, George Scott

Gregory, William Hamilton, Jr.

Guggenheim, Meyer Robert, Sr.

Gulden, Charles, II

Gulden, Charles, Sr.

Gulden, Frank, Jr.

Gulden, Frank, Sr.

Havemeyer, Harry Waldron

Havemeyer, Henry, Sr.

Havemeyer, Henry Osborne

Havemeyer, Horace, Jr.

Havemeyer, Horace, Sr.

Hayward, William Tyson, Jr.

Hayward, William Tyson, Sr.

Hollins, Harry Bowly, Jr.

Hollins, Harry Bowly, Sr.

Hollister, Buell, Sr.

Hubbs, Charles Francis

Huber, Frederick Max, Sr.

Hutton, Edward Francis

Hutton, Marjorie Merriweather Post

Ireland, Rufus J., Sr.

Johnson, Bradish, Jr.

Johnson, Bradish, Sr.

Kalbfleisch, Franklin H.

Keith, Minor C.

Kingsland, George Lovett, Sr.

INDUSTRIALISTS (cont'd)

Kobbe, George Christian

Koehler, Robert H.

Lawrance, Charles Lanier

Lester, Maxwell, Sr.

Liebman, Julius

Lorillard, Dr. George L.

Macy, George Henry

Magoun, Francis Peabody

Magoun, George B.

Maxwell, Henry W.

Mc Kee, John

Mc Kee, William L.

Meeks, Joseph W., Sr.

Mollenhauer, John

Mollenhauer, John Adolph

Morgan, Charles, Sr.

Morgan, John

Oakman, Walter George, Sr.

O'Donohue, Charles A.

Peck, William L.

Perkins, Richard Sturgis, Sr.

Poillon, John Edward

Post, Waldron Kintzing

Powell, David B.

Ranft, Richard, Jr.

Reid, Willard Placide

Riggio, Frank Vincent

Robb, James

Schieren, Charles Adolph, Sr.

Seaman, Frank

Shea, David J.

Smith, Charles Robinson

Swirbul, Leon A.

Thorne, Edwin, II

Thorne, Francis Burritt, Sr.

Thorne, Landon Ketchum, Jr.

Titus, Walter Livingston, Sr.

Todd, William H.

Truslow, Frederick C.

Turnbull, George R.

Valentine, Landon Barrett

Westin, Clarence Frederick, Sr.

White, Raymond S.

Whitney, William Collins

Wilbur, Edward Russell, Sr.

INTELLIGENCE AGENTS

Baldridge, Harry Alexander, Sr.

Gardiner, Robert David Lion

Hyde, Henry Baldwin, II

Johnson, Aymar

Post, Charles Kintzing

Tenney, Charles Henry, Sr.

INVENTORS

Lawrance, Charles Lanier

Van Anden, Frank

JOURNALISTS

Blum, Ethel Mildred Halsey

Ford, Malcolm W.

Fortescue, Granville Roland

Hyde, Marie de LaGrange

Kobbe, Gustave

Page, Walter Hines, Sr.

Vanderbilt, Alva Erskine Smith
 [*later*, Belmont]

MERCHANTS

Arnold, Richard

MERCHANTS (cont'd)

Arnold, William

Blum, Edward Charles

Blum, Robert Edward

Bohack, Henry C.

Conover, Augustus Whitlock, Sr.

Corse, Israel S.

Covell, Charles Heber, Sr.

Creamer, Frank D., Sr.

Creamer, Joseph Byron, Sr.

Gibb, Howard, Sr.

Gibb, John

Gibb, Lewis Mills, Jr.

Gibb, Lewis Mills, Sr.

Gunther, William Henry, Jr.

Jones, Frank Smith

Low, Chauncey E.

MacLeod, Thomas Woodward, Sr.

Maitland, Robert L.

Melville, Frank, Jr.

O'Donohue, Charles A.

Otto, Thomas N.

Parsons, Schuyler Livingston, Sr.

Peters, Harry Twyford, Sr.

Peters, Samuel Twyford

Post, Henry

Richard, Alfred Joseph

Rothschild, Simon Frank

Rubinstein, Ira

Shea, Timothy J., Sr.

Slote, Alonzo

Suydam, Charles

Suydam, John R., Sr.

Titus, Walter Livingston, Sr.

Welles, Benjamin Sumner, Sr.

Westin, Clarence Frederick, Sr.

Williams, Richard H., Sr.

Wilmerding, Lucius Kellogg

MILITARY

Baldridge, Harry Alexander, Sr.

Bates, William Graves

Fortescue, Granville Roland

Post, Charles Kintzing

Robb, James

Smith, Robert Gibson

Titus, James Gulden, Sr.

Yates, Douglas Thomas, Sr.

Yates, Richard George, Sr.

NAVAL ARCHITECTS

Smith, Fred D.

PHYSICIANS

Ash, Dr. Charles F.

Carroll, Dr. Alfred Ludlow

Catlin, Dr. Daniel, Sr.

Garben, Dr. Louis F., Sr.

King, Dr. George Suttie

Lorillard, Dr. George L.

McBurney, Dr. Malcolm

McLaughlin, Dr. Daniel

Moore, Dr. David Dodge

Pasternack, Dr. Richard

Stewart, Dr. George David

Sullivan, Dr. Raymond Peter, Sr.

Vander Veer, Dr. Albert, Jr.

Wagstaff, Dr. Alfred, Sr.

Watt, Dr. James, Sr.

Woolley, Dr. James V. S., Sr.

Wright, Dr. Arthur Mullen

POLITICIANS

Allen, Theodore

Asten, Thomas B.

Belmont, August, Sr.

Belmont, Perry

Brownlie, George

Conover, Daniel D.

Creamer, Frank D., Sr.

Delaney, John Hanlon

Fairchild, Julian Douglas

Gibson, Gregory Martin

Goodrich, William W.

Graham, George Scott

Howell, James Frederick, Sr.

Hulse, The Reverend William Warren

Lawrence, Chester B.

Lemmerman, Fred C.

Lester, Maxwell, Jr.

Ludlow, William Handy, Sr.

Macy, William Kingsland, Sr.

Morrison, George Alexander

Moses, Robert

Nicoll, William

Pardee, Roy Edmund

Post, Regis Henri, Sr.

Proctor, Cecil W.

Reid, Willard Placide

Remsen, Jacob

Robbins, Josiah

Roosevelt, Robert Barnwell, Sr.

Ryan, John T.

Schieren, Charles Adolph, Sr.

Smith, Elward, Sr.

Stanchfield, John Barry, Sr.

Swan, Alden S.

Tenney, Charles Henry, Sr.

Thorne, Landon Ketchum, Sr.

Wagstaff, Alfred, Jr.

Waterbury, Leander

PUBLISHERS

Delaney, John Hanlon

Eaton, James Waterbury, Sr.

Kempster, James H.

Moffitt, William Henry

Page, Walter Hines, Sr.

Reid, John Robert

Roosevelt, Robert Barnwell, Sr.

Slote, Daniel, Jr.

Smith, Virginia Woodhull Otto

Thorne, Landon Ketchum, Jr.

Van Anden, William M., Sr.

Wilbur, Edward Russell, Sr.

RESTAURATEURS

Huber, Frederick Max, Sr.

Oelsner, Rudolph

Titus, James Gulden, Sr.

SHIPPING

Ceballos, Juan Manuel, Sr.

Clyde, William Pancoast, Sr.

Havemeyer, Horace, Sr.

Hawley, Edwin

Isbrandtsen, Hans J.

Mollenhauer, John Adolph

Moran, Eugene Francis, Jr.

Staples, Cyrus E.

Sutton, Effingham B., Sr.

Sutton, Frank

Sutton, Woodruff, Sr.

WRITERS

Andrews, William Loring

Belmont, Perry

Carroll, Dr. Alfred Ludlow

Eaton, James Waterbury, Sr.

Fortescue, Granville Roland

Harbeck, Charles T.

Havemeyer, Harry Waldron

Havemeyer, Louisine Waldron

Hyde, James Hazen

Ireland, John Busteed

King, Dr. George Suttie

Kobbe, Gustave

Moses, Robert

Page, Walter Hines, Sr.

Parsons, Schuyler Livingston, Jr.

Peters, Harry Twyford, Sr.

Post, Marie Caroline de Trobriand

Post, Waldron Kintzing

Puzo, Mario

Roosevelt, Robert Barnwell, Sr.

Smith, Charles Robinson

Stewart, Dr. George David

Strong, Theron George

Sullivan, Dr. Raymond Peter, Sr.

Vanderbilt, Alva Erskine Smith
  [*later*, Belmont]

Welles, Benjamin Sumner, III

Rehabilitative Uses

Non-residential rehabilitative secondary uses of surviving estate houses
listed are current as of 2007. Estates are identified by the original owner.
For subsequent estate owners, see surname entry.

Arnold Manor

Annie Stuart Cameron Arnold estate,
Clovelly, West Islip

Bayard Cutting Arboretum

William Bayard Cutting, Sr. estate,
Westbrook Farm, Great River

Daughters of Wisdom Convent

William Kingsland Macy, Sr. estate,
Islip

Dowling College

William Kissam Vanderbilt, Sr. estate,
Idlehour, Oakdale

Environmental Interpretive Center of
Suffolk County

Harold Hathaway Weekes estate,
Wereholme, Islip

The Gatsby Restaurant

Frank D. Creamer estate,
Islip

The Islip Art Museum

Harry Kearsarge Knapp, Sr. estate,
Brookwood, East Islip

Joint Industry Board of the Electrical Industry

Arthur Keeler Bourne, Sr. estate,
Lake House, Oakdale

Frederick Gilbert Bourne estate,
Indian Neck Hall, Oakdale

Long Island Center for Experimental Art

Harry Kearsarge Knapp, Sr. estate,
Brookwood, East Islip

Long Island Maritime Museum

Anson Wales Hard, Jr. estate,
Meadow Edge, West Sayville

Long Island Yacht Club

George Brownlie estate,
Willow Close, Babylon

Office of Hospital Development,
Good Samaritan Hospital

John Vanderveer estate,
Sunnymead, West Islip
(gardener's cottage)

The Open Gate

Charles Gulden, Sr. estate,
Netherbay, Bay Shore

Sagtikos Manor

Stephanus Van Cortlandt estate,
Sagtikos, West Bay Shore

Southward Ho Country Club

Thomas Adams, Jr. estate,
Ardmore, West Bay Shore

Henry Baldwin Hyde, Sr. estate,
The Oaks, West Bay Shore

Timber Point Country Club	William Laurence Breese estate, *Timber Point*, Great River
The Villas	Richard Ranft, Jr. estate, Bay Shore
West Sayville Golf Course	Anson Wales Hard, Jr. estate, *Meadow Edge*, West Sayville

Listed are only those statesmen and diplomats who resided in the Towns of Babylon and Islip.

Statesmen

Department of Navy (became part of Department of Defense in 1947)

Whitney, William Collins
　　　– Secretary of Navy (Cleveland and Benjamin Harrison administrations)
Islip

Under Secretaries, Assistant Secretaries, and Deputy Secretaries of State –

Welles, Benjamin Sumner, III
　　　– Assistant Secretary of State (Franklin Delano Roosevelt administration)
　　　– Under Secretary of State (Franklin Delano Roosevelt administration)
Welles House, Islip

Diplomats

Belmont, August, Sr.
　　　– United States Charge d' affairs, The Netherlands
　　　– United States Minister to The Netherlands
　　　– Austrian Council General to the United States
Nursery Stud Farm, North Babylon

Belmont, Perry
　　　– Minister to Spain, 1887-1888
Nursery Stud Farm, North Babylon

Guggenheim, Meyer Robert, Sr.
　　　– Ambassador to Portugal, 1953-1954
Firenze Farm, North Babylon

Page, Walter Hines, Sr.
　　　– Ambassador to Court of St. James (Wilson administration)
Bay Shore

Post, Regis Henri, Sr.
　　　– Governor, Territory of Puerto Rico, 1907
Littlewood, Bayport

Roosevelt, Robert Barnwell, Sr.
　　　– Ambassador to The Netherlands
Lotos Lake, Bayport

Diplomats (cont'd)

Taylor, George Campbell
      – Member, United States Embassy at Court of St. James (Lincoln administration)
East Islip

Thorne, Landon Ketchum, Jr.
      – Economic Minister, Office of Foreign Operations, Italy
      – Economic Minister, Office of Foreign Operations, Belgium
The Lodge, West Bay Shore

Welles, Benjamin Sumner, III
      – Chief, Latin American Affairs Division, Department of State, 1920
      – Ambassador to Cuba, 1933
Welles House, Islip

Advisors and Personal Secretaries

Post, Regis Henri, Sr.
      – Auditor, Territory of Puerto Rico, 1903
      – Secretary to the Governor of Puerto Rico, 1904
Littlewood, Bayport

Welles, Benjamin Sumner, III
      – Secretary, United States Embassy in Japan, 1917
Welles House, Islip

Villages

The village references used in this compilation are the current (2007) village or hamlet boundaries and should not be confused with zip code designations. When the owner who contracted for the original construction of the house is known, it is indicated by an asterisk.

AMITYVILLE

Haight, Gilbert Lawrence, Jr.

Ireland, Rufus J., Sr.

Thorn, Edward Floyd–Jones

BABYLON

Blagden, Crawford, Sr.

Bromell, Alfred Henry

Brownlie, George, *Willow Close*

Cox, George, Jr.

deMurias, Fernando Enrique

Evers, Cecil C.

Ford, Malcolm W.

* Foster, Jay Stanley, II

Haff, Albert D.

Hawley, Edwin

Hayward, William Tyson, Jr.

Hepburn, Henry Charles, Jr., *The Firs*

Hepburn, Henry Chester

Howell, Elmer Brown

Howell, Elmer W.

Kalbfleisch, Franklin H., *Larklawn*

Mc Kee, Henry Sellers, II

Morris, Stuyvesant Fish, III

Morse, William Otis

Moses, Robert

Murdock, Uriel Atwood, II

* Post, Henry, *Postholme*

Reid, John Robert, *The Towers*

Reid, Willard Placide, *The Towers*

Remsen, Jacob, *The Harbor*

Shortland, Thomas Francis

Snedeker, Charles V.

Strong, James H. S.

Tappin, Charles L., *Twin Oaks*

Walbridge, Ernest A.

Walbridge, George Hicks

BAYPORT

Allen, Theodore

Baruch, Bernard Mannes, Sr., *Strandhome*

* Behman, Louis C., Sr., *Lindenwalt*

Cox, Stephen Perry, *Arcadia*

Dahl, George W.

* Delaney, John Hanlon

* Edwards, Edward, *White House*

Ely, John R.

Ennis, Thomas

Fortescue, Granville Roland, *Wildholme*

* Foster, William R., Jr., *Strandhome*

Kobbe, George Christian

Koehler, Robert H.

Liebman, Julius

* Macconnell, John B.

Manton, Martin Thomas

Mc Kee, John

* Meeks, Joseph W., Jr.

Melville, Frank, Jr.

Morgan, Charles, Sr.

* Morgan, John, *Idle Hour*

* Payne, Albert

Post, Charles Alfred, *Strandhome*

Post, Charles Kintzing, *Strandhome*

* Post, Regis Henri, Sr., *Littlewood*
  [Post owned a second house in Bayport.]

Post, Waldron Kintzing, *Strandhome*

Post, William Kintzing

BAYPORT (cont'd)

* Purdy, Charles Robert, *Edgemere*

* Roosevelt, Robert Barnwell, Sr., *Lotos Lake*

* Rubinstein, Ira, *Cheap John's Estate*

  Seaman, Frank

  Smith, Fred D.

  Snedecor, James H.

  Staples, Cyrus E.

  Stoppani, Charles F., Jr.

* Stoppani, Charles F., Sr., *Arcadia*

* Stoppani, Joseph H., *Liberty Hall*

  Suydam, Charles

  Suydam, John R., Jr., *Edgewater*

* Suydam, John R., Sr., *Edgewater*

* Todd, William H., *Lenapes Lodge*

  Zerega, John Pierre, Sr., *Littlewood*

BAY SHORE

  Adams, John Dunbar, *Woodlea*

  Aldrich, Spencer, Sr., *Windermere*

  Allison, William Manwaring, Sr.

  Ash, Dr. Charles F.

* Asten, Thomas B.

  Bachia, Richard Augustus, Jr.

  Ballard, Frederick E., Sr.

  Bates, William Graves, *Evergreens*

  Baxter, John Edward

  Bedell, Walter Ellwood

  Belmont, August, III

  Blum, Edward Charles, *Shore Acres*

  Blum, Robert Edward

  Burchell, George W.

* Carroll, Dr. Alfred Ludlow

  Catlin, Dr. Daniel, Sr.

  Ceballos, Juan Manuel, Sr., *Brookhurst Farm*

  Clarkson, William Kemble

  Conover, Augustus Whitlock, Sr.

* Conover, Daniel D.

* Covell, Charles Heber, Sr., *Villa Avalon*

  Dillon, John Allen, Sr.

  Drummond, Howard, *Little House*

  Eastwood, John H.

  Elder, George Waldron, Sr.

  Fairchild, Julian Douglas

* Frank, Emil H., Sr.

  Frothingham, John Sewell

  Garner, Thomas, Jr.

  Garner, Thomas, Sr.

  Garner, William Thorn

  Gibb, Lewis Mills, Jr., *Cedarholme*

* Gibb, Lewis Mills, Sr., *Cedarholme*

  Gibson, Frederick E.

  Gibson, John James

* Gibson, John Joseph

  Goodrich, William W.

  Gordon, Edward

* Guastavino, Rafael, Jr.

  Gulden, Charles, Sr., *Netherbay*

  Gulden, Frank, Jr.

  Gunther, William Henry, Jr.

* Havemeyer, Harry Waldron

* Havemeyer, Horace, Sr., *Olympic Point*

  Hodges, George W., Sr.

  Hubbard, Harmanus B., *Oakhurst*

  Huber, Frederick Max, Sr.

  Hulse, The Rev. William Warren, *Elysian Views*

  Hutton, Edward Francis

  Hutton, Franklyn Laws

  Hyde, James R.

* Hyde, Richard

  Hyde, William J., *White Cottage*

  Johnson, Effingham Lawrance

BAY SHORE (cont'd)

Kelly, James P., *Awixaway*

Kempster, James H., *Westbeach*

King, Dr. George Suttie

Kleinman, David E.

* Knapp, Edward Spring, Sr., *Awixa Lawn*

Kobbe, Gustave

Lawrance, Charles Lanier, *Manatuck Farm*

Lawrance, Francis Cooper, Jr., *Manatuck Farm*

Lawrance, Francis Cooper, Sr., *Manatuck Farm*

Lawrence, Chester B.

Lemmerman, Fred C.

* Lester, Joseph Huntington, *Lestaley*

Lester, Maxwell, Jr.

Lester, Maxwell, Sr., *Four Hedges*

Livingston, Henry Beekman, Jr.

* Low, Chauncey E., *Seaward*

MacLeod, Thomas Woodward, Sr.

Macy, George Henry

Maxwell, Henry W., *Scrub Oaks*

Mildeberger, Elwood, *Oakelwood*

* Mollenhauer, John

* Mollenhauer, John Adolph, *Homeport*

* Montgomery, Richard H.

Myers, Nathaniel

O'Donohue, Charles A., *The Moorings*

* Oelsner, Rudolph

Oppenheimer, Julius

Owens, Joseph Eugene, Sr.

Page, Walter Hines, Sr.

Parsons, William Decatur, *Restina Cottage*

Peck, William L.

Pinkerton, Allan, II

Pinkerton, Robert Allan, Sr., *Dearwood*

Poillon, John Edward

Quinn, Michael

Ranft, Richard, Jr.

Riggio, Frank Vincent, *Riggio House*

Robbins, Josiah

* Robbins, William H., Sr.

* Rothschild, Simon Frank

Ryan, John T.

* Sharp, H. Cecil, *Millcreek*

* Shea, Timothy J., Sr., *O'Conee*

Slote, Alonzo

Slote, Daniel, Jr.

* Smith, Charles Robinson

Snow, Frederick B.

* Strong, Theron George

Sullivan, Dr. Raymond Peter, Sr.

Tenney, Charles Henry, Sr.

Thorne, Francis Burritt, Jr.

* Thurber, Fred C.

Underhill, Edward Beekman, Sr.

Wagstaff, George Barnard

Ward, Edwin Carrington, *Wake Robin*

Weld, Philip Balch

Wood, Henry Duncan, Jr.

Woolley, Dr. James V. S., Sr.

* Wray, William H., *Whileaway*

* Young, Albert, *Awixaway*

BRIGHTWATERS

Gibson, Gregory Martin

Howell, James Frederick, Sr.

Moran, Eugene Francis, Jr., *Shadow Lawn*

Packer, Frederick Little

Pardee, Dwight W.

Parkinson, Thomas Ignatius, Jr.

Phelps, Charles E., *Brightwaters*

Swirbul, Leon A.

Turnbull, John Gourlay, Jr.

Yates, Richard George, Sr.

EAST ISLIP

Bigelow, Edwin Hicks

* Carlisle, Jay Freeborn, Sr., *Rosemary*

Dana, Richard Turner

Duval, Henry Rieman, *Farmouth*

Entenmann, Robert

Gregory, William Hamilton, Jr., *Creekside*

Harbeck, Charles T.
[Harbeck owned two houses in East Islip.]

* Hollins, Gerald Vanderbilt, Sr., *The Hawks*

* Hollins, Harry Bowly, Jr., *Crickholly*

* Hollins, Harry Bowly, Sr., *Meadow Farm*

Hoppin, Bayard Cushing

Johnson, Aymar, *Woodland*

* Johnson, Bradish, Jr., *Woodland*

* Johnson, Edwin Augustus, Sr.

* Johnson, Edwin Augustus, Sr.,
Deer Range Farm
[Johnson built two houses in East Islip.]

Johnson, Lee

* Johnston, James Boorman

* Knapp, Harry Kearsarge, II, *Creekside*

* Knapp, Harry Kearsarge, Sr., *Brookwood*

Knapp, Theodore J., Sr., *Brookwood*

Lawrance, Charles Lanier

* McBurney, Dr. Malcolm

Moran, Amedee Depau

Morgan, Henry, *The Stables*

Morgan, Robert Woodward, Sr.

Nicoll, William

Pinkerton, Robert Allan, II

Plumb, James Ives, *Deer Range Farm*

Plumb, Sara Ives, *Deer Range Farm*

Taylor, George Campbell, *Deer Range Farm*

* Taylor, George Campbell
[Taylor built two houses in East Islip.]

Thorne, Francis Burritt, Sr., *Brookwood*

Wharton, Percival C.

Wharton, William Fishbourne

* Williams, Percy G., *Pine Acres*

Wilmerding, Lucius Kellogg

FIRE ISLAND

Hyde, Henry Baldwin, II

Vander Veer, Dr. Albert, Jr., *Alkmaar Cottage*

GREAT RIVER

* Breese, William Laurence, *Timber Point*

Cutting, Robert Fulton

* Cutting, William Bayard, Sr., *Westbrook Farm*

Davies, Julien Tappan, *Timber Point*

Dempsey, Joseph Francis, Sr.

* Hobbs, Charles Buxton, *River Croft*

Hutchins, Francis Sessions

Lorillard, Dr. George L., *Westbrook Farm*

* Maitland, Robert L., *Westbrook Farm*

Stewart, Dr. George David, *Appin House*

Stewart, James

* Truslow, Frederick C., *Questover Lodge*

* White, Raymond S.

ISLIP

* Atwood, Frederic Lawrence

Atwood, Kimball Chase, Jr., *Mapleton*

Baker, William Dunham

Beard, Anson Mc Cook, Jr.

* Bruce-Brown, Ruth A. Loney, *Bronhurst*

Bull, Henry Worthington

Creamer, Frank D., Sr.

Creamer, Joseph Byron, Sr.

Crothers, Gordon, *La Casetta*

deCoppet, Andre H., *The Willows*

deGoicouria, Albert V.

Dempsey, Joseph Francis, Jr.

* Dick, Adolph M.

ISLIP (cont'd)

Dick, John Henry, *Allen Winden Farm*

Dick, William, *Allen Winden Farm*

Dick, William Karl, *Allen Winden Farm*

Doxsee, James Harvey, Sr.

Egly, Henry Harris

Flint, Sherman, *Evershade*

Garben, Dr. Louis F., Sr.

Gibb, Howard, Sr.

* Gibb, John, *Afterglow*

Graham, George Scott, *Lohgrame*

Gulden, Charles, II

* Gulden, Frank, Jr.

Gulden, Frank, Sr.
 [Gulden owned two houses in Islip.]

Hallock, Gerard, III

* Havemeyer, Henry Osborne, *Bayberry Point*

Havemeyer, Horace, Jr.

Havemeyer, Horace, Sr.

Heckscher, Charles Augustus, Jr.

Hollister, Buell, Sr.

Hollister, Henry Hutchinson, Sr.

Howell, Carlton Bell

Johnson, Bradish Gaillard, Sr.

Johnson, Enfin

Johnson, John Dean

Johnson, Parmenus

Knapp, William K.

Lazare, Andrew

Livingston, Robert Cambridge, III

Lovering, Joseph Sears, Jr.

Macy, William Kingsland, Sr.

McNamee, John

Meeks, Edward B.

Meeks, Joseph W., Sr.

* Moffit, William Henry, *Beautiful Shore*

Moore, Dr. David Dodge

Oakman, Walter George, Sr.

Pardee, Roy Edmund

* Parsons, Schuyler Livingston, Jr.,
 Pleasure Island

* Parsons, Schuyler Livingston, Sr., *Whileaway*

Pasternack, Dr. Richard

Perkins, Richard Sturgis, Sr.

* Peters, Harry Twyford, Sr., *Nearholme*

Peters, Harry Twyford, Sr., *Windholme Farm*

Peters, Samuel Twyford, *Windholme Farm*

Pless, John Anthony, Jr.

Plumb, James Ives, *Shadowbrook*

* Prince, John Dyneley, II

Redmond, Roland

* Russell, William Hamilton, Jr.

* Schieren, Charles Adolph, Sr., *Mapleton*

Scully, Charles B., *Wereholme*

Spaulding, E. B.

Stanchfield, John Barry, Sr., *Afterglow*

Swan, Alden S., *Orowoc*

Tappin, John C.

Tcherepnin, Alexander

Thorne, Edwin, III

Timmerman, Henry Gerlard, *Breeze Lawn*

Titus, James Gulden, Sr.

Titus, Walter Livingston, Jr.

Tobey, Orville Hurd, *Breeze Lawn*

* Tucker, Charles A.

Tucker, Clarence

Valentine, Landon Barrett

Van Anden, Frank

Van Anden, William M., Sr.

* Waterbury, Leander

Webster, Charles D., *Twyford*

* Weekes, Harold Hathaway, *Wereholme*

Welles, Benjamin Sumner, Jr., *Welles House*

Welles, Benjamin Sumner, Sr.

ISLIP (cont'd)

Welles, Benjamin Sumner, III, *Welles House*

Wharton, Richard, *Whileaway*

Wharton, Richard T., Sr., *Whileaway*

* Whitney, William Collins

Williams, Richard H., Sr.

* Wood, Henry Duncan, Sr., *Ellenwood*

Wright, Dr. Arthur Mullen, *Afterglow*

Yates, Douglas Thomas, Sr.

NORTH BABYLON

* Belmont, August, Sr., *Nursery Stud Farm*

Belmont, Perry, *Nursery Stud Farm*

* Corbin, Austin, *Deer Park Farm*

Guggenheim, Meyer Robert, Sr., *Firenze Farm*

Nicholas, Harry Ingersoll, Sr., *Virginia Farm*

Rolston, Roswell, G., *Armagh*

* Sutton, Frank, *North East Farm*

OAKDALE

Aston, W. K.

Bourne, Alfred Severin, Sr.

* Bourne, Arthur Keeler, Sr., *Lake House*

* Bourne, Frederick Gilbert, *Indian Neck Hall*

Burke, Charles Felix

Ludlow, William Handy, Sr.

Ockers, Jacob

* Robert, Christopher Rhinelander, Jr., *Peperidge Hall*

* Vanderbilt, William Kissam, Sr., *Idlehour*

SAYVILLE

Allgood, Andrew Perry de Forest

Baldridge, Harry Alexander, Sr.

Betts, Roland Whitney, *Sunneholm*

Bohack, Henry C.

Bossert, Charles Volunteer

Catlin, John Bernsee, Sr.

* Childs, Eversley, Sr.

* Childs, William Hamlin

Corse, Israel, S., *The Swamp*

Fortescue, Kenyon

* Foster, Andrew D., *Greycote*

* Green, Isaac Henry, II, *Brookside*

* Hayward, Frank Earle, Sr., *Joy Farm*

* Hayward, William Tyson, Sr., *The Anchorage*

* Jones, Frank Smith, *Beechwold*

McLaughlin, Dr. Daniel

Morrison, George Alexander

Otto, Thomas N.

Palmer, Elwell
[Palmer owned a second house in Sayville.]

* Powell, David B., *Cedarshore*

* Powell, Leander Treadwell, *Cedarshore*

Proctor, Cecil W.

* Ridgeway, James W.

Robb, James

* Roosevelt, John Ellis, *Meadow Croft*

* Roosevelt, Robert Barnwell, Jr., *The Lilacs*

Shea, David J., *Beechwold*

Shea, David J., *Wyndemoor*

* Simonds, William Robinson, *Wyndemoor*

Smith, Elward, Jr.

Smith, Elward., Sr.

Smith, Hervey Garret

Smith, Jewett Holt

Smith, Robert Gibson

* Watt, Dr. James, Sr.

Westin, Clarence Frederick, Sr., *Beechwold*

* Wilbur, Edward Russell, Sr., *Beach Grove*

WEST BAY SHORE

* Adams, Thomas, Jr., *Ardmore*

Bossert, Louis, *The Oaks*

Colt, Robert Oliver

Ellis, George Augustus, Jr., *Ardmore*

Gardiner, Robert David Lion, *Sagtikos Manor*

* Hyde, Henry Baldwin, Sr., *The Oaks*

Hyde, James Hazen, *The Oaks*

Isbrandtsen, Hans J.

* Johnson, Bradish, Sr., *Sans Souci*

Johnson, Henry Meyer, *Sans Souci*

Lawrance, John I.

Puzo, Mario

Richard, Alfred Joseph

Thorne, Landon Ketchum, Jr., *The Lodge*

Thorne, Landon Ketchum, Sr., *Thorneham*

Wilmerding, George G.

WEST ISLIP

Andrews, William Loring, *Pepperidges*

Arnold, Alexander Duncan Cameron

* Arnold, Annie Stewart Cameron, *Clovelly*

Arnold, Edward William Cameron, *Oknoke*

* Arnold, Richard, *The Crescent*

Arnold, William, *The Crescent*

Cameron, Edward Miller

Clyde, William Pancoast, Sr.

Davies, Julien Townsend, Sr., *Casa Rosa*

de Forest, James G.

* Dodson, Robert Bowman, *Kanonsioni*

Eaton, James Waterbury, Sr.

Gibson, Cornelia Lott Vanderveer, *Sunnymead*

Havemeyer, Henry, Sr., *Armory*
[Havemeyer owned *Sequatogue Farm*, also in West Islip.]

Heins, John Lewis, Sr.

Hubbs, Charles Francis, *Sequatogue Farm*

Ireland, John Busteed

Keith, Minor C.

Keith, Minor C. R., II

Kingsland, George Lovett, Sr.

Knapp, Shepherd, Sr.

Magoun, Francis Peabody

Magoun, George B.

Magoun, Kinsley

McClure, William, *Clurella*

Mc Kee, William L.

Nicholas, George S., Sr.

Parkinson, Thomas, Ignatius, Sr.

Remsen, Phoenix

Stephens, John L., *Lone Oak*

Stillman, Benjamin D.

Sutton, Effingham B., Sr., *Effingham Pond*

Sutton, Woodruff, Sr., *Sutton Park*

* Thorne, Edwin, II, *Okonok*

Titus, Walter Livingston, Sr.

* True, Benjamin K.

* Turnbull, George R., *The Pines*

Vanderveer, John, *Sunnymead*

* Wagstaff, Alfred, Jr., *Opekeepsing*

* Wagstaff, Dr. Alfred, Sr., *Tahlulah*

Wagstaff, Cornelius DuBois

Yates, Herbert John, Sr., *Onsrufarm*

WEST SAYVILLE

* Hard, Anson Wales, Jr., *Meadow Edge*

America's First Age of Fortune:
A Selected Bibliography

Books listed in this section are, in most instances, different from the listings in the section entitled Selected Bibliographic References to Individual South Shore Estate Owners. Both sections should, therefore, be consulted.

AIA Architectural Guide to Nassau and Suffolk Counties, Long Island. New York: Dover Publications, Inc., 1992.

Aldrich, Nelson W., Jr. *Old Money: The Mythology of America's Upper Class.* New York: Alfred A. Knopf, 1988.

Aldrich, Nelson W., IV. "The Upper Class, Up for Grabs." *Wilson Quarterly* 17:3 (Summer 1993).

Allen, Michael Patrick. *The Founding Fortunes: A New Anatomy of the Super–Rich Families in America.* New York: E. P. Dutton, 1987.

Alsop, Joseph W. *"I've Seen the Best of It: Memoirs"* New York: W. W. Norton & Co., 1992.

Amory, Cleveland. *Celebrity Register: An Irreverent Compendium of American Quotable Notables.* New York: Harper & Row Publishers, 1959. [Published intermittently. Since 1973 it has been edited by Earl Blackwell.]

Amory, Cleveland. *The Last Resorts.* New York: Harper & Brothers, 1952.

Amory, Cleveland. *Who Killed Society?* New York: Harper & Brothers, 1960.

Armour, Lawrence A. *The Young Millionaires.* Chicago: Playboy Press, 1973.

Armstrong, Hamilton Fish. *Those Days.* New York: Harper & Brothers, 1963.

Armstrong, Margaret. *Five Generations.* New York: Harper & Brothers, 1930.

Ashburn, Frank D. *Peabody of Groton.* New York: Coward, McCann & Co., 1944.

Aslet, Clive. *The American Country Home.* New Haven: Yale University Press, 1990.

Auchincloss, Louis. *The Rector of Justin.* Boston: Houghton, Mifflin & Co., 1964.

Auchincloss, Louis. *The Vanderbilt Era: Profiles of a Gilded Age.* New York: The Macmillan Co., 1989.

Bailey, Paul. *Long Island: A History of Two Counties.* New York: Lewis Historical Publishing Co., 1949.

Baker, John C. *American Country Homes and Their Gardens.* Philadelphia: C. Winston, 1906.

Baker, Paul R. *Richard Morris Hunt.* New York: MIT Press, 1980.

Baldwin, Richard P. *Residents: Town of Islip 1720-1865.* Oakdale, NY: William K. Vanderbilt Historical Society of Dowling College, 1989.

Balmori, Diana, Diana McGuire Kostial, and Eleanor M. McPeck. *Beatrix Farrand's American Landscapes: Her Gardens and Campuses.* Sagaponack, NY: Sagapress, 1985.

Baltzel, E. Digby. *The Protestant Establishment: Aristocracy and Caste in America.* New York: Random House, 1964.

Baltzel, E. Digby. *The Protestant Establishment Revisited.* New Brunswick, NJ: New Jersey Transaction Publishers, 1991.

Baron, Stanley Wade. *Brewed in America.* Boston: Little, Brown & Co., 1962.

Barrett, Richmond. *Good Old Summer Days.* Boston: Houghton, Mifflin & Co., 1952.

Batterberry, Michael and Ariane Batterberry. *Mirror, Mirror.* New York: Holt, Rinehart & Winston, 1977.

Bayles, Richard M. *Bayles' Long Island Handbook.* Babylon, NY: privately printed, 1885.

Bayport Heritage Association. *Bayport Heritage.* Dover, NH: Arcadia Publishing Co., 1997.

Beach, Moses Yale. *Wealth and Biography of the Wealthy Citizens of New York City.* New York: The Sun Office, 1845.

Bedford, Stephen and Richard Guy Wilson. *The Long Island Country House, 1870–1930.* Southampton, NY: Parrish Art Museum, 1988.

Beebee, Lucius Morris. *The Big Spenders.* Garden City: Doubleday & Co., Inc., 1966.

Beebee, Lucius. *Mansion On Rails: The Folklore of the Private Railway Car.* Berkeley: Howell–North, 1959.

Beer, Thomas. *The Mauve Decade: American Life at the End of the 19th Century.* New York: Alfred A. Knopf, Inc., 1926.

"Behind the Gates of the Last Estates," *Newsday* September 25, 1986.

Bender, Marilyn. *The Beautiful People.* New York: Coward–McCann, Inc., 1967.

Bendix, Reinhard and Seymour Martin Lipset, ed. *Class, Status and Power.* New York: The Free Press, 1966.

Biddle, Francis. *A Casual Past.* Garden City: Doubleday & Co., Inc., 1961.

Biddle, Francis. *The Llanfear Pattern.* New York: Charles Scribner's Sons, 1927.

Bigelow, Poultney. *Seventy Summers: New York.* 2 vols. Longmans, Green & Co., 1925.

Birmingham, Stephen. *America's Secret Aristocracy.* Boston: Little, Brown & Co., 1987.

Birmingham, Stephen. *The Grandees: America's Sephardic Elite.* New York: Harper & Row Publishers, 1971.

Birmingham, Stephen. *The Grandes Dames.* New York: Simon & Schuster, Inc., 1982.

Birmingham, Stephen. *Our Crowd: The Great Jewish Families of New York.* New York: Harper & Row Publishers, 1967.

Birmingham, Stephen. *Real Lace: America's Irish Rich.* New York: Harper & Row Publishers, 1973.

Birmingham, Stephen. *The Right People: A Portrait of the American Social Establishment.* Boston: Little, Brown & Co., 1968.

Birmingham, Stephen. *The Right Places for the Right People*. Boston: Little, Brown & Co., 1973.

Bloom, Murray Teigh. *Rogues To Riches: The Trouble With Wall Street*. New York: G. P. Putnam's Sons, 1971.

Bolton, Sarah. *Famous Givers and Their Gifts*. New York: T. Y. Crowell & Co., 1896.

Bradley, Hugh. *Such Was Saratoga*. Garden City: Doubleday, Doran & Co., 1940.

Brandon, Ruth. *The Dollar Princesses: Sagas of Upward Nobility, 1870–1914*. New York: Alfred A. Knopf, 1980.

Bremner, Robert H. *American Philanthropy*. Chicago: The University of Chicago Press, 1960.

Bremner, Robert H. *American Social History Since 1860*. New York, 1971.

Brooklyn Blue Book. Brooklyn, NY: Rugby Press, Inc., annual.

Brooklyn Blue Book and Long Island Society Register. Brooklyn, NY: Brooklyn Life Publishing Co., annual.

Brooklyn Blue Book and Long Island Society Register. Brooklyn, NY: Rugby Press, Inc., annual.

Brooks, John. *Once In Galconda. A True Drama of Wall Street 1920–1938*. New York: Harper & Row Publishers, 1969.

Brooks, John. *Showing Off in America*. Boston: Little, Brown & Co., 1981.

Browder, Clifford. *The Money Game In Old New York: Daniel Drew and His Times*. Lexington, KY: University Press of Kentucky, 1986.

Brown, Jane. *Beatrix: The Gardening Life of Beatrix Jones Farrand 1872–1959*. New York: Viking Penguin Books, 1995.

Browne, Irving. *Our Best Society*. New York: Samuel French, 1875.

Burr, Anna Robeson. *The Portrait of a Banker: James Stillman, 1850–1918*. New York: Duffield & Co., 1927.

Burt, Nathaniel. *First Families*. Boston: Little, Brown & Co., 1970.

Byrnes, Rev. Horace W. *Pictorial Bay Shore and Vicinity: A Souvenir*. Bay Shore, NY: privately printed, 1903.

Cable, Mary. *Top Drawer: American Society from Gilded Age to the Roaring Twenties*. New York: Atheneum, 1984.

Cantacuzene, Princess. *My Life Here and There*. New York: Charles Scribner's Sons, 1921.

Capen, Oliver Bronson. *Country Homes of Famous Americans*. Garden City: Doubleday, Page & Co., 1905.

Caro, Robert A. *The Power Broker: Robert Moses and the Fall of New York*. New York: Alfred A. Knopf, 1989.

Carson, Gerald. *The Polite Americans*. New York: William Morrow & Co., 1966.

Chanler, Mrs. Winthrop [Margaret]. *Autumn in the Valley*. Boston: Little, Brown & Co., 1936.

Chanler, Mrs. Winthrop [Margaret]. *Roman Spring*. Boston: Little, Brown & Co., 1934.

Chase, Edna Woolman and Ilka Chase. *Always in Vogue*. Garden City: Doubleday & Co., Inc., 1954.

Churchill, Allen. *The Splendor Seekers: An Informal Glimpse of America's Multimillionaire Spenders – Members of the $50,000,000 Club*. New York: Grosset & Dunlop, 1974.

Churchill, Allen. *The Upper Crust: An Informal History of New York's Highest Society*. Englewood Cliffs, NJ: Prentice Hall, 1970.

Clark, Herma. *The Elegant Eighties*. Chicago: A. C. McClurg & Co., 1941.

Clews, Henry. *Fifty Years in Wall Street*. New York: Irving Publishing Co., 1908.

Close, Leslie Rose. *Portrait of an Era in Landscape Architecture: The Photographs of Mattie Edwards Hewitt*. The Bronx, NY: Wave Hill, 1983.

Conant, Jennet. *Tuxedo Park: A Wall Street Tycoon and the Secret Palace of Science That Changed the Course of World War II*. New York: Simon & Schuster, 2002

Crockett, Albert Stevens. *Peacocks On Parade*. New York: Sears Publishing, 1931.

Crofutt, William A. *The Leisure Class in America*. New York: Arno Press, 1975.

Curtis, George W. *Our Best Society*. New York: G. P. Putnam's Sons, 1899.

Curwen, Henry Darcey, ed. *Exeter Remembered*. Exeter, NH: Phillips–Exeter Academy, 1965.

Darby, Edwin. *The Fortune Builders*. Garden City: Doubleday & Co., Inc. 1986.

Dayton, Abram C. *The Last Days of Knickerbocker Life in New York*. New York: G. P. Putnam's Sons, 1897.

Delano & Aldrich. *Portraits of Ten Country Houses*. Garden City: Doubleday, Page & Co., 1924.

Depew, Chauncey M. *My Memories of Eighty Years*. New York: Charles Scribner's Sons, 1924.

Dickerson, Charles P. *A History of Sayville Community*. Sayville, NY: The Suffolk County News, 1975.

Directory of American Society New York State and the Metropolitan District, 1929. New York: Town Topics, 1928.

Directory of Directors in the City of New York and the Tri–State Area. Southport, CT: Directory of Directors Co., Inc., annual.

Domestic Architecture of H. T. Lindeberg. New York: William Helburn, Inc., 1940.

Domhoff, G. William. *The Bohemian Grove and Other Retreats*. New York: Harper & Row Publishers, 1974.

Domhoff, G. William. *Fat Cats and Democrats*. Englewood, NJ: Prentice–Hall, 1972.

Domhoff, G. William. *The Higher Circles: The Governing Class in America*. New York: Random House, 1970.

Domhoff, G. William. *The Powers That Be: Process of Ruling Class Domination in America*. New York: Random House, 1978.

Downey, Fairfax. *Portrait of an Era*. New York: Charles Scribner's Sons, 1936.

Drury, Roger W. *Drury and St. Paul's: The Scars of a Schoolmaster*. Boston: Little, Brown & Co., 1964.

Eaton, James W. *Babylon Reminiscences*. Babylon, NY: Babylon Publishing Co., 1911.

Eliot, Elizabeth [Lady Elizabeth Kinnaird]. *Heiresses and Coronets*. New York: McDowell, Obolensky, 1959.

Ellet, Elizabeth. *The Queens of American Society*. Philadelphia: Porter & Coates, 1867.

360

Elliott, Maude Howe. *This Was My Newport.* Cambridge, MA: The Mythology Co., 1944.

Elliott, Maude Howe. *Three Generations.* Boston: Little, Brown & Co., 1923.

Elliott, Osborne. *Men at the Top.* New York: Harper & Brothers, 1959.

"Estates and Their Story," *Newsday* December 1, 1965.

Faucigny–Lucinge, Prince Jean–Louis de. *Legendary Parties 1922–1972.* New York: The Vendome Press, 1987.

Ferrell, Merri McIntyre. "Fox Hunting on Long Island." *The Nassau County Historical Society Journal* 54(2001):1-10.

Ferry, John William. *A History of the Department Store.* New York: The Macmillan Co., 1960.

Ferree, Barr. *American Estates & Gardens.* New York: Munn & Co., 1904.

Fisher, Kenneth L. *100 Minds That Made the Market.* Woodside, CA: Business Classics, 1993.

Fiske, Stephen. *Offhand Portraits of Prominent New Yorkers.* New York: George Lockwood & Sons, 1884.

Fleming, Nancy. *Money, Manure & Maintenance: Ingredients for Successful Gardens of Marian Coffin, Pioneer Landscape Architect 1876–1957.* Weston, MA: Country Place Books, 1995.

Forbes, Malcolm and Jeffery Block. *What Happened to Their Children?* New York: Simon & Schuster, Inc., 1990.

Fowler, Marian. *In a Gilded Cage: From Heiress to Duchess.* New York: St. Martin's Press, 1993.

Frelinhuysen, Alice Cooning, et al. *Splendid Legacy: The Havemeyer Collection.* New York: The Metropolitan Museum of Art, 1993.

Fuller, Henry B. *The Cliff Dwellers.* New York: Harper & Brothers, 1893.

Garth, The Rev. William H. *Historical Sketch of St. Mark's: Islip, Long Island.* privately printed, 1928.

Gerard, James W. *My First Eighty–Three Years in America.* Garden City: Doubleday & Co., Inc., 1951.

Geus, Averill Dayton. *The Maidstone Club: The Second Fifty Years 1941 to 1991.* East Hampton, NY: Maidstone Club, 1991.

Gordon, Panmure. *Land of the Almighty Dollar.* London: Frederick Warne & Co., 1892.

Goulden, Joseph, C. *The Money Givers.* New York: Random House Publishers, 1971.

Gouverneur, Marion. *As I Remember: Recollections of American Society During the Nineteenth Century.* New York: D. Appleton & Co., 1911.

Graham, Sheila. *How to Marry Super Rich or Love, Money and the Morning After.* New York: Grosset & Dunlap Publishers, 1974.

Greene, Bert and Philip Stephen Schulz. *Pity the Poor Rich: It's a Losing Battle to Stay on Top But See How They Try.* Chicago: Contemporary Books, 1978.

Gregory, Alexis. *Families of Fortune: Life in the Gilded Age.* New York: Rizzoli International Publications, Inc., 1993.

Griswold, Mac K. and Eleanor Weller. *The Golden Age of American Gardens . Proud Owners . Private Estates . 1890–1940.* New York: Harry N. Abrams, Inc., Publishers, 1991.

Gross, Michael. *740 Park: The Story of the World's Richest Apartment Building.* New York: Broadway Books, 2005.

Gunther, Max. *The Very Rich and How They Got That Way.* New York: Playboy Press, 1972.

Halberstam, David. *The Powers That Be.* New York: Alfred A. Knopf, 1979.

Hall, Edward Tuck. *Saint Mark's School: A Centennial History.* Southborough, MA: Saint Mark's Alumni Association, 1967.

Hamm, Margherita Arlina. *Famous Families of New York.* New York: G. P. Putnam's Sons, 1901.

Harmond, Richard and Vincitorio Gaetano. "Working on the Great Estates." *Long Island Forum* Spring 1988.

Harriman, E. Roland. *I Reminisce.* Garden City: Doubleday & Co., Inc., 1975.

Harriman, Mrs. J. Borden. *From Pinafores to Politics.* New York: Henry Holt & Co., 1923.

Harriman, Margaret Chase. *The Vicious Circle.* New York: Rinehart & Co., 1951.

Harris, Leon. *Merchant Princes: An Intimate History of Jewish Families Who Built Great Department Stores.* New York: Harper & Row Publishers, 1979.

Harrison, Constance Cary. *Recollections Grave and Gay.* New York: Charles Scribner's Sons, 1911.

Harrison, Constance Cary. *The Well–Bred Girl in Society.* Garden City: Doubleday, Page & Co., 1904.

Havemeyer, Harry W. *Along the Great South Bay From Oakdale to Babylon, the Story of a Summer Spa, 1840 to 1940.* Mattituck, NY: Amereon House, 1996.

Havemeyer, Harry W. *East on the Great South Bay: Sayville and Bellport 1860-1960.* Mattituck, NY: Amereon House, 2001.

Havemeyer, Harry W. *Fire Island's Surf Hotel and Other Hostelries on Fire Island Beaches in the Nineteenth Century.* Mattituck, NY: Amereon Ltd., 2006.

Havemeyer, Harry W., "The Story of Saxton Avenue." *Long Island Forum* Winter, February 1, 1990 and Spring, May 1, 1990.

Havemeyer, Harry W. *Merchants of Williamsburg: Frederick C. Havemeyer, Jr., William Dick, John Mollenhauer, Henry O. Havemeyer.* New York: privately printed, 1989.

Havemeyer, Louisine W. *Sixteen to Sixty: Memoirs of a Collector.* New York: Ursus Press, 1993.

Hersh, Burton. *The Old Boys: The American Elite and the Origins of the CIA.* New York: Charles Scribner's Sons, 1992.

Hess, Stephen. *America's Political Dynasties from Adams to Kennedy.* Garden City: Doubleday & Co., Inc., 1966.

Hewitt, Mark Alan. *The Architect & the Country House, 1890–1940.* New Haven: Yale University Press, 1990.

Hoff, Henry B., ed. *Long Island Source Records: From the New York Genealogical and Biographical Record.* Baltimore: Genealogical Publishing, 1987.

Holbrook, Stewart H. *The Age of Moguls.* London: Victor Gollancz, Ltd., 1954.

Holloway, Laura C. *Famous American Fortunes and the Men Who Have Made Them.* New York: J. A. Hill, 1889.

Homberger, Eric. *Mrs. Astor's New York: Money and Social Power in a Gilded Age.* New Haven: Yale University Press, 2002.

Hoogenboom, Ari and Olive Hoogenboom, eds. *The Gilded Age.* Englewood, NJ: Prentice–Hall, 1967.

Hopkins, Alfred. *Modern Farm Buildings.* New York: McBride, Nast & Co., 1913.

Hopkins, Alfred. *Planning for Sunshine and Fresh Air.* New York: Architectural Book Publishing, 1931.

Howath, Susan. *The Rich Are Different.* New York: Simon & Schuster, Inc., 1977.

Howe, Samuel. *American Country Houses of To–Day.* New York: Architectural Book Publishing Co., 1915.

Howell, E. W. *Noted Long Island Homes.* Babylon, NY: E. W. Howell Co., 1933.

Hunt, Freeman. *Lives of the American Merchants.* New York: Hunts' Merchants' Magazine, 1895.

Hunter, Floyd. *The Big Rich and the Little Rich.* Garden City: Doubleday & Co., Inc., 1965.

Ingham, John. *Biographical Dictionary of American Business Leaders.* New York: Greenwood Press, 1983.

Ingham, John and Lynne B. Feldman. *Contemporary Business Leaders: A Biographical Dictionary.* New York: Greenwood Press, 1990.

International Celebrity Register. New York: Celebrity Register Ltd., annual.

Irwin, William Henry, et al. *A History of the Union League Club of New York City.* New York: Dodd, Mead & Co., 1952.

Jaher, Frederic Cople. *The Gilded Elite: American Multimillionaires, 1865 to the Present.* London: Croom Helm, 1980.

Jaher, Frederic Cople, ed. *The Rich, The Wellborn, and The Powerful: Elite and Upper Classes in History.* Secaucus: Citadel Press, 1975.

Jenkins, Alan. *The Rich Rich: The Story of the Big Spenders.* New York: G. P. Putnam's Sons, 1978.

Jennings, Walter Wilson. *20 Giants of American Business.* New York: Exposition Press, 1953.

Josephson, Matthew. *The Money Lords: The Great Finance Capitalists 1925–1950.* New York: Weybright & Talley Publishers, 1972.

Josephson, Matthew. *The Robber Barons...,1861–1901.* New York: Harcourt, Brace, Jovanovich, Publishers, 1934.

Kahn, E. J., III. "The Brahmin Mystique." *Boston Magazine* 75 (May 1983):119–161.

Kaiser, Harvey. *Great Camps of the Adirondacks.* Boston: David R. Godine, Publisher, Inc., 1982.

Kamisher, Lawrence, ed. *One Hundred Years of Knickerbocker History.* Port Washington, NY: Knickerbocker Yacht Club, 1974.

Kavaler, Lucy. *The Private World of High Society: Its Rules and Rituals.* New York: David McKay Co., Inc., 1960.

Kent, Joan Gay. *Discovering Sands Point: Its History, Its People, Its Places.* Sands Point, NY: Village of Sands Point, 2000.

Kirstein, George G. *The Rich: Are They Different?* Boston: Houghton Mifflin & Co., 1968.

Klepper, Michael. *The Wealthy 100: From Benjamin Franklin to Bill Gates – A Ranking of the Richest Americans Past and Present.* Secaucus, NJ: The Citadel Press, 1996.

Knapp, Edward Spring, Jr. *We Knapps Thought It Was Nice.* New York: privately printed, 1940.

Knox, Thomas W. "Summer Clubs on the Great South Bay." *Harper's New Monthly Magazine* July 1880.

Konolige, Kit. *The Richest Women in the World.* New York: The Macmillan Co., 1985.

Konolige, Kit and Frederica Konolige. *The Power of Their Glory: America's Ruling Class: The Episcopalians.* New York: Wyden Books, 1978.

Kouwenhoven, John A. *Partners in Banking: An Historical Portrait of a Great Private Bank, Brown Brothers Harriman & Co., 1818–1968.* Garden City: Doubleday & Co., Inc., 1968.

Kowet, Don. *The Rich Who Own Sports.* New York: Random House, 1977.

Krieg, Joann P., ed. *Long Island Architecture.* Interlaken, NY: Heart of the Lakes Publishing, 1991.

Krieg, Joann P., ed. *Robert Moses: Single–Minded Genius.* Interlaken, NY: Heart of the Lakes Publishing, 1989.

Lamont, Kenneth Church. *The Moneymakers: The Great Big New Rich in America.* Boston: Little, Brown & Co., 1969.

Lampman, Robert J. *The Share of Top Wealth–Holders in National Wealth 1922–1956.* Princeton, NJ: Princeton University Press, 1962.

Lapham, Lewis. *Money and Class in America.* New York: Weidenfeld & Nicolson, 1988.

Lee, Henry J., ed. *The Long Island Almanac and Year Book.* New York: Eagle Library Publications, 1931, 1934.

Lehr, Elizabeth Drexel. *"King Lehr" and the Gilded Age.* Philadelphia: J. B. Lippincott Co., 1935.

Lehr, Elizabeth Drexel. *Turn of the World.* Philadelphia: J. B. Lippincott Co., 1937.

Lewis & Valentine Nursery. New York: Lewis & Valentine Co., 1916.

Lewis, Arnold, et al. *The Opulent Interiors of the Golden Age.* New York: Dover Publications, Inc., 1987.

Libby, Valencia. "Marian Cruger Coffin, the Landscape Architect and the Lady." The House and Garden Exhibition Catalog. Roslyn, NY: Nassau County Museum of Fine Art, 1986.

Lindeman, Eduard C. *Wealth and Culture.* New York: Harcourt, Brace & Co., Inc., 1936.

Livingston, Bernard. *Their Turf: America's Horsey Set and Its Princely Dynasties.* New York: Arbor House Publishers, 1973.

Logan, Andy. *The Man Who Robbed the Robber Barons.* New York: W. W. Norton & Co., 1965.

Long Island Society Register 1929. Brooklyn, NY: Rugby Press, Inc., 1929.

Lowe, Corinne. *Confessions of a Social Secretary.* New York: Harper & Brothers, 1916.

Lucas, Nora. "The Historic Resource Survey for the Period 1900–1940 of the Unincorporated Sections of the Town of North Hempstead." Preservation Computer Services, 1991.

Lucie–Smith, Edward and Celestine Dars. *How the Rich Lived.* New York: Two Continents Publishing Group, 1976.

Lundberg, Ferdinand. *America's 60 Families.* New York: The Vanguard Press, 1937.

Lundberg, Ferdinand. *The Rich and the Super–Rich: A Study in the Power of Money Today.* New York: Lyle Stuart & Co., 1968.

Lundberg, Ferdinand. *"Who Controls Industry?* [pamphlet concerning Richard Whitney case], c. 1938.

Lynes, Russell. *The Domesticated Americans.* New York: Harper & Row Publishers, 1963.

MacColl, Gail and Carol McD. Wallace. *To Marry an English Lord.* New York: Workman Publishing, 1989.

Mackay, Robert B., Anthony K. Baker, and Carol A. Traynor. *Long Island Country Houses and Their Architects 1860–1940.* New York: W. W. Norton & Co., 1997.

Maher, James T. *The Twilight of Splendor: Chronicles of the Age of American Palaces.* Boston: Little Brown & Co., 1975.

Maher, Matthew. "A Study of the Effects of Accelerated Suburbanization [in Nassau–Suffolk] Upon the Social Structure." M. A. thesis, St. John's University, 1982.

Mahoney, Tom and Leonard Stone. *The Great Merchants: America's Foremost Retail Institutions and People Who Made Them Great.* New York: Harper & Row Publishers, 1974.

Marcus, George E. *Lives In Trust: The Fortunes of Dynastic Families in Late Twentieth–Century America.* Boulder, CO: Westview Press, 1992.

Martin, Frederick Townsend. *Things I Remember.* New York: John Lane Co., 1913.

Martin, Frederick Townsend. *The Passing of the Idle Rich.* Garden City: Doubleday, Page, & Co., 1911.

Maxwell, Elsa. *The Celebrity Circus.* London: Allen, 1964.

Maxwell, Elsa. *R. S. V. P.: Elsa Maxwell's Own Story.* Boston: Little, Brown & Co., 1954.

Mayer, Martin. *The Bankers.* New York: Weybright & Talley Publishers, 1974.

Mazzola, Anthony T. and Frank Zachary, ed. *The Best Families: The Town and Country Social Directory, 1846–1996.* New York: Harry N. Abrams, Inc., Publishers, 1996.

McAllister, Ward. *Society As I Have Found It.* New York: Cassell Publishing Co., 1890.

McCash, June Hall. *The Jekyll Island Cottage Colony.* Athens, GA: The University of Georgia Press, 1998.

McCash, William Barton and June Hall McCash. *The Jekyll Island Club: Southern Haven for America's Millionaires.* Athens, GA: The University of Georgia Press, 1989.

McCusker, John J. *How Much Is That in Real Money? A Historical Price Index for Use as a Deflator of Money Values in the Economy of the United States.* Worcester, MA: American Antiquarian Society, 1992.

McKim, Mead, & White. *A Monograph of the Work of McKim, Mead & White 1879–1915.* New York: DaCapo Press, 1985.

McVickar, Harry Whitney. *The Greatest Show on Earth: Society.* New York: Harper & Brothers, 1892.

Metcalf, Pauline C. and Libby Valencia. *The House and Garden.* Roslyn, NY: Nassau County Museum of Fine Art, 1986.

Miller, Frances [Breese]. *More About Tanty.* Southampton, NY: Sandbox Press, 1980.

Miller, Frances [Breese]. *Tanty: Encounter With the Past.* Southampton, NY: Sandbox Press, 1979.

Mills, C. Wright. *The Power Elite.* New York: Oxford University Press, 1956.

Milne, Gordon. *The Sense of Society.* Cranbury, NJ: Fairleigh Dickinson University Press, 1977.

Minnigerode, Meade. *Certain Rich Men.* New York: G. P. Putnam's Sons, 1927.

Monner, Frederick M. *A Local History of Brightwaters From Colonial Times To the Present.* Oswego, NY: 1964.

Montgomery, Maureen E. *Gilded Prostitution: Status, Money and Transatlantic Marriage 1870–1914.* London: Routledge Press, 1989.

Moody, John. *The Masters of Capital: A Chronicle of Wall Street.* New Haven: Yale University Press, 1919.

Morris, Lloyd. *Incredible New York: High Life and Low Life of the Last Hundred Years.* New York: Random House, 1951.

Moses, Robert. *Working For the People.* New York: Harper and Brothers, 1956.

Mountfield, David. *The Railway Barons.* New York: W. W. Norton & Co., 1979.

Myers, Gustavus. *The Ending of Hereditary American Fortunes.* New York: Julian Messner, Inc., 1939.

Myers, Gustavus. *History of the Great American Fortunes.* New York: Random House, 1937.

Nichols, Charles Wilbur de Lyon. *The Ultra-Fashionable Peerage of America: An Official List of Those People Who Can Be Called Ultra-Fashionable in the United States.* New York: George Harjes, 1904.

Noyes, Dorothy McBurney. *The World Is So Full.* Islip, NY: privately printed, 1953.

Obolensky, Serge. *One Man in His Time: The Memoirs of Serge Obolensky.* New York: privately printed, 1958.

O'Connor, Harvey. *The Empire of Oil.* New York: Monthly Review Press, 1955.

O'Connor, Richard. *The Oil Barons: Men of Greed and Grandeur.* Boston: Little, Brown & Co., 1971.

Old Oakdale History, Volume I. Oakdale, NY: William K. Vanderbilt Historical Society of Dowling College, 1983.

The Old Oakdale History, Volume II: Era of Elegance, Part I. Oakdale, NY: William K. Vanderbilt Historical Society of Dowling College, 1993.

Ostrander, Susan A. *Women of the Upper Class*. Philadelphia: Temple University Press, 1984.

Packard, Vance. *The Status Seekers*. New York: David McKay Co., Inc., 1959.

Parsons, Schuyler Livingston. *Untold Friendships*. Boston: Houghton Mifflin Co., 1955.

Patterson, Augusta Owen. *American Homes of Today*. New York: The Macmillan Co., 1924.

Patterson, Jerry E. *Fifth Avenue: The Best Addresses*. New York: Rizzoli International Publications, Inc., 1998.

Patterson, Jerry E. *The First Four Hundred: Mrs. Astor's New York in the Gilded Age*. New York: Rizzoli International Publications, Inc., 2000.

Pearson, Hesketh. *The Marrying Americans*. New York: Coward McCann, Inc., 1961.

Pendrell, Nan and Ernest Pendrell. *How the Rich Live and Whom to Tax*. New York: Workers Library Publishers, Inc., May 1939.

Persons, Stow. *The Decline of American Gentility*. New York: Columbia University Press, 1973.

Phillips, David. *The Reign of Gilt*. New York: James Pott & Co., 1905.

Picturesque Babylon, Bay Shore and Islip. New York: Mercantile Illustrating Co., 1894.

Pless, Princess Mary. *Better Left Unsaid*. New York: E. P. Dutton & Co., 1931.

Pless, Princess Mary. *What I Left Unsaid*. New York: E. P. Dutton & Co., 1936.

Porzelt, Paul. *The Metropolitan Club of New York*. New York: Rizzoli International Publications, Inc., 1982.

Prominent Residents of Long Island and Their Clubs. New York: Edward C. Watson, c. 1916.

Pulitzer, Ralph. *New York Society on Parade*. New York: Harper & Brothers, 1910.

Randall, Monica. *The Mansions of Long Island's Gold Coast*. New York: Rizzoli International Publications, Inc., 1987.

Rattray, Jeannette Edwards. *Fifty Years of the Maidstone Club: 1891–1941*. East Hampton, NY: privately printed, 1941.

Residences Designed by Bradley Delehanty. New York: Architectural Catalogue Co., Inc., 1939.

Rodgers, Cleveland. *Robert Moses, Builder of Democracy*. New York: Henry Holt and Co., 1952.

Roosevelt, Felicia Warburg. *Doers and Dowagers*. Garden City: Doubleday & Co., Inc., 1975.

Roosevelt, Robert Barnwell. *Love and Luck: The Story of a Summer's Loitering on the Great South Bay*. New York: Harper, 1886.

Sachs, Charles L. *The Blessed Isle: Hal B. Fullerton's Image of Long Island, 1827-1927*. Interlaken, NY: Heart of the Lakes Publishing, 1990.

Schlesinger, Arthur M., Jr. *A Life in the 20th Century: Innocent Beginnings, 1917-1950*. Boston: Houghton Mifflin, 2000.

Schnadelbach, R. Terry. *Ferruccio Vitale: Landscape Architect of the Country Place Era*. New York: Princeton Architectural Press, 2001.

Schrag, Peter. *The Decline of the Wasp*. New York: Simon & Schuster, Inc., 1970.

Sclare, Liisa and Donald Sclare. *Beaux–Arts Estates: A Guide to the Architecture of Long Island*. New York: The Viking Press, 1980.

Sedgwick, Henry Dwight. *In Praise of Gentlemen*. Boston: Little, Brown & Co., 1935.

Sedgwick, John. *Rich Kids*. New York: William Morrow & Co., 1985.

Shodell, Elly. *In The Service: Workers on the Grand Estates of Long Island 1890s – 1940s*. Port Washington, NY: Port Washington Public Library, 1991.

Shopsin, William C. and Grania Bolton Marcus. *Saving Large Estates: Conservation, Historic Preservation, Adaptive Re–Use*. Setauket, NY: Society for the Preservation of Long Island Antiquities, 1977.

Simon, Kate. *Fifth Avenue: A Very Social History*. New York: Harcourt, Brace, Jovanovich Publishers, 1978.

Slater, Philip. *Wealth Addiction*. New York: E. P. Dutton & Co., 1980.

Smith, Arthur D. Howden. *Men Who Run America*. New York: Bobbs–Merrill Co., 1936.

Soben, Dennis P. *Dynamics of Community Change; the Case of Long Island's Declining "Gold Coast."* Port Washington, NY: Ira J. Friedman, 1968.

Social Register. New York: The Social Register Association, annual.

Social Register New York. New York: Social Register Association, annual.

Social Register Summer. New York: Social Register Association, annual.

Spinzia, Raymond E. "Society Chameleons:' Long Island's Gentlemen Spies." *The Nassau County Historical Society Journal* 55 (2000):27-38.

Spinzia, Raymond E. and Judith A. Spinzia. "*Gatsby:* Myths and Realities of Long Island's North Shore Gold Coast." *The Nassau County Historical Society Journal* 52 (1997):16–26.

Spinzia, Raymond E. and Judith A. Spinzia. *Long Island's Prominent North Shore Families: Their Estates and Their Country Homes*. vols. I, II. College Station, TX: VirtualBookworm, 2006.

Starace, Carl A. *Book One: Islip Town Records*. Islip, NY: Town of Islip, 1982.

Stevenson, Charles Goldsmith. *But As Yesterday: The Early Life and Times of St. Ann's Church, Sayville, Long Island, New York (1864-1888)*. privately printed, 1967.

Stein, Susan R. *The Architecture of Richard Morris Hunt*. Chicago: University of Chicago, 1986.

Stephens, W. P. *The Seawanhaka Corinthian Yacht Club: Origins and Early History, 1871–1896*. New York: privately printed, 1963.

Swaine, Robert T. *The Cravath Firm and Its Predecessors, 1819–1948.* vols. 1, 2. New York: Ad Press, Ltd., 1946, 1948.

Talese, Gay. *The Kingdom and the Power.* New York: World Publishers, 1969.

Tankard, Judith B. *The Gardens of Ellen Biddle Shipman.* Sagaponack, NY: Sagapress, Inc., 1996.

Tarbell, Ida. *History of Standard Oil Company.* New York: The Macmillan Co., 1925.

Tebbel, John William. *The Inheritors: A Study of America's Great Fortunes and What Happened to Them.* New York: Putnam, 1962.

Teutonico, Jeanne Marie. "Marian Cruger Coffin: The Long Island Estates; a Study of the Early Work of a Pioneering Woman in American Landscape Architecture." M. S. thesis, Columbia University, 1983.

Thompson, Jacqueline. *The Very Rich Book: America's Supermillionaires and Their Money – Where They Got It, How They Spend It.* New York: William Morrow & Co., Inc., 1981.

Thorndike, Joseph J., Jr. *The Very Rich: A History of Wealth.* New York: American Heritage, 1976.

Tishler, William, ed. *American Landscape Architecture: Designers and Places.* Washington, DC: Preservation Press, 1989.

Townsend, Reginald T. *God Pack My Picnic Basket: Reminiscences of the Golden Age of Newport and New York.* New York: Hastings House, 1970.

Townsend, Reginald T. *Mother of Clubs.* New York: Union Club, 1936.

Trachtenberg, Alan. *The Incorporation of America: Culture and Society in the Gilded Age.* New York: Hill and Wang, 1982.

Tuttle, Etta Anderson. *A Brief History of Bay Shore.* privately printed, 1962.

Ulman, Albert. *New Yorkers from Stuyvesant to Roosevelt.* Port Washington, NY: Ira J. Friedman, 1969.

Updike, D. P. *Hunt Clubs and Country Clubs in America.* Cambridge, MA: The Merrymount Press, 1928.

Vanderbilt, Cornelius, Jr. *Farewell to Fifth Avenue.* New York: Simon & Schuster, Inc., 1935.

Vanderbilt, Cornelius, Jr. *Man of the World: My Life on Five Continents.* New York: Crown Publishers, Inc., 1959.

Vanderbilt, Cornelius, Jr. *Palm Beach.* New York: Macaulay, 1931.

Vanderbilt, Cornelius, Jr. *Reno.* New York: Macaulay, 1929.

Vanderbilt, Cornelius, Jr. *Queen of the Golden Age: The Fabulous Story of Grace Wilson Vanderbilt.* New York: McGraw–Hill Book, Co., Inc., 1956.

Van Rensselaer, Mrs. John King. *Newport: Our Social Capital.* Philadelphia: J. B. Lippincott Co., 1905.

Van Rensselaer, Mrs. John King. *New Yorkers of the XIX Century.* New York: F. T. Neely, 1897.

Van Rensselaer, Mrs. John King and Frederic Van De Water. *The Social Ladder.* New York: Henry Holt & Co., 1924.

Van Rensselaer, Peter. *Rich Was Better.* New York: Wynwood Press, 1990.

VanWagner, Judith, et al. *Long Island Estate Gardens.* Greenvale, NY: Hillwood Art Gallery, 1985.

Van Wyck, Frederick. *Recollections of an Old New Yorker.* New York: Liveright, Inc., Publishers, 1932.

Veblen, Thorstein. *The Theory of the Leisure Class: An Economic Study of Institutions.* New York: New Modern Library, 1934.

Views From the Circle: Seventy–Five Years of Groton School. Groton, MA: The Trustees of Groton Schools, 1960.

Wall Street Journal, ed. *American Dynasties Today.* Homewood, IL, c. 1980.

Walker, Stanley. *Mrs. Astor's Horse.* New York: Frederick A. Stokes Co., 1935.

Wecter, Dixon. *The Saga of American Society: A Record of Social Aspiration, 1607–1937.* New York: Charles Scribner's Sons, 1937.

Weeks, George L., Jr. *Isle of Shells.* Islip, NY: Buys Brothers Inc., 1965.

Weigold, Marilyn. *The American Mediterranean: An Environmental, Economic, and Social History of Long Island Sound.* Port Washington, NY: Kennikat Press, 1974.

Weinhardt, Donald H. *Bayport: Fading Views.* Bayport, NY: Bayport Heritage Association, 1986.

Weitzenhoffer, Frances. *The Havemeyers: Impressionism Comes to America.* New York: Harry N. Abrams, Inc., Publishers, 1986.

Wells, Richard A. *Manners, Culture and Dress of the Best American Society.* Springfield, MA: King Richardson & Co., 1894.

White, Samuel G. *The Houses of McKim, Mead, and White.* New York: Rizzoli International Publications, Inc., 1998.

Who's Who In New York State. New York: Lewis Historical Publishing Co., annual.

Williamson, Ellen. *When We Went First Class.* Garden City: Doubleday & Co., Inc., 1977.

Woolson, Abba G. *Woman in American Society.* Cambridge, MA: Roberts Brothers, 1873.

Worden, Helen. *Society Circus: From Ring to Ring With a Large Cast.* New York: Covici, Friede, Publishers, 1936.

Zerbe, Jerome. *The Art of Social Climbing.* Garden City: Doubleday & Co., Inc., 1965.

**Selected Bibliographic References
to Individual South Shore Estate Owners**

This portion of the bibliography contains references not only to the South Shore estate owners, but also to their families and their estates. Since books listed in this section are, in most instances, different from the listings in the general bibliography, America's First Age of Fortune: A Selected Bibliography, both sections should be consulted.

Adams, John Dunbar - Bay Shore - *Woodlea*
> Mackay, Robert B., Anthony K. Baker, and Carol A. Traynor. *Long Island Country Houses and Their Architects 1860-1940.* New York: W. W. Norton & Co., 1997.
> Spinzia, Raymond E. and Judith A. Spinzia. *Long Island's Prominent North Shore Families: Their Estates and Their Country Homes.* vols. I, II. College Station, TX: VirtualBookworm, 2006.
> *Spur* October 1914.

Adams, Thomas, Jr. - West Bay Shore - *Ardmore*
> Havemeyer, Harry W. *Along the Great South Bay From Oakdale to Babylon, the Story of a Summer Spa, 1840 to 1940.* Mattituck, NY: Amereon House, 1996.
> Ruther, Frederick. *Long Island Today.* Hicksville, NY: privately printed, 1909.
> Spinzia, Raymond E. and Judith A. Spinzia. *Long Island's Prominent North Shore Families: Their Estates and Their Country Homes.* vols. I, II. College Station, TX: VirtualBookworm, 2006.

Andrews, William Loring - West Islip - *Pepperidges*
> Byrnes, Horace W. *Pictorial Bay Shore and Vicinity: A Souvenir.* privately printed, 1903.

Aston, W. K. - Oakdale - *Peperidge Hall*
Library of Congress, Washington, DC, has photographs of the estate.
The Nassau County Museum Collection has photographs of the estate.
> Havemeyer, Harry W. *Along the Great South Bay From Oakdale to Babylon, the Story of a Summer Spa, 1840 to 1940.* Mattituck, NY: Amereon House, 1996.
> *Long Island Forum* February 1948.
> *Long Island Forum* December 1957.
> *Long Island Forum* December 1978.
> Mackay, Robert B., Anthony K. Baker, and Carol A. Traynor. *Long Island Country Houses and Their Architects 1860-1940.* New York: W. W. Norton & Co., 1997.
> *The Old Oakdale History, Volume II: Era of Elegance, Part I.* Oakdale, NY: William K. Vanderbilt Historical Society of Dowling College, 1993.
> *Town and Country* December 1921.

Behman, Louis C., Sr. - Bayport - *Lindenwalt*
The Nassau County Museum Collection has photographs of the estate.
> Havemeyer, Harry W. *East on the* Great *South Bay: Sayville and Bayport 1860–1960.* Mattituck, NY: Amereon House, 2001.
> Mackay, Robert B., Anthony K. Baker, and Carol A. Traynor. *Long Island Country Houses and Their Architects 1860-1940.* New York: W. W. Norton & Co., 1997.

Belmont, August, Sr. - North Babylon - *Nursery Stud Farm*
Alterman Library, University of Virginia, Charlottesville, VA, has the Nursery Stud Farm records.
Library of Congress, Washington, DC, has a portion of August Belmont, Sr.'s papers.
Massachusetts Historical Society, Boston, MA, has a portion of August Belmont, Sr.'s papers.
New York Public Library, NYC, has a portion of August Belmont, Sr.'s papers.
Office of the Historian, Town of Babylon, has photographs of the estate.
> Beard, Patricia. *After the Ball: Gilded Age Secrets, Boardroom Betrayals, and the Party That Ignited the Great Wall Street Scandal of 1905.* New York: Harper Collins, 2003.
> Birmingham, Stephen. *The Grandes Dames.* New York: Simon & Schuster, 1982.
> Black, David. *The King of Fifth Avenue: The Fortune of August Belmont.* New York: The Dial Press, 1981.
> Catalogue: Loan Exhibition 1893. National Academy of Design. New York: Knickerbocker Press, 1893.
> Douglas, Roy. "The Great Sale, The Auctioning of August Belmont's Thoroughbreds: 1890-1891." *Long Island Forum* 61 (Spring 1998):24-36.
> Douglas, Roy. "Where They First Saw the Light – August Belmont Nursery Farm and Stud in North Babylon, 1867-1890." *Long Island Forum* 60 (Fall 1997):23-35.

Belmont, August, Sr. - North Babylon - *Nursery Stud Farm* (cont'd)

Gottheil, Richard James Horatio. *Belmont–Belmonte Family: A Record of Four Hundred Years, Put Together From the Original Documents in the Archives and Libraries of Spain, Portugal, Holland, England and Germ*any, 1917.

Havemeyer, Harry W. *Along the Great South Bay From Oakdale to Babylon, the Story of a Summer Spa, 1840 to 1940.* Mattituck, NY: Amereon House, 1996.

Katz, Irving. *August Belmont: A Political Biography.* New York: Columbia University Press, 1968.

Spinzia, Raymond E. and Judith A. Spinzia. *Long Island's Prominent North Shore Families: Their Estates and Their Country Homes.* vols. I, II. College Station, TX: VirtualBookworm, 2006.

Belmont, Perry - North Babylon - *Nursery Stud Farm*

Alterman Library, University of Virginia, Charlottesville, VA, has the Nursery Stud Farm records.

Office of the Historian, Town of Babylon, has photographs of the estate.

Belmont, Perry. *An American Democrat: The Recollections of Perry Belmont.* New York: Columbia University Press, 1940.

Douglas, Roy. "The Great Sale, The Auctioning of August Belmont's Thoroughbreds: 1890-1891." *Long Island Forum* 61 (Spring 1998):24-36.

Douglas, Roy. "Where They First Saw the Light – August Belmont Nursery Farm and Stud in North Babylon, 1867-1890." *Long Island Forum* 60 (Fall 1997):23-35.

Gottheil, Richard James Horatio. *Belmont–Belmonte Family: A Record of Four Hundred Years, Put Together From the Original Documents in the Archives and Libraries of Spain, Portugal, Holland, England and Germ*any, 1917.

Spinzia, Raymond E. and Judith A. Spinzia. *Long Island's Prominent North Shore Families: Their Estates and Their Country Homes.* vols. I, II. College Station, TX: VirtualBookworm, 2006.

Bossert, Louis - West Bay Shore - *The Oaks*

Frederick Law Olmsted National Historic Site, Brookline, MA, has the records of Olmsted's landscape commissions.

Beard, Patricia. *After the Ball: Gilded Age Secrets, Boardroom Betrayals, and the Party That Ignited the Great Wall Street Scandal of 1905.* New York: Harper Collins, 2003.

Cooney, Barbara. *Hattie and the Wild Waves: A Story from Brooklyn.* New York: Viking Press, 1990. [children's book]

Country Life in America July 1903.

Havemeyer, Harry W. *Along the Great South Bay From Oakdale to Babylon, the Story of a Summer Spa, 1840 to 1940.* Mattituck, NY: Amereon House, 1996.

Howell, Liz. *Continuity: Biography 1819-1934.* Sister Bay, WI: The Dragonsbreath Press, 1993.

Mackay, Robert B., Anthony K. Baker, and Carol A. Traynor. *Long Island Country Houses and Their Architects 1860-1940.* New York: W. W. Norton & Co., 1997.

Town and Country October 1903.

Town and Country, 1923.

Bourne, Frederick Gilbert - Oakdale - *Indian Neck Hall*

Avery Architectural and Fine Arts Library, Columbia University, NYC, has the architectural records of Ernest Flagg.

Frederick Law Olmsted National Historic Site, Brookline, MA, has the records of Olmsted's landscape commissions.

Joint Industry Board of the Electrical Industry [present owner] has photographs of the estate.

The Nassau County Museum Collection has estate photographs, architectural plans, and the player rolls for Bourne's Aeolian organ.

Architectural Forum, 1919.

Bacon, Mardges. *Ernest Flagg: Beaux-Arts Architecture and Urban* Reformer. Cambridge, MA: MIT Press, 1986.

Brandon, Ruth. *Capitalist Romance: Singer and the Sewing Machine.* Philadelphia: J. B. Lippincott Co., 1977.

Desmond, H. W. "The Works of Ernest Flagg." *Architectural Record* 11 (April 1902):1-104.

"A Fine Residence." *Suffolk News* III (June 18, 1897):2.

Fordyce, James. "Frederick Bourne and Indian Neck Hall." *Long Island Forum* March and April 1987.

Havemeyer, Harry W. *Along the Great South Bay From Oakdale to Babylon, the Story of a Summer Spa, 1840 to 1940.* Mattituck, NY: Amereon House, 1996.

Hopkins, Alfred. *Modern Farm Buildings.* New York: McBride, Nast & Co., 1913.

Mackay, Robert B., Anthony K. Baker, and Carol A. Traynor. *Long Island Country Houses and Their Architects 1860-1940.* New York: W. W. Norton & Co., 1997.

The Old Oakdale History, Volume II: Era of Elegance, Part I. Oakdale, NY: William K. Vanderbilt Historical Society of Dowling College, 1993.

Bourne, Frederick Gilbert - Oakdale - *Indian Neck Hall* (cont'd)
      Spinzia, Raymond E. and Judith A. Spinzia. *Long Island's Prominent North Shore Families: Their Estates and Their Country Homes.* vols. I, II. College Station, TX: VirtualBookworm, 2006.

Breese, William Laurence - Great River - *Timber Point*
      Havemeyer, Harry W. *Along the Great South Bay From Oakdale to Babylon, the Story of a Summer Spa, 1840 to 1940.* Mattituck, NY: Amereon House, 1996.
      Howell, E. W. *Noted Long Island Homes.* Babylon, NY: E. W. Howell Co., 1933.
      Mackay, Robert B., Anthony K. Baker, and Carol A. Traynor. *Long Island Country Houses and Their Architects 1860-1940.* New York: W. W. Norton & Co., 1997.

Bromell, Alfred Henry - Babylon
      Mackay, Robert B., Anthony K. Baker, and Carol A. Traynor. *Long Island Country Houses and Their Architects 1860-1940.* New York: W. W. Norton & Co., 1997.
      Picturesque Babylon, Bay Shore and Islip. New York: Mercantile Illustrating Co., 1894.

Brownlie, George - Babylon - *Willow Close*
      Country Life in America October 1913.
      Mackay, Robert B., Anthony K. Baker, and Carol A. Traynor. *Long Island Country Houses and Their Architects 1860-1940.* New York: W. W. Norton & Co., 1997.

Carlisle, Jay Freeborn, Sr. - East Islip - *Rosemary*
East Islip Historical Society has photographs of the estate.
Frances Loeb Library, Graduate School of Design, Harvard University, Cambridge, MA, has photographs of the estate.
      Art Property of the Late Mr. & Mrs. Jay F. Carlisle Comprising the Entire Contents of Their County Home "Rosemary" East Islip, Long Island, NY. New York: Parke-Bernet Galleries, Inc., 1938. auction catalog.
      Havemeyer, Harry W. *Along the Great South Bay From Oakdale to Babylon, the Story of a Summer Spa, 1840 to 1940.* Mattituck, NY: Amereon House, 1996.
      Howell, E. W. *Noted Long Island Homes.* Babylon, NY: E. W. Howell Co., 1933.
      Mackay, Robert B., Anthony K. Baker, and Carol A. Traynor. *Long Island Country Houses and Their Architects 1860-1940.* New York: W. W. Norton & Co., 1997.

Ceballos, Juan Manuel, Sr. - Bay Shore - *Brookhurst Farm*
      Byrnes, Horace W. *Pictorial Bay Shore and Vicinity: A Souvenir.* privately printed, 1903.
      Havemeyer, Harry W. *Along the Great South Bay From Oakdale to Babylon, the Story of a Summer Spa, 1840 to 1940.* Mattituck, NY: Amereon House, 1996.
      Spinzia, Raymond E. and Judith A. Spinzia. *Long Island's Prominent North Shore Families: Their Estates and Their Country Homes.* vols. I, II. College Station, TX: VirtualBookworm, 2006.

Clarkson, William Kemble - Bay Shore
      Byrnes, Horace W. *Pictorial Bay Shore and Vicinity: A Souvenir.* privately printed, 1903.
      Mackay, Robert B., Anthony K. Baker, and Carol A. Traynor. *Long Island Country Houses and Their Architects 1860-1940.* New York: W. W. Norton & Co., 1997.
      Picturesque Babylon, Bay Shore and Islip. New York: Mercantile Illustrating Co., 1894.

Conover, Daniel D. - Bay Shore
      Byrnes, Horace W. *Pictorial Bay Shore and Vicinity: A Souvenir.* privately printed, 1903.
      Havemeyer, Harry W. *Along the Great South Bay From Oakdale to Babylon, the Story of a Summer Spa, 1840 to 1940.* Mattituck, NY: Amereon House, 1996.

Cutting, William Bayard, Sr. - Great River - *Westbrook Farm*
Department of Landscape Architecture Documents Collection, University of California, Berkeley, CA, has Beatrix Jones Farrand's landscape records.
East Islip Historical Society has photographs of the estate.
      Frederick Law Olmsted National Historic Site, Brookline, MA, has the records of Olmsted's landscape commissions.
      The Nassau County Museum Collection has photographs of the estate.
      The Bayard Cutting Arboretum Near Heckscher State Park, Great River, Long Island. Babylon, NY: Long Island State Park Commission, 1952.

Cutting, William Bayard, Sr. - Great River - *Westbrook Farm* (cont'd)

Country Life in America July 1934.

Havemeyer, Harry W. *Along the Great South Bay From Oakdale to Babylon, the Story of a Summer Spa, 1840 to 1940.* Mattituck, NY: Amereon House, 1996.

Mackay, Robert B., Anthony K. Baker, and Carol A. Traynor. *Long Island Country Houses and Their Architects 1860-1940.* New York: W. W. Norton & Co., 1997.

Moreland, Caroline. *Iris Origo: Marchesa of Val d-Orcia.* Boston: David R. Godine, 2002.

Origo, Iris. *Images and Shadows: Part of a Life.* New York: Harcourt, Brace, Jovanovich, Inc., 1970.

Roussos, George. "A History and Description of William Bayard Cutting and his Country House *Westbrook*, Great River." Board of Trustees and the Long Island State Park and Recreation Commission, 1984.

Sclare, Liisa and Donald. *Beaux-Arts Estates: A Guide to the Architecture of Long Island.* New York: The Viking Press, 1980.

Spinzia, Raymond E. and Judith A. Spinzia. *Long Island's Prominent North Shore Families: Their Estates and Their Country Homes.* vols. I, II. College Station, TX: VirtualBookworm, 2006.

Dick, John Henry - Islip - *Allen Winden Farm*

The Nassau County Museum Collection has photographs of the estate.

Havemeyer, Doris Dick. *Memoirs of a Lifetime, 1890-1976.* Unpublished manuscript in the possession of the family.

Havemeyer, Harry W. *Along the Great South Bay From Oakdale to Babylon, the Story of a Summer Spa, 1840 to 1940.* Mattituck, NY: Amereon House, 1996.

Havemeyer, Harry W. *Merchants of Williamsburg: Frederick C. Havemeyer, Jr., William Dick, John Mollenhauer, Henry O. Havemeyer.* privately printed, 1989.

Hopkins, Alfred. *Modern Farm Buildings.* New York: McBride, Nast & Co., 1913.

Howell, E. W. *Noted Long Island Homes.* Babylon, NY: E. W. Howell Co., 1933.

Mackay, Robert B., Anthony K. Baker, and Carol A. Traynor. *Long Island Country Houses and Their Architects 1860-1940.* New York: W. W. Norton & Co., 1997.

Rania, Mildred. *Irvin Dick – William Dick and Allied Families.* privately printed, 1966.

Dick, William - Islip - *Allen Winden Farm*

The Nassau County Museum Collection has photographs of the estate.

Havemeyer, Doris Dick. *Memoirs of a Lifetime, 1890-1976.* Unpublished manuscript in the possession of the family.

Havemeyer, Harry W. *Along the Great South Bay From Oakdale to Babylon, the Story of a Summer Spa, 1840 to 1940.* Mattituck, NY: Amereon House, 1996.

Havemeyer, Harry W. *Merchants of Williamsburg: Frederick C. Havemeyer, Jr., William Dick, John Mollenhauer, Henry O. Havemeyer.* privately printed, 1989.

Hopkins, Alfred. *Modern Farm Buildings.* New York: McBride, Nast & Co., 1913.

Howell, E. W. *Noted Long Island Homes.* Babylon, NY: E. W. Howell Co., 1933.

Mackay, Robert B., Anthony K. Baker, and Carol A. Traynor. *Long Island Country Houses and Their Architects 1860-1940.* New York: W. W. Norton & Co., 1997.

Rania, Mildred. *Irvin Dick – William Dick and Allied Families.* privately printed, 1966.

Dick, William Karl - Islip - *Allen Winden Farm*

The Nassau County Museum Collection has photographs of the estate.

Havemeyer, Doris Dick. *Memoirs of a Lifetime, 1890-1976.* Unpublished manuscript in the possession of the family.

Havemeyer, Harry W. *Along the Great South Bay From Oakdale to Babylon, the Story of a Summer Spa, 1840 to 1940.* Mattituck, NY: Amereon House, 1996.

Havemeyer, Harry W. *Merchants of Williamsburg: Frederick C. Havemeyer, Jr., William Dick, John Mollenhauer, Henry O. Havemeyer.* privately printed, 1989.

Hopkins, Alfred. *Modern Farm Buildings.* New York: McBride, Nast & Co., 1913.

Howell, E. W. *Noted Long Island Homes.* Babylon, NY: E. W. Howell Co., 1933.

Mackay, Robert B., Anthony K. Baker, and Carol A. Traynor. *Long Island Country Houses and Their Architects 1860-1940.* New York: W. W. Norton & Co., 1997.

Rania, Mildred. *Irvin Dick – William Dick and Allied Families.* privately printed, 1966.

Dodson, Robert Bowman - West Islip - *Kanonsioni*
Babylon Village Museum, Village of Babylon Historical and Preservation Society, Babylon, NY, has Harold Truesdel Paterson's landscape plans for *Kanonsioni*.
> *American Architect and Building News*, 1906
>> Mackay, Robert B., Anthony K. Baker, and Carol A. Traynor. *Long Island Country Houses and Their Architects 1860-1940.* New York: W. W. Norton & Co., 1997.

Ellis, George August, Jr. - West Bay Shore - *Ardmore*
> Havemeyer, Harry W. *Along the Great South Bay From Oakdale to Babylon, the Story of a Summer Spa, 1840 to 1940.* Mattituck, NY: Amereon House, 1996.
> Ruther, Frederick. *Long Island Today.* Hicksville, NY: privately printed, 1909.

Fairchild, Julian Douglas - Bay Shore
> Byrnes, Horace W. *Pictorial Bay Shore and Vicinity: A Souvenir.* privately printed, 1903.
> Havemeyer, Harry W. *Along the Great South Bay From Oakdale to Babylon, the Story of a Summer Spa, 1840 to 1940.* Mattituck, NY: Amereon House, 1996.
> Mackay, Robert B., Anthony K. Baker, and Carol A. Traynor. *Long Island Country Houses and Their Architects 1860-1940.* New York: W. W. Norton & Co., 1997.
> Spinzia, Raymond E. and Judith A. Spinzia. *Long Island's Prominent North Shore Families: Their Estates and Their Country Homes.* vols. I, II. College Station, TX: VirtualBookworm, 2006.

Flint, Sherman - Islip - *Evershade*
Department of Landscape Architecture Documents Collection, University of California, Berkeley, CA, has Beatrix Jones Farrand's landscape records.
> Spinzia, Raymond E. and Judith A. Spinzia. *Long Island's Prominent North Shore Families: Their Estates and Their Country Homes.* vols. I, II. College Station, TX: VirtualBookworm, 2006.

Ford, Malcolm W. - Babylon
> Spinzia, Raymond E. and Judith A. Spinzia. *Long Island's Prominent North Shore Families: Their Estates and Their Country Homes.* vols. I, II. College Station, TX: VirtualBookworm, 2006.

Fortescue, Granville Roland - Bayport - *Wildholme*
Arlington National Cemetery, Arlington, VA, has Fortescue's military records.
> Havemeyer, Harry W. *Along the Great South Bay From Oakdale to Babylon, the Story of a Summer Spa, 1840 to 1940.* Mattituck, NY: Amereon House, 1996.
> Spinzia, Raymond E. "Those Other Roosevelts: The Fortescues." *The Freeholder* 11 (Summer 2006): 8-9, 16-22.
> Spinzia, Raymond E. and Judith A. Spinzia. *Long Island's Prominent North Shore Families: Their Estates and Their Country Homes.* vols. I, II. College Station, TX: VirtualBookworm, 2006.

Foster, Jay Stanley, II - Babylon
Babylon Village Museum, Village of Babylon Historical and Preservation Society, Babylon, NY, has photographs of the estate.
> *Picturesque Babylon, Bay Shore and Islip.* New York: Mercantile Illustrating Co., 1894.

Frank, Emil H., Sr. - Bay Shore
> Byrnes, Horace W. *Pictorial Bay Shore and Vicinity: A Souvenir.* privately printed, 1903.
> Mackay, Robert B., Anthony K. Baker, and Carol A. Traynor. *Long Island Country Houses and Their Architects 1860-1940.* New York: W. W. Norton & Co., 1997.

Gibb, Howard, Sr. - Islip
The Nassau County Museum Collection has photographs of the estate.
> Byrnes, Horace W. *Pictorial Bay Shore and Vicinity: A Souvenir.* privately printed, 1903.
> Havemeyer, Harry W. *Along the Great South Bay From Oakdale to Babylon, the Story of a Summer Spa, 1840 to 1940.* Mattituck, NY: Amereon House, 1996.
> Spinzia, Raymond E. and Judith A. Spinzia. *Long Island's Prominent North Shore Families: Their Estates and Their Country Homes.* vols. I, II. College Station, TX: VirtualBookworm, 2006.

Gibb, John - Islip - *Afterglow*
The Nassau County Museum Collection has photographs of the estate.
> Byrnes, Horace W. *Pictorial Bay Shore and Vicinity: A Souvenir.* privately printed, 1903.
> Havemeyer, Harry W. *Along the Great South Bay From Oakdale to Babylon, the Story of a Summer Spa, 1840 to 1940.* Mattituck, NY: Amereon House, 1996.
> Mackay, Robert B., Anthony K. Baker, and Carol A. Traynor. *Long Island Country Houses and Their Architects 1860-1940.* New York: W. W. Norton & Co., 1997.
> Spinzia, Raymond E. and Judith A. Spinzia. *Long Island's Prominent North Shore Families: Their Estates and Their Country Homes.* vols. I, II. College Station, TX: VirtualBookworm, 2006.

Green, Isaac Henry, II - Sayville - *Brookside*
> Currie, Constance Gibson. "Isaac H. Green, Long Island Architect and his Brookside." *Long Island Forum* 63 (Summer 2000):5-15

Guggenheim, Meyer Robert, Sr. - North Babylon - *Firenze Farm*
Library of Congress, Washington, DC, has a portion of Meyer Robert Guggenheim, Sr.'s correspondence in its Harry Frank Guggenheim collection.
Office of the Historian, Town of Babylon, has photographs of the estate.
> Davis, John Hagg. *The Guggenheims: An American Epic.* New York: William Morrow & Co., Inc.,1978.
> Hoyt, Edwin P. *The Guggenheims and the American Dream.* New York: Funk & Wagnalls, 1967.
> Lomask, Milton. *Seed Money: The Guggenheim Story.* New York: Farrar, Straus & Co., 1964.
> O'Connor, Richard. *The Guggenheims: The Making of an American Dynasty.* New York: Covici Friede Publishers, 1937.
> Spinzia, Raymond E. and Judith A. Spinzia. *Long Island's Prominent North Shore Families: Their Estates and Their Country Homes.* vols. I, II. College Station, TX: VirtualBookworm, 2006.
> Tebbel, John. *An American Dynasty: The Story of the McCormicks, Medills and Pattersons.* New York: Greenwood Press, 1968.
> Unger, Irwin and Debi Unger. *The Guggenheims: A Family.* New York: Harper Collins Publishers, 2005.

Gulden, Charles, Sr. - Bay Shore - *Netherbay*
> Byrnes, Horace W. *Pictorial Bay Shore and Vicinity: A Souvenir.* privately printed, 1903.
> Havemeyer, Harry W. *Along the Great South Bay From Oakdale to Babylon, the Story of a Summer Spa, 1840 to 1940.* Mattituck, NY: Amereon House, 1996.

Haight, Gilbert Lawrence, Jr. - Amityville
> Howell, E. W. *Noted Long Island Homes.* Babylon, NY: E. W. Howell Co., 1933.

Harbeck, Charles T. - East Islip
Frederick Law Olmsted National Historic Site, Brookline, MA, has the records of Olmsted's landscape commissions.
> Havemeyer, Harry W. *Along the Great South Bay From Oakdale to Babylon, the Story of a Summer Spa, 1840 to 1940.* Mattituck, NY: Amereon House, 1996.

Havemeyer, Henry, Sr. - West Islip - *Sequatogue Farm*
> Byrnes, Horace W. *Pictorial Bay Shore and Vicinity: A Souvenir.* privately printed, 1903.
> Havemeyer, Harry W. *Along the Great South Bay From Oakdale to Babylon, the Story of a Summer Spa, 1840 to 1940.* Mattituck, NY: Amereon House, 1996.

Havemeyer, Henry Osborne - Islip - *Bayberry Point*
The Nassau County Museum Collection has photographs of the Bayberry Point houses.
New York Metropolitan Museum of Art, NYC, has a portion of the Havemeyer art collection.
University of Michigan, Museum of Art, Ann Arbor, MI, has a portion of the Havemeyer art collection.
> Burnett, Robert N. "Henry Osborne Havemeyer." *Cosmopolitan* 34 (April 1903):701-704.
> Frelinghuysen, Alice Cooney. *Splendid Legacy: The Havemeyer Collection.* New York: New York Metropolitan Museum of Art, 1993.
> "Furnishings and Decorations From the Estate of Mrs. H. O. Havemeyer." New York: American Art Association and the Anderson Galleries, Inc., 1930. auction catalog
> Havemeyer, Harry W. *Along the Great South Bay From Oakdale to Babylon, the Story of a Summer Spa, 1840 to 1940.* Mattituck, NY: Amereon House, 1996.
> Havemeyer, Harry W. *Merchants of Williamsburg: Frederick C. Havemeyer, Jr., William Dick, John Mollenhauer, Henry O. Havemeyer.* privately printed, 1989.

Havemeyer, Henry Osborne - Islip - *Bayberry Point* (cont'd)

Havemeyer, Harry W. "The Story of Saxton Avenue." *Long Island Forum* Winter, February 1, 1990 and Spring, May 1, 1990.

"Henry O. Havemeyer — Venice." *The New York Times Sunday Supplement* May 23, 1897:14.

"The H. O. Havemeyer Collection." New York: New York Metropolitan Museum of Art Annual Report, 1958.

H. O. Havemeyer Collection of Paintings, Prints, Sculpture, and Objects of Art. New York: New York Metropolitan Museum of Art, 1931. auction catalog

Mackay, Robert B., Anthony K. Baker, and Carol A. Traynor. *Long Island Country Houses and Their Architects 1860-1940*. New York: W. W. Norton & Co., 1997.

Rania, Mildred. *Irvin Dick — William Dick and Allied Families*. privately printed, 1966.

Sternstein, Jerome L. "Corruption in the Gilded Age: Nelson W. Aldrich and the Sugar Trust" in *Capital Studies* (vol. 6) William Maury, ed. Washington, DC: Capitol Historical Society, 1978.

Weitzenhoffer, Frances. *The Havemeyers: Impressionism Comes to America*. New York: Harry N. Abrams, Inc., 1986.

Havemeyer, Horace, Sr. - Bay Shore - *Olympic Point*

Frederick Law Olmsted National Historic Site, Brookline, MA, has the records of Olmsted's landscape commissions.

Catlin, Daniel, Jr. *Good Work Well Done: The Sugar Business Career of Horace Havemeyer, 1903-1956*. privately printed, 1988.

Havemeyer, Doris Dick. *Memoirs of a Lifetime, 1890-1976*. Unpublished manuscript in the possession of the family.

Havemeyer, Harry W. *Along the Great South Bay From Oakdale to Babylon, the Story of a Summer Spa, 1840 to 1940*. Mattituck, NY: Amereon House, 1996.

Havemeyer, Harry W. "The Story of Saxton Avenue." *Long Island Forum* Winter, February 1, 1990 and Spring, May 1, 1990.

Hopkins, Alfred. *Modern Farm Buildings*. New York: McBride, Nast & Co., 1913.

Impressionist Paintings and Drawings From the Estate of Doris D. Havemeyer. New York: Sotheby Park Bernet, Inc., 1983. auction catalog

Mackay, Robert B., Anthony K. Baker, and Carol A. Traynor. *Long Island Country Houses and Their Architects 1860-1940*. New York: W. W. Norton & Co., 1997.

Rania, Mildred. *Irvin Dick — William Dick and Allied Families*. privately printed, 1966.

Spinzia, Raymond E. and Judith A. Spinzia. *Long Island's Prominent North Shore Families: Their Estates and Their Country Homes*. vols. I, II. College Station, TX: VirtualBookworm, 2006.

Weitzenhoffer, Frances. *The Havemeyers: Impressionism Comes to America*. New York: Harry N. Abrams, Inc., 1986.

Havemeyer, Louisine Waldron Elder - Islip - *Bayberry Point*

The Nassau County Museum Collection has photographs of the Bayberry Point houses.

New York Metropolitan Museum of Art, NYC, has a portion of the Havemeyer art collection.

University of Michigan, Museum of Art, Ann Arbor, MI, has a portion of the Havemeyer art collection.

Frelinghuysen, Alice Cooney. *Splendid Legacy: The Havemeyer Collection*. New York: New York Metropolitan Museum of Art, 1993.

"Furnishings and Decorations From the Estate of Mrs. H. O. Havemeyer." New York: American Art Association and the Anderson Galleries, Inc., 1930. auction catalog

Havemeyer, Harry W. *Along the Great South Bay From Oakdale to Babylon, the Story of a Summer Spa, 1840 to 1940*. Mattituck, NY: Amereon House, 1996.

Havemeyer, Louisine W. "The Prison Special, Memories of a Militant." *Scribner's Magazine* 71 (June 1922):665.

Havemeyer, Louisine W. "The Waking of Women." Typescript of speech by Louisine W. Havemeyer, 1924-1925. In possession of family.

Havemeyer, Louisine W. *Sixteen to Sixty: Memoirs of a Collector*. New York: Ursus Press, 1993. [reprint]

Havemeyer, Louisine W. "The Suffrage Torch, Memories of a Militant." *Scribner's Magazine* 71(May 1922):528.

Hourwich, Rebecca. "An Appreciation of Mrs. Havemeyer." *Equal Rights* 14 (February 2, 1929).

Mackay, Robert B., Anthony K. Baker, and Carol A. Traynor. *Long Island Country Houses and Their Architects 1860-1940*. New York: W. W. Norton & Co., 1997.

Rania, Mildred. *Irvin Dick — William Dick and Allied Families*. privately printed, 1966.

Spinzia, Raymond E. and Judith A. Spinzia. *Long Island's Prominent North Shore Families: Their Estates and Their Country Homes*. vols. I, II. College Station, TX: VirtualBookworm, 2006.

Weitzenhoffer, Frances. *The Havemeyers: Impressionism Comes to America*. New York: Harry N. Abrams, Inc., 1986.

Hollins, Harry Bowly, Sr. - East Islip - *Meadow Farm*
Frederick Law Olmsted National Historic Site, Brookline, MA, has the records of Olmsted's landscape commissions.
>Havemeyer, Harry W. *Along the Great South Bay From Oakdale to Babylon, the Story of a Summer Spa, 1840 to 1940.* Mattituck, NY: Amereon House, 1996.
>Mackay, Robert B., Anthony K. Baker, and Carol A. Traynor. *Long Island Country Houses and Their Architects 1860-1940.* New York: W. W. Norton & Co., 1997.
>*Old Oakdale History, Volume I.* Oakdale, NY: William K. Vanderbilt Historical Society of Dowling College, 1983.

Hoppin, Bayard Cushing - East Islip
>Havemeyer, Harry W. *Along the Great South Bay From Oakdale to Babylon, the Story of a Summer Spa, 1840 to 1940.* Mattituck, NY: Amereon House, 1996.
>Spinzia, Raymond E. and Judith A. Spinzia. *Long Island's Prominent North Shore Families: Their Estates and Their Country Homes.* vols. I, II. College Station, TX: VirtualBookworm, 2006.

Hubbard, Harmanus B. - Bay Shore - *Oakhurst*
Architectural Record, 1897.
>Mackay, Robert B., Anthony K. Baker, and Carol A. Traynor. *Long Island Country Houses and Their Architects 1860-1940.* New York: W. W. Norton & Co., 1997.

Hubbs, Charles Francis - West Islip - *Sequatogue Farm*
>Byrnes, Horace W. *Pictorial Bay Shore and Vicinity: A Souvenir.* privately printed, 1903.
>Spinzia, Raymond E. and Judith A. Spinzia. *Long Island's Prominent North Shore Families: Their Estates and Their Country Homes.* vols. I, II. College Station, TX: VirtualBookworm, 2006.

Huber, Frederick Max, Sr. - Bay Shore
>Havemeyer, Harry W. *Along the Great South Bay From Oakdale to Babylon, the Story of a Summer Spa, 1840 to 1940.* Mattituck, NY: Amereon House, 1996.
>Howell, Liz. *Continuity: Biography 1819-1934.* Sister Bay, WI: The Dragonsbreath Press, 1993.

Hulse, The Reverend William Warren - Bay Shore - *Elysian Views*
>Byrnes, Horace W. *Pictorial Bay Shore and Vicinity: A Souvenir.* privately printed, 1903.

Hutton, Edward Francis - Bay Shore
>Byrnes, Horace W. *Pictorial Bay Shore and Vicinity: A Souvenir.* privately printed, 1903.
>*Catalogue of a Fine Collection of Calligraphic Books and Manuscripts: The Property of Mrs. E. F. Hutton of New York City.* London: Southeby & Co., 1922. auction catalog
>Carpenter, Donna Sammons and John Feloni. *The Fall of the House of Hutton.* New York: Henry Holt & Co., 1989.
>Havemeyer, Harry W. *Along the Great South Bay From Oakdale to Babylon, the Story of a Summer Spa, 1840 to 1940.* Mattituck, NY: Amereon House, 1996.
>Spinzia, Raymond E. and Judith A. Spinzia. *Long Island's Prominent North Shore Families: Their Estates and Their Homes.* vols. I, II. College Station, TX: VirtualBookworm, 2006.
>Sterngold, James. *Burning Down the House: How Greed, Deceit, and Bitter Revenge Destroyed E. F. Hutton.* New York: Summit Books, 1990.
>Steven, Mark. *Sudden Death: The Rise and Fall of E. F. Hutton.* New York: New American Library, 1989.

Hutton, Franklyn Laws - Bay Shore
>Byrnes, Horace W. *Pictorial Bay Shore and Vicinity: A Souvenir.* privately printed, 1903.
>Carpenter, Donna Sammons and John Feloni. *The Fall of the House of Hutton.* New York: Henry Holt & Co., 1989.
>Eldridge, Mona. *In Search of a Prince: My Life With Barbara Hutton.* London: Sedgwick & Jackson, 1988.
>Havemeyer, Harry W. *Along the Great South Bay From Oakdale to Babylon, the Story of a Summer Spa, 1840 to 1940.* Mattituck, NY: Amereon House, 1996.
>Heyman, C. David. *Poor Little Rich Girl: The Life and Legend of Barbara Hutton.* Secaucus, NJ: Lyle Stuart, Inc., 1984.
>Spinzia, Raymond E. and Judith A. Spinzia. *Long Island's Prominent North Shore Families: Their Estates and Their Country Homes.* vols. I, II. College Station, TX: VirtualBookworm, 2006.
>Sterngold, James. *Burning Down the House: How Greed, Deceit, and Bitter Revenge Destroyed E. F. Hutton.* New York: Summit Books, 1990.

Hutton, Franklyn Laws - Bay Shore (cont'd)
Steven, Mark. *Sudden Death: The Rise and Fall of E. F. Hutton*. New York: New American Library, 1989.
Van Rensselaer, Philip. *Million Dollar Baby: An Intimate Portrait of Barbara Hutton*. New York: G. P. Putnam's Sons, 1979.

Hyde, Henry Baldwin, II - Fire Island
National Archives and Records Administration, Washington, DC, John E. Taylor Collection, has information on Hyde's activities in the OSS.
Beard, Patricia. *After the Ball: Gilded Age Secrets, Boardroom Betrayals, and the Party That Ignited the Great Wall Street Scandal of 1905*. New York: Harper Collins, 2003.
Brown, Anthony Cave. *The Last Hero: Wild Bill Donovan*. New York: Time Books. 1980.
Casey, William. *The Secret War Against Hitler*. Washington, DC: Regnery Gateway, 1988.
Hyde, Henry Baldwin, II. Unpublished manuscript of his experiences as Chief of OSS in Algeria.
Persico, Joseph E. *Piercing the Reich*. New York: The Viking Press, 1979.
Spinzia, Raymond E. "Society Chameleons: Long Island's Gentlemen Spies." *The Nassau County Historical Society Journal* 55 (2000):27-38.

Hyde, Henry Baldwin, Sr. - West Bay Shore - *The Oaks*
Frederick Law Olmsted National Historic Site, Brookline, MA, has the records of Olmsted's landscape commissions.
Alexander, William. *A Brief History of the Equitable Society: Seventy Years of Progress and Public Service*. New York: The Equitable Life Assurance Society of the United States, 1929.
Bailey, Carlyle R. *The Equitable Life Assurance Society of the United States 1859-1964*. (2 vols.) New York: The Equitable Life Assurance Society of the United States, 1967.
Beard, Patricia. *After the Ball: Gilded Age Secrets, Boardroom Betrayals, and the Party That Ignited the Great Wall Street Scandal of 1905*. New York: Harper Collins, 2003.
Country Life in America July 1903.
Havemeyer, Harry W. *Along the Great South Bay From Oakdale to Babylon, the Story of a Summer Spa, 1840 to 1940*. Mattituck, NY: Amereon House, 1996.
Henry Baldwin Hyde: A Biographical Sketch. New York: The DeVinne Press, 1901.
Mackay, Robert B., Anthony K. Baker, and Carol A. Traynor. *Long Island Country Houses and Their Architects 1860-1940*. New York: W. W. Norton & Co., 1997.
Old Oakdale History, Volume I. Oakdale, NY: William K. Vanderbilt Historical Society of Dowling College, 1983.
Parkinson, Thomas Ignatius. *"Equitable" of the U. S.; What Henry B. Hyde Started in 1859*. New York: Newcome Society in North America, 1950.
Rousmaniere, John. *The Life and Times of the Equitable*. New York: The Stinehour Press, 1995.
Town and Country October 1903
Town and Country, 1923.

Hyde, James Hazen - West Bay Shore - *The Oaks*
Baker Library, Harvard University, Cambridge, MA, has a portion of Hyde's papers.
Cooper Union Museum, The Smithsonian National Museum of Design, NYC, has a portion of Hyde's art collection.
Frederick Law Olmsted National Historic Site, Brookline, MA, has the records of Olmsted's landscape commissions.
The Long Island Museum of American Art, History and Carriages in Stony Brook, has Hyde's coach.
New York Historical Society, NYC, has a portrait of Hyde, photographs, and a portion of his papers.
Alexander, William. *A Brief History of the Equitable Society: Seventy Years of Progress and Public Service*. New York: The Equitable Life Assurance Society of the United States, 1929.
Amory, Cleveland. *Who Killed Society?* New York: Harper Brothers, Publishers, 1960.
Baker, Paul R. *Stanny: The Gilded Life of Stanford White*. New York: The Free Press, 1989.
Bailey, Carlyle R. *The Equitable Life Assurance Society of the United States 1859-1964*. (2 vols.) New York: The Equitable Life Assurance Society of the United States, 1967.
Beard, Patricia. *After the Ball: Gilded Age Secrets, Boardroom Betrayals, and the Party That Ignited the Great Wall Street Scandal of 1905*. New York: Harper Collins, 2003.
Beebee, Lucius. *The Big Spenders*. Garden City: Doubleday & Co., Inc., 1966.
Beebee, Lucius. *Mansions On Rails: The Folklore of the Private Railway Car*. Berkeley, CA: Howell–North, 1959.
Birmingham, Stephen. *Our Crowd: The Great Jewish Families of New York*. New York: Harper & Row Publishers, 1967.
Birmingham, Stephen. *Real Lace: America's Irish Rich*. New York: Harper & Row Publishers, 1973.
Brough, James. *Princess Alice: A Biography of Alice Roosevelt Longworth*. Boston: Little, Brown & Co., 1975.

Hyde, James Hazen - West Bay Shore - *The Oaks* (cont'd)
    Cooper Union for the Advancement of Science and Art, New York − Museum for the Arts Decoration.
        "Four Continents From the Collection of James Hazen Hyde." New York: Cooper Union Museum, 1961.
    Country Life in America July 1903.
    "Fine French Furniture and Objects of Art, Paintings, Tapestries, Rugs: Property of Patrice Hennasy, Mrs.
        Myron Schafer, Mrs. Eileen Allen, James Hazen Hyde and Other Owners." New York: Parke−Bernet
        Galleries, Inc., 1949. auction catalog
    Gerard, James W. *My First Eighty-Three Years in America: The Memoirs of James W. Gerard.* Garden
        City: Doubleday & Co., Inc., 1951.
    Gregory, Alexis. *Families of Fortune: Life in the Gilded Age.* New York: Rizzoli International Publications,
        1993.
    Harvey, George. *Henry Clay Frick: The Man.* privately printed, 1936.
    Havemeyer, Harry W. *Along the Great South Bay From Oakdale to Babylon, the Story of a Summer Spa,*
        1840 to 1940. Mattituck, NY: Amereon House, 1996.
    Howell, Liz. *Continuity: Biography 1819-1934.* Sister Bay, WI: The Dragonsbreath Press, 1993.
    Kennan, George. *E. H. Harriman: A Biography.* Boston: Houghton Mifflin, 1922.
    Lehr, Elizabeth Drexel. *"King Lehr" and the Gilded Age.* Philadelphia: J. B Lippincott Co., 1935.
    Logan, Andy. *The Man Who Robbed the Robber Barons.* New York: W. W. Norton & Co., Inc., 1965.
    Lundberg, Ferdinand. *America's 60 Families.* New York: The Vanguard Press, 1937.
    Mackay, Robert B., Anthony K. Baker, and Carol A. Traynor. *Long Island Country Houses and Their*
        Architects 1860-1940. New York: W. W. Norton & Co., 1997.
    Matz, Mary Jane. *The Many Lives of Otto Kahn.* New York: The Macmillan Company, 1963.
    Morris, Lloyd. *Incredible New York: High Life and Low Life of the Last Hundred Years.* New York:
        Random House, 1951.
    Myers, Gustavis. *The Ending of Hereditary American Fortune.* New York: Julian Messner, Inc., 1939.
    The New York Times July 27, 1959:25.
    Rousmaniere, John. *The Life and Times of the Equitable.* New York: The Stinehour Press, 1995.
    Swanberg, W. A. *Pulitzer.* New York: Charles Scribner's Sons, 1967.
    Town and County October 1903.
    Town and Country, 1923.
    Vanderbilt, Cornelius, Jr. *Queen of the Golden Age: The Fabulous Story of Grace Wilson Vanderbilt.* New
        York: McGraw−Hill Book Co., Inc., 1956.
    Weeks, George L., Jr. *Isle of Shells.* Islip, NY: Buys Brothers, Inc., 1965.

Hyde, Richard - Bay Shore
    Byrnes, Horace W. *Pictorial Bay Shore and Vicinity: A Souvenir.* privately printed, 1903.
    Havemeyer, Harry W. *Along the Great South Bay From Oakdale to Babylon, the Story of a Summer Spa,*
        1840 to 1940. Mattituck, NY: Amereon House, 1996.
    Mackay, Robert B., Anthony K. Baker, and Carol A. Traynor. *Long Island Country Houses and Their*
        Architects 1860-1940. New York: W. W. Norton & Co., 1997.

Johnson, Aymar - East Islip - *Woodland*
East Islip Historical Society has photographs of the estate.
Frederick Law Olmsted National Historic Site, Brookline, MA, has the records of Olmsted's landscape commissions.
    Havemeyer, Harry W. *Along the Great South Bay From Oakdale to Babylon, the Story of a Summer Spa,*
        1840 to 1940. Mattituck, NY: Amereon House, 1996.
    Mackay, Robert B., Anthony K. Baker, and Carol A. Traynor. *Long Island Country Houses and Their*
        Architects 1860-1940. New York: W. W. Norton & Co., 1997.

Johnson, Bradish, Jr. - East Islip - *Woodland*
East Islip Historical Society has photographs of the estate.
Frederick Law Olmsted National Historic Site, Brookline, MA, has the records of Olmsted's landscape commissions.
    Havemeyer, Harry W. *Along the Great South Bay From Oakdale to Babylon, the Story of Summer Spa,*
        1840 to 1940. Mattituck, NY: Amereon House, 1996.
    Mackay, Robert B., Anthony K. Baker, and Carol A. Traynor. *Long Island Country Houses and Their*
        Architects 1860-1940. New York: W. W. Norton & Co., 1997.

Johnson, Bradish, Sr. - West Bay Shore - *Sans Souci*

Bradish Johnson Plantation Records 1819-1822 and Times Books for 1868 and 1880.

Byrnes, Horace W. *Pictorial Bay Shore and Vicinity: A Souvenir.* privately printed, 1903.

Gibson, Dennis A. *A Guide to the Microfilm Collection of Early Louisiana State Records, 1731-1903.* Lafayette, LA: The University of Southwestern Louisiana, 1970.

Havemeyer, Harry W. *Along the Great South Bay From Oakdale to Babylon, the Story of a Summer Spa, 1840 to 1940.* Mattituck, NY: Amereon House, 1996.

Lambert, Rick. "An Oral History of Whitney Plantation." Unpublished transcript of an oral interview of Anthony Tassis in March 1990. Louisiana Division of Historic Preservation.

Mackay, Robert B., Anthony K. Baker, and Carol A. Traynor. *Long Island Country Houses and Their Architects 1860-1940.* New York: W. W. Norton & Co., 1997.

Menn, Joseph Karl. *The Large Slaveholders of Louisiana – 1860.* New Orleans: Pelican Publishing Co., 1964.

Picturesque Babylon, Bay Shore and Islip. New York: Mercantile Illustrating Co., 1894.

Johnson, Henry Meyer - West Bay Shore - *Sans Souci*

Byrnes, Horace W. *Pictorial Bay Shore and Vicinity: A Souvenir.* privately printed, 1903.

Havemeyer, Harry W. *Along the Great South Bay From Oakdale to Babylon, the Story of a Summer Spa, 1840 to 1940.* Mattituck, NY: Amereon House, 1996.

Mackay, Robert B., Anthony K. Baker, and Carol A. Traynor. *Long Island Country Houses and Their Architects 1860-1940.* New York: W. W. Norton & Co., 1997.

Johnson, John Dean - Islip

Emory University Library, Atlanta, GA, Special Collections, has a log of the *Wanderer.*

Library of Congress, Washington, DC, has a file of material on the *Wanderer.*

National Archives, Washington, DC, has a register of the *Wanderer* dated June 1858.

Calonius, Erik. *The Wanderer: The Last American Slave Ship and the Conspiracy That Set Its Sails.* New York: St Martin's Press, 2006.

Wells, Gordon. *Port Jefferson: The Story of a Village.* Port Jefferson, NY: Historical Society of Greater Port Jefferson, 1985.

Wells, Tom Henderson. *The Slave Ship Wanderer.* Athens, GA: University of Georgia Press, 1968.

Johnston, James Boorman - East Islip

Frederick Law Olmsted National Historic Site, Brookline, MA, has the records of Olmsted's landscape commissions.

Havemeyer, Harry W. *Along the Great South Bay From Oakdale to Babylon, the Story of a Summer Spa, 1840 to 1940.* Mattituck, NY: Amereon House, 1996.

Jones, Frank Smith - Sayville - *Beechwold*

The Nassau County Museum Collection has photographs of the estate.

Havemeyer, Harry W. *East on the Great South Bay: Sayville and Bayport 1860–1960.* Mattituck, NY: Amereon House, 2001.

Mackay, Robert B., Anthony K. Baker, and Carol A. Traynor. *Long Island Country Houses and Their Architects 1860-1940.* New York: W. W. Norton & Co., 1997.

Knapp, Harry Kearsarge, II - East Islip - *Creekside*

Havemeyer, Harry W. *Along the Great South Bay From Oakdale to Babylon, the Story of a Summer Spa, 1840 to 1940.* Mattituck, NY: Amereon House, 1996.

Howell, E. W. *Noted Long Island Homes.* Babylon, NY: E. W. Howell Co., 1933.

Knapp, Edward Spring. *We Knapps Thought It Was Nice.* privately printed, 1940.

Mackay, Robert B., Anthony K. Baker, and Carol A. Traynor. *Long Island Country Houses and Their Architects 1860-1940.* New York: W. W. Norton & Co., 1997.

Knapp, Harry Kearsarge, Sr. - East Islip - *Brookwood*

East Islip Historical Society has photographs of the estate.

The Nassau County Museum Collection has photographs of the estate.

Havemeyer, Harry W. *Along the Great South Bay From Oakdale to Babylon, the Story of a Summer Spa, 1840 to 1940.* Mattituck, NY: Amereon House, 1996.

Knapp, Edward Spring. *We Knapps Thought It Was Nice.* privately printed, 1940.

Mackay, Robert B., Anthony K. Baker, and Carol A. Traynor. *Long Island Country Houses and Their Architects 1860-1940.* New York: W. W. Norton & Co., 1997.

Lemmerman, Fred C. - Bay Shore
    Byrnes, Horace W. *Pictorial Bay Shore and Vicinity: A Souvenir.* privately printed, 1903.
    Mackay, Robert B., Anthony K. Baker, and Carol A. Traynor. *Long Island Country Houses and Their Architects 1860-1940.* New York: W. W. Norton & Co., 1997.
    Picturesque Babylon, Bay Shore and Islip. New York: Mercantile Illustrating Co., 1894.

Lorillard, Dr. George L. - Great River - *Westbrook Farm*
    Garland, John. "The Legacy and Fall of Westbrook Farms." M. S. thesis, Hofstra University, Hempstead, NY, 1994.
    Havemeyer, Harry W. *Along the Great South Bay From Oakdale to Babylon, the Story of a Summer Spa, 1840 to 1940.* Mattituck, NY: Amereon House, 1996.
    Mackay, Robert B., Anthony K. Baker, and Carol A. Traynor. *Long Island Country Houses and Their Architects 1860-1940.* New York: W. W. Norton & Co., 1997.
    Sclare, Liisa and Donald. *Beaux-Arts Estates: A Guide to the Architecture of Long Island.* New York: The Viking Press, 1980.
    Whittlock, Lavern A. "The Story of Westbrook." *Long Island Forum* September 1986.

McBurney, Dr. Malcolm - East Islip
Avery Architectural and Fine Arts Library, Columbia University, NYC has photographs of the estate.
East Islip Historical Society has photographs of the estate.
McIlwaine Collection, Avery Architectural and Fine Arts Library, Columbia University, NYC, has the architectural records of Delano and Aldrich.
    Architectural Forum 29 (August 1918).
    Havemeyer, Harry W. *Along the Great South Bay From Oakdale to Babylon, the Story of a Summer Spa, 1840 to 1940.* Mattituck, NY: Amereon House, 1996.
    Mackay, Robert B., Anthony K. Baker, and Carol A. Traynor. *Long Island Country Houses and Their Architects 1860-1940.* New York: W. W. Norton & Co., 1997.
    Noyes, Dorothy McBurney. *The World Is So Full of a Number of Things.* privately printed, 1956.

McClure, William - West Islip - *Clurella*
    Byrnes, Horace W. *Pictorial Bay Shore and Vicinity: A Souvenir.* privately printed, 1903.
    Havemeyer, Harry W. *Along the Great South Bay From Oakdale to Babylon, the Story of a Summer Spa, 1840 to 1940.* Mattituck, NY: Amereon House, 1996.

Moffitt, William Henry - Islip - *Beautiful Shore*
The Nassau County Museum Collection has photographs of the estate.
    Havemeyer, Harry W. *Along the Great South Bay From Oakdale to Babylon, the Story of a Summer Spa, 1840 to 1940.* Mattituck, NY: Amereon House, 1996.

Mollenhauer, John - Bay Shore
    Havemeyer, Harry W. *Along the Great South Bay From Oakdale to Babylon, the Story of a Summer Spa, 1840 to 1940.* Mattituck, NY: Amereon House, 1996.
    Havemeyer, Harry W. *Merchants of Williamsburg: Frederick C. Havemeyer, Jr., William Dick, John Mollenhauer, Henry O. Havemeyer.* privately printed, 1989.
    Rania, Mildred. *Irvin Dick – William Dick and Allied Families.* privately printed, 1966.

Mollenhauer, John Adolph - Bay Shore - *Homeport*
    Havemeyer, Harry W. *Along the Great South Bay From Oakdale to Babylon, the Story of a Summer Spa, 1840 to 1940.* Mattituck, NY: Amereon House, 1996.
    Havemeyer, Harry W. *Merchants of Williamsburg: Frederick C. Havemeyer, Jr., William Dick, John Mollenhauer, Henry O. Havemeyer.* privately printed, 1989.
    Hopkins, Alfred. *Modern Farm Buildings.* New York: McBride, Nast & Co., 1913.
    Mackay, Robert B., Anthony K. Baker, and Carol A. Traynor. *Long Island Country Houses and Their Architects 1860-1940.* New York: W. W. Norton & Co., 1997.
    Picturesque Babylon, Bay Shore and Islip. New York: Mercantile Illustrating Co., 1894.
    Rania, Mildred. *Irvin Dick – William Dick and Allied Families.* privately printed, 1966.

Moses, Robert - Babylon
Bard, Erwin W. *The Port of New York Authority.* New York: Columbia University Press, 1942.
Caro, Robert A. *The Power Broker: Robert Moses and the Fall of New York.* New York: Alfred A. Knopf, Inc., 1974.
Kieley, John B. *Moses on the Green.* Tuscaloosa, AL: University of Alabama Press, 1959.
Krieg, Joann P., ed. *Robert Moses Single-Minded Genius.* Interlaken, NY: Heart of the Lakes Publishing, 1989.
Lines, Jon J., Ellen L. Parker, and David C. Perry. *Building Twentieth Century Public Works Machine: Robert Moses and the Public Authority.* Chicago: The Institute of Public Works History, 1987.
Mackay, Robert B., Anthony K. Baker, and Carol A. Traynor. *Long Island Country Houses and Their Architects 1860-1940.* New York: W. W. Norton & Co., 1997.
Rodgers, Cleveland. *Robert Moses: Builder for Democracy.* New York: Henry Holt and Co., 1952.
Spinzia, Raymond E. and Judith A. Spinzia. *Long Island's Prominent North Shore Families: Their Estates and Their Country Homes.* vols. I, II. College Station, TX: VirtualBookworm, 2006.

Myers, Nathaniel - Bay Shore
Country Life in America, 1932.
Mackay, Robert B., Anthony K. Baker, and Carol A. Traynor. *Long Island Country Houses and Their Architects 1860-1940.* New York: W. W. Norton & Co., 1997.

Nicholas, Harry Ingersoll, Sr. - North Babylon - *Virginia Farm*
Havemeyer, Harry W. *Along the Great South Bay From Oakdale to Babylon, the Story of a Summer Spa, 1840 to 1940.* Mattituck, NY: Amereon House, 1996.
Spinzia, Raymond E. and Judith A. Spinzia. *Long Island's Prominent North Shore Families: Their Estates and Their Country Homes.* vols. I, II. College Station, TX: VirtualBookworm, 2006.

Oakman, Walter George, Sr. - Islip
Havemeyer, Harry W. *Along the Great South Bay From Oakdale to Babylon, the Story of a Summer Spa, 1840 to 1940.* Mattituck, NY: Amereon House, 1996.
Mackay, Robert B., Anthony K. Baker, and Carol A. Traynor. *Long Island Country Houses and Their Architects 1860-1940.* New York: W. W. Norton & Co., 1997.
Spinzia, Raymond E. and Judith A. Spinzia. *Long Island's Prominent North Shore Families: Their Estates and Their Homes.* vols. I, II. College Station, TX: VirtualBookworm, 2006.

O'Donohue, Charles A. - Bay Shore - *The Moorings*
Byrnes, Horace W. *Pictorial Bay Shore and Vicinity: A Souvenir.* privately printed, 1903.
Spinzia, Raymond E. and Judith A. Spinzia. *Long Island's Prominent North Shore Families: Their Estates and Their Country Homes.* vols. I, II. College Station, TX: VirtualBookworm, 2006.

Packer, Frederick Little - Brightwaters
Library of Congress, Washington, DC, has four of Packer's wartime posters.

Page, Walter Hines, Sr. - Bay Shore
Byrnes, Horace W. *Pictorial Bay Shore and Vicinity: A Souvenir.* privately printed, 1903.
Hendrick, Burton J. The *Life and Letters of Walter H. Page* (3 vols.). Garden City: Doubleday, Page & Company, 1925.
Spinzia, Raymond E. and Judith A. Spinzia. *Long Island's Prominent North Shore Families: Their Estates and Their Country Homes.* vols. I, II. College Station, TX: VirtualBookworm, 2006.

Parsons, Schuyler Livingston, Jr. - Islip - *Pleasure Island*
Havemeyer, Harry W. *Along the Great South Bay From Oakdale to Babylon, the Story of a Summer Spa, 1840 to 1940.* Mattituck, NY: Amereon House, 1996.
Parsons, Schuyler Livingston, Jr. *Untold Friendships.* Boston, MA: Houghton Mifflin Co., 1955.

Parsons, Schuyler Livingston, Sr. - Islip - *Whileaway*
The Nassau County Museum Collection has photographs of the estate.
Havemeyer, Harry W. *Along the Great South Bay From Oakdale to Babylon, the Story of a Summer Spa, 1840 to 1940.* Mattituck, NY: Amereon House, 1996.
Parsons, Schuyler Livingston, Jr. *Untold Friendships.* Boston, MA: Houghton Mifflin Co., 1955.

Peck, William L. - Bay Shore
       Byrnes, Horace W. *Pictorial Bay Shore and Vicinity: A Souvenir.* privately printed, 1903.

Peters, Harry Twyford, Sr. - Islip - *Windholme Farm*
Olin Library, Cornell University, Ithaca, NY, has Ellen Biddle Shipman's landscape records.
Shelburn Museum, Shelburn, VT, has items from the Peterses' home including: a trade sign with a three-
    dimensional horse with blanket; 1820 English mochaware pepper shakers and bowl; a brass teapot with tilt-top;
    1829 English candle reflectors, inkstand, and candle stand; English Staffordshire decorated cow creamers; 1840
    English Staffordshire rabbit.
       American Architect and Building News, 1916.
       Country Life In America, 1912.
       Havemeyer, Harry W. *Along the Great South Bay From Oakdale to Babylon, the Story of a Summer Spa,*
          1840 to 1940. Mattituck, NY: Amereon House, 1996.
       Hopkins, Alfred. *Modern Farm Buildings.* New York: McBride, Nast & Co., 1913.
       Mackay, Robert B., Anthony K. Baker, and Carol A. Traynor. *Long Island Country Houses and Their*
          Architects 1860-1940. New York: W. W. Norton & Co., 1997.
       Peters, Harry Twyford. *American on Stone; The Other Printmakers to the American People; A Chronicle of*
          American Lithography Other Than That of Currier and Ives, From Its Beginning Shortly Before 1820
          to Years When Commercial Single-Stone Hand-Colored Lithography Disappeared From the American
          Scene. Garden City: Doubleday, Doran & Co., Inc., 1931.
       Peters, Harry Twyford. *California on Stone.* Garden City: Doubleday, Doran & Co., 1935.
       Peters, Harry Twyford. *Currier and Ives: Printmakers to the American People.* Garden City: Doubleday,
          Doran & Co., Inc., 1942.
       Presentation of the New York Historical Society's Gold Medal for Achievement in History to Harry Twyford
          Peters, Dec. 8, 1947. New York: New York Historical Society, 1948.

Peters, Samuel Twyford - Islip - *Windholme Farm*
Olin Library, Cornell University, Ithaca, NY, has Ellen Biddle Shipman's landscape records.
       American Architect and Building News, 1916.
       Country Life in America, 1912.
       Havemeyer, Harry W. *Along the Great South Bay From Oakdale to Babylon, the Story of a Summer Spa,*
          1840 to 1940. Mattituck, NY: Amereon House, 1996.
       Hopkins, Alfred. *Modern Farm Buildings.* New York: McBride, Nast & Co., 1913.
       Mackay, Robert B., Anthony K. Baker, and Carol A. Traynor. *Long Island Country Houses and Their*
          Architects 1860-1940. New York: W. W. Norton & Co., 1997.
       Spinzia, Raymond E. and Judith A. Spinzia. *Long Island's Prominent North Shore Families: Their Estates*
          and Their Country Homes. vols. I, II. College Station, TX: VirtualBookworm, 2006.

Pinkerton, Allan, II - Bay Shore
       Havemeyer, Harry W. *Along the Great South Bay From Oakdale to Babylon, the Story of a Summer Spa,*
          1840 to 1940. Mattituck, NY: Amereon House, 1996.
       Horan, James D. *The Pinkertons: The Detective Dynasty That Made History.* New York: Crown
          Publishers, Inc., 1967.
       Mackay, Robert B., Anthony K. Baker, and Carol A. Traynor. *Long Island Country Houses and Their*
          Architects 1860-1940. New York: W. W. Norton & Co., 1997.
       Spinzia, Raymond E. and Judith A. Spinzia. *Long Island's Prominent North Shore Families: Their Estates*
          and Their Country Homes. vols. I, II. College Station, TX: VirtualBookworm, 2006.

Plumb, James Ives - Islip - *Shadowbrook*
The Nassau County Museum Collection has photographs of the estate.

Prince, John Dyneley, II - Islip
Olin Library, Cornell University, Ithaca, NY, has Ellen Biddle Shipman's landscape records.
       American Architect and Building News, 1916.
       Hopkins, Alfred. *Modern Farm Buildings.* New York: McBride, Nast & Co., 1913.

Robert, Christopher Rhinelander, Jr. - Oakdale - *Peperidge Hall*
Library of Congress, Washington, DC, has photographs of the estate.
The Nassau County Museum Collection has photographs of the estate.

> Havemeyer, Harry W. *Along the Great South Bay From Oakdale to Babylon, the Story of a Summer Spa, 1840 to 1940.* Mattituck, NY: Amereon House, 1996.
> *Long Island Forum* February 1948.
> *Long Island Forum* December 1957.
> *Long Island Forum* December 1978.
> Mackay, Robert B., Anthony K. Baker, and Carol A. Traynor. *Long Island Country Houses and Their Architects 1860-1940.* New York: W. W. Norton & Co., 1997.
> *The Old Oakdale History, Volume II: Era of Elegance, Part I.* Oakdale, NY: William K. Vanderbilt Historical Society of Dowling College, 1993.
> *Town and Country* December 1921.

Roosevelt, John Ellis - Sayville - *Meadow Croft*
Office of Suffolk County Historian, Great River, NY, has photographs, a printed booklet, and historical specifications of the estate collected for historical designation.
Theodore Roosevelt Association, Oyster Bay, NY, has John Ellis Roosevelt's scrapbook.

> Harmond, Richard P. and Donald H. Weinhardt. "John Ellis Roosevelt of Meadow Croft." *Long Island Forum* 51 (Fall 1988).
> Havemeyer, Harry W. *East on the Great South Bay: Sayville and Bayport 1860–1960.* Mattituck, NY: Amereon House, 2001.
> Mackay, Robert B., Anthony K. Baker, and Carol A. Traynor. *Long Island Country Houses and Their Architects 1860-1940.* New York: W. W. Norton & Co., 1997.
> "Monograph on Meadow Croft, the Former John E. Roosevelt Estate, Sayville, Long Island." Suffolk County Parks Department, Division of Cultural and Historic Services, 1984. unpublished booklet.
> Spinzia, Raymond E. and Judith A. Spinzia. *Long Island's Prominent North Shore Families: Their Estates and Their Country Homes.* vols. I, II. College Station, TX: VirtualBookworm, 2006.

Roosevelt, Robert Barnwell, Jr. - Sayville - *The Lilacs*
Office of Suffolk County Historian, Great River, NY, has vertical file material and photographs of the estate.

> Havemeyer, Harry W. *East on the Great South Bay: Sayville and Bayport 1860–1960.* Mattituck, NY: Amereon House, 2001.
> Mackay, Robert B., Anthony K. Baker, and Carol A. Traynor. *Long Island Country Houses and Their Architects 1860-1940.* New York: W. W. Norton & Co., 1997.
> Spinzia, Raymond E. and Judith A. Spinzia. *Long Island's Prominent North Shore Families: Their Estates and Their Country Homes.* vols. I, II. College Station, TX: VirtualBookworm, 2006.

Roosevelt, Robert Barnwell, Sr. - Bayport - *Lotos Lake*
Office of Suffolk County Historian, Great River, NY, has vertical file material and photographs of the estate.

> Bleyer, Bill. "The Forgotten Roosevelt." *Newsday* October 6, 1985:10-12, 25.
> Harmond, Richard P. "Lost and Found." *Long Island Historical Journal* 7 (Fall 1994):125-9.
> Harmond, Richard P. "Robert Barnwell Roosevelt and the Early Conservation Movement." *Theodore Roosevelt Association Journal* 14 (2).
> Harmond, Richard P. and Donald W. Weinhardt. "Robert Barnwell Roosevelt on the Great South Bay." *Long Island Forum* 50 (August/September 1987):164-71.
> Havemeyer, Harry W. *East on the Great South Bay: Sayville and Bayport 1860–1960.* Mattituck, NY: Amereon House, 2001.
> Spinzia, Raymond E. "Those Other Roosevelts: The Fortescues." *The Freeholder* 11 (Summer 2006): 8-9, 16-22.
> Spinzia, Raymond E. and Judith A. Spinzia. *Long Island's Prominent North Shore Families: Their Estates and Their Country Homes.* vols. I, II. College Station, TX: VirtualBookworm, 2006.

Shea, David - Sayville - *Wyndemoor*
The Nassau County Museum Collection has photographs of the estate.

Simonds, William Robinson - Sayville - *Wyndemoor*
The Nassau County Museum Collection has photographs of the estate.

Smith, Charles Robinson - Bay Shore
> Mackay, Robert B., Anthony K. Baker, and Carol A. Traynor. *Long Island Country Houses and Their Architects 1860-1940.* New York: W. W. Norton & Co., 1997.
> *Picturesque Babylon, Bay Shore and Islip.* New York: Mercantile Illustrating Co., 1894.

Stanchfield, John Barry, Sr. - Islip - *Afterglow*
The Nassau County Museum Collection has photographs of the estate.
> Byrnes, Horace W. *Pictorial Bay Shore and Vicinity: A Souvenir.* privately printed, 1903.
> Mackay, Robert B., Anthony K. Baker, and Carol A. Traynor. *Long Island Country Houses and Their Architects 1860-1940.* New York: W. W. Norton & Co., 1997.
> Spinzia, Raymond E. and Judith A. Spinzia. *Long Island's Prominent North Shore Families: Their Estates and Their Country Homes.* vols. I, II. College Station, TX: VirtualBookworm, 2006.

Stewart, James - Great River
The Nassau County Museum Collection has photographs of the estate.
> Mackay, Robert B., Anthony K. Baker, and Carol A. Traynor. *Long Island Country Houses and Their Architects 1860-1940.* New York: W. W. Norton & Co., 1997.

Taylor, George Campbell - East Islip
East Islip Historical Society has photographs of the estate.
The Long Island State Parks Commission has photographs of the estate.
> Havemeyer, Harry W. *Along the Great South Bay From Oakdale to Babylon, the Story of a Summer Spa, 1840 to 1940.* Mattituck, NY: Amereon House, 1996.
> Mackay, Robert B., Anthony K. Baker, and Carol A. Traynor. *Long Island Country Houses and Their Architects 1860-1940.* New York: W. W. Norton & Co., 1997.

Thorne, Landon Ketchum, Sr. - West Bay Shore - *Thorneham*
Frances Loeb Library, Graduate School of Design, Harvard University, Cambridge, MA, has photographs of the estate.
Innocenti and Webel landscape records are located at their office in Locust Valley.
Queensborough Public Library, Long Island Collection, Jamaica, NY, has Thorne family records including genealogical notes c. 1920-1929.
> *Architectural Annual, 1929.* New York: Architectural League of New York, 1929.
> Havemeyer, Harry W. *Along the Great South Bay From Oakdale to Babylon, the Story of a Summer Spa, 1840 to 1940.* Mattituck, NY: Amereon House, 1996.
> Hilderbrand, Gary R. *Making a Landscape of Continuity: The Practice of Innocenti & Webel.* Cambridge, MA: Harvard University Graduate School of Design, 1997.
> Howell, E. W. *Noted Long Island Homes.* Babylon, NY: E. W. Howell Co., 1933.
> Mackay, Robert B., Anthony K. Baker, and Carol A. Traynor. *Long Island Country Houses and Their Architects 1860-1940.* New York: W. W. Norton & Co., 1997.
> Sclare, Liisa and Donald. *Beaux-Arts Estates: A Guide to the Architecture of Long Island.* New York: The Viking Press, 1980.

Thurber, Fred C. - Bay Shore
> *Architectural Record,* 1897.
> Mackay, Robert B., Anthony K. Baker, and Carol A. Traynor. *Long Island Country Houses and Their Architects 1860-1940.* New York: W. W. Norton & Co., 1997.

Timmerman, Henry Gerlard - Islip - *Breeze Lawn*
The Nassau County Museum Collection has photographs of the estate.
> Byrnes, Horace W. *Pictorial Bay Shore and Vicinity: A Souvenir.* privately printed, 1903.
> Mackay, Robert B., Anthony K. Baker, and Carol A. Traynor. *Long Island Country Houses and Their Architects 1860-1940.* New York: W. W. Norton & Co., 1997.

Truslow, Frederick C. - Great River - *Questover Lodge*
The Nassau County Museum Collection has photographs of the estate.
> Mackay, Robert B., Anthony K. Baker, and Carol A. Traynor. *Long Island Country Houses and Their Architects 1860-1940.* New York: W. W. Norton & Co., 1997.

Tucker, Charles A. - Islip

> Byrnes, Horace W. *Pictorial Bay Shore and Vicinity: A Souvenir.* privately printed, 1903.
> Havemeyer, Harry W. *Along the Great South Bay From Oakdale to Babylon, the Story of a Summer Spa, 1840 to 1940.* Mattituck, NY: Amereon House, 1996.
> Hopkins, Alfred. *Modern Farm Buildings.* New York: McBride, Nast & Co., 1913.

Turnbull, George R. - West Islip - *The Pines*

> Byrnes, Horace W. *Pictorial Bay Shore and Vicinity: A Souvenir.* privately printed, 1903.
> Mackay, Robert B., Anthony K. Baker, and Carol A. Traynor. *Long Island Country Houses and Their Architects 1860-1940.* New York: W. W. Norton & Co., 1997.

General References to Vanderbilt Family

[*see also* references to individual Vanderbilt family members]

Biltmore Estate, Asheville, NC, has material collected from all Vanderbilt families in their archives.
Melville Library, SUNY Stony Brook, LI, has the National Woman's Party papers on microfilm.
New York State Library, Albany, NY, has Cornelius Vanderbilt's six–volume will.
Newport Historical Society, Newport, RI, has material relating to Woman Suffrage events held in Newport by Alva Vanderbilt Belmont.
The Preservation Society of Newport County, Newport, RI, has Alva Vanderbilt's personal scrapbook of newspaper clippings about the March 26, 1883, Masque Ball held at 660 Fifth Avenue, New York City.
Queens College Library, Historical Collection, Flushing, NY, has Vanderbilt family records, including 1699 tax rolls and a deposit of 1790–1840 material.
Sewall–Belmont House [National Woman's Party Headquarters], Washington, DC, has scrapbooks pertaining to Alva Vanderbilt Belmont and photographs of the Vanderbilt family.
Suffolk County Vanderbilt Museum and Planetarium archives, Centerport, LI, has photographs of the Vanderbilt family and an album of photographs of Alva Vanderbilt Belmont's house *Beacon Towers,* taken by Samuel H. Gottscho. The Gottscho collection is also in the Avery Architectural and Fine Arts Library, Columbia University, NYC, and in the Library of Congress, Washington, DC. Also included in the collection at the Vanderbilt Museum is an album with Alva Vanderbilt Belmont's funeral photographs and newspaper clippings.

> Allen, Armin Brand. *The Cornelius Vanderbilts of the Breakers: A Family Retrospective May 27 – October 1, 1995.* Newport: The Preservation Society of Newport County, 1995.
> Andrews, Wayne. *The Vanderbilt Legend: The Story of the Vanderbilt Family, 1794–1940.* New York: Harcourt, Brace and Co., 1941.
> Auchincloss, Louis. *The Vanderbilt Era: Profile of a Gilded Age.* New York: Charles Scribner's Sons, 1989.
> Baker, Paul. *Richard Morris Hunt.* Cambridge: The MIT Press, 1980.
> Beebee, Lucius. *The Big Spenders.* Garden City: Doubleday & Co., Inc., 1966.
> Belmont, Alva Vanderbilt. "Are Women Really Citizens?" *Good Housekeeping* September 1931.
> Belmont, Alva Vanderbilt. "Belief in Women Is Belief in Women's Suffrage." *Women's Magazine* December, 1909.
> Belmont, Alva Vanderbilt. "How Can Woman Get the Suffrage?" *The Independent* 31 (March 1910).
> Belmont, Alva Vanderbilt. "Jewish Women in Public Affairs." *American Citizen* May 1913.
> Belmont Alva Vanderbilt. " The Liberation of a Sex." *Hearst's Magazine* April 1913.
> Belmont Alva Vanderbilt. "New Standards for Business Women." *Business Woman's Magazine* January 1915.
> Belmont, Alva Vanderbilt. *One Month's Log of the Seminole.* New York: privately printed, 1916.
> Belmont, Alva Vanderbilt. Foreword to article by Christable Pankhurst, "Story of the Woman's War." *Good Housekeeping* November 1913.
> Belmont, Alva Vanderbilt. "Unpublished 1917 Autobiography of Alva Vanderbilt Belmont." In Wood Collection, Huntington Library, San Marino, California.
> Belmont, Alva Vanderbilt. "Unpublished 1933 Autobiography of Alva Vanderbilt Belmont." In Matilda Young Papers, Special Collections Department, William R. Perkins Library, Duke University, Durham, North Carolina.
> Belmont, Alva Vanderbilt. "What the Woman's Party Wants." *Collier's* 23 (December 1922).
> Belmont, Alva Vanderbilt. "Why I Am a Suffragist." *The World To–Day* October 1911.
> Belmont, Alva Vanderbilt. "Woman's Right to Govern Herself." *North American Review* 190 (November 1909).

Belmont, Alva Vanderbilt. "Woman Suffrage as It Looks To–Day." *The Forum* March 1910.

Belmont, Alva Vanderbilt. "Women as Dictators." *Ladies Home Journal* September 1922.

"Belmont to Sell Belcourt." *New York Herald Tribune* December 30, 1908. [Newport estate]

"Brookholt on the Market." *The New York Times* January 6, 1909:1. [Uniondale estate]

Burden, Shirley. *The Vanderbilts in My Life: A Personal Memoir.* New Haven: Ticknor & Fields, 1981.

"Buys Chateau in France: Mrs. O. H. P. Belmont Plans to Live Abroad, Newport Hears." *The New York Times* September 4, 1926:5.

Field, Frederick Vanderbilt. *From Right to Left: An Autobiography.* Westport, CT: L. Hill, 1983.

Foreman, John and Robbe Pierce Stimson. *The Vanderbilts and the Gilded Age: Architectural Aspirations, 1879–1901.* New York: St. Martin's Press, 1991.

Fowler, Marian. *In a Gilded Cage: From Heiress to Duchess.* New York: St. Martin's Press, 1994.

Gavan, Terrence. *The Newport Barons.* Newport: Pineapple Publications, 1988.

Geidel, Peter. "Alva E. Belmont: A Forgotten Feminist." Ph.D. dissertation, Columbia University, 1993.

Goldsmith, Barbara. *Little Gloria . . . Happy At Last.* New York: Alfred A. Knopf, 1980.

Kaiser, Harvey H. *Great Camps of the Adirondacks.* Boston: David R. Godine, 1982.

Keeler, Rebecca T. "Alva Belmont: Exacting Benefactor for Women's Rights." Ph.D. dissertation, University of South Alabama, 1987.

King, Robert B. *The Vanderbilt Homes.* New York: Rizzoli International Publications, Inc., 1989.

Lane, Wheaton. *Commodore Vanderbilt: An Epic of the Steam Age.* New York: Alfred A. Knopf, 1942.

MacColl, Gail and Carol McD. Wallace. *To Marry an English Lord: Or, How Anglomania Really Got Started.* New York: Workman Publishing, 1989.

MacDowell, Dorothy K. *Commodore Vanderbilt and His Family: A Biographical Account of the Descendants of Cornelius and Sophia Johnson Vanderbilt.* privately printed by Dorothy K. MacDowell, 1700 Fifth Avenue W., Hendersonville, NC., 1989.

"Mrs. Belmont's Funeral." *The New York Times* January 27, 1933.

"Mrs. O. H. P. Belmont Buys a Lighthouse." *The New York Times* February 1, 1924:19.

"Mrs. O. H. P. Belmont Dies at Paris Home." *The New York Times* January 26, 1933.

The Old Oakdale History, Volume I. Oakdale, NY: William K. Vanderbilt Historical Society of Dowling College, 1983.

The Old Oakdale History, Volume II: Era of Elegance, Part I. Oakdale, NY: William K. Vanderbilt Historical Society of Dowling College, 1993.

Patterson, Jerry E. *The Vanderbilts.* New York: Harry N. Abrams, Inc., Publishers, 1989.

Rector, Margaret Hayden. *Alva, That Vanderbilt–Belmont Woman.* Wickford, RI: The Dutch Island Press, 1992.

Sloane, Florence Adele. *Maverick In Mauve.* Garden City: Doubleday & Co., Inc., 1983.

Smith, Arthur D. *Commodore Vanderbilt: An Epic of American Achievement.* New York: Robert M. McBride & Co., 1927.

Spinzia, Raymond E. "In Her Wake: The Story of Alva Smith Vanderbilt Belmont." *The Long Island Historical Journal* 6 (Fall 1993):96–105.

Spinzia, Raymond E. and Judith A. Spinzia. *Long Island's Prominent North Shore Families: Their Estates and Their Country Homes.* vols. I, II. College Station, TX: VirtualBookworm, 2006.

Stasz, Clarice. *The Vanderbilt Women: Dynasty of Wealth, Glamour and Tragedy.* New York: St. Martin's Press, 1991.

Stein, Susan R. *The Architecture of Richard Morris Hunt.* Chicago: The University of Chicago Press, 1986.

Swanberg, W. A. *Whitney Father, Whitney Heiress.* New York: Charles Scribner's Sons, 1980.

"To Build Belmont Hospital: Mrs. O. H. P. Belmont the Sponsor for One as a Memorial." *The New York Times* September 17, 1909:1.

Vanderbilt, Arthur T. *Fortune's Children: The Fall of the House of Vanderbilt.* New York: William Morrow & Co., Inc., 1989.

Vanderbilt, Cornelius, Jr. *Farewell to Fifth Avenue.* New York: Simon & Schuster, Inc., 1935.

Vanderbilt, Cornelius, Jr. *Man of the World: My Life on Five Continents.* New York: Crown Publishers, Inc., 1959.

Vanderbilt, Cornelius, Jr. *Queen of the Golden Age: The Fabulous Story of Grace Wilson Vanderbilt.* New York: McGraw–Hill Book Co., Inc., 1956.

Vanderbilt, Gloria. *Black Knight, White Knight.* New York: Alfred A. Knopf, 1987.

Vanderbilt, Gloria. *Once Upon a Time.* New York: Alfred A. Knopf, 1985.

Vanderbilt, Gloria Morgan and Lady Thelma Furness. *Double Exposure: A Twin Autobiography.* New York: David McKay Co., Inc., 1958.

Vanderbilt, Gloria Morgan. *Without Prejudice.* New York: E. P. Dutton, 1936.

Van Rensselaer, Philip. *The Vanderbilt Women.* Chicago: Playboy Press, 1978.

Vichers, Hugo. *Gladys: Duchess of Marlborough.* New York: Holt, Rinehart & Winston, 1979.

"Belmont to Sell Belcourt." *New York Herald Tribune* December 30, 1908. [Newport estate]

"Want Wall Removed: Hempstead Board Denies Mrs. Belmont's Right to Fence Beach." *The New York Times* September 20, 1918:15.

"What the Woman's Party Wants." *Collier's* December 23, 1922.

Vanderbilt, William Kissam, Sr. - Oakdale - *Idlehour*

American Institute of Architects, Washington, DC, has architectural sketches of *Idlehour*.

Biltmore Estate, Ashville, NC, has material collected from all Vanderbilt families in their archives.

Culver Pictures, Hollywood, CA, has photographs of *Idlehour*.

Dowling College Library, Historical Collection, Oakdale, NY, has a photographic archive of the estate and family.

Library of Congress, Manuscript Division, Washington, DC, has a portion of Marlborough Papers.

The Long Island Museum of American Art, History and Carriages in Stony Brook has Vanderbilt's Chariot D'Orsay carriage.

The New York Historical Society, NYC, has the log of Vanderbilt's yacht *Valiant*.

Octagon Museum of American Architectural Foundation, Prints and Drawings Collection, Washington. DC, has photographs of the original *Idlehour*.

Queens College Library, Historical Collection, Flushing, NY, has Vanderbilt family records, including 1699 tax rolls and a deposit of 1790-1840 material.

Suffolk County Vanderbilt Museum and Planetarium archives, Centerport, LI, has photographs of the Vanderbilt family and an album of photographs of Alva Vanderbilt Belmont's house *Beacon Towers,* taken by Samuel H. Gottscho. The Gottscho collection is also in the Avery Architectural and Fine Arts Library, Columbia University, NYC, and in the Library of Congress, Washington, DC. Also included in the collection at the Vanderbilt Museum is an album with Alva Vanderbilt Belmont's funeral photographs and newspaper clippings.

"The Alva." *Historic Preservation* August 6, 1892.

Architectural Record October–December 1895.

Balsan, Consuelo Vanderbilt. *The Glitter and the Gold.* New York: Harper & Brothers, 1952.

Beard, Patricia. *After the Ball: Gilded Age Secrets, Boardroom Betrayals, and the Party That Ignited the Great Wall Street Scandal of 1905.* New York: Harper Collins, 2003.

Belmont, Alva Vanderbilt. One Month's Log of the Seminole. New York: privately printed, 1916.

Belmont, Alva Vanderbilt. "Unpublished 1917 Autobiography of Alva Vanderbilt Belmont" In Wood Collection. Huntington Library, San Marino, CA.

Belmont, Alva Vanderbilt. "Unpublished 1933 Autobiography of Alva Vanderbilt Belmont" In Matilda Young Papers, Special Collections Department, William R. Perkins Library, Duke University, Durham, NC.

Brough, James. *Consuelo: Portrait of an American Heiress.* New York: Coward, McCann & Geoghegan, Inc., 1979.

"Burial in Britain for Mrs. Balsan." *New York Times* December 12, 1964.

Havemeyer, Harry W. *East on the Great South Bay: Sayville and Bayport 1860–1960.* Mattituck, NY: Amereon House, 2001.

"*Idle Hour* [*Idlehour*]." *Locust Valley Leader* May 25, 1979.

"*Idle Hour* [*Idlehour*] Art Sale Yields $132,962.50." *New York Herald Tribune* May 1, 1926.

"*Idle Hour* [*Idlehour*] Art to Be Sold." *New York Herald Tribune* March 18, 1926.

"*Idle Hour* [*Idlehour*] Bought by Realty Operators." *New York Herald Tribune* January 7, 1926.

"Idle Hour [*Idlehour*] Development Brochure," exclusive sales agents E. A. White Organization, 225 West 34th Street, NYC, for Edmund G. and Charles F. Burke, Inc., owners, 146 Pierrepont St., Brooklyn, NY.

"*Idle Hour* [*Idlehour*]: The Estate of William K. Vanderbilt." *Architectural Record* 13 (May 1903).

"*Idle Hour* [*Idlehour*]: The Estate of William K. Vanderbilt." *Architectural Record* June 1903.

"*Idle Hour* [*Idlehour*] Treasures Bring $34,290 at Sale." *New York Herald* Tribune April 30, 1926.

"*Idle Hour* [*Idlehour*]: The William K. Vanderbilt, Sr. Estate." *Gold Coast* June 1981.

Vanderbilt, William Kissam, Sr. - Oakdale - *Idlehour* (cont'd)

Indiana Limestone Company. "The W. K. Vanderbilt Home: An Example of Exquisitely Carved Gray Indiana Limestone." Bedford, IN: Indiana Limestone Co., 1929. [refers to New York City house]

Kahn, E. J. "A Reporter at Large: A Place to Think (Peace Haven)." *New Yorker* March 16, 1940.

Mackay, Robert B., Anthony K. Baker, and Carol A. Traynor. *Long Island Country Houses and Their Architects 1860-1940*. New York: W. W. Norton & Co., 1997.

Marlborough, Duchess of [Consuelo Vanderbilt Balsan]. "Hostels for Women." *The Nineteenth Century and After* 1911:858–66.

Marlborough, Duchess of [Consuelo Vanderbilt Balsan]. "The Position of Woman," Parts 2, 3, 10. *North American Review* 89 (1909):180–93, 351–59, 11–24.

Marlborough, Duchess of [Consuelo Vanderbilt Balsan]. "Saving the Children." Lady Priestly Memorial Lecture, National Health Society, June 29, 1916.

Marilyn Estates, Inc. "*Idle Hour* [*Idlehour*] Mansion Built by W. K. Vanderbilt: Located at Oakdale, Long Island, Offered for Immediate Sale or Lease." New York: Marilyn Estates, Inc., 1936.

Maxwell, Elsa. *R.S.V.P.: Elsa Maxwell's Own Story*. Boston: Little Brown and Co., 1954.

Oakdale Club: A Residential Club Located at Oakdale Long Island. privately printed, nd.

Old Oakdale History, Volume I. Oakdale, NY: William K. Vanderbilt Historical Society of Dowling College, 1983.

Old Oakdale History, Volume II: Era of Elegance, Part I. Oakdale, NY: William K. Vanderbilt Historical Society of Dowling College, 1993.

Prost, L. H. "*Collection de Madame et du Colonel Balsan* (Paris: c. 1930). Sale Catalogue of the Estate of Lady Sarah Consuelo Spencer–Churchill." Doyle, New York, 2001.

Rector, Margaret Hayden. *Alva, That Vanderbilt Woman: Her Story as She Might Have Told It*. Wickford, RI: The Dutch Island Press, 1991.

Sclare, Liisa and Donald Sclare. *Beaux-Arts Estates: A Guide to the Architecture of Long Island*. New York: The Viking Press, 1980.

Spinzia, Raymond E. "In Her Wake: The Story of Alva Smith Vanderbilt Belmont." *The Long Island Historical Journal* 6 (Fall 1993):96–105.

Spinzia, Raymond E., Judith A. Spinzia, and Kathryn E. Spinzia. *A Guide to New York's Suffolk and Nassau Counties*. New York: Hippocrene Books, 1991 (revised).

Spinzia, Raymond E. and Judith A. Spinzia. *Long Island's Prominent North Shore Families: Their Estates and Their Country Homes*. vols. I, II. College Station, TX: VirtualBookworm, 2006.

Stuart, Amanda Mackenzie. *Consuelo and Alva Vanderbilt: The Story of a Daughter and a Mother in the Gilded Age*. New York: Harper Collins Publishers, 2005.

"Vanderbilt Sues *Idle Hour* [*Idlehour*] Buyers." *New York Herald Tribune* December 12, 1923.

Van Pelt, John V. "A Monograph of the William K. Vanderbilt House, Richard Morris Hunt Architect," *Architectural Record* September 1925. [discusses New York City house]

"When *Idle Hour* [*Idlehour*] was Peace Haven." *Long Island Forum* October and November 1980.

Wagstaff, Dr. Alfred, Sr. - West Islip - *Tahlulah*

Queensborough Public Library, Long Island Collection, Jamaica, NY, has records for Christ Episcopal Church [known locally as the "Wagstaff Church"], West Islip.

Havemeyer, Harry W. *Along the Great South Bay From Oakdale to Babylon, the Story of a Summer Spa, 1840 to 1940*. Mattituck, NY: Amereon House, 1996.

"Hanging Out: Stereographic Prints From the Collection of Samuel Wagstaff, Jr., at the J. Paul Getty Museum, October 13 through November 11, 1984." Providence, RI: Bell Gallery, List Art Center, Brown University, 1984.

Weekes, Harold Hathaway - Islip - *Wereholme*

Office of the Suffolk County Historian has photographs of the estate.

Original architects' model of *Wereholme* is currently located in the house.

Havemeyer, Harry W. *Along the Great South Bay From Oakdale to Babylon, the Story of a Summer Spa, 1840 to 1940*. Mattituck, NY: Amereon House, 1996.

Mackay, Robert B., Anthony K. Baker, and Carol A. Traynor. *Long Island Country Houses and Their Architects 1860-1940*. New York: W. W. Norton & Co., 1997.

Spinzia, Raymond E. and Judith A. Spinzia. *Long Island's Prominent North Shore Families: Their Estates and Their Country Homes*. vols. I, II. College Station, TX: VirtualBookworm, 2006.

Weld, Philip Balch - Bay Shore
      Byrnes, Horace W. *Pictorial Bay Shore and Vicinity: A Souvenir.* privately printed, 1903.
      Spinzia, Raymond E. and Judith A. Spinzia. *Long Island's Prominent North Shore Families: Their Estates and Their Country Homes.* vols. I, II. College Station, TX: VirtualBookworm, 2006.

Welles, Benjamin Sumner, III - Islip - *Welles House*
Franklin Delano Roosevelt Library, Hyde Park, NY, has a portion of Benjamin Sumner Welles III's papers.
      Gellman, Irwin F. *Secret Affairs: FDR, Cordell Hull, and Sumner Welles.* New York: Enigma Books, 2002.
      Spinzia, Raymond E. "Sumner Welles: Brilliance and Tragedy." *The Freeholder* 9 (Winter 2005):8-9, 22.
      Spinzia, Raymond E. and Judith A. Spinzia. *Long Island's Prominent North Shore Families: Their Estates and Their Country Homes.* vols. I, II. College Station, TX: VirtualBookworm, 2006.
      Welles, Benjamin. *Sumner Welles: FDR's Global Strategist.* New York: St. Martin's Press, 1997.

Whitney, William Collins - Islip
Library of Congress, Washington, DC, has William Collins Whitney's papers.
The Nassau County Museum Collection includes photographs of his Westbury estate.
      "The Fabled Past: The Whitneys of Westbury." *The North Shore Journal* 13 (May 27, 1982) n.p.
      "Furniture & Works of Art – Architectural Elements of the Residence of the Late Helen Hay Whitney, 972 Fifth Avenue, New York." New York: Parke–Bernet Galleries, Inc., 1946. auction catalog [New York City house]
      Hirsh, Mark D. *William C. Whitney: Modern Warwick.* New York: Dodd, Mead & Co., 1948.
      Hoyt, Edwin P. *The Whitneys: An Informal Portrait, 1635–1975.* New York: Weybright & Talley Publishers, 1976.
      Klepper, Michael. *The Wealthy 100: From Benjamin Franklin to Bill Gates – A Ranking of the Richest Americans Past and Present.* Secaucus, NJ: The Citadel Press, 1996.
      McKim, Mead & White. *A Monograph of the Work of McKim, Mead & White 1879–1915.* New York: DaCapo Press, 1985. [New York City house]
      Spinzia, Raymond E. and Judith A. Spinzia. *Long Island's Prominent North Shore Families: Their Estates and Their Country Homes.* vols. I, II. College Station, TX: VirtualBookworm, 2006.
      Swanberg, W. A. *Whitney Father, Whitney Heiress.* New York: Charles Scribner's Sons, 1980.

Wray, William H. - Bay Shore - *Whileaway*
      Byrnes, Horace W. *Pictorial Bay Shore and Vicinity: A Souvenir.* privately printed, 1903.
      Mackay, Robert B., Anthony K. Baker, and Carol A. Traynor. *Long Island Country Houses and Their Architects 1860-1940.* New York: W. W. Norton & Co., 1997.
      Picturesque Babylon, Bay Shore and Islip. New York: Mercantile Illustrating Co., 1894.

Wright, Dr. Arthur Mullen - Islip - *Afterglow*
The Nassau County Museum Collection has photographs of the estate.
      Byrnes, Horace W. *Pictorial Bay Shore and Vicinity: A Souvenir.* privately printed, 1903.
      Mackay, Robert B., Anthony K. Baker, and Carol A. Traynor. *Long Island Country Houses and Their Architects 1860-1940.* New York: W. W. Norton & Co., 1997.
      Spinzia, Raymond E. and Judith A. Spinzia. *Long Island's Prominent North Shore Families: Their Estates and Their Country Homes.* vols. I, II. College Station, TX: VirtualBookworm, 2006.

Biographical Dictionaries Master Index 1975–1976. Detroit: Gale Research Co., 1975.

Biography and Genealogy Master Index 1981–1985. Detroit: Gale Research Co., 1985.

Biography and Genealogy Master Index 1986–1990. Detroit: Gale Research Co., 1990.

Biography and Genealogy Master Index 1991–1995. Detroit: Gale Research Co., 1995.

Brooklyn Daily Eagle Online 1841-1902, Internet

Current Biography Yearbook. New York: The H. W. Wilson Co. [selected volumes]

Dow Jones News Internet Retrieval.

The Eagle and Brooklyn: The Record of the Progress of the Brooklyn Daily Eagle. 2 vols.
　　　Brooklyn, NY: The Brooklyn Eagle, 1893.

Levy, Felice, ed. *Obituaries on File.* New York: Facts on File, 1979.

Lexis Nexis Academic Universe, Internet.

Malone, Dumas, ed. *Dictionary of American Biography.* NY: Charles Scribner's Sons, 1935.

The National Cyclopaedia of American Biography. Clifton, NJ: James T. White & Co., 1984.

Newsday Internet Retrieval.

New York State's Prominent and Progressive Men. 2 vols. New York: New York Tribune, 1900.

The New York Times Index. New York: The New York Times. [annual obituaries from 1979–1997]

The New York Times Obituaries Index, vol. 1, 1858–1968. New York: The New York Times, 1970.

The New York Times Obituaries Index, vol. 2, 1969–1978. New York: The New York Times, 1980.

Prominent Families of New York. New York: The Historical Co., 1898.

Standard and Poor's Register of Corporations, Directors and Executives. Charlottesville, VA:
　　　Standard and Poors, Inc. [selected volumes]

Who's Who in America. Chicago: Marquis Who's Who, Inc. [selected volumes]

Who's Who in Finance and Industry. Chicago: Marquis Who's Who, Inc. [selected volumes]

Who's Who in New York. New York: Lewis Historical Publishing Co. [selected volumes]

Who's Who in New York City and State. New York: L. R. Hamersly Co., 1904–1960 [selected volumes]

Who's Who in the East. Chicago: Marquis Who's Who, Inc. [selected volumes]

Who's Who of American Women. Chicago: Marquis Who's Who, Inc. [selected volumes]

Who Was Who in America with World Notables. New Providence, NJ: Marquis Who's Who, Inc.
　　　[selected volumes]

Atlas of Babylon, Bay Shore and Islip. Wendelken and Co., 1888.

Atlas of the Ocean Shore of Suffolk County. E. Belcher Hyde, Inc., 1915.

Dolph's Street, Road and Land Ownership Map of Suffolk County. New York: Dolph & Stewart, 1929.

Hagstrom Map of Western Suffolk County. Maspeth, NY: Hagstrom Map Co., Inc., 1996.

Hagstrom's Street, Road and Landownership Atlas of Suffolk County, Long Island, Western Half. New York: Hagstrom Co., Inc., 1944.

Real Estate Reference Map of a Part of Suffolk County, Long Island, N.Y.: Comprising of the Townships [Towns] of Huntington, Smithtown, Babylon and Islip. New York: E. Belcher Hyde, Inc. Engineers Publishers, 1931.

American Architect and Building News, 62

American Splendor: The Residential Architecture of Horace Trumbauer, 105, 106 all

Architectural Record, 118, 264 middle, 265 top, 274, 276 top left, and bottom right and left, 277 left top and bottom

Bayport Historical Association, 3, 14, 65, 68, 76, 157, 166 top, 170, 207, 210, 211, 214 bottom, 226, 239, 245, 251

Marjorie Wilson Candiano, 191

Country Life in America, 183, 200 bottom

East Islip Historical Society, 1, 10, 36 all, 37, 48, 81, 111, 121, 124, 136 top, 165, 168, 188, 201 bottom, 204 top, 205, 222, 255 both, 263, 264 top right, and lower left and right, 279, 280, 287, 292, 298

John Vanderveer Gibson, 87 both, 278

Charles Hayward, 108

Hicks Nursery, 202

Elizabeth Huber Howell, 120 top

Carl Ilardi, 258

Gary Lawrance, 293

Library of Congress, 223 both, 233 top, 262 both

Long Island Rail Road, 44

Long Island Today, 67

Richard A. Milligan, 209, 284

Nassau County Division of Museum Services, 17 bottom, 147 top right and left

New York State Office of Parks, Recreation, and Historic Preservation, 174

Noted Long Island Homes, 31, 52, 53, 61, 97 top, 145, 264 top left

Pictorial Bay Shore and Vicinity: A Souvenir, 5, 15, 39, 43, 45, 82, 83 bottom, 119, 120 bottom, 123, 127, 132, 141, 155, 160, 162, 167, 169, 175 bottom, 176, 187 bottom, 198 bottom, 206, 215, 221, 229 top, 270, 271, 297

Picturesque Babylon, Bay Shore and Islip, 70, 75 lower right, 235

Helena Parsons Hallock Pless, 97 bottom

Sayville Public Library, 138, 193, 212, 234, 238, 289

Raymond E. Spinzia, xi, xii, 2, 4, 6, 7 bottom right, 11 top and bottom, 16, 17 top, 22, 26, 27, 28, 30 all, 32 both, 33, 34, 41, 46, 47, 50, 51, 57, 58, 59, 60, 64, 66, 69, 73, 74, 77, 79 both, 83 top, 84, 86, 88, 90, 92, 93, 94, 95, 99 both, 100, 102, 103, 104, 107 bottom, 110, 112, 113, 114, 129, 130, 131, 136 bottom, 139, 142, 144, 146, 147 middle, bottom right and left, 158, 163, 166 bottom, 171, 173 both, 175 top, 177, 178 both, 180, 186, 187 top, 189 both, 190, 192, 197, 198 top, 200 top, 201 top, 204 bottom, 214 top, 216, 219, 224, 227, 229 bottom, 230, 231, 232 both, 233 bottom, 236, 241, 243, 246, 248, 249 top, 256, 257, 259, 260, 261, 265 bottom, 266, 268, 269 bottom, 275, 276 top right and middle, 277 middle, top, and bottom right, 281, 282, 283, 285, 291, 294, 296, 299, 301

Suffolk County Historical Society Museum, 185

Peter Titus, 12, 56, 78, 300 top

Town and Country, 125

Town of Babylon Historian, 7 top left, 18, 20, 21, 91

Untold Friendships, 196 both

Village of Babylon Historical and Preservation Society, 75 all except lower right, 107 top, 217, 249 bottom, 253, 269 top

Douglas Thomas Yates, Sr., 300 bottom

About the Authors

Judith and Raymond Spinzia are former Long Island residents, now residing in central Pennsylvania. Their first book, *Long Island: A Guide to New York's Suffolk and Nassau Counties* (New York: Hippocrene Books, 1988; 1991, revised), is a standard reference book which has been used as a textbook for teaching Long Island history and can still be found in almost all public libraries and schools on Long Island. A third (revised) edition of the guidebook is scheduled to be published in 2007.

The Spinzias write and speak, jointly and separately, on a variety of Long Island-related subjects including the North and South Shore estates, Tiffany stained-glass windows, and the Vanderbilts of Long Island. On several occasions their lectures have been chosen by the radio station of *The New York Times*, WQXR, as the cultural event of the day in the New York Metropolitan area. Additionally, they have been featured on local television and radio programs and in articles published by *The New York Times, Newsday*, and other regional newspapers.

The Spinzias served as Long Island history consultants for a local cable television channel that, in an effort to encourage local interest, aired material from their guidebook twice daily. They also were consultants for a Japanese television network for a documentary on Louis Comfort Tiffany and contributed material to the Arts and Entertainment Network's "Biography" series for its presentations on the Vanderbilt and Tiffany families.

Their two-volume companion work to this South Shore book, *Long Island's Prominent North Shore Families: Their Estates and Their Country Homes*, was published in 2006. Ordering information and sample pages for both this volume and the North Shore work can be found by visiting the Spinzias' website **spinzialongislandestates.com.**